Yul Brynner

International Film Stars
Series Editor: Homer B. Pettey and R. Barton Palmer

This series is devoted to the artistic and commercial influence of performers who shaped major genres and movements in international film history. Books in the series will:

- Reveal performative features that defined signature cinematic styles
- Demonstrate how the global market relied upon performers' generic contributions
- Analyse specific film productions as case studies that transformed cinema acting
- Construct models for redefining international star studies that emphasise materialist approaches
- Provide accounts of stars' influences in the international cinema marketplace

Titles available:

Close-Up: Great Cinematic Performances Volume 1: America
edited by Murray Pomerance and Kyle Stevens

Close-Up: Great Cinematic Performances Volume 2: International
edited by Murray Pomerance and Kyle Stevens

Chinese Stardom in Participatory Cyberculture
by Dorothy Wai Sim Lau

Geraldine Chaplin: The Gift of Film Performance
by Steven Rybin

Tyrone Power: Gender, Genre and Image in Classical Hollywood Cinema
by Gillian Kelly

Film Stardom in Southeast Asia
edited by Jonathan Driskell

Diana Dors: Film Star and Actor
by Martin Shingler

Yul Brynner: Exoticism, Cosmopolitanism and Screen Masculinity
by Susanna Paasonen

www.euppublishing.com/series/ifs

Yul Brynner

Exoticism, Cosmopolitanism and Screen Masculinity

Susanna Paasonen

EDINBURGH
University Press

Edinburgh University Press is one of the leading university presses in the UK. We publish academic books and journals in our selected subject areas across the humanities and social sciences, combining cutting-edge scholarship with high editorial and production values to produce academic works of lasting importance. For more information visit our website: edinburghuniversitypress.com

© Susanna Paasonen, 2023, 2024

Edinburgh University Press Ltd
13 Infirmary Street
Edinburgh EH1 1LT

First published in hardback by Edinburgh University Press 2023

Typeset in 12/14 Arno and Myriad by
IDSUK (Dataconnection) Ltd

A CIP record for this book is available from the British Library

ISBN 978 1 4744 9794 7 (hardback)
ISBN 978 1 4744 9795 4 (paperback)
ISBN 978 1 4744 9796 1 (webready PDF)
ISBN 978 1 4744 9797 8 (epub)

The right of Susanna Paasonen to be identified as the author of this work has been asserted in accordance with the Copyright, Designs and Patents Act 1988, and the Copyright and Related Rights Regulations 2003 (SI No. 2498).

Contents

Figures   vi
Acknowledgements   viii

Chapter 1: A fantastic figure   1
Chapter 2: Flexible origins and exotic displays   15
Chapter 3: A royal presence   48
Chapter 4: Bodily assets, or, 'S-E-X'   75
Chapter 5: Strong, silent, ethnic types   107
Chapter 6: Cosmopolitan commitments   136
Chapter 7: Man, beast, machine   165
Chapter 8: Performance style, posturing, and camp   196
Chapter 9: An afterlife – et cetera, et cetera, et cetera   223

References   242
Index   282

Figures

Figure 2.1	Brynner as Vicola in *Port of New York* (1949)	20
Figure 2.2	Brynner as Irani, Russian, Indian, 'Cajun,' Yugoslav, German, Mexican, and Ukrainian	34
Figure 3.1	King Mongkut in his introduction scene	54
Figure 3.2	The Orientalist charms of King Mongkut	55
Figure 3.3	The ornamental, vengeful Rameses II	64
Figure 3.4	The dashing pirate king Lafitte	66
Figure 3.5	King Solomon among Orientalist temptations	68
Figure 4.1	Brynner as usher to Hell in *Le testament d'Orphée* (1960)	78
Figure 4.2	An invitation to dance, followed by planned flagellation	93
Figure 4.3	Brynner topless in *The Brothers Karamazov* (1958), *Kings of the Sun* (1963), *The Long Duel* (1967), and *The File of the Golden Goose* (1969)	95
Figure 4.4	Chief Black Eagle, detained	97
Figure 5.1	Riding crops in *Anastasia* and *The Journey*	110
Figure 5.2	The statuesque, butch Taras Bulba	114
Figure 5.3	Bounine and Stoloff in Cossack fashions	117
Figure 5.4	Jules Gaspard d'Estaing	122
Figure 5.5	Brynner as Arab, Japanese-Polish-American, Israeli, and German (*Escape from Zahrain*, *Flight from Ashiya*, *Cast a Giant Shadow*, and *Triple Cross*)	125
Figure 5.6	Zooming in (*The Long Duel* and *The File of the Golden Goose*)	127
Figure 6.1	Brynner with Maroussia and Aliosha Dimitrievitch (in *Anastasia* and *The Ed Sullivan Show*)	149

Figure 7.1	Brynner shot in chiaroscuro in *The Brothers Karamazov*, *Invitation to a Gunfighter*, and *The Double Man*	167
Figure 7.2	Chris Adams and *Westworld* robot	172
Figure 7.3	Sabata, a gunslinger with flair	177
Figure 7.4	Evil and jovial grins (*The Light at the Edge of the World* and *Catlow*)	179
Figure 7.5	The diabolical Captain Kongre	181
Figure 7.6	A fantasy sex robot	186
Figure 7.7	Carson, a man-statue	188
Figure 7.8	Marciani at a strip show	190
Figure 8.1	Striking poses in *The King and I*, *The Ten Commandments*, and *Taras Bulba*	202
Figure 8.2	Yul Brynner: the centerpiece. Clockwise from top left: *The King and I*, *Surprise Package*, *Taras Bulba*, *Kings of the Sun*, *Solomon and Sheba*, *The Ten Commandments*, *Invitation to a Gunfighter*, *The Buccaneer*, and *Anastasia*	205
Figure 8.3	Rameses, Nefertiri, and Moses in chains	207
Figure 8.4	Visual gags in *Once More, with Feeling!*	209
Figure 8.5	The evil Chairman	213
Figure 8.6	An alluring torch singer	214
Figure 9.1	Brynner's posthumous anti-smoking ad	231
Figure 9.2	Yul Brynner statue in Vladivostok. Photograph by Rock Brynner (Wikipedia, Creative Commons License 3.0)	233
Figure 9.3	Google Image search results for Yul Brynner GIFs	238

Acknowledgements

In the course of working on this book, I have more than once tried to trace the origins of my long-term fascination with Yul Brynner – not least since these have been regularly inquired about by those who have found my interest a puzzlement. This took root in my early teens when browsing my mother's fan magazines of the late 1950s and early 1960s featuring articles, comics, romantic short stories, advice columns, colorful posters, and gossipy bits on internationally and regionally established film and pop stars. Within these visual galleries, Brynner made the occasional appearance, and invariably stood out. As it took years for me to see any of his film work, my initial fascination had to do with his specific aesthetic and look. To a large extent, it is this interest in Brynner's star persona and its visual display that inspired the work for this book more than three decades later.

This is something of a labor of love, a project that I vaguely entertained since my undergraduate days in film and television studies, and for which I have collected materials out of unspecified interest ever since. It was, however, not until much later that I put some of this in writing, the outcome of which was published in the journal *Screen* (2019, 60, no. 2) as 'Striking Poses: The Fantastic Body of Yul Brynner,' and which forms the general thematic basis for this book. During the COVID-19 lockdowns I eventually opted for a longer format for my Yul investigation so that it is fair to describe the project as both extracurricular and escapist in the refuge that archival research offered during the pandemic.

Throughout, my Yul project has enjoyed remarkably warm and enthusiastic support from friends, colleagues, and editors. I have been delighted by the joyful engagement and encouragement, both given the degree to which my research profile is detached from film history and the degree to which the topic at hand is niche within film history and stardom studies as such. First of all, thanks go to my very dear and fabulous friend, Adrianne Wortzel, who once described this project as arising from a 'petri dish of lust.' Debates over the accuracy of this definition aside, Adrianne's extended enthusiasm and interest in, as well as her help with archival access for, this project have been unparalleled, and ever so appreciated. I would also like to extend my warmest thanks to John Mercer for all the support and for sharing his accumulated wisdom on male sex symbols, and to Will Straw for his help with some of the films, for understanding and supporting cinematic fetishes, such as mine, and for also commenting on the manuscript. I am further indebted to Hanna Järvinen, Minna Långström, and Mari Pajala who all took the time to carefully read the manuscript. Their generosity has truly meant a lot and their observations and suggestions have helped to make the book stronger. Suurkiitokset.

The very final stretches of archival work for this book were conducted during my stay as Hunt-Simes Visiting Chair in Sexuality Studies at Sydney Social Sciences and Humanities Advanced Research Centre (SSSHARC), University of Sydney, spring 2022: huge thanks to Kane Race and Lee Wallace for hosting me. Homer B. Pettey and Barton Palmer, the editors of the International Film Stars series, received my proposal with collegial warmth that took me very much by surprise: it has been a pleasure working with you, and the Press. Thank you, Henry MacAdam, for reaching out with your collaborative *The Gladiators vs. Spartacus* project, Tom Apperley for helping with *Playboy* archives, and Hannu Salmi for aid with *Elokuva-aitta*. For cheering me on, many, many thanks to Ricky Barnes, Joyce Goggin, Kylie Jarrett, Kati Åberg, and the collective of the International Institute for Popular Culture (IIPC) at University of Turku: you have all been stellar. And kudos to Ville Hurskainen for helping me spot much detail in film work.

Chapter 1

A fantastic figure

'For the first time, here is an actor with a personality as big as the vast CinemaScope screen,' enthused the British fan magazine, *Picturegoer*, in September 1956, predicting that Yul Brynner would become the biggest name in Hollywood as 'the animal magnetism of the man is something that must be experienced to be believed.'[1] This was the year that catapulted Brynner to international film stardom through his roles as 'the King of Siam' in the Hollywood rendition of the Rodgers and Hammerstein musical, *The King and I* (Walter Lang, 1956); as Pharaoh Rameses II in the popular Biblical epic, *The Ten Commandments* (Cecil B. DeMille, 1956); and as a former Russian white general in *Anastasia* against Ingrid Bergman (Anatole Litvak, 1956): all three films were released within a period of six months. Although he had become a major Broadway star with the runaway success of *The King and I* in 1951, Brynner now seemed to be virtually everywhere, starring in eleven films and doing a cameo in a twelfth by 1960.

His was a novel film star aesthetic, one expansively and opaquely exotic, in-your-face masculine, and intense in its physical presence. 'There are things about Yul Brynner which reach out and grab you,' *Saturday Evening Post* reported in 1958: 'First, there are his eyes – burning, hypnotic, ripe-olive brown. Then there's his head, which is (and this will come as a surprise to nobody) shaved as clean as a seven-and-a-half-pound egg.'[2] The mesmerized writer was not alone in his ruminations. Musing over the actor's 'flattish nose,' 'flaring nostrils,' and 'fawnlike ears,' *Collier's* concluded that his 'totally hairless skull plus the electricity he discharges with his slightest movement give Brynner the effect of a young Tartar colonel in one of Genghis Khan's crack cavalry regiments.'[3]

A head initially shaved for the Broadway premiere of *The King and I* was Yul Brynner's most striking singular physical feature that set him apart from his contemporaries and rendered him instantaneously recognisable. Yet his presence was identified as striking also more broadly: 'Beneath that fabulous dome, fierce eyes smolder above Asian cheek-bones and brazenly flared nostrils,' wrote the scandal tabloid, *Hush-Hush*.[4] *Picturegoer* further enthused over his larger-than-life persona:

> 'Extraordinary people,' said Yul Brynner, 'in extraordinary pictures.' It's his recipe for success. And he himself is the best example of the first ingredient. Study him, even slightly, and you begin to be reminded of one of the black-and-white puzzle-drawings in a child's magazine. You know the kind: 'Portrait of a giant. Find the boy – find the philosopher – find the hidden human …'
>
> Brynner is all of these – but first you have to see past the staggering appearance. Giant is apt for every aspect of his public personality. The fellow isn't, like many younger stars, just a fashionable figment of acclaim. He is prodigious. He is also something of a chameleon.[5]

Although Brynner stood no more than 1.73 meters (5 feet 7 inches) tall, he was characterised as 'giant' by virtue of his personality and presence. For his part, director Cecil B. DeMille described Brynner as 'the most powerful personality I've ever seen on the screen – a cross between Douglas Fairbanks Sr., Apollo, and a little bit of Hercules.'[6] These descriptions make for an appropriate start to a book exploring the different layers of Brynner's film star image and its transformations over time. Their hyperbolic flourish, no matter how fantastic, was not exceptional, as such. Excess in Brynner's star persona ranged from accounts of animal magnetism and electric sex appeal to the fascinated detailing of his voracious appetite, incredible energy, and intense physical presence. It was standard for 1950s Hollywood stars to be made to stand out from the crowd as extraordinary individuals in terms of their corporeal assets and personae alike. Brynner was, nevertheless, more committed to this project of personality construction than most. Early on, he recounted a piece of advice received from his old friend, the artist Jean Cocteau, 'When you become a star [...] be sure of one thing. That your public relations never let people think that you go to the bathroom.' Brynner went on:

> He gave me a wonderful key. It is an actor's job to create illusions, to deal in make-believe. You will see actors in magazines looking not only like everybody else in everyday life, but even sloppier somehow. You see Miss Helen Hayes cooking an old tired *pizza*. You see Katharine Cornell puttering in the garden, pulling a worm out of the ground. Really! I think this is absolutely dismal.[7]

Cocteau's advice, which was to be reiterated in many interviews and character profiles since, speaks of heightened awareness of stardom as a performance extending well beyond the screen and stage as a matter of professional responsibility. Brynner embraced the public role of star as a fabricator and teller of tales, just as he made extensive efforts to construct and retain a sense of mystery about his persona and early life. When it came to family origins or his place of birth, Brynner was a particularly advanced illusion-maker: not only did he depict a range of ethnic otherness onscreen, but he also freely remixed exotica in his autobiographical accounts that unfolded as ever-changing variations, partly, but not exclusively, to obscure his Russian roots in Cold War-era Hollywood. Improvisations in imaginative autobiographical detail afforded Brynner's screen appearances with additional frisson and mythical aura even if, by the mid-1960s, they also risked marking him on anachronistic terms since their manifest artificiality gestured toward the elaborate fabrications of a bygone Hollywood studio era.

A catalog of work

Brynner's first major stage role was in the 1946 Broadway musical *Lute Song* as the Chinese Tsai-Yong, and he is probably best remembered for his role as King Mongkut in *The King and I*, which he performed onstage 4,625 times during 1951–1955 and 1976–1985, practically till the end of his life: he won a Tony Award for the role as featured actor in 1952 and a special Tony in 1985. In 1957, he was nominated for, and won, the Academy Award for best actor for the musical's film version.

His was an exceptionally dramatic career trajectory, one starting with being the talk of Hollywood town in 1956, entering the top listings of All-American film favorites and enjoying international popularity in Europe and Asia alike.[8] His films nevertheless soon entered a decline in terms of both their commercial and critical success, *The Magnificent Seven* (John Sturges, 1960) and *Westworld* (Michael Crichton, 1973) being exceptions to the rule. By 1967, despite Brynner still actively making films, the *Playboy* feature 'Sex Stars of the Fifties' framed him as very much the star of a generation past, writing that, '[o]lder female filmgoers fantasized affairs with such sophisticated Continental types as Yul Brynner, whose polished pate became a new international sex symbol.'[9] And, by 1969, he was featured in an article on actors who had managed to retain their star status and high fees despite mainly appearing in flops.[10] The question of Brynner's film stardom is, however, more complex than such a narrative summary of sharp ascent and gradual descent allows for.

Brynner's film career spanned from 1940s film noir to 1950s Technicolor studio epics, 1960s Westerns and spy films, and 1970s action and science fiction; starting as the smooth-talking, suave, urbane, and murderous head of an opium smuggling ring with *Port of New York* (László Benedek, 1949) and ending as a retired, vengeful New York mob hitman in *Death Rage* (*Con la rabbia agli occhi*, Antonio Margheriti, 1976). Between these two roles as New Yorkers, Brynner appeared onscreen as military figures and revolutionary leaders of shifting – Russian, Iranian, German, Indian, Ukrainian, Mexican, Yugoslav, Mexican, Native American, Arab – origins, as pirates both gallant and sadistic, as hired guns and gunslinger robots, as secret agents and military men, and as Egyptian, Israeli, and Siamese kings.

From the *mise-en-scène* of Orientalist desire in *The King and I* where his decorative, authoritative, and muscular king evokes forbidden interracial desire in a widowed British schoolteacher, to his strutting and stomping alpha masculine Cossack in *Taras Bulba* (J. Lee Thompson, 1962), the tragic 'Creole' dandy gunslinger, Jules Gaspard d'Estaing, of unsurpassed technical skill and destructive rage in *Invitation to a Gunfighter* (Richard Wilson, 1964), and his vocally sparse post-apocalyptic street fighter in *The Ultimate Warrior* (Robert Clouse, 1975), Brynner's roles were standouts. This was, firstly and obviously, an issue of him mostly having star billing, and hence being the key focus of attention. Secondly, it involved his particular performance style foregrounding physical presence and expressive gesticulation over the nuances of dialogue. Thirdly, and no less importantly, it had to do with how his characters were routinely othered in ethnic and racial terms *vis-à-vis* the films' primary North American audience. Communicating, at turns, melancholy, egoism, heroism, aggression, and deadly vehemence, Brynner's figure was cast as an object of erotic desire and visual contemplation. The overall appeal of this figure was reflected in, and amplified by, creative narrations of the actor's own background, persona, and presence.

Brynner's exotic 'off-white' European star persona came wrapped up in barbaric undertones while also connoting Continental sophistication.[11] His elastic positioning in Hollywood's racial taxonomy – was he Mongolian, Romani, French, Swiss, Russian? – made him suitable for playing most types except for those of well-rounded, all-American heroes, whereas in the European co-productions of the 1960s and 1970s he was considered American enough to play the part, or otherwise a good fit in terms of their mixed international casts and target audiences. Considerations of cultural appropriation – the ethics and politics involved in taking on elements, styles, identities, and histories of a culture other than one's own – are more than warranted in analysing Brynner's onscreen appearances in yellowface, brownface, and redface. While attending to these concerns, this book nevertheless builds on the argument that his star image was rich in ambiguity in ways that render it resistant to critiques aiming to fix its overall dynamics. That is to say, while this book engages in contextual and representational critique, it also holds onto the logic of both/and, so as to account for the paradoxical and incommensurate elements comprising Brynner's star image.

Recurring elements

Following Richard Dyer's classic analysis, star images, as 'constructed personages in media texts,' involve both variation – because an actor playing the same role over and over again may eventually have limited appeal – and cohesion reducible to identifiable traits and characteristics.[12] Hence, for example, Doris Day's (neé Doris von Kappelhoff) idiosyncratic wholesome perkiness, cleanliness, and healthy appetite; or the athletic, groomed ideal American masculinity of her co-star, Rock Hudson (born Roy Harold Scherer Jr.) whose public image was only later steeped in queer overtones.[13] Permanently marked by his breakthrough role as King Mongkut, Brynner's star image wove together exoticism, masculinity, and cosmopolitanism, so that despite his roles being diverse, there was cohesiveness to it.[14] Performance-wise, this image built on bodily aesthetics and gestures resulting in an intense, often dramatically stylized onscreen presence.

In order to map out Brynner's star image, I focus on performative elements recurring and varying over time: the types he played, the gestures he deployed, the ways in which his body was framed and depicted, and the kinds of templates that were used for making sense of it to the cinemagoing public. Here, I broadly build on Will Straw's exploration of cinema as an archive of gestures, presence, performance styles, specific faces and bodies, as well as their transformation over time.[15] Analytically, when mapping out the work of a singular actor, this means focusing much less on the narratives or aesthetics of any of their films than tracing repetitions and variations in performances across them. This further means foregrounding the work of physical appearance, presence, and action from which individual performances emerge, so as to shift analytical emphasis from an actor's function in diegesis and narrative, and from narrative and representational analysis as such, to the repetitive and flexible aspects of bodily display as elements that matter in their own right. Throughout, my interest revolves around Brynner's figure, its onscreen displays, and media reception.

Following this methodological principle, I engage with the entire catalog of Brynner's films. In what follows, I explore his cinematic oeuvre from films defined as classics to mostly forgotten B-films; forty productions in total. My attention further extends from leading roles to cameo appearances while also addressing some of his television work and cataloging his unrealised yet rumoured film projects. While some of Brynner's films – such as his breakthrough vehicle, *The King and I* – are examined more attentively than others, I focus largely on introductory scenes establishing the overall tone and style of his characters as they make themselves first known to viewers. For reasons evident enough, introduction scenes are key to not only laying out the defining features of a character but to establishing an actor's overall presence within the film narrative. They set the tone for characters which, in most of Brynner's work, do not drastically transform or develop in the course of ensuing narrative action. And since he largely played variations of a type – especially so from the 1960s on – there is much repetition to his characters, the tracing of which I argue to be central for understanding his star image. In sum, my overall methodological approach foregrounds recurring patterns. In terms of visual thinking, I further take my cue from Varpu Rantala's work on cinematic iconographies of addiction where she maps out gestural, postural, and compositional repetitions across films and visualises these as composites.[16] Consequently, many illustrations in this book are pairs or composites pointing out recurring similarities in Brynner's gestures, poses, and presences across films.

To date, Brynner has not been an object of much scholarly interest, which makes this the first academic monograph on the topic. When his persona and work have been addressed, this has mainly been in connection with screen masculinity, Hollywood Russianness, *The King and I*, and his plans as film producer.[17] While drawing on these bodies of research, this book focuses squarely on the fantastic figure of Yul Brynner: his corporeal presence, performance style, and self-representation as it connects to his film roles and other public activities, and as it moves from lavish studio productions to small-budget ventures, documentary work for the UNHCR, and Broadway stage revivals. A focus on Brynner's figure is to an extent mandatory, given how contemporaneous media both foregrounded and feasted on accounts of his physique, vitality, and sex appeal. Once it entered public consciousness, the notion of Brynner as an 'egg-bald panther' with hypnotizing eyes whose 'arrogant masculinity lingers' in irresistible ways followed him, in different variations, for the rest of his life – and even beyond.[18] And if there was tenacity to the tropes through which his star image was framed, the same applied to his overall performance style. Across Brynner's onscreen appearances, displays of masculinity were amplified by the actor's low voice, trademark baldness, and erect posture, as well as by his gestural and emotive registers, recurrent poses and stares.

Film work forms only one component of any actor's 'extensive, multimedia, intertextual' star image.[19] Source-wise, this book also builds on biographical accounts, Brynner's own published books, television, magazine, newspaper, and radio interviews, as well as a broad range of print sources ranging from trade press news to gossip columns, film and theater reviews, cover features, adverts, exposés, and other ephemera. Since my interest lies in Brynner's international star image, US print sources have been supplemented with British, Canadian, French, Finnish, and Australian ones, English-language papers published in India, Hong Kong, and Israel, as well as a light sprinkling of others. These vary from leading national newspapers to regional ones, film and fan magazines, industry papers, women's magazines, and a range of other periodicals. As this book was written during the global COVID-19 pandemic involving limited mobility within partial lockdowns, the scope of available sources has been largely, albeit not exclusively, limited to digital archives.

This paves the way for a more specific methodological note. I downloaded some 5,000 sources from digital print media history archives, the most relevant of which – about one fifth – have been included and are duly marked in the list of references. While focusing especially on the active years of Brynner's film career, these searches covered his early theater and television work of the 1940s and expanded to the current day in order to make sense of how he has been posthumously remembered. The width and range of digital databases facilitates explorations of historical material in scales impossible to achieve through manual means. Metadata and scanned files enabling keyword searches make it possible to trace both the circulation of syndicated content across newspapers (especially in the United States and Canada) and repetitions occurring in independently produced material since magazines routinely borrowed and modified content published somewhere else.

At the same time, such an expansive approach to historical sources means focusing primarily on items comprising keyword hits: these may be scans of film reviews, news items, or features isolated from the spreads in which they originally appeared. Alternatively, these may be scans of entire pages and, in some instances, it is possible to browse entire issues. Contextual nuance and care are nevertheless virtually impossible to balance with a large number of sources, unless the effort at hand comprises one's life's work. Studying such independent items, even at scale, makes it hard to understand the specificities of the publications involved, or to estimate the relative visibility of any particular film star within them.

With Finnish fan and film magazines, I resorted to the more traditional method of browsing through physical volumes starting at 1956 and ending at 1963, by which time mentions of Brynner and his films had practically ceased. This contextual insight made it possible to compare Brynner's overall visibility to those of his contemporaries in a context where he never became a top star even as mentions of him randomly dotted the gossip columns. In these magazines, Brynner had much less visibility than, for example, his co-stars Ingrid Bergman, Charlton Heston, Sal Mineo, or Tony Curtis. Brynner lost slightly in visibility to Sidney Poitier and hands down to Rock Hudson, Marlon Brando, Elizabeth Taylor, and Jayne Mansfield – and even to John Saxon and Tab Hunter. While it is beyond the scope of this book, and that of most single-authored enterprises, to explore several such linguistically and culturally bound popular publics, attending to them is key in studies of international film stardom. In the three Finnish periodicals I examined, Brynner was the focus of only four features and garnered no praise for his acting: he adorned one cover and starred in two additional 'fan posters' over the eight-year time span.[20] All this speaks of status comparable to his *The Brothers Karamazov* co-stars, Claire Bloom and Maria Schell: recognized but far from the brightest of celestial bodies. The chances are for the case to be similar in other local European contexts (and beyond) where national and regional cinemas regularly stole Hollywood's thunder, and where fan magazines offered letter templates in a number of languages for readers to write to their favorite stars.[21] Even though US materials dominate my historical sources due to their sheer volume and accessibility, focusing exclusively on them would have risked a biased perspective on Brynner's international star standing.

Ambiguities

Introducing Brynner to its American female readership in 1956, at the cusp of his cinematic fame, *Collier's* positioned him as a new kind of film star:

> By long-established standards, a screen hero's character must be white, a screen villain's black. Brynner's forthcoming roles, however, will show him portraying characters who are simultaneously black *and* white: rather villainous heroes or somewhat heroic villains afflicted with a kind of appealing schizophrenia.[22]

While the article focused on the diverse shades of gray in Brynner's film roles – such as the polygamous King of Siam, 'arrogant, yet humble, cruel yet achingly sympathetic,' or *Anastasia*'s scheming Russian general/nightclub owner of amorous intent – Brynner was also regularly positioned between black and white on racial terms, as an obscurely foreign star. *Collier's* further extended such ambiguity to his persona, with Deborah Kerr, his co-star in *The King and I*, characterizing it as 'a mixture of opposites.'[23] The appeal of most film star images builds on what Judith Mayne identifies as 'constant reinvention, the dissolution of contraries, the embrace of wildly opposing terms.'[24] In the case of Yul Brynner, such contingency and incongruity was particularly glaring, from accounts of his persona to his screen and stage work, and back again.

Brynner's star image – as construed on the basis of media reception and representation, biographical accounts, and onscreen performances – is rich in ambiguity. To summarize just some of this: he was a long-term special consultant for the UNHCR who promoted awareness of global refugee crises while also playing highly exoticized characters in brownface; an advocate for the rights of Romani, he consistently tapped into Gypsy exoticism to fuel his star image; an actor whose later film catalog was rich in killings and mauling he, nonetheless, disavowed gratuitous violence for disrespecting the value of human life and harmfully affecting more impressionable audience members.[25] Described as both an egoistic hedonist with a penchant for an exclusive jet-set lifestyle and the most disciplined and hard-working professional imaginable, he was a man loved by 'every leading lady who ever worked with him' – 'Children worship him. Audiences swoon at him' – yet he was also considered 'arrogant, ponderous, manipulative, demanding, prevaricating, and temperamental.'[26] Toward interviewers, '[h]e [could] be exasperatingly evasive and disarmingly cooperative. Sometimes [...] both at practically the same time.'[27]

Contrasting views of his personality abounded, with some saying Brynner had an excellent sense of humor while others described him as a humorless 'Uncle Scrooge, the king of tightwads,' the stingiest and nastiest of men in Hollywood and 'the king of mean.'[28] Known for his fondness of children, he was dedicated to helping orphans and was caring towards his junior stage colleagues or, alternatively, the kind to punch a child actor in the gut instead.[29] Though a self-proclaimed perfectionist, he turned in a series of performances which were considered variations of a type. He was a loving, engaged parent who, paradoxically, virtually disinherited his children, including the ones he had adopted only a decade before: 'regal and grand and authoritative'; 'kind and generous and attentive.'[30]

From the 1950s, Brynner began expressing acute boredom and tedium over being steadily typecast in the roles of 'bastards with a heart of gold' and with journalists repeatedly asking him the very same questions – and, as Hedda Hopper put it four years before his Hollywood fame, 'Yul is the sort of chap who, when he gets bored, toddles off to Bali or some such place.'[31] Yet he embraced and specialized in precisely such roles of bastards, eventually performing one onstage thousands of times, at the rate of eight shows a week. Manifestly disinterested in his own looks and arguing that men preening themselves in front of mirrors were unmasculine, Brynner was gossiped to never stray 'too far from a full-length mirror' himself.[32]

It is undoubtedly the case that any person's life and career are rife with contradiction in how their actions and persona are seen by others: perspectives vary, people change, and the social contexts for making sense of all this remain in continual flux. When outlining Yul Brynner's star image, as is the task of this book, it has not been my aim to resolve such tensions, let alone to reconstruct an underlying truth under the mass of conflicting representations. Differing narrations and attempts at uncovering the facts of Brynner's life were, after all, key to the constitution of his star persona from the outset, and have remained so to the current day.[33] Profiles, interviews, and exposés routinely represented conflicting accounts of Brynner's character and origin in order to discredit some and establish others – and, on many an occasion, managed doing both at once. In this sense, ambiguity was very much the stuff that made and fuelled his star image. It is the thick narrative layer of Brynner's public image, peppered with paradox, that this book focuses on.

Ambiguity, in sum, here means refusing to pin down one's objects of study to a singular perspective or analytical outcome: that they can simultaneously mean, afford, and effect different things that need to be accounted for, or at least be presented as available avenues for cultural analysis. This makes it possible to think through conflicting dynamics without doing away with irreconcilable tensions between or within them. Such a perspective necessitates forms of interpretation accommodating contradiction and simultaneity – of things potentially being *both and*.[34] Achieving this is admittedly easier said than done, yet this is my general rationale in exploring Brynner's film stardom.

I suggest that some of the ambiguities of Brynner's star image can be tied in with post-World War II notions of cosmopolitanism, namely the belief in a global human community, irrespective of national borders, which the modern notion of human rights is based on. While this political notion of cosmopolitanism underpinned Brynner's humanitarian activities advancing the rights of refugees, his reluctance to identify with any culture or nationality implied a more vernacular, personal cosmopolitan outlook. In order to make sense of this, I build on cosmopolitanism as a contextual framework for untangling the different, often seemingly incompatible, layers of Brynner's star image, from his public advocacy work to his flamboyant ethnic onscreen spectacles and shifting autobiographical fabulations. Paradoxically, liberal cosmopolitanism promoting universal human rights came here entwined with the appeal of the foreign and the exotic that his public persona operated and played with.

Thematic threads

Structure-wise, this book takes a thematic rather than linear approach. Each following chapter approaches his star image from a different perspective, through a different contextual framing and in connection with different sets of source material. While I briefly outline Brynner's biography in Chapter 2, this book does not set out to narrate a life story.[35] And while there is chronological order to how his films are examined within individual chapters, this does not apply to his entire body of work – so that, for example, his two comedies of 1960 are discussed as late as Chapter 8.

Exploring Brynner's diverse narrations of origin, Chapter 2 also provides an overview of his unrealised and realised film roles in the context of Hollywood's Production Code governing racial displays, and addresses his interest in film production and directing. Chapter 3 focuses on Brynner's kingly roles: his tenacious identification with the part of King Mongkut, the Orientalist templates that he was confined to and played with, as well as his performances in the lavish historical studio films *The Ten Commandments*, *Solomon and Sheba*, and *The Buccaneer*.

Chapter 4 zooms in on Brynner's physical assets and his positioning as a sex symbol oozing 'sex appeal to females from six to sixty.'[36] It explores press accounts of his physique, baldness, appetite, and animal magnetism that were in generous supply. The chapter further extends to media gossip on his private life and considers his star image in the context of contemporaneous male bodily displays by the likes of Kirk Douglas and Anthony Quinn. Moving closer to the bulk of Brynner's film work, Chapter 5 explores his diverse ethnic displays, inquiring after the stakes involved in taking on Russian roles during the Cold War, and tracks continuities and repetitions across his geographically diverse yet often similar characters. Changing gears somewhat dramatically, Chapter 6 addresses Brynner's humanitarian work and advocacy through the lens of cosmopolitanism. Discussing his media work for the UNHCR, his Romani affiliation and advocacy, and even his pan-ethnic cookbook, the chapter further explores his cosmopolitan style, flair, and jet-set lifestyle. This combination, I argue, is the stuff of ambiguity.

Returning more squarely back to his film oeuvre, Chapter 7 focuses on masculinity and screen violence in Brynner's spy thrillers, Westerns, action and science fiction films of the 1960s and 1970s. Considering connections between his roles as spies, gunfighters, warriors, and robots, the chapter also discusses emergent debates on screen violence and the question of ageing for a star whose brand was premised on physical prowess and desirability. Bringing together many strands cutting through the preceding chapters, Chapter 8 foregrounds Brynner's performance style with a focus on repetitions and stylizations. Focus-wise, it moves from the impact of Brynner's acting teacher, Michael Chekhov, to the shortcomings of his comic techniques and the camp aspects of his later work, including a drag cameo number in *The Magic Christian* (Joseph McGrath, 1969).

Finally, Chapter 9 looks at Brynner's afterlife: his identification with the role of King Mongkut, his posthumous anti-smoking ad, obituaries, biographies, and other forms of public remembrance, as well as the vernacular ways in which his idiosyncratic gestures and features are circulated on online platforms. Varying in their themes, scopes, and approach, these chapters are united in their focus on Brynner's star image: its fabrication, flexibility, reappearance, and overall ambiguity. The story begins with mythic, elusive origins.

Notes

1. *Picturegoer*, 15 September 1956a.
2. *Saturday Evening Post*, 22 November 1958.
3. *Collier's*, June 1956, 34.
4. *Hush-Hush*, July 1957, 33.
5. *Picturegoer*, 17 January 1959.
6. *Newsweek*, 19 May 1958, 103.
7. *Redbook*, May 1957, 96, emphasis in the original.
8. On listings of Hollywood favorites, see *The Hollywood Reporter*, 14 September 1956; *St. Petersburg Times*, 31 December 1956; *Picturegoer*, 8 June 1957; *Studio Survey*, 28 August 1957; *Boxoffice*, 16 February 1959; *The Hollywood Reporter*, 5 May 1959. On international popularity, see *The Hollywood Reporter*, 27 December 1957; *Elokuva-aitta* 24, 1958a; *The Hollywood Reporter*, 10 May 1961; *The Hollywood Reporter*, 17 July 1961. As discussed in Chapter 2, Brynner's birthplace was regularly identified as Sakhalin, which may have contributed to him being embraced as a 'Japanese' star, *The Korea Times*, 16 February 1975.
9. *Playboy*, January 1967, 101.
10. *San Francisco Examiner*, 20 September 1969.
11. On female off-white European Hollywood actors, see Negra 2001.
12. Dyer 1979, 109.
13. McDonald 2013; Mercer 2015. See also Hirsch 2010.
14. To quote a dictionary insert, 'His image – exotic, often sinister, and foreign, yet virile, masculine, and authoritative – was undeniably linked to his physique, his Eurasian facial features, but most especially his bald head.' Doll 2005, 168.
15. Straw 2011.
16. See Rantala 2016.
17. E.g., Cohan 1997; Robinson 2007. As producer, Brynner's key projects were *The Magnificent Seven* (which he ultimately did not produce) and the unrealised *The Gladiators* that feuded with Kirk Douglas's *Spartacus*. On the former, and on Brynner's early career, see Hannan 2015; on the latter, see MacAdam and Cooper 2020. This book builds loosely on Paasonen 2019. In addition, the popular reference work, *Ultimate Warrior: The Complete Films of Yul Brynner* examines the actor's full filmography with a side of biographical information, Dabell and Dabell 2019.

18. *Screenland*, May 1957, 53, 71.
19. Dyer 2004, 3.
20. With the exception of a handful of feature articles discussed in Chapter 4, Brynner was mainly present in short-format 'fan chart' introductions, gossip inserts, film reviews and promotions. E.g., *Ajan sävel* 46, 1958; *Ajan sävel* 21, 1959; *Ajan sävel* 29, 1960; *Ajan sävel* 5, 1961; *Elokuva-aitta* 3, 1957; *Filmitähti* 2, 1957; *Ajan sävel* 45, 1960; *Elokuva-aitta* 6, 1957; *Elokuva-aitta* 8, 1957.
21. In Finland, these came in English, German, French, and Italian. *Ajan sävel* 11, 1959. In addition, Swedish and Finnish studio contact details were provided. *Ajan sävel* 11, 1957.
22. *Collier's*, June 1956, 33, emphasis in the original.
23. Ibid., 34.
24. Mayne 1993, 138.
25. E.g., archival interviews in the documentary film *Les mille et une vies de Yul Brynner*, 2019; film violence is further addressed in Chapter 7.
26. *LA Times*, 10 August 1975.
27. *The Chattanooga Times*, 19 January 1958.
28. *The London Standard*, 10 October 1985; Jacobs and Stadiem 2004, 226; *The Telegraph*, 9 July 2020.
29. Here, Sal Mineo's personal essay is particularly elaborate. *Photoplay*, October 1957; see also *Collier's*, June 1956, 38; *Screenland*, May 1957, 71; *Elokuva-aitta* 15, 1958; Brynner 1989, 59. Gut-punching is the account of Anthony Rapp: *Out*, 1 February 1994; *People*, 5 April, 2019.
30. Brynner 1989, 246; Brynner 2010, 8; his children did all inherit, even though the estate was left to his fourth wife, Kathy Lee, see Capua 2006, 158.
31. *Cinépanorama*, July 1959; *LA Times*, 30 September 1952.
32. See Chapter 5; Langella 2012, 54.
33. E.g., *Behind the Scenes*, 28 March 1957; *Hush-Hush*, July 1957; *Saturday Evening Post*, 22 November 1958; *LA Times*, 10 August 1975; *Courier-Post*, 13 October 1985; *South China Morning Post*, 25 February 1990; *The Telegraph*, 9 July 2020.
34. I have elaborated on this at length elsewhere, see Paasonen 2021.
35. For those interested in life stories, there are four biographies to choose from, plus two documentary films: Robbins 1987; Brynner 1989; Brynner 2006; Capua 2006; *Yul Brynner: The Man Who Was King*, 1995; *Les mille et une vies de Yul Brynner*, 2019.
36. *Screenland*, January 1960, 68.

Chapter 2

Flexible origins and exotic displays

Spinning his autobiographical narrative freely as improvisations and variations that never cohered to a single story, Yul Brynner was a self-made man in a rather literal sense. His pan-ethnic star image was fuelled by constantly transforming stories of origin and background, some of which were grounded in fact; others not. In one prominent variation, his mother was a Romanian Gypsy who either had or had not died at his birth.[1] In others, she was Bessarabian or half-Romani while his father was half-Jewish, half-Mongolian, or Swiss.[2] Brynner was born either on the island of Sakhalin or among a group of nomadic Roma in an undefined location, under the stars; named either Yul Khan, Thaidje Khan, or Yul Taidje-Khan, his family of royal line either descending from – or having survived the rule of – Ghengis Khan.[3] The first name 'Yul' was arguably handed down from his great-great-great-great-grandfather, its meaning in Mongolian being 'Beyond the Hills,' or 'Beyond the Horizon... what you can't see.'[4]

Brynner was brought up in either Beijing or Paris, or both, touring Europe with a circus group or a band of Gypsy performers – or perhaps as a minstrel.[5] Other narrative variations included Buddhist monk training in China, philosophy and science degrees at the Sorbonne, combined with multiple doctorates, a black belt in judo, early service as cavalryman and a stint as driver for the Loyalists in the Spanish Civil War resulting in imprisonment and an early loss of hair.[6] An obituary writer notes how, '[t]o some, he presented himself as an orphan, to others as a child of privilege. He was either self-taught or a PhD.' Meanwhile, Brynner's accent gave few clues: 'It was unplaceable – too thick to be French, too liquid to be Chinese.'[7]

Diverse tales of origin were key to the construction of Brynner's public image as a decidedly foreign actor, yet one with geographically unspecific roots. Richly embellished autobiographical details and inventive artist names were standard fare in 1950s Hollywood, where fantastic personalities had been coined for amplifying star glamour ever since the studios were established three decades prior. Alien origins, both actual and fabricated, held erotic and exotic allure while also constraining careers in multiple ways. The ethnic flexibility of Brynner's star image – his seeming ability to move between, cross over, and occupy a range of positions without being bound to any single one – revolved around his overall physical look, accented English, as well as his well-acknowledged proclivity for fabulated autobiographies that involved a denial of Russian roots in favour of hybrid, nomadic, and opaque ones. Such narrations offered degrees of personal privacy and helped to draw attention away from his city of birth, Vladivostok, which could have anchored him in unfavourable ways in Cold War Hollywood. 'The facts of my existence have almost nothing to do with the realities of my life,' Brynner was quoted stating: 'I'm willing to discuss what I am doing but not who I was.'[8] '"Everyone," he says impatiently in that undefinable European accent, "is always saying we want the facts! It bores the bejesus out of me. [...] My life is art and imagination. The realities of my life are what is happening on stage."'[9]

This chapter first charts Brynner's narratives of origin, starting with factual detail, as largely presented by his son and biographer, Rock Brynner.[10] Juxtaposing these with the actor's own narrations and their circulation in the press, I explore the composition of his star image as an alien and exotic one. Brynner's biography certainly had more than a faint streak of romance to it, even as his self-narrations expanded to a different plane of myth and mystery by the time he rose to major Broadway – and subsequent Hollywood – fame. It is these narrations that affect how his star image became composed. Since film roles, whether rumored or realized, are of similar importance to how star personae come about, the second part of this chapter offers an overview of Brynner's various film projects, both actualized and hypothetical, and concludes with a discussion of his directing and production plans.

Not from around here

According to Rock Brynner's biography, the actor-to-be was born on 11 July 1920 in Vladivostok, in the Far Eastern Republic – nominally an independent state of the Russian Soviet Federated Socialist Republic – bordered by China and Korea.[11] While born into a wealthy, prominent, local family, he also had German and Swiss ancestry: he held a Swiss passport courtesy of his paternal grandfather, Jules Brynner, an industrialist and key figure in the founding and development of the city of Vladivostok. His birth name, Yuliy Briner, was in homage to his grandfather (rather than any mythical Mongolian ancestors) and shortened to Yul.

Jules Brynner had left his native country early on, working on ships and doing trade in Shanghai and Yokohama before landing in the Russian Far East where he would become the owner of several mines in Manchuria. Representative of mercantile cosmopolitanism,[12] Brynner's grandfather spoke German, French, English, Mandarin, and Japanese. In 1882, he married Natalya Kurkutova, an orphan raised by Mikhail Yankovsky, an exiled Polish count and a central player in local politics; it was through Kurkutova, granddaughter of a half-Buryat merchant, that Brynner could lay claim to some Mongolian heritage. Brynner's father, Boris, continued in family business and local politics while his inherited Swiss citizenship (momentarily) helped to shelter the family fortune after the October Revolution of 1917. He married Maria Dimitrievna Blagovidova, known as Marousia, who came from Russian intelligentsia and was a trained musical stage performer from the Petrograd Conservatory: through her maternal grandfather, Brynner could be associated with Jewish roots.[13]

In 1923, Boris Brynner left his family for Catharina Kornakova, a younger actress of the Moscow Art Theatre and later teacher of the Stanislavski method, leading a mobile international Euro-Asian lifestyle with a base in the Chinese-controlled Harbin, and later Shanghai.[14] In 1927, Marousia, her mother, Yul, and his older sister Vera – later a classical singer – migrated to Harbin to escape Stalin's regime, the presence of which was increasingly felt in East Siberia. It was at the Harbin YMCA that Brynner started playing the guitar at the age of ten. As Japanese troops began to approach in 1932, the family relocated to Paris via Shanghai, joining the substantial community of exiled White Russians already residing in the city. Brynner was sent to an elite boarding school, yet quickly relocated to a lycée in the city – the family still being financially supported by the industrialist father and, occasionally, by his brother. Rather than focusing on his formal education, Brynner met the Dimitrievitches, a Romani family of musicians and, at the age of twelve, joined their troupe performing Russian Roma music at the club Raspoutine. Two years later, he began training as a trapeze artist at Cirque d'Hiver, developing a stage character as a melancholy flying clown. This career was cut short by an accident at the age of seventeen as Brynner fell from the trapeze and broke several bones from leg to shoulder, risking permanent damage: in later accounts, the injury translated as him breaking 27 or 47 bones, or 'practically every bone in his body.'[15]

Consuming opium for both recreational purposes and for pain relief, Brynner met Jean Cocteau when the artist approached him for drugs at a nightclub. Brynner went on to befriend both the artist and others from his circle, such as the actor Jean Marais and Pablo Picasso. He continued to work at Cirque d'Hiver as a clown, yet his ambitions shifted to acting. Living on his own at the age of seventeen, he joined Georges and Ludmilla Pitöeff's Théâtre des Mathurins as an apprentice, stage-hand, carpenter, wig-maker, and bit-part player. As his mother, now diagnosed with leukemia, wanted to see her sister who was still living in Harbin, Brynner accompanied her and spent time with his father in Shanghai in 1938, training to play the ball game Jai Alai and enjoying the occasional tiger hunt.[16] Returning to Europe the following year, Brynner joined Mikhail (later Americanized to Michael) Chekhov's Moscow Art Theatre in Devon and took acting classes with the group. Despite doing his theatrical training in Paris, England, and the United States, it was with Russian mentors – the Pitöeffs and Chekhov, once a student of Konstantin Stanislavski – that he learned his craft.

With the war approaching Paris in 1940, Brynner and his mother boarded a ship for Manhattan where his sister Vera was already living. On arrival, he joined the Chekhov Players in Connecticut, doing small touring plays on college campuses, learning English, and making a modest Broadway debut as clown in Shakespeare's *Twelfth Night* late in 1941 as Youl Bryner.[17] Unable to enlist in the army due to health reasons after Pearl Harbor, Brynner joined the Office of War Information, broadcasting bulletins in French to the resistance movement in France and, in Russian, war-related news to the Soviet Union. Meanwhile, to make ends meet, he worked as a model for fashion photographers and art students; he also played the role of the southerner, Andre, in the 1943 Broadway play *The Moon Vine*, and appeared in some of Ludmilla Pitoëff's (short-lived) plays, all the while performing regularly at New York nightclubs.[18]

In 1942, Brynner met the actor Virginia Gilmore, once teen girlfriend of director Fritz Lang who had recently starred in Jean Renoir's *Swamp Water* and who had promised to help him with his English skills.[19] The two married in 1944 and he became a US citizen the same year. Through his war-time radio work, Brynner made contacts with people in early television. In 1944, he first appeared in a CBS children's show, *Mr. Jones and His Neighbors*, followed by performances in a range of programs, gradually rising through the ranks until he became an assistant director. In 1949, Brynner and Gilmore launched their own half-hour afternoon television show, *We're On* (often referred to as *Mr. and Mrs.*), for the New York-based WNBT, where they mainly interviewed Broadway stage and screen performers.[20] Brynner was appointed producer-director with CBS the same year working on current affairs, television theater, and suspense, in shows such as *Danger, Studio One, Starlight Theatre, Actor's Studio*, and *Omnibus*.[21] During this time, he was not altogether absent from the stage, returning to Broadway in the 1946 musical, *Lute Song*, liberally adapted from 'the ancient Chinese classic, "Pi-Pa-Kik",' which he claimed to have first seen as a child in 'his native Peking.'[22] In 1948, Brynner was cast as Prince Nikolai against four Russian ballerinas in *Dark Eyes*: the play continued to tour Britain where the press identified him (in surprisingly straightforward manner) as 'a young Russian.'[23]

Brynner's film debut was in 1949 in the documentary-style film noir *Port of New York* depicting the struggle of federal agents against an opium smuggling ring, led by his suave villain, Paul Vicola. The film was made before Brynner shaved off his thinning hair and, interestingly, his accent came across as lighter than in any other film role since (as discussed in Chapter 5, his other characters all spoke the same). Vicola was soft-talking, smooth, suave, sinister, and decidedly bad – evoking acute fear in the female protagonist whom he later strangles when he suspects a leak. As such, the character was not-too-distant kin to Dr. Nestri, whom Brynner played the same year in a *Studio One* live drama episode, 'Flowers from a Stranger,' with his hair toned white for instant aging effect. In this rare surviving example of Brynner's 1940s television work, he played a 50-something-year-old concentration camp survivor and renowned psychotherapist, who devised schemes of both a romantic and murderous nature aimed at the (equally) traumatised female lead character. Vicola and Nestri each have a looming, menacing presence, though the latter is one of manic gestures, obsessive longing, and ultimate mental collapse rather than cold restraint. Given Brynner's argued preference for the roles of villains over those of heroes, under different circumstances these could have become the types for him to specialize in.[24]

Figure 2.1 Brynner as Vicola in *Port of New York*

Many critics considered his performance as Vicola, along with those of the rest of the cast in the *Port of New York*, as good, even if standard and methodical, some going as far as to describe his elegant, cold 'screen menage' outstanding in combining 'the suavity of Charles Boyer with the craftiness of Peter Lorre.'[25] The French Boyer – who was to join Brynner in the cast of the 1958 *Buccaneer* and the 1969 *The Madwoman of Chaillot* (directed by Bryan Forbes) – was known for romantic, glamorous leads and as Ingrid Bergman's ill-intentioned husband in *Gaslight* (George Cukor, 1944). Meanwhile, the Hungarian Lorre was cast by Hollywood in sinister, offbeat supporting roles. Coded as an amalgamation of the two, Brynner was introduced to film fans as European-foreign and menacing, yet also a tad charming. Complimenting his 'unusual look,' *Variety* saw him as standing 'out as a cultured heavy, exploiting a good voice and unusual look to register as a novel personality,' even as *Daily News* labeled Vicola as borderline comic in his overdone 'stalking about.'[26] Despite mainly neutral reviews and efforts, such as a promotional tour with radio interviews, 'Miss Port of New York' and 'Miss Port of Boston' beauty contests, 'a three-hour parade of ship-floats, sound-trucks and bannered cars,' department store window displays, and giveaways such as 'dope capsules,' cards, and 'wanted' posters featuring Brynner's face, *Port of New York* failed to make much of an impact.[27]

It was not until the Broadway success of *The King and I* that Brynner gradually left his by now well-established and well-paid television job, and it was also the play that launched his Hollywood career (see Chapter 3). Although his claim of having made more than a thousand television shows is fantastical, given the modest volume of early programming alone, Brynner had broad directorial experience across genres.[28] Even after becoming a star, he continued to plan a 'repertory company of outstanding Hollywood and Broadway personalities' for CBS and, as late as 1958, a 'playhouse' project of television films in collaboration with United Artists and Walter Mirisch (of the Mirisch Corporation).[29] As discussed below, Brynner expressed an interest in quitting acting before the musical's film version even started shooting, repeating this desire to move back behind the camera for years to come.[30]

Despite possibly taking some classes at the Sorbonne before the war and joining a master's seminar in Philosophy at Northwestern University in 1955 when touring with *The King and I*, Brynner had little formal education.[31] At Northwestern, he also enrolled in photography classes, eventually developing a professional skillset and joining the renowned Magnum Photo co-operative. His behind-the-scenes shots were published in *Life* magazine and *New York Herald Tribune* and, in 1960, he published a book of documentary photographs from refugee camps together with Inge Morath (see Chapter 6).[32] He also worked on film sets as photographer.³³ Brynner was a naturalized US citizen until 1965 when he gave up his citizenship for tax reasons, having already resided in Switzerland for several years.³⁴ After Gilmore divorced him in 1960, he was married to women of Yugoslavian-Chilean, French, and Malaysian origins, fathering a total of three children and adopting a further two (see Chapter 6).³⁵

Slippery narratives

In 1956, *The Washington Post* identified Brynner's year of birth as 1915 and his birthplace as Sakhalin:

> [A]n island off the coast of Northern Japan, unpleasantly close to Siberia. His mother was a Romanian gypsy, who died giving birth to him. His father was a Mongolian, Taije Khan who had been educated in Switzerland and had become a Swiss citizen with the Swiss name of Brynner. [...] working on his own he had acquired B.A. and M.A. degrees from the Sorbonne in Paris and is now studying for a doctorate at the same institution. Somewhere along the way he also absorbed eight languages fluently – not an accent in any of these – and can talk pretty well in another eight.³⁶

Since Brynner spoke accented English, this narrative had an unstable basis to start with, even though he was, indeed, a polyglot. The article presents one example of how Brynner's biographical details unfolded in the media as contingent variations of recurring characters, settings, and themes. These narrations were successful to the degree that obituaries, later dictionaries and reference works continued to offer different details of his life – birth year and given names included.³⁷ Even when journalists were offered factual tidbits, such as Brynner having Japanese cousins (his grandfather Jules had fathered a child in Yokohama before sailing off to Vladivostok), they hardly knew what to trust.³⁸

Brynner's proclivity for spinning tales of exotic origin was recognized early on in his career so that, over the decades, journalists regularly both commented on their lack of veracity and unsuccessfully pushed him to set the record straight: his reputation as an unwilling, resistant, and difficult interviewee remained with him for the decades to come. The 1957 tabloid exposé, 'The Awful Truth about Yul Brynner,' exhibited little suspension of disbelief:

Flexible origins and exotic displays 23

> When this angular-faced, amber-eyed, flat-nosed Mongolian mountebank opens his mouth, *anything* is liable to come out of his mouth – and usually does [...] At a swanky cocktail party in New York's theatrical district [...] Yul described a childhood of Oriental splendor in a palace in Outer Mongolia, surrounded by dusky slaves and voluptuous, slant-eyed dancing girls. 'It was natural for me to play the role of the king in *The King and I*,' says Yul. 'I learned about being a king at a very early age.'[39]

Combining factual detail with the blatantly fantastic, Brynner's stories of origin resulted in fabulation in constant motion where recognizable features repeated in patterned yet unpredictable ways. For the most part, his self-fashioning meant alignment with the nomadic Romani, yet in some variations his background was one of wealth and privilege left for the freedom of a touring artist's life. In one retelling, he was sent from Asia to France without any family at all: 'I made the voyage from Yokohama to Marseilles alone, in charge of the ship's doctor. It was a fantastically wonderful trip for a little boy.'[40] This unstable narrative web extended from his early days of stardom to later biographical accounts. Describing and mocking the 'ten or twelve weird stories in circulation' about his beginnings in a 1958 *Saturday Evening Post* interview, Brynner denied telling any of these himself:

> Looking me squarely in the eye – and when Brynner looks you squarely in the eye, there is a noticeable impact, you can almost hear a click – he said, 'If you took the trouble to trace those stories, you'd find that none of them was really told by me. They came out of conversations someone is supposed to have had with me, but when writers come to me to verify them, I tell each of them, "Yes, that's true." [...] 'No matter what story I tell them,' he said, 'writers invent things about me, and once they've invented them they believe them. They tell these tales at a dinner party, and they become part of the Brynner story. I don't want to embarrass anyone, so who am I to take the trouble to deny all this fiction? In fact, I enjoy it.'[41]

Similar glee was evident in a 1959 French television interview with the journalist Pierre Dumayet who inquired which of the dozen or so stories the actor himself preferred. With a grin, Brynner responded that the version he particularly loved identified him as a Swiss-Mongolian born in Brooklyn.[42] Such glee, in combination with the range and quality of his origin stories, obviously means that neither Brynner nor, indeed, pretty much anyone else was invested in them being taken as accurate fact. Rather, journalistic probes and explorations render evident the pleasures involved in witnessing such narratives cross, intermesh with, and contradict one another.

Attempting to uncover the actual state of affairs behind the curtain of fabrication, *Redbook* magazine titled its 1957 feature 'Self-Made Mystery Man,' introducing its subject as an individual of rare imagination: 'Yul Brynner alters his life story to suit his mood of the moment. Here are the facts (?) about this "average clean-cut Mongolian boy".'[43] Such articles became something of a genre of their own, often riffing off one another and recycling semi-identical quotes: by 1958, a *Picturegoer* reader excited by these colorful retellings was keenly awaiting a film on Brynner's life.[44] All this suggests that the issue was less one of providing the correct facts than that of feeding elusive tales of the actor's background and persona to prop up his public appeal. Furthermore, given how Brynner was defined as a 'Broadwayite' (in a play on 'Muscovite') during his stage breakthrough, and how his facial features and accent were later identified as 'Slavic,' suggests that his origins may not have been much of an actual mystery.[45]

Stories of exotic background and self-mythologizing habits sold papers. Since Brynner's factual life story was colorful to start with, it did not take much embellishing for it to read as fantastic – the narrative presented in the 1957 fan magazine *Picture Show*, for example, was largely factual (except for identifying the actor as six feet tall).[46] Across interviews, profiles, and exposés, Brynner was quoted as highlighting the importance of keeping his private life – family and childhood – away from the public eye so that florid stories afforded degrees of privacy. 'Brynner has succeeded in mystifying the people and glamorizing himself to an extent not approached even by Greta Garbo,' wrote *Redbook*, which went on to quote him arguing the issue was that of drawing a line between his public and private personae: 'and I have my fun while drawing the line.'[47] He also wanted to be firmly in control of the story. When Brynner's sister, Vera, set some of the record straight in a *Newsweek* cover feature focusing on the actor, he became incensed enough to cut off communication with her until she was dying of cancer.[48]

Expansive language skills were one central element of Brynner's star persona. In 1956, *Collier's* described 'Vira Dharmawara, who is spiritual adviser to the Throne of Cambodia' visiting Brynner on the set of *The King and I* and the two conversing 'on spiritual issues in English, French, Chinese, Mongolian, Russian, Spanish, German, Italian, and Hungarian.'[49] Combining cultural and intellectual capital with linguistic prowess, the flabbergasted journalist situated Brynner as a man of the world, eloquent on virtually any topic and in virtually any language. Accounts of Brynner's first language varied, yet Russian was not on the cards – on occasion, he argued to have never been to Russia.[50] His first language was identified as either Mandarin, Cantonese, or Romani, followed by Mongolian learnt from a paternal grandmother and a range of other languages (Malay, Korean, Japanese, Thai, possibly Hungarian); the eighth language could have been French, the ninth Russian taught by a kind emigrant actor in Paris, the tenth and final was English.[51] He was also believed to have spoken Serbo-Croat fluently enough to act as interpreter on the set of *Battle of Neretva* (Veljko Bulajić, 1969), as well as to need only a little brushing up for 'his German, Italian and Spanish' to fare just fine.[52] According to Brynner's son, his language skills encompassed Russian, French, English, and some Romani, as well as a little Korean, Mandarin, and Cantonese which he learned when young.[53]

When promoting *Le Serpent / Night Flight from Moscow* (Henri Verneuil, 1973; a film where he uses his three major languages) on French television, Brynner claimed to speak a total of eleven languages by virtue of having lived in different parts of the world. He further explained being poor at regional accents since he already had an accent in all the languages he spoke, so that 'it becomes impossible to impose another accent on top of mine.' When inquired about his first language, Brynner argued that he did not even know:

> I have a rather undefinable accent, as you can hear: I have a bit of an accent in French, I have a little bit of an accent in English, and also in other languages, and I don't know where these accents come from. They surely come from me.[54]

Brynner can be interpreted as saying that he in fact had no first language, just as he did not have a country of origin allowing for a sense of national identity. Alternatively, he can be seen to say that accents were merely one facet or expression of his persona signalling the individual uniqueness of a self-made man. In another 1970s interview, he claimed not to be 'a man from nowhere' but rather a man with extraordinarily mobile roots:

> [V]ery profound roots that go back very far. It's this that has made it possible for me to move without being uprooted. It's this that's allowed me to move as much as I moved in all of my young youth, even in my second youth […] I continue to move even now because my roots are so expansive.[55]

Being a man of strong yet mobile roots meant not being fixed through narratives of ancestry but rather weaving through and tapping into any given number of them. As discussed in Chapter 6, fictitious Romani roots, adopted during his teens through his affiliation with the Dimitrievitch family, grew particularly central to Brynner's self-presentation.[56]

Fabricated stars

In order to craft larger-than-life personae, studio-era Hollywood freely reinvented names and biographical details while personal characteristics operating as star trademarks were highlighted though their repetitive display. Such refashioning was the work of both studio publicity departments and agents paid to promote their clients' thespian goods. During the silent era, for example, Fox studio publicity transformed Theodosia Goodman of Cincinnati to the mysterious Theda Bara, daughter of a French actress – or, possibly, that of an Arabian princess – and an Italian sculptor, born and raised in 'the shadow of the Sphinx.'[57] Daughter of Polish and Swiss Jewish immigrants, Goodman was refashioned into the quintessential foreign vamp emanating sexual danger and Orientalist allure: even her new name was presented as an anagram for 'Arab death.'[58] Here, Orientalism – which, following Edward Said's argument – operates as a tactic of othering that positions the Orient as an object for the Occident to know and control, offered ample tropes to recycle and build on (see Chapter 3).[59]

The authenticity of such florid origin stories was publicly doubted from the outset, with fan magazines skeptically probing gaps between stars' onscreen images and offscreen personae. In other words, fabricated star images were understood to be part and parcel of Hollywood's overall logic of entertainment, escapism, and fantasy.[60] This general skepticism helps to explain reactions to Brynner's biographical accounts, as these extended from journalistic accounts to readers' letters, such as the one published in *Redbook*:

> After reading the fascinating account of Yul Brynner's many past lives ('Self-Made Mystery Man' – May), I am convinced that Brynner must have been born in a small town in Connecticut – acquiring his vast knowledge of languages in a public library, his delightful oriental characteristics on an imaginary trip to Shangri-La, and his gypsy mother while she wandered on the way to the corner store.[61]

Brynner's self-invention followed established Hollywood patterns of mobility, exoticism, Orientalism, and artifice, yet in a somewhat off-sync manner. First, his star image was not a product of studio publicity since its basic elements had been laid out during the run of *Lute Song* and, in particular, with his stage success in *The King and I*.[62] In the publicity surrounding *Lute Song*, which toured until 1947, Brynner was variously identified as a 'young Eurasian,' 'part Chinese,' 'Swiss citizen who is also Gypsy-Mongol,' and as a physically excellent choice for the Oriental role.[63] Occasionally, Brynner simply identified as American when inquired about his nationality, possibly tapping into the notion of the US as 'the great melting pot' (even though he eventually gave up citizenship).[64] When caught telling contradictory tales of origin, Brynner, according to one biographer, would simply state being 'a joint, worldwide, national and international citizen of the earth.'[65]

Second, Brynner was free to shape his star image by virtue of not being under exclusive contract with any studio but working with Fox, Paramount, and MGM in 1956 alone. To the extent that it was possible for any actor of the era to coin, Brynner's star persona was his own volatile creation that no agent could really alter, even though it was profoundly shaped by both the range of roles available to him and the ways in which his star image was framed in the press. Third, by the time that he ascended to film stardom, dramatic and romantic stories of origin of the kind that were popular from the 1910s to the 1940s had already grown passé. Even as Brynner's flamboyant self-imaginings guaranteed him steady, and at times intense public attention, these also risked marking him in anachronistic ways as a creature of Hollywood past. Consider, for example, a 1962 newspaper article addressing his autobiographical narrations (in past tense, even though these were still very much ongoing):

> For a long time Brynner perplexed and baffled Hollywood. He took a deep pride in confusing the publicists and columnists with the facts of his background. At one time, he claimed to be a member of the Czarist family, and permitted the press department of the studio to grind out endless stories about the aristocratic glamor of his background.[66]

Redbook similarly wrote that '[s]everal years ago he was part Russian and was born in Russia, but he changed his mind about that.'[67] There are no early mentions of Russian roots, either romanticised or more prosaic, attributed to Brynner in the press sources I scoured for this book. This does not mean that such mentions did not exist, merely that their public visibility was easily overridden by alternative retellings. Be that as it may, the overall fluidity, inner contradiction and excess of Brynner's autobiographical stories rendered his ethnic or national origins ones best guessed. This allowed for him to overcome typecasting as that which he demonstrably was, a first-generation immigrant from Soviet Russia, albeit one of heterogeneous heritage. Describing it a 'star's duty' to be 'a man of mystery' in a 1959 *Picturegoer* article, Brynner merely denied such origins: 'There is no Russian blood in my veins. But I am part Mongolian and that is a common strain in the USSR. I spent my childhood in Peking and Paris.'[68] It was not until 1972, following an article in the Soviet newspaper, *Izvestia*, that he admitted being Russian – 'but only partly.'[69]

In 1950s Hollywood, Russianness itself had become a career-killing liability and being identified as such risked being typecast in a narrow range of roles.[70] In a polarized geopolitical imaginary where anti-communist and anti-Russian sentiments intermeshed, 'Russians were particularly dangerous because as educated white people they could "pass" for members of in-group; their "otherness" was in many ways invisible, unless revealed by English spoken with a strong Russian accent.'[71] Noël Coward, Brynner's long-time friend and co-star in *Surprise Package* (Stanley Donen, 1960) characterized his accent as 'rhythmical Americanese marinated in borscht.'[72] This accent nevertheless failed to identify or fix him as Russian, even as references to the actor's 'Mongol eyes crossing in narrow slits' and 'Slavic accent rumbling' repeated for decades to come.[73]

Brynner's unwillingness to be pinned down in terms of nationality, I suggest, should not be understood merely as a straightforward pre-emptive response to anti-Russian sentiments in 1950s US. It remains a fact that Brynner left Vladivostok at any early age for Harbin, then Shanghai, Paris, and New York, and that he could be characterized as Russian only in the partial sense of immediate family. If anything, his background was cosmopolitan. In Paris, he took on a Romani identity and, in the United States, his vague Europeanness, complete with mentions of Sorbonne degrees, afforded levels of sophistication and elegance which, albeit starkly at odds with his presumed barbarian Mongol heritage, were of an equally alien kind. Siberia and Outer Mongolia worked as dramatic backdrops of birth and partial origin but much less as defining markers of identity. Brynner's son suggests as much, arguing that 'his essence was that of a man without a country.'[74] Brynner's cross-continental background functioned as a springboard for his self-fashioning as a cosmopolitan man of the world who, by implication, could play just about any man in the world.

An alien star in demand

With Brynner's Broadway fame, speculations of his casting in various film productions began to circulate. In 1951, he signed an exclusive deal with Paramount, which upped the ante on his potential film roles and meant that he was generously promoted in a similar way to the studio's other promising newcomers, such as Audrey Hepburn and Rosemary Clooney.[75] Around this time, Brynner was still balancing Broadway stardom with his work as a director at CBS.[76] Some years before his final screen breakthrough Brynner was already a recognizable celebrity actor who was considered to need merely the right kind of role for his star to truly take off. In a well-developed plan in 1952, he was to be reintroduced to film audiences in Billy Wilder's *A New Kind of Love* as a 'rugged Soviet ballet dancer (as important to Stalin as Joe DiMaggio is to America)' in a role originally designed for Maurice Chevalier against either Audrey Hepburn or Katharine Hepburn: the film was to be shot in Venice.[77]

It is telling of Brynner's status in early 1950s Hollywood that *A New Kind of Love* was very much planned as a star vehicle to showcase an actor 'utterly different from anyone who has ever been in pictures' – a man exotic 'in the most masculine sense imaginable' of French, Scandinavian, Chinese, and Gypsy background.[78] Brynner reportedly wrote two songs for the film, with the plan of accompanying himself with a guitar.[79] As the production was postponed and eventually canceled, Brynner received compensation of $100,000 in 1953, his Paramount contract ending later the same year.[80] Had Brynner's second film appearance ever been as a rugged Soviet ballet dancer, it is possible that his star image would have become more fixed along Russian lines. This, however, was not to be.

In terms of star image, potential, rumored yet aborted projects matter in terms of understanding the range and type of roles that a performer has been considered a good fit for – and, in 1950s and 1960s Hollywood, both gossip and potential projects were in ample supply. With Brynner, it was clear well before the film premiere of *The King and I* (and while still starring in the musical play) that his star image was not only masculine but exotic and alien in equal measure. And, since Brynner was already in his 30s, he was not eyed for the roles of young men. As early as 1951, he was rumored to be the preferred lead actor in a Mahatma Gandhi biopic.[81] Soon after, Louella Parsons envisioned him as the perfect fit for the role of a refugee Romanian gigolo marrying an American schoolteacher in Tijuana in the musical remake of *Hold Back the Dawn* (Mitchell Leisen, 1942).[82] Other proposed early alternatives included the role of a Cossack in a film set in pre-Soviet times, 'tiki'-themed *South Seas Story* with Audrey Hepburn, the role of Pontius Pilate in *Pilate's Wife*, and a cameo in the star-studded stage comedy, *Main Street to Broadway*.[83] In 1953, Brynner – rather than Kirk Douglas – was rumored to play Vincent van Gogh in *Lust for Life* while Brynner and Charlton Heston were both proposed for the role of the American missionary, Reverend Davidson, in *Rain / Miss Sadie Thompson*.[84] Rumours also circulated of him being a great fit for the role of 'colourful beggar Hajj' in the musical comedy *Kismet* set in Baghdad (directed in 1955 by Vincente Minnelli) and for John Huston's unrealised bullfighting film, *The Matador*.[85]

These potential projects, some of which were passing mentions and others in the planning, ranged from biographical films of notable men of international origins to various kinds of adventurers and men of action. His lead role in the romantic biopic, *Omar Khayyam*, was discussed as something of a set deal in 1954 (the film was eventually released in 1957, starring the Hungarian-American Cornel Wilde): Brynner was also reported to be eyed for 'the top heavy role, Yosidah' in the Biblical film, *Joseph and His Brethren*; for a lead in a Georges Simenon adaptation, *A Woman of New York*; and to be considering a role in *Nijinsky Story*.[86] News of him starring in the Carlo Ponti and Dino de Laurentiis biblical epic, *Judith and Holofernes*, with Silvana Mangano as Judith against his Holofernes, started circulating in 1952, and continued for some years.[87] The producers had recently finished *Ulysses* with Kirk Douglas and Anthony Quinn and went on to make the 1954 *Attila* with Quinn as the Hun.[88] This suggests that Brynner was considered suitable for leading masculine roles in historical epics before Cecil B. DeMille cast him for *The Ten Commandments* in 1954. By the time the news broke of Brynner being the first actor recruited by DeMille, this was described as a 'striking, not to say astonishing, casting coup' involving 'the top-flight personality and actor of the Broadway stage.'[89]

Other high-profile projects were simultaneously discussed. In 1955, Brynner was said to be the first pick for the role of Napoleon (a role eventually played by Herbert Lom) in the de Laurentiis and Ponti

Paramount production, *War and Peace* (also starring Audrey Hepburn, Henry Fonda, Mel Ferrer, and Oscar Homolka) and as the lead for a television series based on the Jean Gabin vehicle, *Pépé le Moko* (Julien Duvivier, 1937).[90] In July 1956, soon after the successful premiere of *The King and I* but before either *The Ten Commandments* or *Anastasia* made it to the screens, Brynner was rumored for the title role in Darryl Zanuck's semi-documentary CinemaScope film, *The Secret Crimes of Josef Stalin*, his screen tests being, according to Louella Parsons, 'more Stalin than the Old Joe himself.'[91] The actor soon denied these claims, arguing that he 'wouldn't touch the role for anything in the world' and that he drew the line at impersonating 'the most cruel tyrant of all time.'[92]

Since the film was never made, it is difficult to estimate the extent to which Brynner was considered for the role, yet it is easy enough to see why he would not have found it altogether appealing. With Stalin recently dead, his successor Nikita Khrushchev had denounced his political purges, even as knowledge of the terror within the Gulag, the Soviet prison camp system, was yet to become public. The film promised to focus on Stalin's early activities as paid assassin and bank robber, and to explore the claim that 'the dictator murdered his second wife.'[93] No matter how barbaric the King of Siam or Rameses II may have been, they fit the broad mold of a 'bastard with a heart of gold' – the type that Brynner came to identify as his specific niche, and which he played for much of his career in variations ranging from Third Reich and Soviet colonels to gunslinger outlaws.[94] However, being cast as Stalin, whose heart was far from golden, would have been an unnecessary risk to take, especially in the early stages of his film career. It might also have been personally an unpleasant one, given his family history of loss and forced migration.

In further plans, Brynner was to take on leading roles in biopics of the British Regency-era clown Grimaldi, Houdini, Mussolini, Giuseppe Garibaldi, Kemal Atatürk, and Buddha (under the direction of either King Vidor or David Lean), as well as the role of Kublai Khan in *Marco Polo* (against either Brigitte Bardot or his *Solomon and Sheba* co-star, Gina Lollobrigida).[95] A range of literary adaptations were also proposed: *China Story* written by Pearl Buck; Darryl F. Zanuck's *Chez Pavan* set in a lively Parisian hotel, based on a bestselling novel; adaptations of French novels *The Return of Cinders* and *Face to Face*, both with Simone Signoret, and Alphonse Daudet's *The New Adventures of Tartarino* with Jayne Mansfield; an adaptation of *The Voyage of the Lucky Dragon* on Japanese fishermen caught in the fallout of the first H-Bomb at Bikini; William Goetz's *Time of the Dragons* meant to 'continue the Japanese kick he started with *Sayonara*'; the Viking epic, *The Tallest Ships*, also proposed for Kirk Douglas; adaptation of Berkely Mather's action-packed *The Achilles Affair*, as well as the male lead against Audrey Hepburn in the adaptation of Phyllis Hastings's novel, *Rapture in My Rags*, an 'offbeat story of a farm girl with no one to love who falls in love with a scarecrow until a cynical farm labourer comes along and she transfers her affections to him.'[96]

Yet other unrealised projects of the late 1950s and early 1960s involved biblical themes and exotic action as roles in *The Greatest Story Ever Told* (a biblical epic eventually directed by George Stevens in 1965 and starring Max von Sydow as Jesus, Charlton Heston as John the Baptist, and Telly Savalas as Pontius Pilate), a 'pirate yarn' titled *Captain Sin* and *The Night-Comers*, an action film based on a novel by Eric Ambler set on a Southeast Asian island undergoing a coup.[97] At this point, Brynner was a desired choice for romantic leading roles: Leo McCarey eyed him for *An Affair to Remember* (released in 1957, with Cary Grant and Deborah Kerr), and Billy Wilder for *Love in the Afternoon* (out the same year, with Gary Cooper and Audrey Hepburn)[98]. Plans were also reported for biblical epics *Joshua and Reba* and *Barabbas* with de Laurentiis, the latter co-starring Simone Signoret; *The White Rajah*, a biopic of Sir James Brooke, the colonial British ruler of Salawak, Malaysia, where he would most likely have played the Sultan of Brunei against Robert Mitchum's lead; a story of an 'eccentric oil tycoon'; a 'Nepalese' role in *The Mountain is Young* based on a novel by Han Suyin; the lead in a World War II biopic *The Sam Magill Story*; roles in *Monte Carlo Mob* and *The Battle of the Bulge*; the part of Crazy Horse in *The Day Custer Fell*, as well as a biopic of the Genghis Khan.[99]

There were discussions of Brynner joining forces with Tony Curtis well before making *Taras Bulba* (J. Lee Thompson, 1962) together in 'Milton Sperling's Cinerama-with-a-story, *Cinerama Circus*,' the two playing the roles of a lion tamer and high-wire artist, respectively.[100] In 1959, Brynner was rumoured to star against Dorothy Dandridge – one of Hollywood's few Black female stars – in an adaptation of Gustave Flaubert's *Salammbo* as 'Halmicar, father of Hannibal, in a yarn about the First Punic War.'[101] The 1960 Marilyn Monroe vehicle, *Let's Make Love*, was first written for Brynner, who was to play a Greek industrialist (a role eventually re-tailored for Yves Montand).[102] And, in the 1970s, discussions were underway for the roles of General Moshe Dayan in a David Ben-Gurion biopic on the birth of Israel; Caesar in a Federico Fellini film; a 'submarine pirate in a yet untitled film dealing with a true-life World War II adventurer'; as well as a role in the volcano disaster film, *Day the World Ended*.[103] Within these rumored projects, Brynner's potential parts were those of foreign leaders and men of action in an ever-shifting range of ethnicities.

In 1957, Byla Productions, an independent production company that Brynner had set up with *Anastasia* director Anatole Litvak the previous year, announced a distribution deal with Paramount, making him co-producer. Their first, and only, finished film was *The Journey* (made with MGM in 1959), with unrealised plans for shooting *Two Different Worlds* in Istanbul and Paris the following year.[104] In 1967, it was announced that Brynner had established a production company, Danube Films, with *Villa Rides* director Buzz Kulik in order to make a film on the life of Otto von Bismarck (later the plan included Carlo Ponti).[105] Since Atatürk and Bismarck were roles that Brynner was arguably specifically interested in portraying, his earlier turning down of the role of Stalin had little to do with aversion towards playing political leaders, or 'great men.' And since the ethnic scale of his actualized film roles was as broad as that of unrealised ones, he seemed to have little opposition to being typecast in exotic parts.

Now this, now that

As an actor, Brynner could be considered an 'auteur' in the sense of being 'responsible for and exercised significant control' over his star image and onscreen roles.[106] Or, as an obituary writer put it, '[h]is roles were often no more than starring vehicles for the character he had established – the glamorous, dominant mystery man whose smooth bald head had started a new fashion.'[107] It was nevertheless blatantly clear from the parts that he was offered that limitations did apply.

To present Brynner's actualized roles in the form of a listing: onscreen, his body was Thai in *The King and I* (1956); then Egyptian in *The Ten Commandments* (1956); Russian in *Anastasia* (1956), *The Brothers Karamazov* (Richard Brooks, 1958), *The Journey* (Anatole Litvak, 1959), and *Le Serpent / Night Flight from Moscow* (1973). It continued to transform to French in *The Buccaneer* (Anthony Quinn, 1958); Israeli in *Solomon and*

Sheba (King Vidor, 1959) and *Cast a Giant Shadow* (Melville Shavelson, 1966); Cossack in *Taras Bulba* (1962) and *Romance of a Horsethief* (Abraham Polonsky, 1971); Arab in *Escape from Zahrain* (Ronald Neame, 1962); German in *Morituri* (Bernhard Wicki, 1965) and *Triple Cross* (Terence Young, 1966); Iranian in *The Poppy is also a Flower* (Terence Young, 1966); Indian in *The Long Duel* (Ken Annakin, 1967); Mexican in *Villa Rides* (Buzz Kulik, 1968), and *Adíos, Sabata / Indio Black* (Frank Kramer, 1970); and Yugoslav in *Battle of Neretva* (1969).

Figure 2.2 Brynner as Irani, Russian, Indian, 'Cajun,' Yugoslav, German, Mexican, and Ukrainian.

When Brynner's characters were American, they came in diverse ethnic hues as his body re-emerged as French-American in *The Sound and the Fury* (Martin Ritt, 1959); Greek-American in *Surprise Package* (1960); Native American in *Kings of the Sun* (J. Lee Thompson, 1963); Japanese-Polish-American in *Flight from Ashiya* (Michael Anderson, 1964); 'Cajun' in *Invitation to a Gunfighter* (Richard Wilson, 1964), *The Magnificent Seven* (John Sturges, 1960), and *Return of the Seven* (Burt Kennedy, 1966); and as Italian-American in *Death Rage* (1976) and, possibly, in *Port of New York* (1949). The role of the egocentric conductor, Victor Fabian in *Once More, with Feeling!* (Stanley Donen, 1960) was simply cosmopolitan, so that no particular ethnic profiling was necessary. In 1960, Brynner did a cameo in Jean Cocteau's *Le testament d'Orphée* as an usher to Hell primly dressed in a tuxedo and speaking in accented French: together with Alain Resnais and Jean Marais, he also helped to finance the film.[108] His other cameo as a female torch singer in *The Magic Christian* (1969) was a lip-synch.

On some occasions – as in his roles as CIA agent Dan Slater in *The Double Man* (Franklin J. Schaffner, 1967), the secret service agent Pete Novak in *The File of the Golden Goose* (Sam Wanamaker, 1969), and the outlaw thief Jed Catlow in *Catlow* (Sam Wanamaker, 1971) – no specific explanation was given for his accent beyond Novak's name pointing to East European origins. In *Fuzz* (Richard A. Colla, 1972), it added to the mystery of his deaf blackmailer character, even as 'Sardo' – deaf in Spanish – came linguistically coded and, in *The Light at the Edge of the World* (Kevin Billington, 1971), to that of his diabolic pirate captain, Jonathan Kongre. In *The Ultimate Warrior* (Robert Clouse, 1975) set in post-apocalyptic New York and also starring the Swedish Max von Sydow, accents no longer mattered since the world as we know it had already come to an end. Accents were a similar non-issue among the entertainment robots of *Westworld* (Michael Crichton, 1973) and *Futureworld* (Richard T. Heffron, 1976). And since *The Madwoman of Chaillot* (Bryan Forbes, 1969) was set in Paris with an English-speaking cast, his accent needed as little explaining as Katharine Hepburn's, Danny Kaye's, Charles Boyer's, Giulietta Masina's, or Oskar Homolka's.

Starting from his accent, the sense of the unspecified alien was central to Brynner's star image in ways that created both opportunities and constraints in him being cast as imported goods. In 1947, Universal had reportedly turned down Brynner's screen test due to his overtly Oriental looks.[109] These looks worked in his favour in *The King and I* and the actor systematically amplified them through tongue-in-cheek self-narrations as a 'clean-cut Mongolian boy.'[110] After his performance as King Mongkut, classifiable as yellowface, Brynner moved to brownface and a plethora of ethnicities without ever playing a corn-fed WASP hero. If, following Richard Dyer, film stars are 'embodiments of the social categories in which people are placed and through which we make our lives – categories of class, gender, ethnicity, religion, sexual orientation, and so on,' with Brynner many such categories remained in perpetual motion.[111] Both the range and degree of stylization that his performances involved evoke the basic yet complex question connected to the politics of representation: who stands in for whom, who speaks on behalf of whom, and under which historical conditions.[112]

Even as his film career grew highly successful, Brynner, white yet not entirely so, was a desirable studio-era proxy for performers whose explicit otherness prevented them from being cast in major parts within the system's segregationist, racist hierarchies. These hierarchies extended to the internal divisions within whiteness, as marked by features and accent alike, so that Brynner's roles spoke of both the inner instability of whiteness and its power as a means of systemizing bodily difference within social organization.[113] He played characters of virtually any ethnicity, building on the established convention of white stars – such as Douglas Fairbanks or John Barrymore of years past – participating in 'masquerades of ethnicity' with 'the help of a healthy suntan or a little makeup,' often in romanticized settings of 'tents and towers, kings, and castles.'[114] At the same time, he brought an extra off-white frisson to such displays.

Sarah Berry points out that Hollywood studio-era exoticism and ethnic stereotyping were premised on the existence of 'a category of nonethnic whiteness' on the one hand, and on interconnected myths of racial purity and dangers of 'mixed blood,' on the other. This segregationist ideology entailed 'ethnic simulacra' performed by white actors.[115] It is noteworthy that the advent of Technicolor and the overall shift to color film production resulted in even more emphasis being placed on exotic plots and characters so that the racial dynamics cutting through the studio era remained, and were steadily reified, as non-white actors were very seldom cast in leading roles.[116] And as studios tried to lure audiences with lavish widescreen spectacles set in exoticized, faraway lands of the kind that television could not offer, ethnic displays in brownface remained abundant.

This had much to do with the Hays Office that regulated the standards of decency in Hollywood through the Production Code from 1930 till 1968. While largely remembered for the limitations it set on sexual depiction – as in the acceptable length of kisses, suggestive dialogue, and degrees of undress – the Code equally regulated depictions of racial miscegenation by governing possible plots and casting options connected to romantic scenes in highly concrete terms.[117] By the mid-1950s the Code's effect was beginning to slowly weaken, yet it took another decade for it to be abandoned largely due to the financial pressure to screen more straightforward sexual content.

As Brynner's stardom took flight, the American civil rights movement was gathering momentum. Meanwhile, Hollywood comprised its own social reality where non-white professionals were almost exclusively excluded from film production, where Black actors had a narrow choice of roles, where films largely skirted around issues of social justice, and where the Code conditioned acceptable displays of sexuality and race.[118] The romantic pairing of white women with non-white men was a persistent topic of concern, given that 'colored' men had been construed as a sexual threat for decades and that interracial marriage was illegal in several US states till 1967.[119] Carlos E. Cortés notes that post-World War II Hollywood turned its attention to 'evils at home' by recycling tropes of threat posed to white women by racialized men – a threat that could nevertheless be avoided by the narrative being situated in distant lands, in the distant past, among the royalty, or any combination thereof.[120] These were the sorts of roles that Brynner largely, albeit not exclusively, played in the 1950s and 1960s.

A director at heart

In a 1959 interview made during the filming the comedy of *Once More, with Feeling!*, Brynner noted that Hollywood tends to create a specific formula for each of its stars: 'And I think that the formula towards which I was most pushed was to play a type that is extremely hard, even mean, with a heart of gold. And that can become very boring.'[121] Even as he would have wished to play roles that were more interesting and fun, Brynner continued, incoming offers only involved the same kinds of parts. He further argued that acting was not a career that he had chosen to start with. Rather, he wanted to return to his work as director and step away from the spotlight in order to reclaim freedom as a private citizen:

> I don't like the attention, I don't like not being able to walk down the street without being noticed. At this, you could tell me to let my hair grow, to wear a hat or a moustache, but nothing works any more. Even if I had a beard, a hat and dark glasses, it would make no difference.[122]

While this obviously was not a decision that he stuck to, Brynner had declared himself tired of acting as early as 1955, expressing a desire to move back behind the camera since film is 'strictly a director's medium' and directing, in comparison to acting, is 'like leading a symphony orchestra as compared to playing a fiddle.'[123] As Hedda Hopper pointed out, '[i]t's a fine bit of irony that the man who doesn't want to act any more should be the supreme star of the motion picture industry.'[124] For its part, Paramount announced plans for his directorial debut before *The King and I* or *The Ten Commandments* were released.[125]

In 1956, Brynner and Gilmore established their own independent company, Alciona – its logo designed by Jean Cocteau – in order to gain more control over future projects.[126] This involved an obvious financial incentive, given that the actor vocally critiqued and disparaged studio management as 'parasites' and 'overpaid professionals' throughout his career.[127] This dislike manifested in manifold ways: his son, for example, mentions Brynner having a graphic designer make a version of the 20th Century Fox's logo reading '16th Century Fucks' and giving out thus decorated matchboxes even before working with the studio on *The King and I*.[128] Alciona soon announced a $25 million collaboration with United Artists on eleven films, with Brynner starring in eight and directing 'one or two,' and Martin Ritt – Brynner's early collaborator at CBS – directing several.[129] The deal was exceptionally large, even unprecedently lavish. It basically spoke of Brynner's bargaining power as Hollywood's Next Big Thing and gave him the freedom to allocate the funding across projects as he pleased.[130]

Together with Paul Radin, Alciona's executive vice president, Brynner identified UA as the company allowing the 'greatest amount of creative autonomy' and freedom.[131] This was not hugely surprising, given that the company had initially been founded by major early Hollywood stars and directors (Charlie Chaplin, D.W. Griffiths, Mary Pickford, and Douglas Fairbanks Sr.) in order to gain more artistic and financial autonomy.

UA's broad operating principle was to finance and distribute films by independent production companies. Along with Columbia Pictures, it thrived as this became a general trend in late studio-era Hollywood, and the company was instrumental to how the system became undone.[132] The plan was for Brynner to receive ten percent of the films' gross income starting with the Spartacus slave revolt narrative, *The Gladiators*, but as the project got postponed due to conflicts with Kirk Douglas's rivaling production and eventually unraveled (see Chapter 4), *The Magnificent Seven* moved to the forefront of Brynner's plans.[133]

Initially, it was Brynner who was named as not only the star in but also the director of the 1959 *The Buccaneer*. He stepped down due to what was described as a conflict between these two roles (but which, in fact, involved a conflict with the producer, DeMille) and Quinn – DeMille's then son-in-law who had played a supporting role in the 1938 version – took over.[134] Despite rumours of friction on set, there was rapport between the two men, and the plan was for Quinn to direct first *The Gladiators* and then *The Magnificent Seven* for Alciona – or, alternatively, for Brynner to direct and for Quinn to act in the latter.[135] Brynner's most notable success in developing film projects was to be with the latter film, adapted from Akira Kurosawa's 1954 *Seven Samurai* into a Western by screenwriter Louis Morheim.[136]

Since Kurosawa's film was released in the United States as *The Magnificent Seven* in 1956, and identified as having been influenced by the American Western, the adaptation was not quite as surprising as it may have initially seemed.[137] UA, troubled by delayed and messy pre-production, eventually pulled its support for Alciona and rights were shifted over to the Mirisch Company, which produced the film together with Alpha Productions, an independent company owned by the film's director, John Sturges. Quinn then (unsuccessfully) sued both Brynner and UA in 'the biggest lawsuit ever brought by one actor against another,' arguing that there had been a verbal agreement to jointly acquire the rights to the Japanese original, and that this had been Quinn's idea.[138] Since the film was, despite its rocky start, a box office success grossing $9 million in its first year alone, with Brynner retaining a cut of something like $1 million, the dispute was no trifle.[139]

Other potential (or rumored) Alciona projects included Alphonse Daudet's novel *The Nabob* with Brynner as 'an oriental potentate,' 'the adventurer Jansoulet, who returns with a fortune from Tunis to Paris' (also rumored to star Brigitte Bardot), a film on the battle of Alamo with Alan

Ladd, collaboration with Richard Brooks (the director of *The Brothers Karamazov*), and television work with UA.[140] In 1958, news of Brynner and Litvak planning a film about the 'mad king' Paul I, the son and successor of Catherine the Great on the Russian throne, with Brynner in the title role, began to circulate: the film was indeed in the planning for years, with Abraham Polonsky (who was also working on *The Gladiators*) as screenwriter.[141] None of these projects came into fruition and, in 1959, Brynner relocated Alciona to Switzerland for tax purposes.[142]

In 1961, Alciona and Mirisch announced a deal of three films to be distributed through UA: these included *Kings of the Sun* (plugged as *The Mound Builders*, 1963) and an unrealised biopic of a British soldier working with elephants in Burma, titled either *Bandoola* or *Elephant Bill* to be filmed in Sri Lanka (then Ceylon).[143] *Return of the Seven* was most likely part of this pact (the case with *Cast a Giant Shadow* is more unclear, given Brynner's minor role). Around this time, Brynner bought remake rights to Sacha Guitry's 1934 film, *Le Roman d'un tricheur* (*Memoir of a Cheater*) and the adaptation of the play *Portrait of a Murder* was also on the cards: despite such plans, his directorial ambitions were never realized outside of television and he never became a producer beyond *The Journey* (with Byla) and Alciona's 11-film deal with UA became undone.[144] Brynner's lavish share of *The Magnificent Seven* afforded by the collaboration with Mirisch, combined with the hardships involved in attempts at getting the project off the ground first with Alciona, point to reasons behind this. Mirisch was known for its generous deals, and collaboration freed Brynner from the labor involved on the production side of things. Brynner's choice of projects was, by and large, based on the available fees.[145] This tactic was hardly exceptional by Hollywood standards and its benefits must have been obvious ever since Brynner received $1 million for largely rehashing his performances in *The Ten Commandments* and *Anastasia* for the 1959 *Solomon and Sheba* (see Chapter 3).[146]

Rumors of Brynner directing Broadway musicals – Rodgers and Hammerstein's *The Flower Drum Song* and *My Indian Family* based on a Pearl Puck novel – circulated in 1958 but were never realised.[147] While Richard Brooks wanted Brynner to star in a contemporary Broadway interpretation of Jean-Paul Sartre's *Lucifer and the Lord* in 1957, it is not clear whether he ever entertained the idea, having already transitioned to the big screen.[148] It was not until 1974 that Brynner returned to the stage (with *The Odyssey*, later renamed *Home Sweet Homer*) and he quit making films two years later: this decision was obviously impacted by the volume and quality of roles available to an actor in his mid-50s, and the continuing audience allure that his King Mongkut held. To understand how Brynner was able to collect the kinds of pay checks that he did and – much more centrally in terms of this book's focus – the kind of star image that he had, it is however necessary to circle back and to zoom in on his signature role in *The King and I*.

Notes

1. *New Yorker*, 21 April 1951; Capua 2006, 3–4.
2. *The NY Times*, 27 April 1977; *LA Times*, 10 August 1975.
3. *The Washington Post*, 2 September 1956; *Bidoun*, Fall 2005; *Picturegoer*, 9 April 1960; *NY Herald Tribune*, 24 February 1946; *The Boston Globe*, 25 November 1949; *Cosmopolitan*, May 1957, 36.
4. *The Boston Globe*, 25 November 1949; *Picture Show*, 3 September 1955; *Minneapolis Tribune*, 9 July 1951.
5. *The NY Times*, 4 December 1960; *Top Spot*, 6 June 1959; *The Washington Post*, 11 October 1985; *Screenland* May 1957; *LA Times*, 10 October 1985, 36.
6. *Top Spot*, 6 June 1959; *SF Examiner*, 23 February 1958; *Papua New Guinea Post*, 1 September 1962; *The Guardian*, 23 March 1974; *The Toronto Star*, 22 February 1975; *The Vancouver Sun*, 14 December 1962; *NY Herald Tribune*, 24 February 1946; *The Boston Globe*, 25 November 1949.
7. *The Washington Post*, 11 October 1985a.
8. *NY Herald Tribune*, 24 April 1958.
9. *The SF Examiner*, 12 December 1982a.
10. Brynner 1989; Brynner 2006.
11. This section builds on Brynner 2006, Kindle edition, and, to a lesser extent, on his earlier biography, Brynner 1989, throughout.
12. Wollen 1994, 190.
13. Marousia's grandfather, a doctor, had converted to the Russian Orthodox Church. It should be noted that state discrimination against Judaism was extensive in pre- (and post-) revolutionary Russia: limitations applied to political participation and educational opportunities alike.
14. In addition to Brynner 2006, see also *Australian Women's Weekly*, 28 February 1973.
15. *NY Herald Tribune*, 20 January 1957; *Screenland*, May 1957, 71; *LA Times*, 29 October 1955; *Picturegoer*, 24 January 1959.
16. The Brynner family enterprise continued to operate from Shanghai where Boris Brynner died in 1948; the remaining fortune was lost in the Chinese revolution.
17. For an overview of Brynner's stage work of the 1940s, see Capua 2006, 172–4; Dabell and Dabell 2019, 250.
18. *Variety*, 17 February 1943.
19. Brynner also took diction classes with Alice Crowther, who was affiliated with the Chekhov Players. *Australian Women's Weekly*, 3 April 1957.

20. *Broadcasting*, 7 February 1949; *Variety*, 9 February 1949. For listings of his television work, see Brynner and Pages 2010d, 244–5; Capua 2006, 176–8; Dabell and Dabell 2019, 245–9.
21. *Broadcasting*, 22 August 1949; *The Lincoln Journal*, 28 August 1949; *The Hollywood Reporter*, 22 December 1950; *The Cincinnati Enquirer*, 28 October 1950. Brynner himself identified his television work starting as early as 1942–1943, but this seems unlikely. *Saturday Evening Post*, 22 November 1958, 84.
22. *Variety*, 19 December 1945; *St. Louis Dispatch*, 5 November 1946; *The Boston Globe*, 13 January 1946.
23. *Variety*, 31 March 1948; *The Tatler*, 21 January 1948; *The Tatler*, 17 December 1947.
24. *The Boston Globe*, 25 November 1949.
25. *Sun*, 9 April 1951; *The Boston Globe*, 25 November 1949; *The NY Times*, 3 February 1950; *NY Herald Tribune*, 3 February 1950; *Showmen's Trade Review*, 26 November 1949; *LA Times*, 7 December 1949; *The Hollywood Reporter*, 23 November 1949; *Boxoffice*, 3 December 1949.
26. *Variety*, 23 November 1949, 25; *Daily News*, 3 February 1950.
27. *Showmen's Trade Review*, 31 December 1949.
28. *LA Times*, 28 August 1955; *NY Herald Tribune*, 19 December 1955. His last work as television director seems to have been in 1953. Brynner and Pages 2010d, 244.
29. *LA Times*, 17 June 1951; *Variety*, 1 January 1958.
30. E.g., *LA Times*, 16 May 1954.
31. *Saturday Evening Post*, 22 November 1958, 25, 81.
32. *Life*, 28 May 1956 featured a multi-page feature, titled 'King and His Camera,' with behind-the-scenes photographs on the making of *The King and I*. See also *NY Herald Tribune*, 11 March 1956; *NY Herald Tribune*, 7 February 1958. A selection of his photographic work has been published in Brynner 1996; Brynner and Pages 2010a; Brynner and Pages 2010b; Brynner and Pages 2010c. It was also featured as an exhibition in 2012. *The Times*, 11 January 2012; *Harper's Bazaar*, February 2012.
33. In 1957, Brynner shot the Cary Grant and Sophia Loren vehicle, *Houseboat*, for European magazines. He is often listed as doing a cameo in the 1961 *Goodbye Again* starring Ingrid Bergman, Yves Montand, and Anthony Perkins and directed by Anatole Litvak, but is not, in fact, anywhere to be spotted in the film, even though he did photography on set. Litvak also recruited him to do photography for the 1962 *Five Miles to Midnight*, with Perkins and Loren: these commissions were partly favours to friends. *The Hollywood Reporter*, 16 September 1957; *The Hollywood Reporter*, 9 November 1960; *NY Herald Tribune*, 4 December 1960, 3; *The Montreal Gazette*, 24 January 1962; *Elokuva-aitta* 9, 1962.
34. In the press, Brynner explained that the decision was motivated by the need to have the same citizenship as his wife and daughter so as to avoid the risk of international tensions splitting up the family. E.g., *The NY Times*, 22 June 1965; Brynner 1989, 167–8.
35. *LA Times*, 27 March 1960.
36. *The Washington Post*, 2 September 1956.
37. Doll 2005.

38. *The Montreal Gazette*, 27 July 1962; *The Vancouver Sun*, 9 October 1979. It should be noted that the truth came a little embellished, as Brynner argued to have spent childhood summers in Kyoto 'to escape cold of Peking,' *Variety*, 18 July 1962.
39. *Behind the Scenes* 1957 19, emphasis in the original.
40. *Saturday Evening Post*, 22 November 1958, 85.
41. Ibid.
42. *Cinépanorama*, 11 July 1959.
43. *Redbook*, May 1957, 31.
44. E.g., *Cosmopolitan*, May 1957; *The Pittsburgh Press*, 24 March 1957; *Behind the Scenes*, 28 March 1957; *Hush-Hush*, July 1957; *Picturegoer*, 8 March 1958.
45. *Daily Telegraph*, 17 June 1951.
46. *Picture Show*, 4 May 1957.
47. *Redbook*, May 1957, 32.
48. Brynner 1989, 113–4, 175; *Newsweek*, May 1958, 100. Vera Bryner, who retained the original spelling of the family name, disclosed similar facts already in *Redbook*, May 1957, 33. She died in 1967.
49. *Collier's*, June 1956, 38; the encounter was faithfully paraphrased in *Picturegoer*, 17 January, 1959.
50. *The Sketch*, 1 August 1956, 109.
51. *The NY Times*, 27 April 1977; *The Chattanooga Times*, January 19 1958; *Cosmopolitan*, May 1957 36; *The Hollywood Reporter*, 1 June 1951; *Radioscopie* 1974.
52. *LA Times*, 9 December 1968; *Picture Show*, 21 July 1956.
53. Brynner 2006, Kindle edition.
54. *Midi trente*, 10 November 1972.
55. *Radioscopie*, 1974.
56. These were reiterated as something of a fact as late as in the 2019 biographical documentary *Les mille et une vies de Yul Brynner*.
57. Negra 2001, 62; Studlar 2011, 123.
58. Studlar 2011, 124.
59. Said 1995.
60. Studlar 2011, 125, 129, 131–4.
61. *Redbook*, August 1957.
62. Palmer 2010, 11; Brynner 1989, 40.
63. *Meridien Record*, 8 December 1945; *The Brooklyn Citizen*, 7 February 1946; *NY Herald Tribune*, 24 February 1946; *The Boston Globe*, 13 January 1946; *Variety*, 19 December 1945; *The Windsor Star*, 13 May 1947.
64. *LA Times*, 18 May 1954.
65. Robbins 1987, 2.
66. *Toronto Daily Star*, 22 December 1962.
67. *Redbook*, May 1957, 31.
68. *Picturegoer*, 24 January 1959.
69. *The Austin Statesman*, 2 July 1972.
70. Robinson 2007, 152.
71. Ibid., 6.
72. Robbins 1987, 2.
73. *The Washington Post*, 14 December 1974.

74. Brynner 2006, Kindle edition.
75. *The Hollywood Reporter*, 28 December 1951; *The Hollywood Reporter*, 2 February 1953a.
76. He was reportedly planning a Fu Manchu TV series about the Chinese supervillain; *The Hollywood Reporter*, 17 July 1951. Based on a series of novels by the British author Sax Rohmer, *Fu Manchu* (which was to become recognised as a racist trope) had already made several onscreen appearances, played probably most notoriously by Boris Karloff in 1932.
77. *LA Times*, 9 June 1952; *LA Times*, 9 August 1952; *NY Herald Tribune*, 14 October 1952; *The Independent Exhibitors Film Bulletin*, 29 December 1952; *LA Times*, 17 January 1953; *The Hollywood Reporter*, 8 August 1952.
78. *LA Times*, 26 October 1952.
79. *LA Times*, 19 June 1952.
80. *The NY Times*, 6 February 1953; *LA Times*, 9 February 1953; *The Hollywood Reporter*, 10 February 1953; *The Hollywood Reporter*, 1 October 1953.
81. *St. Petersburg Times*, 13 December 1951.
82. *SF Examiner*, 6 November 1952.
83. *LA Times*, 13 October 1952; *The Hollywood Reporter*, 11 February 1953; *The Hollywood Reporter*, 13 October 1953; *The Montreal Gazette*, 11 December 1952.
84. *LA Times*, 30 October 1953; *LA Times*, 14 March 1953; *Variety*, 1 April 1953. This would have been a remake of the 1932 screen adaptation of a W. Somerset Maugham short story, also rumored to star Rita Hayworth and to be shot on the South Seas.
85. *LA Times*, 27 June 1953; *LA Times*, 19 June 1954.
86. *The Hollywood Reporter*, 24 May 1954; *The Hollywood Reporter*, 7 April 1954; *The Hollywood Reporter*, 2 February 1953b; *The Hollywood Reporter*, 10 September 1954; to be precise, rumors of the latter film had already started circulating in 1952, *The Hollywood Reporter*, 2 October 1952.
87. *LA Times*, 8 November 1952; *LA Times*, 7, October 1953; *LA Times*, 28 May 1954; *The Hollywood Reporter*, 4 March 1954; *The Hollywood Reporter*, 10 March 1954.
88. *LA Times*, 11 October 1953.
89. *LA Times*, 6 October 1953.
90. *The Hollywood Reporter*, 19 May 1955; *The Hollywood Reporter*, 2 February 1955.
91. *The SF Examiner*, 2 July 1956.
92. *Variety*, 11 July 1956; *The Hollywood Reporter*, 9 July 1956; *LA Times*, 9 July 1956b. Other actors considered for the part included James Mason and Kirk Douglas. *The Hollywood Reporter*, November 27 1956.
93. *The NY Times*, 21 June 1956.
94. *NY Herald Tribune*, 12 June 1958; *Radioscopie* 1974; *The Washington Post*, 14 December 1974.
95. *LA Times*, 15 November 1956; Hannan 2015, Kindle edition; *The Hollywood Reporter*, 3 February 1959; *The Washington Post*, 22 February 1959; *The SF Examiner*, 11 July 1962; *LA Times*, 22 January 1957; *Boxoffice*, 5 February 1962; *The Hollywood Reporter*, 27 December 1955; *The Hollywood Reporter*, 14 August 1962; *Toronto Daily Star*, 1 June 1957; *LA Times*, 6 July 1962; *Variety*, 8 February 1961; *The Hollywood Reporter*, 29 March 1961; *Variety*, 26 April 1961.

96. *LA Times*, 22 January 1958; *The Washington Post*, 19 September 1961; *The Hollywood Reporter*, 16 November 1959; *Variety*, 1 November 1961; *Variety*, 5 July 1961; *The Hollywood Reporter*, 2 July 1958; *LA Times*, 15 August 1958; *The Hollywood Reporter*, 1 July 1960; *The Hollywood Reporter*, 4 October 1962; *Nepean Times*, 19 April 1962; *St. Petersburg Times*, 14 April 1957.
97. *The Hollywood Reporter*, 22 June 1961; *The Hollywood Reporter*, 31 July 1956; *The Hollywood Reporter*, 23 December 1957.
98. Eyman 2020, 290, 321.
99. *The Hollywood Reporter*, 2 February 1961; *The Hollywood Reporter*, 31 March 1959; *The NY Times*, 12 August 1958; *The NY Times*, 11 November 1958; *The Hollywood Reporter*, 13 February 1961; *The Hollywood Reporter*, 9 October 1958; *The Hollywood Reporter*, 10 October 1961; *Variety*, 24 July 1968; Hannan 2015, Kindle edition; *Australian Jewish Times*, 19 August 1960. Hannan 2015 also mentions the potential role of Aristotle Onassis in *Tosca* against Maria Callas in 1968 (this being the year that Onassis married Jacqueline Kennedy).
100. *The Hollywood Reporter*, 7 November 1958.
101. *The Hollywood Reporter*, 22 July 1959.
102. *The Austin Statesman*, 27 August 1960. Gregory Peck, Cary Grant, Charlton Heston, Rock Hudson, and Jimmy Stewart also reportedly refused the role. *Australian Women's Weekly*, 1 May 1963, 15. The New York Public Library hosts Earl Hammond's 1965 screen manuscript for a Brynner and Betty Grable starrer *Stay Out of Berlin!* but there is no evidence of the project having ever entered pre-production (Grable's last film role was in the 1955, *How to Be Very, Very Popular*, although she did stage work till the late 1960s).
103. *Australian Jewish Times*, 10 October 1974; *Boxoffice*, 5 May 1975; *The Toronto Star*, 22 February 1975; *The Hollywood Reporter*, 16 June 1978. The latter film was also rumored to star Charlton Heston and was eventually realised as *When Time Ran Out . . .* (James Goldstone, 1980). While these listings of rumored projects are lengthy, I am not claiming them to be complete, given constraints in archival access. Furthermore, the listings do not distinguish between ideal casting options discussed by producers, proposed projects, and ones that actually entered negotiations.
104. *The Hollywood Reporter*, 9 April 1957; *Variety*, 10 April 1957; *Picture Show*, 6 July 1957. Initially launched as Alby Pictures with *The Journey*, Byla productions was named after Brynner's and Litvak's initials.
105. *LA Times*, 2 December 1967; *Variety*, 8 May 1968, 46.
106. Lennon 2012.
107. *The Guardian*, 11 October 1985.
108. *Variety*, 22 July 1959; *Elokuva-aitta* 15, 1959; Brynner 1996, 134.
109. *The Boston Globe*, 11 October 1985.
110. *The Globe and Mail*, 11 October 1985.
111. Dyer 2004, 16.
112. Shohat 1995, 166.
113. Dyer 1997, 19–20.
114. Studlar 1989, 30.
115. Berry 2004, 182.

116. Ibid., 193.
117. Maillard 2018, 2651–3; on the Production Code and white racial fantasies, see Courtney 2005.
118. Quinn 2011; Palmer 2010a, 3, 6; Abramson 2008, 194.
119. Cortés 1991, 21–2.
120. Ibid., 1991, 27–8.
121. *Cinépanorama*, 11 July 1959.
122. Ibid.
123. *LA Times*, 28 August 1955; *The Calgary Herald*, 20 July 1956.
124. *LA Times*, 24 November 1957.
125. *The NY Times*, 9 February 1956.
126. Alciona came from *alkyón*, Greek for halcyon (hence the logo was that of a bird). Brynner 2006, Kindle edition. This was arguably also the name of Brynner's first boat. *Variety*, 12 September 1956.
127. E.g., *Newsweek*, 19 May 1958, 103; *London Life*, 27 August 1966, 25. Such mentions were abundant.
128. Brynner 1989, 85. Brynner's disenchantment with the studio was also more specifically connected to his first wife Virginia Gilmore, a Fox contract actor, practically losing her career after marrying him without the studio's permission.
129. *The NY Times*, 23 December 1957; *South China Morning Post*, 24 December 1957; see also *Broadcasting*, 28 August 1950.
130. Commenting on the deal's scale, Brian Hannan argues that '[c]alling what the actor had in mind audacious was like referring to the Titanic as a big ship. Yul Brynner envisaged himself as a mogul. Harnessing his Oscar-winning talent and box office prowess to his unproven skills as a producer and director, Brynner sought to position himself as a major player.' The analysis, however, is debatable, given that it was routine for star actors to set up their own production companies and also since Brynner's commitment to prioritizing his work as producer and director was far from consistent or solid (as far as I see, this was never something he prioritized). Furthermore, there can be no access to how Brynner may or may not have envisaged himself as a movie mogul. Hannan 2015, Kindle edition.
131. *Variety*, 12 February 1958. UA also worked with Kirk Douglas's Bryna, see Fenwick 2020.
132. On UA since year 1951, see Balio 2009.
133. *Newsweek*, 19 May 1958, 102; *The NY Times*, 13 May 1958. On an in-depth analysis of the production of *The Magnificent Seven*, see Hannan 2015. For an equally careful exploration of *The Gladiators*, see MacAdam and Cooper 2020.
134. *The Hollywood Reporter*, 5 April 1956; *LA Times*, 5 April 1956; *NY Herald Tribune*, 22 April 1956; *Variety*, 4 June 1958; *Motion Picture Exhibitor*, 27 November 1957.
135. *LA Times*, 3 February 1958; *LA Times*, 12 March 1958; Hannan 2015, Kindle edition. As Hannan points out, there were also discussions of Litvak directing.
136. *Variety*, 5 February 1958. There was bidding around the manuscript by Brynner's Quinn's and Kirk Douglas's production companies. Hannan 2015, Kindle Edition.
137. *The NY Times*, 25 November 1956; *LA Times*, 16 May 1958.
138. *The Hollywood Reporter*, 2 February 1960; *The Washington Post*, 21 February 1960; *Variety*, 10 February 1960a; *The Hollywood Reporter*, 5 February 1960a; MacAdam

and Cooper 2020, 52. Some years later, Quinn further sued Alpha, Mirisch, and United Artists. Quinn, however, lost the case. *Variety*, 25 November 1964; *The Times*, 24 July 2004.
139. *LA Times*, 6 July 1961; *LA Times*, 26 September 1963; Hannan 2015, Kindle edition.
140. *The NY Times*, 17 October 1958; *Variety*, 22 October 1958; *Picturegoer*, 17 January 1959; *Elokuva-aitta* 24, 1958b; *The Calgary Herald*, 9 April 1959; *St. Petersburg Times*, 7 May 1958; *Variety*, 25 December 1957; *Broadcasting*, 20 December 1957; *Variety*, 1 January 1958.
141. *The NY Times*, 7 December 1958; *LA Times*, 2 November 1959; *The Hollywood Reporter*, 2 November 1959; *Variety*, 4 November 1959; *Elokuva-aitta* 19, 1959, 17; MacAdam and Cooper 2020, 216–17, 228, 265, 290.
142. *Variety*, 4 February 1959a.
143. MacAdam and Cooper 2020, 280; *Variety*, 14 June 1961; *Variety*, 16 May 1962; *Variety*, 4 July 1962; *The Hollywood Reporter*, 28 June 1962; *South China Morning Post*, 5 December 1963; *The Montreal Gazette*, 9 September 1963; *Variety*, 1 January 1964; *Variety*, 8 December 1965.
144. *Variety*, 22 December 1963; *Le Monde*, 29 December 1965; Hannan 2015, Kindle edition.
145. This is highlighted in Brynner 1989, and was especially the case after the making of *Taras Bulba* (1962).
146. See also MacAdam and Cooper 2020, 170–1.
147. *The Hollywood Reporter*, 24 April 1958; *The Hollywood Reporter*, 30 July 1958.
148. *Variety*, 24 July 1957.

Chapter 3

A royal presence

Brynner played King Mongkut on stage from 1951 to 1955 and, intermittently, from 1976 to 1985, onscreen in 1956, and on television in the 1972 thirteen-episode series, *Anna and the King*. The kingly trope continued in biographies; the 1987 *Yul Brynner: The Inscrutable King* and the 1989 *Yul: The Man Who Would Be King*; in the co-authored 1983 *Yul Brynner Cookbook: Food Fit for the King and You*; the 1995 made-for-television documentary, *The Man Who Was King*; and in a virtually endless array of newspaper and magazine articles addressing the actor and his legacy (see Chapter 9). Despite the spectrum of parts that Brynner played during his career, he remained tenaciously associated with his excessive and stylized interpretation of King Mongkut, the historical Siamese ruler made Broadway character. In journalistic mentions of Brynner spanning from the 1950s to the current day, only mentions of his bald head repeat with the same frequency as kingly allusions.

Examining Orientalism and masculinity in both the narrative of *The King and I* and in Brynner's screen presence, this chapter zooms in on the royal trope cutting through his star image. In doing so, it further examines the kingly reverberations in his roles as Pharaoh Rameses II, the 'buccaneer king' Jean Lafitte,[1] and King Solomon in top-budget 1950s Hollywood studio spectacles that marked the early part of his career and fame.

An Oriental attraction

Steeped in myth, cosmopolitanism, and exoticism from the outset, Brynner's star image framed him as imported goods, a 'product of the Mysterious East' operating with a different kind of logic – and constraint – than that governing the lives of regular Americans.[2] Within 1950s American culture, Brynner, in his son's words, 'almost constituted a new species. Even his name was a mystery: one cannot confidently guess from which continent those three syllables emerged, for they are neither European nor Oriental.'[3] Brynner himself argued that the name was 'common enough in Outer Mongolia.'⁴ His was a project of self-exoticizing that made use of broad Orientalist tropes, often in highly playful, over-the-top manner.

His 1951 role as King Mongkut in the stage musical *The King and I* was obviously elementary to how this project came about. A key reason for Brynner being cast in the part was Mary Martin, the star of *Lute Song* and later *South Pacific*, recommending him to Richard Rodgers and Oscar Hammerstein as a natural fit for the part. At this point, Brynner was not entirely unknown on Broadway, having won the 1946 Most Promising Actor Donaldson Award (nowadays known as the Tony) for his first Oriental role.⁵ Although short-lived, *Lute Song* was greeted with a critical reception appreciative of its 'rare and colourful beauty' and visual magnificence: Brynner's performance as a Chinese poet was described as captivating and the actor as 'just right' for the part, courtesy of his Oriental roots.⁶ In accounts credited to Martin, when Brynner auditioned for *Lute Song* he sat down in the lotus position

> with his guitar and started playing and singing like a gypsy. His voice had such excitement, such poise. I loved him and we signed him right away. He was wonderful as an Oriental. His chiseled face is beautiful and he moves like a cat.⁷

Or, alternatively, newspaper sources suggest, after squatting on the floor, Brynner continued to 'write with a brush, Chinese-style,' being 'more Oriental than Fu-Manchu and, of course, a virile-looking man.'⁸ These descriptions bear uncanny resemblance to Rodgers's account of Brynner auditioning for *The King and I*: 'Out came a partially baldheaded, muscular fellow with a bony, oriental-like face. He scowled at us, then sat down cross-legged tailor fashion in the middle of the stage.'⁹ Brynner had then continued to perform Russian Roma songs to apparently convincing effect. In Hedda Hopper's florid retelling, he 'twangled his guitar, let out a pagan yell and leaped into the air.'¹⁰ 'Or so the legend goes,' Brynner himself remarked, having narrated similar versions of the event himself.¹¹ Since both the moment of Brynner's discovery and his casting in these Oriental roles were key in the construction of his star image, the attention paid to them comes as no surprise. As further discussed in Chapter 4, recycled quotes attributed to people both named and anonymous were standard practice in film journalism, resulting in repetitions and variations communicating more or less the same thing. The quotes associated with Brynner's auditions essentially suggest an organic fit between these roles and his persona, physical assets, and skill – even as Brynner was initially reluctant to play King Mongkut, preferring instead to focus on his career as a television director.[12] A biographer reiterates:

> The role of the king was perfect for him. It involved several aspects of his own personality and his experiences as an artist, such as the mystery about his Oriental origins, his ability to sing and play the guitar, his exotic look and his magnetic charisma. On stage these combined elements transformed him into a real monarch. He delivered the lines with an accent that was a mix of all the languages he knew.[13]

The issue, then, was seen to go beyond a good fit between the actor and the role toward something that resulted in more than the sum of its parts, namely a star image where the actor's persona and role intimately merged, despite Brynner's features requiring further Oriental amplification through body paint and stage makeup. Promotional stills for the 1951 Broadway play exhibit him elaborately and dramatically made up, dressed in ornamental Thai silks designed by Irene Sharaff, sporting ankle bracelets and radical eyebrows in what was to become his trademark pose – legs apart, hands on hips, chin up, upper-body muscles tensed, bare-chested, and on his face a grim, determined stare. Defined as 'half Mongolian and half French,' Brynner made for a 'sensational discovery.'[14]

In *The King and I*, Brynner's still nascent Orientalist self-branding met a quintessentially Orientalist romantic narrative so that one supported and amplified the other. The 1951 musical, like the 1956 film, tells the story of the British governess, Anna Leonowens, her arrival in Bangkok with her son, her introduction to the royal court, and her engagement within its politics as an advocate of abolition resistant to the rituals of prostration in front of the king. As the narrative progresses, Anna forms warm bonds with the royal children and wives, also growing closer to the temperamental, all-powerful king while having an unresolved conflict concerning her own house that was promised yet not provided. Before the romantic hues of their relationship can fully develop or any racial lines become crossed, the king dies of a 'broken heart.'

The story is very liberally based on historical events. Born in Colonial India in 1831, Anna Harriette Leonowens, the child of a British 'farm boy/soldier' and an Indian 'mixed-race army brat,' refashioned herself into a genteel Victorian lady and worked in the Siamese court for six years in the 1860s, first teaching the royal wives and children and later serving as the king's scribe.[15] In 1870, she published a memoir, *The English Governess at the Siamese Court*, detailing her life in court, from the habits of the harem to etiquette and ceremonies, Bangkok city life, Siamese art and religious habits, combining memory with fabrication and standard Orientalist tropes.[16] One of the book's chapters is dedicated to describing Somdetch P'hra Paramendr Maha Mongkut, the Supreme King of Siam, prone to 'capricious provocations of temper' yet also broadly learned, endlessly energetic and progressive in his policies.[17] 'Capable at times of the noblest of impulses, he was equally capable of the basest actions,' she writes, probing the hierarchies of the royal harem and then shifting to anecdotes detailing the king's arrogance, inquisitiveness, 'morbid egotism, various and keen annoyance,' and his conflicts with European ambassadors.[18]

Leonowens's colorful memoirs continued with the 1872 *Romance of the Harem*. In her introduction to the book's 1991 edition, Susan Morgan characterizes it as bizarre and of dubious veracity: 'Around *The Romance of the Harem* and around its author shimmer the gaudily alluring veils of misinformation, contradiction, obscurity, and denunciation.'[19] Leonowens's memoirs are personal travelogues detailing the sights and habits of Oriental lands through British imperialist eyes, values, and tropes. In this historical context, the harem operated as an Orientalist figure rich in sensationalist, erotic titillation.[20] As Inderpal Grewal points out, colonial literature, of which travelogues formed a central part, made use of the harem as the opposite of the home, rendering it a moral construct for supporting and symbolizing division and conflict between the East and the West, the monogamous and the polygamous, the Christian and the not.[21] Nineteenth-century colonial travelogues generically depicted the adventures of European protagonists in exotic lands and among alien people, both of which were presented as mysteries to be resolved and governed.[22] This was explicitly the case with the story of Miss Anna bringing Western principles of modern (if not democratic) modes of governance and thought to an Oriental court, fighting for her right to a home as opposed to her allocated place in the harem.

In 1944, Margaret Landon fictionalized Leonowens's two memoirs in her bestselling novel *Anna and the King of Siam*, offering a further romanticized account of life in the Siamese court in times past, while weaving in her own experiences of living in Thailand as the wife of an American missionary.[23] Landon's book (which also appeared as a condensed version with *Reader's Digest*) was adapted to the screen in a 1946 film starring the Englishman Rex Harrison as King Mongkut and the Kentucky-born Irene Dunne as Miss Anna. Following its success, Hammerstein then adapted the book into the Broadway musical that launched Brynner's career. Susan Brown argues that these versions 'firmly entrenched the popular perception of Leonowens as the proper English lady who undertook single-handedly to "civilize" the king and court of Siam,' further amplifying the imperialist tones of the original work.[24]

For her part, Christina Klein explores *The King and I*'s narrative in connection with Cold War geopolitics and the asymmetrical power differentials of modernisation. For her, Miss Anna was, despite her crisp Queen's English, Americanized – as is evident in the use of *Uncle Tom's Cabin* as a show within a show, or as something of a *mise en abyme*. She further argues that Hammerstein's own liberal racial politics resulted in excising 'much of Leonowens's and Landon's ethnocentric and racist language,' so that the '"yellow-peril" characterizations of the 1946 film' were bypassed and the narrative was transformed 'into a heterosexual romance of unconsummated trans-racial love.'[25] Following these lines of analysis, *The King and I* emerges as a colonial narrative foregrounding Miss Anna's soft power that results in the death of the Oriental monarch incapable of balancing his tyrannical forms of rule steeped in tradition with the dictates of Western modernism.

Leonowens's memoirs, Landon's book, its film adaptation and Rodgers and Hammerstein's musical were all firmly targeted at Western (largely American) audiences, their appeal owing to familiar tropes of barbaric yet infantilized polygamous rulers, female sexual slavery, and lush royal splendor, as envisioned in nineteenth-century travelogues, novels, and visual arts.[26] As such, they were explicitly part and parcel of the Orientalist project of imagining Asia and North Africa expansively as a site 'of romance, exotic beings, haunting memories and landscapes, remarkable experiences.'[27] The notions of Oriental despotism, cruelty, and sensuality highlighted in the reception of *The King and I* and, indeed in that of Brynner as its star, speak of the persistent appeal and presence of colonial imagination that also provided support for 1950s US Asian foreign policy.[28]

The Broadway premiere of *The King and I* was received with enthusiasm, with critics praising its exotic visual splendor and overall spectacular qualities.[29] Identifying the play as 'a colourful, Oriental pageant in superb taste,' the British *Sketch* continued to compliment Brynner's performance as the King 'who alternatively shocks Anna with his Oriental arrogance and barbaric ferocity, and appeals to her with his loneliness, tenderness and desire to improve himself and his people' – the narrative being, by and large, that of the perceived burden of a white woman's civilizing mission among the Orientals.[30]

At this point, Gertrude Lawrence was the show's star. Brynner was commended for his physicality, 'sinewy, panther-like grace,' vital presence and dynamic performance style, even as his singing skills and mumbled diction garnered less praise.[31] As Lawrence died of cancer in 1952, Brynner succeeded her in star billing. For *The New York Times*, his 'combination of surface ruthlessness and inner hunger and gratitude' was altogether superb and his Mongkut put 'a solid floor under the whole production.'[32] *The Hollywood Reporter* chimed in during the play's run in Los Angeles: 'Every complimentary adjective could be attached to his magnificent performance.'[33]

Yet not all reviewers were enthusiastic. Despite Brynner being the clear winner of the 1951 *Variety* critics survey, the paper somewhat begrudgingly described his physical fit for the part, his 'appearance and sort of savagery' being the kind that 'femme audiences obviously dote on,' yet characterized his acting as 'harsh and lacking in charm.'[34] Identifying Brynner's corporeal presence and look, rather than his professional skillset as the source of successful characterization, the critique was among the first of many similar ones to come (see Chapter 8). It is equally noteworthy that key terms meandering through Brynner's career were already in place before his film career took off: Orientalist descriptions of characteristic savagery, sex appeal, and bestial feline movements repeated and grew more elaborate as the years progressed. The same applied to critiques of his physical presence eclipsing thespian skill.

King on the big screen

By the time the musical made it to the big screen, Brynner had played the role 1,246 times on Broadway, in addition to an eighteen-month nation-wide tour covering thirty cities: he had also won 'the Donaldson, the Antoinette Perry and the Critics' Circle Awards' for the part.[35] Both the play's box office success and Brynner's own ascendence to fame made him the unquestioned 'perfect' choice for King Mongkut, with rumors of the pending production circulating by year 1954 – even as Marlon Brando was very much eyed for the part.[36] Brynner's sense of control over the role, and over the film's entire production, was such that he was said to have left little room for its director, Walter Lang. Rather than being malleable to Lang's suggestions, Brynner reportedly managed the filming, and even the casting: this had to do with his professional experience as a television director but even more with his own sense of mastery over the material.[37] When Lang was nominated for an Academy Award for best director for his work, Deborah Kerr (the film's Miss Anna, and star headliner) sent Brynner a wire congratulating him on the achievement.[38]

The King and I feasts on the aesthetic magnificence of an imagined Siamese court with the aid of Sharaff's historically studied costume design in CinemaScope 55 screen format and the rich hues of DeLuxe Color film. If the play was applauded for its colorful visual opulence, these aspects were further boosted by the film's lavish studio *mise-en-scène* so that its 'pictorial magnificence' redoubled: 'every shot is a honey, now a shimmer, now a dazzle of color.'[39] Hedda Hopper enthusiastically endorsed the result as 'one of the most beautiful pictures ever seen,' identifying Brynner as a 'combination of Jack Barrymore, Valentino and Clark Gable'; a 'half-barbaric king' of 'great strength and an endearing naivete.'[40] The Hollywood Reporter was equally excited by Brynner as 'masculinity personified,' describing the film's 'sensual magnificence' and 'animal magnetism' between the King and Miss Anna with gusto: 'a great love story, with all the sex and glamour of an exotic Oriental background.'[41]

King Mongkut makes his first entrance sitting cross-legged on a gilded throne attending to his daily duties of governance as Miss Anna, freshly arrived in Bangkok, insists on conversing with him against all royal protocol.

Figure 3.1 King Mongkut in his introduction scene

The spacious hall is lavishly decorated in shades of yellow, ochre, and gold: the King himself is clad in a black top decorated with opals, his slippers richly embroidered, and his face made up for an effect both brown and wildly Oriental. Interrupted in his activities, Mongkut glares in dismay, rises up, places his hands on his hips, and begins sizing up the new governess whom he then takes to meet the royal wives. As the scenography shifts to hues of pink, the King, hand on one hip and aggressively gesturing and pointing with the fingers of the other hand, orders Miss Anna to do as she is told. The King stands on a cushioned pedestal, his arms now folded, now hands on his hips, as the royal children make their entrance, kneeling and bowing down to show him their respect, one by one. The overall mode is stylized, fantastic, opulent, exaggerated, and lightly comic. The introductory scene establishes the King as an exotic, dominant, and somewhat child-like character of pointy staccato gestures and statuesque poses who speaks English without articles – less to imitate a Thai accent than to match popular American conceptions of Oriental parlance. Like 'Chinglish' deployed by white actors in yellowface, this accent is a figment of Hollywood imagination.[42] In later scenes, as Mongkut's clothing changes into looser decorative silk and he starts to exhibit more of his shaved, muscular torso, the Oriental ruler becomes more explicitly framed as a sexual sight.

Figure 3.2 The Orientalist charms of King Mongkut

Film reviewers were full of enthusiasm: 'It's hard to take one's eyes off this astonishing artist'; 'Something sensational has just happened on the screen! Yul Brynner has arrived, at last. And I can't remember such a terrific actor-impact since Marlon Brando and, before him, Gregory Peck':[43]

> It is not often that we discover a masterly new actor in a musical show, but this agreeable surprise occurs in the case of *The King and I* (Carlton). Yul Brynner is not only one of the most exciting personalities to appear on the screen since James Dean and Marlon Brando. He is an actor of tremendous power and discipline. I cannot tell you whether his performance bears any likeliness to a real King of Siam, never having encountered such a person: but I do know for certain that it suggests the right kind of king for this particular play, bears out the clear intentions of the script, and makes a whole man, a huge man, a man one must believe be, out of this odd mixture of pride, barbarism, warmth, eagerness to learn and 'puzzlement'.[44]

As superlatives flowed and critics raved, the production was further lauded as a 'breath-taking, eye-filling,' 'great artistic triumph' that was both predicted to be, and became, an 'outstanding box office attraction.'[45] Critiques of Brynner's performance grew more muted as he was established as the 'inevitable and in all ways perfect King.'[46] While credited largely for the same things as in the stage performance – his physique and overall 'femme appeal' – the camera was also found to increase the attractiveness of his 'handsomeness of features and subtlety of expression.'[47] The impression he made was described simply as 'staggering': 'We've never before seen an actor with such animal vigor and forceful sex appeal.'[48] Brynner was, in sum, firmly installed as the centrepiece of the 'ravishingly pretty' film as 'the most vital and colourful personality of any screen today' radiating 'an infectious charm' of libidinal overtones.[49] Critical voices panning the film as tiresome 'sumptuous idiocy' remained scarce, the enthused tones of *New York Herald Tribune* being more representative:[50]

> It is Brynner who gives the movie its animal spark, its coiled tension. He is every inch an Oriental king, from the eloquent fingers that punctuate his commands to the sinewy legs and bare feet with which he stalks about the palace, like an impatient leopard.
> His eyes glower with imperial rage, they widen with boyish curiosity, they dance with amusement at his own simple jokes, and on his death couch they are heavy with resignation and accumulated wisdom. This is a rare bit of acting – Brynner is the king, and you don't forget it for a second.[51]

In the light of the enthusiastic reception of both the Broadway play and the Hollywood musical, Brynner, himself 'a mixture of half a dozen of nationalities,' was indeed seen as 'every inch an Oriental king' by the standards of mid-1950s American critics and audiences.[52] He quite perfectly fit the Orientalist templates that the role required as a 'captivating combination of grace and arrogance and infantilism' with an 'instinct for barbarism.'[53] While contemporary press mainly stuck to mentioning three of the king's main characteristics ('childlike, cruel and lovable'[54]), he was equally associated with bare-chested, whip-waving sex appeal of the 'desert romance' tradition – a popular genre written by women for women 'with oriental subplots and oriental landscapes in which the prototype heroine was English and the hero a sensual foreigner, usually Arab, Latin, or Mediterranean (or at least appearing to be so).'[55] Unabashed Orientalism was not an issue: critics had more reservations about the plot where 'the Western white governess has to condescend to the Eastern coloured king.'[56]

Casting politics

It is noteworthy that Brynner won the Academy best actor award for this extravagantly stylized performance as a tyrannical, yet child-like Oriental ruler who expresses his inner thoughts and feelings through song and dance – and that he did so over Laurence Olivier in *Richard III* (Laurence Olivier, 1955), Kirk Douglas in *Lust for Life* (Vincente Minnelli, 1956), and both James Dean and Rock Hudson in *The Giant* (George Stevens, 1956). All in all, the film garnered nine Academy Award nominations, winning five: in addition to Brynner's, these were for art direction, cinematography, scoring, sound recording, and Sharaff's costume design. In addition, the film's soundtrack remained on the charts for a whopping 274 weeks, speaking to its acute and notably broad popular appeal.[57] Such a favorable reception was not available in Thailand where the film, similarly to the later re-imaginations of Leonowens's life in Siam, was banned, with Brynner's performance in particular identified as 'buffoonish and backward.'[58]

The film's cast included no key performers of Thai origin. The Broadway actor Terry Saunders and the Shanghai-born Judy Dan played royal wives, the Filipino-American Patrick Adiarte featured as the Crown Prince Chulalongkorn, and Carlos Rivas, a Texan of German and Mexican origins, was cast as the Burmese courtier, Lun Tha. The part of the Burmese slave girl, Tuptim, was played by the Puerto Rican Rita Moreno, born Rosa Dolores Alverío Marcano ('Moreno' translates as 'brown,' 'dusky,' or 'dark-coloured'). Moreno's star image at this point combined sex and innocence, oscillating between the tropes of 'Latin vamp' and 'Latina next door': she was also recurrently typecast in stereotypical 'barefoot roles' as biracial African or Native American women.[59] The overall casting policy was hardly exceptional in 1950s Hollywood, the film's blatantly stylized artifice of the studio-imagined Siam being equally haphazard in its cultural accuracy. In any instance, no amount of diversity in casting could have altered the Orientalist logic of the narrative itself. The same applied to the play where, in Virginia Brynner's (née Gilmore) words, the cast had been chosen 'primarily for some elusive quality and the feeling that it would inspire in the audience,' the performers being 'mostly Oriental – Chinese, Japanese, and Korean. There were also children of Philippine, Puerto Rican, and Spanish heritage.'[60]

As *The King and I* toured Britain in 1953, the king was 'neatly' played by the Czech-born Herbert Lom; in New York, the American Alfred Drake took over and, after Brynner's death, the part was briefly played by the eloped Soviet ballet dancer-choreographer superstar, Rudolf Nureyev.[61] It was not until the signing of the British Jonathan Pryce for the part of the 'one-half French, one-half Vietnamese wheeler-dealer' in the 1990 production of *Miss Saigon* that more vocal debates on Broadway's racial casting policies started to play out.[62] It took even longer for concerns over cultural appropriation, ethnic stereotyping, and racially segregating casting to become issues of broader public concern.

Hailed in the press around the premieres of *The King and I* and *The Ten Commandments* as 'the 1956 equivalent of Rudolph Valentino in the realm of fearless dynamic sex appeal,' Brynner built his star image on a longer legacy of exotic and erotic masculinity of the foreign kind.[63] In studio-era Hollywood, the logic of sexualized ethnic othering applied to Hollywood stars of both genders (the gender system in place being highly binary). 'Sexual licentiousness and exoticism' were mapped onto non-white stars in inner hierarchies separating dangerous ethnic others from the titillatingly hot-blooded.[64] As Ernesto Chávez points out, since the 1920s, each 'national and ethnic group had its part in Hollywood's racial and racist script,' which resulted in both stereotyping of national and ethnic groups and in typecasting that locked performers into specific types of roles along national, ethnic, and racial lines.[65]

The tendency was not entirely uniform. Early Mexican-born stars such as Dolores del Río and Lupe Vélez, for example, were not characterized through the kinds of stereotypes that eventually grew standard ('Latin bombshell'; 'hot tamale') but rather in terms of sophistication, glamour, and refined elegance: they were cast as European aristocrats inasmuch as peasants, 'native girls,' and fiery, tempestuous ethnic characters.[66] In some instances, the star's ethnic re-invention was a means to undo marks of difference so as to allow for flexibility in casting beyond racialized lines, as in Margarita Cansino of Spanish and Irish-American origins being remade into Rita Hayworth, the all-American 'Love Goddess.'[67] There was, then, constant yet largely one-way traffic at the borders of whiteness, with light-skinned actors taking on virtually any ethnicity and nationality, including the kinds of racialized roles that Brynner specialized in.[68]

By the late 1950s when Brynner's persona was probed in the media as the 'Asian Valentino,' there was a plethora of templates to model these accounts on.[69] Valentino's sex appeal had been rooted in his Italian origins giving way to the more expansive figure of 'Latin Lover.' His major screen success was as Sheik Ahmed Ben Hassan (revealed in the film to be of Spanish and British heritage so as not to disturb the racial lines of sexual desire).[70] As a variation of desert romance, *The Sheik* (George Melford, 1921) largely defined his star image through the Orientalist fantasy of 'female slaves and their despotically attractive Oriental masters.'[71] Examining Valentino's star image, Gaylyn Studlar ties it in with 'a wider web of popular discourses that linked the exotic to the erotic in forging a contradictory sexual spectacle of male ethnic otherness within a xenophobic and nativist culture.'[72] Like Valentino's sex-saturated star image some decades earlier, Brynner's was foreign in ways that set him apart from his contemporaries by 'promising the danger and excitement of everything that was uncommon' for American audiences.[73] Valentino's otherness, in contrast to Brynner's, was however femininized and his star image could not move beyond his positioning as a sex object – or, to rephrase, while Brynner was certainly positioned as an exotic sex object, his star image was not fully subsumed by this.[74] His breakthrough role as Siamese king against the English Miss Anna amply gestured towards the legacy of desert romance, even as his star image was not confined to it.

Cosmopolitanism and Orientalism

One way to frame Brynner's star image and its evident appeal is in reference to popular cosmopolitanism as mundane and occasionally stylized traffic in the alien and exotic – as on the sights seen on a cinema screen or the commodity selections of a department store. Addressing such displays, Mica Nava examines the attraction and eroticism of exoticness that, while steeped in racism, allows for experiencing and consuming difference (through visual and other means). In doing so, she calls for distinguishing between exoticizing and colonializing imaginations, even as these two have historically fed into, and supported, one another.[75] Nava's analysis focuses specifically on women's fascination with racialized otherness, as in Valentino's and the ballet dancer Vatslav Nijinsky's cosmopolitan masculine displays. Both performers were hailed as phenomena due to their physicality – appearance, motion, gesture, beauty, body aesthetic – yet both were also labeled as effeminate on homophobic terms.[76] While Brynner's star figure had little resemblance with those of either Valentino or Nijinsky, it is noteworthy how references to the former stuck, as well as how terminology applied to the latter was also recycled in building his star image. Nijinksy of Ballets Russes fame was known for his exotic parts but he was equally exoticized for and through Russianness.[77]

The success of Ballets Russes' European and North American tours around year 1910, most notably with the staging of Nikolai Rimski-Korsakov's *Schéhérazade*, owed largely to the company's particular brand of Orientalism – 'vibrating, brilliantly coloured, erotic, violent and exciting.'[78] Encapsulating this fascinating otherness, the star dancer Nijinsky was characterized in the press as 'half cat, half snake,' frightening and fascinating in his ornamental clothing and makeup.[79] Addressing *Schéhérazade*'s Orientalism, dance historian Hanna Järvinen argues that the critics' characterizations of wild and exotic luxurious savagery well exceeded the show's plot derived from *The Thousand and One Nights*. Rather, the issue was that of the orientalization of Russia premised on a Western sense of cultural supremacy – of Russians being classed as Europe's last barbarians; childlike, primitive, and distinct as such from the Occident.[80] Building on Richard Dyer's examination of whiteness as not merely involving a binary division among the white and the non-white but also entailing hierarchies within whiteness between 'those white and those not-white-enough,' Järvinen points out the precarious position of Russians within such boundary work. Even as Russians were identified as white in twentieth-century racist taxonomies, 'Russia was in the East, and easily included in the Orient.'[81]

Orientalist imaginaries are key to understanding Brynner's particular brand of cosmopolitanism and off-white Europeanness suggestive of ethnic flair.[82] Born in the Russian Far East yet secure in his partial Swiss ancestry, his was a star image not unequivocally white, playing with Oriental qualities and refusing attempts to fix it on national, racial, or ethnic terms. Brynner's star persona stretched the boundary work between the Orient and then Occident by occupying diverse, constantly shifting positions. This speaks of both privilege connected to self-identification and the impact of typecasting and othering on his star image. Thus understood, Brynner was both a subject and object of Orientalist imagination.

For it was also the actor, and not merely his roles, that was identified as magnetically barbarian.[83] As further discussed in Chapter 4, Orientalist animal comparisons were in ample use when describing Brynner's star persona, sex appeal, and carnal appetite. When commenting on his secretary arguably describing him as 'the most beautiful animal I've ever met' in 1959, Brynner stated that, 'People mainly call me an odd kind of an animal, according to the press [...] all sorts of animal, and just simply an animal.'[84] It was nevertheless the large cats – panthers, tigers, and the occasional lion – that he was most identified with. Such characterizations emerged early on and repeated throughout Brynner's career, as in a 1974 article describing his 'special energy,' 'primitive quality,' and 'sensual quality that draws one in and unsettles at the same time. [...] Even as he sits talking, relaxing, there is a tension, a strength about him almost like a panther in repose.'[85] Such descriptions were not too far a cry from the tropes used to chart Nijinsky's Russian-Oriental charms.[86]

Staging the Orient

As the 'perfect King,' the Euro-Siberian Brynner was a good enough match for the pick-and-mix aesthetics of Hollywood Siam, which one critic defined as those of an 'Oriental wedding cake.'[87] Another described the set:

> [Built] in Siamese style, which is probably the gaudiest style in the world. It also includes an Egyptian type of temple, some Babylonian pillars of fire, and array of fountain like the New York World's Fair, vast floor of shiny marble, and a small jungle of tropical foliage.[88]

Explicitly a figment of studio-era Hollywood imagination, the set design was representative of collage-like Orientalist imagination fusing together elements from different places, times, and cultures into a spectacle optimized for cinematic visual pleasure.[89] Here, the design made use of Orientalist 'exoticizing formalism that cared little and knew even less about the cultures from which it extracted its aesthetic resources.'[90] In the 1910s, the nascent film industry joined in the fashionable wave of exoticism, aesthetically inspired by the costuming and staging of Ballets Russes in films such as *Intolerance* (D.W. Griffiths, 1916) featuring a fantastically decadent Babylon; the Theda Bara vehicle, *Cleopatra* (J. Gordon Edwards, 1917); and, obviously, *The Sheik*.[91] The trend continued in the design of Orientalist cinemas, such as Grauman's Egyptian and Chinese theaters, finished in 1922 and 1926, respectively.[92]

At this point, Orientalism had been in vogue for decades in Europe and North America, from Egyptomania to Chinoiserie and Japonaiserie, and more undefined, eclectic forms of exoticisms. These trends are easy enough to track in nineteenth century painting, architecture, and consumer culture, from World Exhibitions to department store window displays (Siam shared a pavilion with Japan and China as early as the 1867 Paris Universal Exhibition under the personal supervision of King Mongkut, the country hosting its own pavilion in many an expo since).[93] Displays and sales of imported arts, crafts, and consumables – as well as Western manufactured goods appropriating their styles – fed an expansion of commodified Orientalism especially catering to the middle class. As Gaylyn Studlar points out, Orientalism held strong appeal in American 'consumer advertising, dance, the decorative arts, fashion, movie palace architecture, literature, theater, and vaudeville' showcasing 'exotic picturesque qualities' as cultural products toyed with the tropes of sexual decadence, immorality, primitivity, and perversity associated with the non-West.[94]

Even as Orientalism grew less fashionable around the time of World War II, the appeal of eastern splendor and exoticism did not simply fade away. *Lute Song* was a straightforward example of Chinoiserie, *The King and I* of broader Orientalism, and Brynner's next film, *The Ten Commandments*, fully tapped into Egyptomania: all involved the othering of their alluring and decorative male leads. The 1956 *Ten Commandments* was Cecil B. DeMille's remake of his own silent, lavish 1923 film once extolled as 'one of the greatest, if not the greatest, picture which has ever been filmed.'[95] Expanding to full Technicolor in some of the largest film sets ever built, employing 25,000 extras, and costing over $13 million to make, *The Ten Commandments* was the most expensive film to date and, at three hours and thirty-nine minutes, of equally epic length.[96] Combining Biblical spectacle with Egyptian Orientalism, the film was promoted, and largely received, as a meticulously researched and historically accurate account of biblical events, even as its massive largesse was also a point of critique.[97]

As R. Barton Palmer points out, 'blockbuster Technicolor films shot in one of the era's several innovative widescreen formats' were one means of tackling the increasingly challenging economic conditions that the studio system found itself in: such 'glamorous, extravagant spectacles' bordered on the retrograde in often being either similar to, or – like *The Ten Commandments* – direct remakes of 'the epic spectaculars of late 1920s cinema.'[98] With 'elaborate, expensive production values (especially the proverbial "cast of thousands"),' these films exploited their historical license to display 'the scantily clad human body,' employing for the purpose 'performers with obvious physical gifts' – such as Yul Brynner.[99] At the same time, *The Ten Commandments* was pious to the point of fervor. Even as the mammoth *Cleopatra* (Joseph L. Mankiewicz, 1963) had yet to be made, some critics identified *The Ten Commandments* as a cinematic museum-piece of the kind to take one's grandmother to.[100] The film's artistic merit, a Finnish reviewer argued, 'is the same as that of the picture boards I recall being used to enliven religion classes at first grades' – the difference being that 'DeMille's pictures also move and talk. But one can only recommend the film to completely illiterate and untaught folks.'[101]

DeMille cast Brynner as Rameses II on the basis of his Broadway performance in *The King and I*, basically seeing the prince-turned-pharaoh in King Mongkut and persuading the actor to take the part during an impromptu meeting backstage in his dressing room.[102] Brynner's Rameses was variously lauded as 'expert' and avoiding caricature, 'unquestionably apt and complementary to a lusty and melodramatic romance,' yet also 'rock-visaged' and too similar to his King Mongkut.[103] While some described the film as hollow and empty at heart ('Dance-girls and dogma don't mix'), its spectacular appeal translated internationally at the box-office so that the two films that launched Brynner's career were both highly successful, elaborate, wide-screen spectacles, *The Ten Commandments* becoming the highest grossing film of the year.[104]

Rameses is first seen looking out from a palace, brooding as he debates the state of inheritance with his father, the ruling Pharaoh who has a soft spot for Moses (Charlton Heston), his sister's son – a prince who is

Figure 3.3 The ornamental, vengeful Rameses II

freshly victorious in battle. Topless, adorned in armbands, belt, neckplate, rings, pleated skirt, and a gold-decorated prince's scalp lock, Rameses established himself as not only ornamental and masculine but also as power-hungry, jealous, and vengeful – an impression further solidified in the scenes that follow, where he stiffly vows to beat Moses to the crown and has no qualms about flogging and starving armies of Hebrew slaves to achieve his monumental building mission. Rameses smirks but does not smile. Meanwhile, his masculinity remains undisturbed by the gold-trimmed dresses and capes he wears.

As the 'fine baleful brute of a Pharoah one had expected he would be,' Brynner played a variation of a type, even though Rameses was more straightforwardly bad, 'a figure of cool, calculated and imperturbable evil' than Mongkut.[105] Both of his early kingly roles were marked by similar 'arrogant sensuality,' hauteur, and colorful Orientalist costuming while being far from identical – not least because the vengeful Rameses would have been unlikely to break into song and dance.[106] Given that the role of Rameses already involved degrees of typecasting, these two films branded Brynner's star image – on exotic and semi-barbarically masculine terms – as one to shine in these kinds of sand-and-sequins spectacles. His third 1956 role in *Anastasia*, rife with Russo-Parisian elegance and menace alike, both broke with and supported this image (see Chapter 5).

Cutting a royal figure

In 1958, Charlton Heston and Brynner re-joined forces in *The Buccaneer*, produced under DeMille's supervision. The former was cast as General Andrew Jackson and the latter as the flamboyant French pirate captain Jean Lafitte, leader of a crew of a thousand, during the American War of Independence against the British. The film has the two men forming an alliance as Lafitte, enamored with the Governor's daughter, aims for respectability and joins the fight in exchange for a promise of citizenship. As he fails to achieve this, Lafitte returns to the sea, his crew, and marauding ways. Given the co-starring bill of Brynner and Heston, references to *The Ten Commandments* were unavoidable, with one critic summing up the film in the imaginary subtitle, 'How Moses and the King of Siam Won the Battle of New Orleans.'[107]

Lafitte was no average sea marauder but veritable pirate royalty – a role befitting Brynner: 'an old hand at kingly roles,' who sings folksongs in French and joins in formal dances with practiced ease as a 'portrait of dashing nonchalance.'[108] Shot in Technicolor and VistaVision, *The Buccaneer* was initially planned as a musical and retains much of the aesthetic: it is indeed in full color and makes full use of the studio re-enactments of pirate ships, the houses of the well-to-do, and the Louisiana swamplands – for which fifty moss-hung trees were reportedly transported from the bayous for authentic effect.[109] Sporting a wig and a dandy mustache, Brynner's Lafitte makes his first entrance at a makeshift market where the bourgeoisie arrive in bright-colored, feather-decorated finery to hackle over looted valuables. A fight breaks out among the pirates, initiated by the sassy, fast-tempered Bonnie Brown (Claire Bloom, who had already co-starred with Brynner in the 1958 *The Brothers Karamazov*). Dressed in gray tights, black leather boots, a blue coat with green ornaments, and a ruffled white shirt, the mischievous Lafitte spars with his fellow pirates, using his walking stick as a prop weapon with masterly ease. As the Governor's daughter (Inger Stevens) arrives in a carriage, he stands, transfixed, and then changes gears, bringing their 'little show' to an end. The mood is merry and quintessential Hollywood: Lafitte is established as a leading figure of great charm around whom the social action, and especially the women, cluster.

Figure 3.4 The dashing pirate king Lafitte

The lavish costuming adds to the overall sense of heightened artifice and fantastic qualities which contemporary critics were quick to point out – along with the film's poor script, slow rhythm, belabored style, and dialogue pitched at 'sub-teenage level.'[110] As the 'rollicking pirate,' Brynner 'cut the dashing figure' but also made 'a theatrical role even more theatrical with his posturings' while 'his unaccustomed hairiness detracts from the interest of his unusual face and seems to eliminate the dignity usually found in his graver moments.'[111] Lafitte was, despite his violent profession, 'a suave cosmopolite' cut from familiar cinematic fabric, 'like some hero of a romantically fashioned, lavishly illustrated picture book.'[112] For one critic, the character presented the 'combination of a seagoing Robin Hood and a seagoing Al Capone'; another saw Brynner as playing 'Douglas Fairbanks Jun. playing a pirate,' and a third as exhibiting 'the flashing sex appeal of a latter day Valentino.'[113]

With a $6 million production budget, *The Buccaneer* was 'the biggest picture of the year.'[114] Extensively advertised with an additional $1.2 million, it nevertheless failed to become a box office sensation (DeMille died soon after the film's premiere).[115] Similarly to *The Ten Commandments*, *The Buccaneer* came across as dated in its lavish and stiff studio artifice.[116] Such concerns did not lift with Brynner's next historical epic – quite the contrary. As Tyrone Power died in November 1958 of heart failure in Spain when shooting a fight scene for *Solomon and Sheba*, an epic set in biblical times detailing the doomed attraction between the wise king and the Queen of Sheba, Brynner was cast as his replacement. The film was some three quarters ready at the time of Power's abrupt demise, and his scenes needed to be redone.[117] Courtesy of hefty insurance, Brynner was paid the exorbitant sum of $1 million for salvaging the film.[118] It is understandable that Brynner, fresh from two major kingly roles, was considered a natural fit in sharing some, if not much, of Power's masculine star quality.[119] Contra Power's 'gentle, introspective' style, *Cosmopolitan* wrote, Brynner was 'virile and direct, with the impact of a pile driver [...] like someone about to crack a whip.'[120] For Brynner, the decision to take on the role was largely a financial one, as the salary gave him the freedom to leave his first marriage and relocate to Europe.[121] According to reports, he bought both a Mercedez Benz 190SL and a Rolls Royce with the earnings, baptising them 'Solomon' and 'Sheba,' respectively.[122]

Solomon and Sheba is a lavish spectacle of the old school kind, freely spun from an Old Testament story of wise King Solomon's seduction by an Ethiopian queen, played by the Italian Gina Lollobrigida. One of King Vidor's last works, it communicates a familiar Hollywood feel going 'right back to the spectacles of the silent days': 'the film is busy, crowded, huge, tremendous. Thousands of extras trash around, and the battle scenes call for the assistance of the Spanish army. The voice of Jehovah, stereophonically recorded, booms in your ear from loudspeakers in the auditorium.'[123] All in all, the film's technical execution, and especially its spectacular format of Super Technirama 70, gained more positive critical attention than its narrative or execution as 'an inflated Biblical Western.'[124] The film nevertheless had popular appeal among the audience. All four films discussed in this chapter were expensive studio productions distributed in widescreen copies making use of the technical opportunities on offer. Context-wise, this had to do with the film industry's battle with the ever-growing popularity of television: compared to the small black and white TV screens and poor audio quality, studio spectacles offered lavish, rich color, panoramic vistas, and booming sound.[125] These were premium productions aiming to dazzle: their royal palaces, vast armies, pirates, and attractive lead stars were equally alluring.

Figure 3.5 King Solomon among Orientalist temptations

Solomon and Sheba shares the monumental desert and palace grandeur of *The Ten Commandments* yet also caters for an Orientalist twist of harems and erotic seduction. *The New York Times* described the film as 'pseudo-lustful' and originating 'from the jewel-in-the-navel and the lady-in-the-bathtub school of films':

> Indeed, its high point is an orgy, one of those pre-DeMille affairs in which a mob [...] go into a splurge of tub-thumping and shimmy-shaking while their queen dances wildly in their midst, invoking virility and fertility, and girls and fellows rush off squealing into the woods. It is the sort of erotic nonsense that was ridiculous thirty years ago.[126]

The critic was not alone in arguing for the film's general lack of attraction. A second reviewer reported having laughed out loud at this scene of 'shocking pagan orgy' and a third pondered as to its remix qualities: 'The choreography of this dance is curiously reminiscent with its tom-tom background of Pawnee or maybe Arapahoe influences, blended with somebody's conception of some Iron Age fertility rite.'[127] 'For some reason,' wrote a Finnish critic, 'American filmmakers have decided it's inappropriate to make a good film out of biblical topics. No – it must absolutely be excessively pathos-filled, overtly sentimental and anti-psychological. As additional spice, it must have widescreen lechery or battle, or preferably both.'[128] Yet others compared the film's 'deathly opulence,' with that of 'the posher funeral parlors' and complained that Brynner's listless, 'drearily disinterested portrayal' of Solomon approximated a human tableau.[129]

Solomon makes his first entrance in a chariot drawn by two white horses, dressed in black decorative leather armor, an ornamental headdress, and a cape to protect him against the natural elements of the desert, as if gesturing towards Rameses's (final, fatal) chariot trip to the desert to chase after Moses and his people. A battle with the Egyptians looms close and even as his brother, the army-leader Adonijah (the British, albeit Saint Petersburg-born George Sanders), mocks his skills on the field, arguing that Solomon is better suited to the singing of songs, he joins the army and later comes to his brother's rescue. Solomon, thus introduced as jovial, humble, and brave, is seen speaking of the importance of peace and soldierly respect against his brother's unscrupulous warring ways, and is soon announced as the heir to the throne, usurping Adonijah. A soft-spoken man of principle and justice, Solomon is to be driven to near ruin by his passion for Sheba, only to be rescued by his faith in a monotheistic god that he serves, and whom she also comes to recognize as her lord and savior.

Commenting on Brynner's 'faintly Russian accent' and the melange of Lollobrigida's Italian and Sanders's British ones giving the Israelites 'an astonishingly multilingual sound,' *New York Herald Tribune* further pondered about his lackluster performance as 'Solomon walking through his harem, touching wives' faces with all the passion of a housewife feeling grapes at the supermarket.' The complaint continued:

> It would not be fair to blame Brynner for the performance he tries to wrench out of such material, but his face does remain assiduously immobile throughout, perhaps out of some respect for the clear-headedness of Solomon. In most of his close-ups he is in a brown study, but as with Rodin's 'The Thinker' we never get a very clear idea what he's in a study about.[130]

King Solomon's stern musings were indeed similar in poise, gesture, and expression to those of Rameses II's brooding revenge and mourning over the loss of his only son, even as the Israelite is markedly the more sympathetic of the two. Trade paper reviews were somewhat favorable, describing Brynner's performance as 'surprisingly subdued' and nuanced, even as there was broad consensus over his poor fit for the part.[131] In particular, reviewers had issues with Solomon's lack of erotic appeal that went very much against Brynner's sexualized star image (discussed in Chapter 4), and of the film's marketing as a 'tale of love and lust'; a 'passion-filled story of the leader of a people who succumbs to the intoxicating wiles of a pagan queen.'[132]

> As a king who by tradition had a thousand wives, whose favourite scent, according to harem gossip, is attar of roses, he gives a strange impression not only of monogamy but chastity. Without the love story, there isn't much of *Solomon and Sheba* except a huge, garish spectacle, hollow at the heart.[133]

The just Solomon of poetic qualities represents the opposite end of the spectrum to the tyrannical Rameses, with Lafitte and King Mongkut occupying positions in between: they are all unquestionable leaders, ornamental in their displays, and vigorously heterosexual in their tastes. Brynner's kingly profile did not extend to further films, even as his performances continued to be as ones of men of authority and, on occasion, those of luxury. Meanwhile, as discussed in Chapter 9, his royal presence was to be long felt onstage in *The King and I* revivals starting in 1976 and ending only shortly before the actor's death in 1985. Before arriving at this point, however, broad expanses of Brynner's career and stardom remain to be explored, continuing with the pressing question of his bodily presence and sex appeal. To this end, the following chapter zooms in on the actor's positioning as a sex symbol.

Notes

1. *St. Petersburg Times*, 15 December 1958.
2. *Cosmopolitan*, May 1957, 35.
3. Brynner 1989, 18.
4. *Top Spot*, 25 April 1959.
5. *The Daily Telegraph*, 24 July 2001.
6. *The Washington Post*, 28 May 1947; *Daily News*, 7 February 1946; *The Washington Post*, 25 May 1947; *The Wall Street Journal*, 8 February 1946. The same definition was applied to his role as King Mongkut, *Town & Country*, May 1951, 93.
7. *Courier-Post*, 13 October 1985; *Newsweek*, 19 May 1958, 100.
8. *LA Times*, 26 June 1951; *Daily News*, 30 March 1957; *The SF Examiner*, 12 December 1982a, 44.
9. Quoted in Robbins 1987, 40.
10. *LA Times*, 26 June 1951.
11. *Philadelphia Daily News*, 25 June 1981; one of Brynner's own narrations can be heard in an archived excerpt from BBC's 1972 radio show, *Be My Guest*.
12. E.g., *Saturday Evening Post*, 22 November 1958, 82; *Daily Record*, 30 December 1984; *The SF Examiner*, 12 December 1982a, 44; *Philadelphia Daily News*, 25 June 1981.
13. Capua 2006, 36.
14. *Daily Telegraph*, 19 May 1951.
15. Morgan 2008, 31. Morgan's biography traces Leonowens's life in detail.
16. See Kaplan 1995.
17. Leonowens 1873, 237–40.
18. Ibid., 247, 265.
19. Morgan 1991, ix.
20. Lewis 2019, 174–6; Kaplan 1995, 38; Studlar 1997, 48–51.
21. Grewal 1996; Said 1995, 201, 204.
22. Said 1994, 202–3.
23. Klein 2003, 194.
24. Brown 1995, 589.
25. Klein 2003, 195. This version also foregrounds female friendship, see Donaldson 1990.
26. Bernstein 1997, 3.
27. Said 1995, 1.
28. Ibid., 206–8; Klein 2003; Țion 2021, 51.
29. E.g., *Variety*, 4 April 1951; *The Globe and Mail*, 30 March 1951; *The Billboard*, 7 April 1951; *Harper's Bazaar*, April 1951.
30. *The Sketch*, 6 June 1951; Shohat 1997, 40.
31. *Variety*, 4 April 1951; *The Billboard*, 10 March 1951; *NY Herald Tribune*, 30 March 1951; *The Wall Street Journal*, 2 April 1951; *The Billboard*, 7 April 1951; *Variety*, 16 July 1952.
32. *The NY Times*, 5 October 1952.
33. *The Hollywood Reporter*, 19 May 1954.

34. *NY Herald Tribune*, 17 May 1951; *Variety*, 29 October 1952.
35. *The Washington Post*, 10 October 1985; *South China Morning Post*, 8 November 1967.
36. *The SF Examiner*, 25 October 1954, *LA Times*, 21 May 1954; *Cosmopolitan*, May 1957, 37; also Hannan 2015, Kindle edition.
37. See also Deborah Kerr in the 1995 documentary film, *Yul Brynner: The Man Who Was King*.
38. *Newsweek*, May 1958, 103; *Toronto Daily Star*, 24 May 1958.
39. *The NY Times*, 29 June 1956; *Tribune*, 5 October 1956; also *Cosmopolitan*, August 1956, 20.
40. *LA Times*, 2 June 1956; *LA Times*, 9 July 1956a.
41. *The Hollywood Reporter*, 29 June 1956.
42. On 'Chinglish' and 'off-white' yellowface, see Ma 2020.
43. *The Sketch*, 26 September 1956; *Picturegoer*, 15 September 1956b.
44. *The Observer*, 16 September 1956.
45. *The Independent Film Journal*, 7 July 1956; *The Independent Exhibitors Film Bulletin*, 9 July 1956.
46. *Motion Picture Herald*, 30 June 1956.
47. *Variety*, 4 July 1956; *The NY Times*, 29 June 1956.
48. Wanda Hale's superlative review for *Daily News* on 29 June 1956 was reprinted verbatim as paid advert in the same paper on 2 July 1956. The quote here is from the advert.
49. *The Tatler*, 26 September 1956; *The Jerusalem Post*, 10 January 1957.
50. *Le Monde*, 23 January 1957.
51. *NY Herald Tribune*, 29 June 1956.
52. *Beverley Times*, 24 December 1958.
53. *Modern Screen*, October 1956, 10.
54. *Picture Show*, 13 October 1956, 12.
55. Nava 2007, 36; see also Burge 2020; Studlar 1989, 24–5.
56. *Tribune*, 5 October 1956.
57. Klein 2003, 194.
58. *Christian Science Monitor*, 27 December 1999. Even so, it was reported that the King of Thailand invited Brynner for a visit during the first run of the Broadway show: the meeting failed to take place, arguably due to shooting schedules. In 1985, Queen Sirikit attended the show with an entourage of 45, meeting its stars backstage. *LA Times*, 3 June 1955; *The Globe and Mail*, 18 March 1985; *South China Morning Post*, 18 March 1985; Klein 2003, 221.
59. Beltrán 2009, 76–7.
60. *Good Housekeeping*, July 1955, 118.
61. *The Manchester Guardian*, 9 October 1953; *Daily News*, 13 May 1953; *LA Times*, 16 September 1989; *The Globe and Mail*, 25 August 1989. Nureyev's performance garnered an overwhelmingly negative reception.
62. *Philadelphia Inquirer*, 13 August 1990.
63. *The Washington Post*, 3 July 1956; comparisons to Valentino were repeated in *Cosmopolitan*, May 1957, 35.
64. Berry 2004, 188–90.

65. Chávez 2011, 523.
66. Rodríguez 2011, 70–3.
67. McLean 1993.
68. Rodríguez 2011, 74.
69. *Hush-Hush*, July 1957.
70. Studlar 2011, 124.
71. Studlar 1989, 24.
72. Ibid., 23.
73. Brynner 1989, 83.
74. Studlar 1989, 21
75. Nava 2007, 25–6
76. For a detailed historical analysis of Nijinsky's star image, see Järvinen 2014.
77. Nijinsky was Polish.
78. Ibid., 28.
79. Ibid., 30.
80. Järvinen 2020, 76–8.
81. Ibid., 79, 77; see also Tlostanova 2008 and, on the ambiguity of Orientalism in Russia, van der Oye 2010.
82. Negra 2001.
83. Capua 2006, 64.
84. *Cinépanorama*, 11 July 1959.
85. *The Washington Post*, 14 December 1974.
86. See Järvinen 2014.
87. *Monthly Film Bulletin* 1956.
88. *NY Herald Tribune*, 29 June 1956.
89. Shohat 1997, 47–8.
90. Bush 2013, 193.
91. Shohat 1997, 23–7; Studlar 1997, 100–1; Bernstein 1997, 4.
92. For a careful analysis of early cinema and histories of Egyptomania, see Lant 1992.
93. Martin 2019, 137–43.
94. Studlar 2011, 118.
95. *Pasadena Evening Post*, 23 October 1923.
96. *The Washington Post*, 22 November 1956; *Cosmopolitan*, November 1956. For lengthy coverage of the film's scale and execution, see *American Cinematographer*, November 1956.
97. A dutiful listing of DeMille's '40-year' historical research is provided in *The Montreal Gazette*, 8 March 1957; see also *Elokuva-aitta* 16, 1958.
98. Palmer 2010a, 13.
99. Ibid.
100. *Sight and Sound*, Winter 1957; *The Jerusalem Post*, 20 December 1960.
101. *Elokuva-aitta* 16, 1958, 20.
102. *Saturday Evening Post*, 22 November 1958, 82.
103. *Variety*, 10 October 1956; *Le Monde*, 21 January 1958; *NY Herald Tribune*, 9 November 1956; *The NY Times*, 9 November 1956; *Cosmopolitan*, November 1956; *LA Times*, 28 October 1956; *The Independent Exhibitors Film Bulletin*, 15 October 1956.

104. *Variety*, 4 December 1956; *The Times of India*, 23 January 1958; *The NY Times*, 10 November 1956.
105. *The Manchester Guardian*, 28 February 1958; *Australian Jewish News*, 22 December 1967.
106. *Picturegoer*, 28 December 1957.
107. *The Washington Post*, 18 December 1958.
108. *SF Examiner*, 14 December 1958; *The Hollywood Reporter*, 12 December 1958, 3.
109. *The Hollywood Reporter*, 15 October 1957. Apparently making the film a musical was Brynner's idea (as he was set to either direct or co-direct it). See Hannan 2015, Kindle edition.
110. *The Washington Post*, 18 December 1958; *Variety*, 17 December 1958; *South China Morning Post*, 20 October 1959; *The Independent Exhibitors Film Bulletin*, 22 December 1958.
111. *Picturegoer*, 9 May 1959; *South China Morning Post*, 20 October 1959.
112. *Variety*, 17 December 1958; *Seventeen*, December 1958.
113. *SF Examiner*, 19 December 1958; *The Manchester Guardian*, 25 June 1959; *The Hollywood Reporter*, 12 December 1958, 4.
114. *SF Examiner*, 14 December 1958; *St. Petersburg Times*, 15 December 1958.
115. *Variety*, 26 November 1958; *The Hollywood Reporter*, 24 November 1958; *Monthly Film Bulletin* 1959b.
116. For a scathing critique of *The Ten Commandments*' old-fashioned feel, see *Le Monde*, 21 January 1958.
117. *LA Times*, 17 November 1958.
118. *Variety*, 9 March 1960.
119. On Power's star image, see Kelly 2021.
120. *Cosmopolitan*, August 1959, 14.
121. Brynner 2006, 293; *The Vancouver Sun*, 30 June 1959.
122. *The Hollywood Reporter*, 10 February 1959.
123. *The Globe and Mail*, 28 December 1959; *The Observer*, 1 November 1959.
124. *Le Monde*, 19 December 1959; *The Guardian*, 9 June 1960; *Picture Show*, 31 October 1959; *Monthly Film Bulletin* 1959c.
125. See Lipton 2021, part VII.
126. *The NY Times*, 26 December 1959.
127. *The Tatler*, 11 November 1959; *NY Herald Tribune*, 26 December 1959.
128. *Elokuva-aitta* 7, 1960.
129. *The Washington Post*, 30 December 1959; *Picturegoer*, 31 October 1959.
130. *NY Herald Tribune*, 26 December 1959.
131. *Variety*, 4 November 1959a; *The Independent Exhibitors Film Bulletin*, 4 January 1960; *Australian Women's Weekly*, 23 December 1959.
132. *The Independent Exhibitors Film Bulletin*, 31 August 1959, 16.
133. *The Observer*, 1 November 1959.

Chapter 4

Bodily assets, or, 'S-E-X'

> Brynner has a rumbling yet staccato voice, like a bass viol in a barrel. He has a big smile, and perfect teeth show through thick, sensuous lips. His large brown eyes have often been described as hypnotic. He has an electromagnetic personality, a devil-may-care manner that may be part Brynner, part Lafitte.
>
> — Gene Handsaker, *The Chattanooga Times*

Starting with his Broadway hit where Brynner, 'bald, magnetic, graceful as a great cat' was credited for making women swoon 'over his shining dome and smouldering eyes,' his star image was firmly grounded in physical presence, sex appeal, and baldness.[1] 'What does this man got?', *Cosmopolitan* wondered in 1957, then answering its own question by quoting an anonymous female fan: 'It's a surge of power like electric current. Women can feel it.'[2] Brynner's star persona was built on an unabashed display of bodily goods and stylized poses complete with taut muscles and hard, fixed stares. Whether adorned in elaborately decorated Oriental costumes of silks and pelts, the elegant apparel of a dandy, or little else than a leather loincloth, his bodily presence was designed to stand out.

Masculine appeal and heterosexual prowess became key to Brynner's star image while, at around the same time – and in equally mythical manner – his fantastic, cosmopolitan tales of origin became central to its constitution. Mapping the secret of his appeal in their 1956 cover feature, 'Yul Brynner: Why Do Women Find Him Irresistible?', *Collier's* – in a familiar rhetorical move – evoked the figure of Rudolph Valentino.

> In the 30 years since his death, Hollywood has been longing for a successor to the Great Lover. Every foreign-born actor with good looks and dark eyes who turns up there gets measured as a possibility. The fact that Brynner is unquestionably a fine actor doesn't interest the magnates nearly as much as whether or not he can set womanhood in the mass on fire. Does he have what back in Valentino's days was referred to as IT, and later became known as Sex Appeal?[3]

Other writers joined in with a resounding 'yes.' Identifying Brynner as 'the sexiest bald-headed man in the world,' 'Rudolph Valentino and Elvis Presley rolled into one,' 'the bald man's Apollo Belvedere [...] acme of manly beauty and virile elegance' and an 'egg-bald panther of a man' of 'almost hypnotic appeal,' the press made broad – and deliberately hyperbolic – use of exotic and animalistic tropes.[4] 'Some men, like Charles Boyer, exude a soft Continental effete type of charm,' the *Daily News* quoted an unidentified film director as saying, but:

> Yul's lure is that of a sleek tiger crouching for the spring [...] And that strong, bony head of his, as prominent as any animal's, enhances the overall effect of sadistic beast of prey – neither realizing nor measuring its own overpowering strength.[5]

This chapter examines Brynner's star image through depictions of his physique and sex appeal, from bare-chested cinematic displays to rumors of his affairs with both women and men, his early nude shots and the dissonant erotic quests featured in his films. Starting with his trademark baldness, it attends to Brynner's ambiguous positioning as a sex symbol in late studio-era Hollywood. It further looks at the logic of repetition – and practices of outright plagiarism – characteristic of 1950s and 1960s film journalism that shaped his star image.

'The Golden Egg-Head'

Reminiscing about Brynner for a made-for-television documentary, Constance Towers, who played Miss Anna in the Broadway revival of 1976–1978, foregrounds two of his characteristics – baldness and sex appeal – as well as their combined force: 'Here was a man who's bald. He had the courage and the security to be totally bald and yet be one of the sexiest men that women will today tell you [...] is the sexiest man I've ever seen.'[6] It is, in fact, hard to underestimate the role that Brynner's hairstyle played in his star image, as well as the extent to which baldness came to define it. Consider, for example, the 1956 *Washington Post* article 'Yul: Bald, Bold and Big at Box Office' addressing his sex appeal and body aesthetic:

> The hottest matinee idol Hollywood has turned out in years is bald, 41 years old, happily married, not tall and half Mongolian. His name is Yul Brynner and he is so far removed from the accepted standard

> of male attraction that the publicity drum beaters of the movie capital are completely revising their mating calls.
>
> Brynner's background is fabulous, his foreground is spectacular and his future promises to be rich beyond belief. It took Twentieth Century Fox's *The King and I*, the most expensive movie musical ever made and now breaking box office records, to demonstrate that a man can look like Yul and still make female audiences flutter [...] five years after his stage click he strode on screen, almost shockingly virile, floridly colorful, bald as a billiard ball and entirely original. Whereupon the Geiger sex-counters of movie feminine audiences reacted exactly as the feminine Broadway audience had.[7]

Although he had hair or wore a toupee for four screen roles, a clean-shaven head was Brynner's most striking singular physical feature. While male baldness is hardly a rarity as such, the hairstyle was exceptional in Hollywood where toupees and other aids were routinely used to disguise thinning hair and where few 'dreamed that a baldheaded man – any baldheaded – could have and even exude sex appeal.'[8] Brynner first shaved off his hair for the role of King Mongkut in 1951 at the recommendation of its costume designer, Irene Sharaff, arguably to gesture towards the years that the king had spent in a Buddhist monastery.[9] In a 1979 television interview promoting the London stage run of *The King and I*, Brynner casually identified this as a lucky experiment that 'could've turned out terrible – because, you know, the shape of the head is not necessarily the most attractive thing in the world. Not in every case. It could've been a disaster.'[10] Brynner then stuck with the style, in the overblown phrasing of a biographer, transforming 'baldness from a common blemish into an outstanding trademark. Suddenly, after a razor cut, Yul Brynner became one of the sexiest actors in film history, representing the most authentic and irresistible image of masculinity.'[11]

Baldness was considered striking enough for Brynner to respond to seemingly endless interview questions concerning it: rumors of him shaving with a sabre, questions probing the frequency of his trimming habits, and queries as to the libidinal impact of baldness on women were repeated with notable frequency from the 1950s. This rhetorical gesture was recurrent to the point of being a default: in 1958, an Associated Press writer simply identified the actor's baldness as 'the logical place to start an interview.'[12] The topic came up irrespective of context. The following year, *The Manchester Guardian* published a satirical essay dedicated to the relentless avalanche of questions that Brynner faced on his baldness and 'controlled panther-like gait' even when trying to discuss his acting methods and professional

Figure 4.1 Brynner as usher to Hell in *Le testament d'Orphée* (1960)

plans.¹³ And, in 1965, *The Jerusalem Post* reported Brynner's arrival to shoot *Cast a Giant Shadow*, jumping from discussing his familiarity with the Zionist paramilitary organization, Haganah, to his grooming routines: 'Brynner confessed that his hair requires constant tonsorial care: he keeps it bald by running an electronic shaver over it every morning.'¹⁴ His hairstyle remained a primary interview topic well into the 1970s.¹⁵

Brynner's baldness was extensively used as visual element in film posters, as in promotional shots for *Once More, with Feeling!* where Kay Kendall's teased hair peeps behind Brynner's bald dome to a comical troll doll effect,¹⁶ or in the Italian poster of *The Double Man* simply displaying two of Brynner's heads against a red background. Meanwhile, the fact of his hairstyle inspired a seemingly endless range of tongue-in-cheek verbal bravado among journalists and columnists:

> With his pate gleaming attractively in full flesh-orama, Yul is a sight to make strong women palpitate. Not since Guy Kibbee [a comic actor of the 1930s and 1940s] has any movie star so unblushingly exposed his elongated forehead, and never before in Holly-history has there been a lockless lover.¹⁷

One article after another experimented with word games to further highlight the state of affairs: hence *Top Spot*'s 'The Eggman: Spotlight on Yul Brynner,' *Hush-Hush*'s 'Bald Facts about Yul Brynner's Secret Life,' and *Newsweek*'s 'Yul Brynner – Golden Egghead.'[18] The latter's cover featured a close-up of Brynner, cropped from the top of his head to the bridge of his nose, accompanied with the text, 'Bald but Big at the Box Office.' Casual references to Brynner's baldness punctuated film reviews, news items, and interviews almost as something of compulsory gesture that at times took over the article in question. The abovementioned *Hush-Hush*, for example, spent a full page addressing his hairstyle, its popularity, and originality by industry standards: 'When Brynner first appeared on the scene in the glory of his total baldness with the sheen of a bowling ball circling his head like a halo, show business was stunned, both by his baldness and boldness.'[19]

Brynner became a perennial figure and standard reference in articles on male baldness, from pieces on hair loss and dandruff avoidance, to columns identifying his choice 'to clip off his crop' going over 'like a bowling ball in a new alley' as an exception to the common rule.[20] He emerged as the disinterested one in pieces on male Hollywood stars' novel hairstyles; as the one who, on receiving his Academy Award, made Jerry Lewis 'run his fingers through *his* crewcut'; as the one who made women 'quiver like jelly [...] when that clean-shaven cranium first appeared on the screen,' and as the one whose head 'has become a shining symbol of hope to millions of bald men who'd like to believe they can still say hello to romance even though they've had to say goodbye to their hair.'[21] In the course of all this, a 'Yul Brynner hairstyle' was established as a jokey, roundabout vernacular means for connoting baldness in the international press.[22] Meanwhile, his onscreen appearances in a hairpiece in *The Sound and the Fury* and *The Buccaneer* were considered newsworthy as such, them being similar to 'seeing one of Reubens's ladies in a crinoline.'[23]

Baldness rendered Brynner instantaneously recognizable on the pages of any film magazine. In the winter of 1957, a Finnish fan magazine printed a full-page picture of the actor, accompanied by nothing else but the caption, 'YUL BRYNNER, new bare-headed male idol for teenage girls.'[24] The following year, a brief cover feature, 'How do you like Yul?' elaborated on rumors of barbers' traffic slowing down due to his popularity and weighed views for and against the hairstyle.[25] Nevertheless, in the cover image, Brynner wore a straw hat. A later feature came with a centerfold fan poster of Brynner as Solomon – that is, in a wig.[26] When listing Brynner's personal info to a fan in 1963, the editor further added, 'Let's see if we can find a picture of Yul with hair close-by – hopefully!'[27] And, indeed, the accompanying photo was a promotional still from *The Sound and the Fury*. On the one hand, Brynner was introduced as the bald one, and his baldness was picked up in virtually all mentions of him in Finnish film magazines. On the other hand, the editorial choices of using photos of Brynner in wigs is suggestive of aesthetic aversion towards his trademark style. The same applies to *Picturegoer* using a photo of Brynner as Jean Lafitte for its 1959 cover (this was their only cover featuring the actor).[28]

The choice to opt for a shaved head was certainly distinctive by contemporary standards, and there were no Hollywood parallels. The Austrian-American actor and director Erich von Stroheim performed bald – as well as with hair – but his star image was never that of an Oriental seducer or a man of action, and he could hardly have been considered a sex symbol. The Greek-American actor Telly Savalas, whose career picked up in the 1960s, became known for his baldness, low voice, and macho action roles. Some of his flamboyance resembled Brynner's exotic bluster, yet Savalas's fame as a 'middle-aged sex symbol' remained on the much more modest scale of B-movies and television work.[29]

Brynner himself expressed studied disinterest in commenting on his hairstyle: this was unsurprising as such queries were constant. In an article entirely dedicated to answering a reader's question on his actual state of hair, the actor nevertheless encouraged balding men to shave it all off and argued for the hairstyle's quintessentially masculine quality: 'Warriors in ancient times and modern wrestlers shave their skulls to impart a ferocious cast to their features. A bald head is virile. The so-called crowning glory is a woman's boast.'[30] Further elaborating on the theme in *Photoplay*, Brynner described hair as a mere prop similar to a uniform or a spear. However, 'combing hair is a lot of nonsense for a man. I can't stand to see a man in front of the mirror, arranging his hair like a woman, putting a wave in it. Ugh!'[31] This firm binary gender framing separating minimalist masculinity from ornamental femininity re-emerged in an interview done while shooting *The Journey*:

> There are very few men in the movies these days. [...] Very few real men want to be actors. The results of show business are very unpleasant to a real man. The attention a movie star gets, which is pleasant to a woman, is boring to a man. [...] A real man is judged not on how he looks but how he behaves. Cutting your hair off is only another expression of masculinity. It shows you don't care. And I don't care.[32]

Brynner approached the topic of his baldness with haughty fatigue, suggesting that an interest in one's own looks does not befit a manly man, and by positioning himself as someone above such trivial feminine matters. Writing on male Hollywood glamour in 1957, Thomas Wiseman nevertheless doubted Brynner's claim that 'if a man had to think of his looks he was beyond improving', suggesting that the actor in fact thought a great deal about the 'powerful and pagan appearance' that his baldness allowed for.[33] This is a fair guess since physical goods are key corporeal currency within the economies of any film stardom. Acknowledging this would nevertheless have created a dent in Brynner's self-cultivated image of blasé self-assured masculinity where baldness equalled the lack of feminine vanity and made him ever more the man.

Insatiable physicality, plus press remix

Brynner was reported to never sleep more than five hours a night, four when working, his 'atomic energy' aided by the use of an oxygen tank placed in his dressing room or trailer for warding off physical fatigue.[34] Fan magazines characterized him as 'a tremendously vital male [...] bursting with energy':

> [A] superhuman being who pursues his work and his manifold hobbies with furious gusto. He is such a perfectionist that he must get to the professional level quickly in each one – photography, stamp collecting, water-skiing, Yoga, philosophical studies, chef of exotic dishes, designing and building modern furniture, languages, collecting ballads from around the world and singing them to his own guitar accompaniment.[35]

Accounts of exceptional physical energy and intensity met descriptions of animal insatiability in Brynner having five, or possibly six, large meals a day.[36] In 1957, *Redbook* opened its cover feature with an incredulous report on the actor's gastronomic preferences:

> At precisely five o'clock every morning [...] a bald-headed man in his thirties wakes up with the tormenting conviction that he is starving to death. This is the fabulous Yul Brynner [...] who is being widely hailed as the most exciting male on the screen since Rudolph Valentino.
> At five o'clock, Brynner stalks his kitchen and begins the day. His breakfast consists of a large steak, sometimes two, washed down

with coffee. Before nine o'clock, tigerish hunger smites him again and he tides himself over until 12 o'clock with a few large meat sandwiches. For lunch he has chops, steak, turkey, or roast beef and this may get him by until two o'clock when he sends out for sandwiches and cake. In the afternoon he refreshes himself several times with snacks. At dinner Yul eats large helpings of roast beef, with bread, potatoes and dessert. He has a snack before bedtime and goes to sleep at once. He would take a nap after lunch, he says, but can barely doze off before hunger disturbs him.

The preoccupation with eating does not affect Brynner's remarkably photogenic physique. He stands just under six feet, weighs 180, and is muscled like an athlete. On stage and in motion pictures he is frequently seen shirtless, exposing rippling pectorals and hard round arms. In a tight sport shirt Brynner has only to stride – he walks like a cat – through the Paramount restaurant to inspire warm breathing among secretaries, an effect on women which is apparently universal.[37]

Fast forward to 1978, a journalist returned to the topic of his 'legendary' appetite: 'Huge steaks, salads, whole chickens, a leg of lamb, large pieces of pie. Not so much, you say. Listen – that's for breakfast.'[38] Reading press accounts of Brynner, such as these, makes evident their recurrent themes and repetitions, so that a saturation point for thematic analysis seems quick to reach. This is partly since writers routinely quoted previously published articles and interviews, and partly since such repetitions and emphases were key to the construction of star images to start with. 'As a loyal fan of this actor,' a *Cosmopolitan* reader wrote in 1957, 'I constantly scan magazines for write-ups on him; however, I've found most of the articles about him amazingly similar in form and content.'[39] Paradoxically, the reader then went on to compliment the magazine's recent feature for offering original content, despite it catering much that was already familiar.

Syndicated content, such as Hedda Hopper's and Louella Parsons' columns, had broad circulation and they served as sources for gossip published in other countries, just as English-language fan magazines were sourced for similar periodicals elsewhere.[40] In other words, liberal repurposing extended beyond linguistic divides. The Finnish film magazine *Elokuva-aitta*, for example, first introduced Brynner around the time of the local premiere of *The King and I* in a two-page article, 'Bald-headed Yul Brynner mesmerises women,' the contents of which were, by and large, appropriated from the British fan magazine, *Picturegoer*, and which recycled well-tested tropes:

> The newest novelty in Hollywood, too: a charmer without hair! Dark eyes, masculine features, supple presence of a panther and the height of 183 cm – all this is all right but … The top of his head shines bright as a wintery glacier indeed.[41]

In 1961, *Ajan sävel* published a multi-page feature, much of which was lifted from *Picturegoer*'s earlier three-part article, from his hairstyle to diverse tales of origin, great appetite, language skills, and serious interests ('he studies church history in his spare time').[42] This seems to have been less a case of syndicated content and more one of liberal citational practices, since author names were either absent or replaced with local ones.[43] And, as is probably evident at this point, even when articles presented original content, writers made use of stock expressions and characterizations, as when *Elokuva-aitta* interviewed Brynner in Vienna: 'This hero is of surprisingly small frame but undeniably a magnet of a man,' with a 'strong-featured yet sensitive face and panther-like, simultaneously soft and steely presence.'[44]

Broadly following the logic of remix, namely the sampling and recombination of previously published elements to coin novel content, writers borrowed soundbites from one another without identifying their sources: some of these elements were repeated verbatim, and others as more or less creative variations. This resulted in near-identical characterizations repeating over time, and at times parallel to one another, the sources of which were opaque to start with. In 1956, *Collier's* quoted Brynner's former CBS production assistant on his charms: 'He's so dramatic! He can say "Hello" in the most incredibly romantic way. It knocks you out. There's an awful lot of animal to this man. He walks like a panther.'[45] The description soon became something like common currency repeated in *Picturegoer* and thrice in *Screenland* by 1960 (where his animalism and ability to charm women speechless with a 'hello' were presented as both known facts and a quote from a young girlfriend).[46] Brynner's allure was further seen to extend to female journalists collecting themselves to confront 'this symbol of kingly male arrogance and stare into his burning, hypnotic, ripe-olive brown eyes.'[47]

Excess and penchant for bodily pleasure were never far from the construction of the actor's star persona: 'Yul Brynner is a tremendously vital man, bursting with energy and curiosity, pugnacious, restless, voracious, a breaker of rules, an original.'[48] Whether haunted by a tigerish hunger or having the motions of a panther, his persona was recurrently sketched out as excessively energetic, amazingly virile, and mysteriously captivating. 'Animal magnetism' was a characteristic offered by an anonymous studio employee when questioned about Brynner's appeal for a *Photoplay* feature on his bald-headed charms:

> It's a strange combination of almost brute strength and subtle gentle tenderness. He takes complete command when he comes into a room. [...] He doesn't look at you. He stares at you. It's a strange experience. Those eyes seem to pierce you. Most women become almost transfixed, as if they were hypnotized.
>
> Yul's appeal to the feminine world is – let's face it – S-E-X. Ask any girl what she thinks of him, and it comes out something like 'grrr.'[49]

Film scholar Steve Cohan argues that this article, authored by Army Archerd, could 'make sense of the actor's bald pate only by picturing it as a kind of phallus,' leading to overcompensation in descriptions of 'the excessive, unregulated physicality of his entire body.'[50] Whatever the libidinal tensions involved may be, it is noteworthy that the more hyperbolic accounts of Brynner's sex appeal (Archerd's included) were often penned by male journalists who used quotes attributed to anonymous women to communicate the public's spellbound fascination with Brynner. This was also the case in *Newsweek*'s rather critical 1958 cover feature:

> 'He's ugly magnetic,' one ardent feminine fan said recently, and added with savage glee, 'Look at his face. The bone structure suggests cruelty and women love it. There are very few male animals like him.' [...] 'He's a man's man *and* a woman's man.' [...] 'You can look into his eyes and go back centuries' [...] 'He has such fire.' [...] 'He would be the most attractive man alive even if he grew grass on his head.'[51]

In such florid accounts, the mere fact of Brynner's facial bone structure, vaguely suggestive of Asian heritage, was mapped onto an Orientalist sexual imagination rich in barbarism, primitivity, and masculine aggression of the kind that dotted many of his onscreen roles. This animal appeal then seemed to evoke savage features in female fans as something of a primitive reverberation.

Gossip and cosmopolitan sexualities

Media accounts of Brynner's sex appeal broadened into rumours of sexual exploit so that, in a 1957 exposé, 'According to Yul, who looks upon his boudoir battles as no more than the due of his invincible charm, the time he has spent horizontally occupied would have killed an ordinary man.'[52] Quoting Deborah Kerr, Brynner's co-star in *The King and I* and *The Journey* describing his '*oodles* of sex appeal,' the article continued to address the difficulty of telling the man apart from the myth:

> Every one of Brynner's friends has a different story to tell about Yul and his exploits, and the different versions have only one thing in common – they all invest Yul with the charm of a Don Juan, the strength of a Samson, and the morals of a tomcat.[53]

The exposé wove through inflated narratives of sexual prowess to present the reader with a more boring truth of monogamous domesticity while still leaving room for salacious, gossipy details, such as Brynner, during the shooting of *The Ten Commandments*, striding,

> majestically up to one of the female extras, a beautiful blonde called Tanya, who played the part of a slave girl in the film. He balanced himself like a tiger on the balls of his feet, and harshly ordered the trembling girl to his dressing room, as imperiously as any Pharaoh could have wished.[54]

In this account, the actor and the role fused together, the actor using his role and star presence to pressure an extra for sex to the general merriment of his male colleagues (and magazine readers). In a contemporary perspective, this nevertheless comes across as something of a toxic brew.[55] Stories of sexual exploits supported Brynner's exotic and masculine image, even – or, perhaps, especially – when tapping into tropes of authoritarian domination reminiscent of Orientalist imageries of sexual savagery. Or, as an anonymous 'lady admirer' put it in *Cosmopolitan*,

> You can't picture this man ever knuckling under to some woman. I suppose there must be a strong streak of masochism in me – but I adore being bullied. Brynner is a pantherish gent who would never take No for an answer. Of course, it's hard to tell whether it's the man or the roles he plays – but I get the message. I'm his if he'll have me.[56]

Sex appeal and sexual prowess were central constituents of Brynner's star image, yet he also managed degrees of privacy so that his personal affairs were relatively seldom the stuff of extensive public contemplation. Here, ample rumors surrounding his pending divorce from Virginia Gilmore, combined with gossip of his affairs with both 'a 19-year-old Austrian starlet' and his future wife, Doris Kleiner, were notable exceptions.[57]

These rumors were not unfounded as Lark Tilden was born in 1959, the Brynners divorced in 1960, and Kleiner and Brynner married some days later. Rumours also circulated of affairs with a young anonymous French model and with Ingrid Bergman when filming *Anastasia* – the vehicle for a return to Hollywood following her virtual blacklisting for leaving her husband and child for the director Roberto Rossellini in 1950.[58]

Despite some rough patches, Brynner seems to have been favored by key Hollywood gossip columnists.[59] Louella Parsons, Hedda Hopper, and Joyce Haber all wrote chatty pieces on him indicating the intimacy of regular phone calls, meetings, and overall chumminess.[60] This is not to say that these columnists did not gossip about Brynner – this being, after all, their very trade. Their relative restraint nevertheless remains in sharp contrast to later biographies and other posthumous forms of reminiscence. Or, to rephrase, while rumors of sexual exploits played a part in building Brynner's virile star image, most of his high-profile trysts were only made public later when their overall attention value – like Brynner's star image – had largely faded. These rumors were also broader in their suggested scope.

Biographers write of 'a brief but spirited affair' with Judy Garland, another with Nancy Davis (later the US First Lady) when appearing in *Lute Song*, and a third with Joan Crawford during *The King and I*'s first Broadway run.[61] The latter liaison did not fully fly under the gossip radar: Hopper insinuated that the couple was seen 'openly together' and *Photoplay* reported of Crawford being rumored to 'break up the home of Yul Brynner and Virginia Gilmore. The King of Broadway and the Queen of Hollywood – a juicy tidbit.'[62] Both Anita Ekberg and Gina Lollobrigida later listed Brynner among their lovers and Rock Brynner further mentions witnessing his father's intimate interactions with both Marilyn Monroe and Bergman.[63] Claire Bloom, his co-star in *The Brothers Karamazov* and *The Buccaneer*, dedicated a section of her memoirs to their affair, detailing Brynner's need 'to be surrounded by an adoring harem of women,' their getaways to Cecil B. DeMille's 'Paradise' ranch, and to Paris visiting Dimitrievitch's nightclub for an evening of vodka and song, and Brynner ultimately shifting his attentions to Kim Novak.[64]

Writing on both Crawford and Brynner denying any romantic arrangements in 1951, *The Hollywood Reporter* then moved to the topic of Marlene Dietrich as a potential 'woosome twosome,' the couple having been spotted together in 'conspicuous boites at the Copa and the Stork' while Brynner explained that the two had met in Paris two decades prior and had merely recently renewed their old friendship.⁶⁵ Dietrich remains probably the best known of Brynner's Hollywood affairs even if, at the time, the level of rumor remained relatively subdued – possibly since she was nineteen years his senior.⁶⁶ According to Rock Brynner, the affair started in the early 1940s, the two meeting at a New York club (the aptly titled Blue Angel) where Brynner sang Russian Roma songs in his first job in the new country.⁶⁷ For her part, Dietrich's daughter, Maria Riva, dates the meeting to 1951 and describes her mother furnishing a hideaway apartment with Siamese silks and proudly displaying the smears of body paint on the king-sized bed following Brynner's daily visits. In her account, the volatile affair lasted four years until Brynner ended things, Dietrich consequently hating him with venom till her death.⁶⁸

Dietrich's close friend and magazine publisher Leo Lerman claims that the couple met through Noël Coward.⁶⁹ Coward, who had turned down the Broadway role of King Mongkut, was friends with the show's star Gertrude Lawrence who then introduced him to Brynner (while, according to her daughter, having an affair with Brynner herself).⁷⁰ In his posthumously published diaries, Lerman describes acting as go-between for Dietrich and Brynner, listening to her laments and delivering her baked goods to his stage door.⁷¹ Lerman writes of first meeting Brynner himself when the latter was still with Michael Chekhov's theater company: 'a catlike young man, sinewy – was he Oriental? Part Oriental? Kurdish? – something so exotic I could not say quite what he was, but what he definitely was, and knew it fully, was a charmer.'⁷² He further mentions Brynner's affair with Hurd Hatfield, a fellow actor at Chekhov's, best known for his leading role in *The Picture of Dorian Gray* (Albert Lewin, 1945).⁷³

The anecdote is not an isolated one. In his memoirs of his life with Salvador Dalí, Carlos Lozano, actor, dancer, and gallery owner, writes of Brynner and Kirk Douglas socializing with the artist and his entourage when filming *The Light at the Edge of the World* in Spain (Brynner had met Dalí already in 1930s in Paris in Cocteau's company).⁷⁴ Lozano reminisces that he felt fortunate to make it to dinner 'with a grasp of my dignity' after a previous encounter with Brynner and, in a suitably surrealist fashion, of the actor 'wandering around the suite all afternoon not knowing whether to seduce me or Donyale Luna [the actor and model] who, for some reason never disclosed, had been lying on a bed of fresh fish.'⁷⁵ Perhaps the best-known homoerotic Brynner anecdote involves an affair with Manuel Puig, the future author of *The Kiss of the Spider Woman*, who was assistant on the set of *Once More, with Feeling!*⁷⁶

The veracity of memoirs and biographies detailing Brynner's affairs with men are no different from those involving women, even as the volume of the latter easily outweighs the former. There is a tendency, especially in popular historiography, to disavow accounts of gay, lesbian, and bisexual interests and attachment among the Hollywood elite as salacious, hostile gossip.[77] With bisexual preferences, there is the additional issue of their visibility being eclipsed by both heterosexual norms and gay and lesbian identity politics.[78] Since similar standards do not apply to straight trysts, this speaks of deep bias in what attachments and desires count, what becomes remembered, and how we envision the past and the sexual lives possible within it. In other words, the issue is one of frames and limits of imagination pertaining to both sexuality and history. That a cluster of queer narratives exists in connection with Brynner – one involving diary notes, autobiographies, and biographies drawing on interviews – speaks of an expansion of his star image from ardent womanizer to more polymorphous sex appeal and sexual agency.

Having freshly moved from Paris to New York, Brynner worked as an artist's model and, in 1942, posed for a series of nudes for George Platt Lynes, a fashion photographer known for his portraits of gay artists who was, at this point, focusing increasingly on the naked male body. In some shots, Brynner simply stands and faces the camera for full frontal exposure. In others, he sits and reclines on a plywood construction against a white background with a towel in his hand in a setting gesturing towards a bathhouse, his body carefully lit as an object of visual contemplation. Platt Lynes produced a broad series of male nudes – 600 of which the sexologist Alfred E. Kinsey collected – that were not publicly exhibited for decades.[79] These nudes – prints of which remain in circulation, and which have since been reprinted, not least with a gay male audience in mind[80] – make Brynner an exception among major Hollywood stars in the degrees of flesh bared for the camera, even while his partly exposed body was to become very much key to the construction of his star image as a staunchly heterosexual, insatiably virile Casanova; 'the bald Don Juan.'[81]

As one of the full-frontal shots was printed in Andy Warhol's *Interview* magazine in 1977, Brynner shrugged off the shoot as something he had done for money, and that hardly mattered.[82] There is little reason to doubt the financial motivation involved, the shoot happening soon after Brynner's immigration to the United States. It should, nevertheless, be noted that the connection between the photographer and the model may not have been entirely random as their social networks entangled. In the 1930s, Platt Lynes photographed Jean Cocteau who drew Brynner's portrait around the same time (and several times after). Both Cocteau and Brynner (now fully clothed) posed for the British Cecil Beaton, whom Platt Lynes also photographed. A friend and colleague of Platt Lynes's at *Vogue*, Beaton was also an Oscar-winning film and stage costume designer known especially for his work on musicals, and a star in the firmament of queer high society.[83]

Considering Brynner's social connections and sex appeal beyond heteronormative templates opens up an angle to that which Ken Plummer discusses as cosmopolitan sexualities: an outlook committed to acknowledging plurality, difference, and the co-existence of sexual lifeworlds. As an extension, or aspect, of cosmopolitanism, such pluralism focuses attention on multiplicities that exist in any given time and place, and foregrounds respect towards the diversity of sexual lives.[84] Cosmopolitanism has, historically, been a quality of large cities and connected to travel between them, so that sexual cultures have been both highly local and fluid in how they extend and connect – something that Brynner's cross-Atlantic social affiliations also suggest.[85] Friends with the British Coward and the French Cocteau[86] alike, Brynner was part of an international social circuit where promiscuity was not rare among members of any gender and where heterosexuality was not a strict norm – Dietrich herself (another friend of Cocteau's) being known for her omnivorous appetites.[87]

A sex symbol

In 1955, Hedda Hopper announced that Brynner was to take on an additional role in *The Ten Commandments* as the first man, tastefully nude and anonymised, in the film's prequel: 'Since Adam was prewardrobe, they'll have to fall back on fig leaves and beard.'[88] The prequel was never screened (probably never shot) yet Brynner's previous experience as nude model and his ease with cinematic bodily displays do not exclude the possibility of one having been in the planning.

Film scholar Mark Gallagher conceptualizes cinematic sex appeal as dependent on the 'exposure and display of the body, as well as on a range of performative signs that comprise his or her idiolect.'[89] Sex appeal then involves a set of traits repeated, highlighted, and recognized across an actor's body of work, and possibly showcased or magnified through technical, narrative, and tonal means. In a straightforward sense, Yul Brynner's sex appeal was built through recurrent displays of his partly exposed, muscular body, toned by early trapeze work, long-term yoga practice, and a passion for water skiing. In his roles as tyrannical Oriental rulers, Brynner's appearance was decoratively spectacular to start with, his routinely bared arms, chest, and midriff adding to the overall spectacle.

Sex appeal results from bodily work and, as a component of star image, it is bolstered through narrative accounts and descriptions of both performers and their performances – as in the myriad accounts of Brynner's animal, primitive, and mesmerising magnetism. Yet sex appeal alone does not a sex symbol make. Will Scheibel defines sex symbol as a 'celebrity image that derives its dominant meaning and affect from sex.'[90] A sex symbol entails a truncation of a kind where sex overshadows the actor's other characteristics and features, mastery of the dramatic arts included. John Mercer further points out that a sex symbol is 'a symbol (or perhaps more accurately a synecdoche) for prevalent attitudes towards sex' and hence a matter of cultural norms and values:

> So rather than the assumption that sex symbols exist merely because they are 'sexy', it is rather more that specific celebrities are (or become) containers into which sets of meanings and anxieties around sex and sexuality can be poured, or a metaphorical surface on to which desires can be projected.[91]

As such a container or surface, Brynner was foreign and off-white: perhaps European, perhaps barbarically Mongol, perhaps something else. In the 1950s US, the in-your-face masculinity of his onscreen characters communicated the allure and risk of transgression in terms of both ethnicity and sexuality (as in King Mongkut's obvious libidinal interracial appeal to Miss Anna). Brynner's sexualized exoticism, as displayed in his film work, was amplified through verbal means in the press. Meanwhile, the actor himself expressed fatigue over his labeling as a sex symbol.[92] This involved similar masculine haughtiness as his approach to the topic of his shaved pate.

> On the subject of his own sex appeal he is suitably scornful, as becomes an austere philosopher and man of action. Once asked what he had that women found so fascinating, he replied: 'How should I know? I'm not a woman...'[93]

Commenting on his frustration with how his star image was framed as late as 1974, Brynner (aged 54) argued for due professional respect. Meanwhile, the journalist elaborated on his exotic persona, summing up some of the dilemma in the process:

> 'I have a kind of senior position in the business,' he explains. 'Forty-one years. I'm not a starlet. I do get insulted if I'm treated like one. Some of the talentless people in the press, they treat me like an animal in a zoo, or a male Jayne Mansfield.' He glowers, his Mongol eyes closing to narrow slits, and skewers a piece of raw fish.[94]

Jayne Mansfield, of course, was a film star known less for her acting than for her sex symbol and Playboy Playmate status, promotional stunts, personal life, colorful biographical tales, striking costumes, extravagant lifestyle, and trademark high squeals.[95] By 1974, Mansfield had been dead for years, her career having suffered a steep decline in the 1960s.[96]

A sex symbol is, in a literal sense, objectified for the visual gratification of viewers. At the same time, it is not accurate to say that an actor classified as a sex symbol is merely an objectified product lacking agency. Any simple binary between sexual subjectivity and objectification is reductive, given the routine, mundane ways in which people frequently move between positions as objects and subjects, possibly occupying both at once, as we dress, groom, and adorn ourselves, fulfil mandated work tasks, or try to physically appeal to others.[97] Jessica Hope Jordan makes a similar argument in her analysis of Mansfield's star image, showing how her positioning as a sexualized visual commodity also involved her ability to manipulate and craft her star image, as Mae West had done some decades earlier.[98] Brynner's positioning as a sex symbol involved the kind of reductive pigeonholing that he saw as drawing attention away from his professional skill. At the same time, sex appeal was elementary to Brynner reaching the level of stardom that he enjoyed: it would hardly be fair to say that he played no knowing part in how all this played out.

Offbeat romance

Brynner's screen characters held firm erotic appeal even as none of his films could be classified as romance. In a recurrent theme moving from *Anastasia* to *The Sound and the Fury*, *Surprise Package*, and beyond, his macho characters intimidated the leading women who then fell for their charms without much wooing, while, at the same time, these men exhibited vulnerability and tenderness in accordance with the 'bastards with a heart of gold' trope that the actor preferred. To the extent that these were romantic leads, their modus operandi was, as a *Picturegoer* reader noted in 1957, to mask desire 'by indifference and disdain.'[99] For Hedda Hopper, Brynner and Bergman's love scenes in *Anastasia*, 'in which he doesn't speak the word of love or put a hand on her, are something for all actors to study.'[100]

Rather than doing conventional love scenes, Brynner argued for stagings of sexual desire and intent through looks and gestures so that kisses or any other physical contact were unnecessary. He explained his method in response to the journalist's musings on the 'Shall We Dance?' number in *The King and I* being 'one of the sexiest scenes ever filmed': 'When I reached out to ask Deborah to dance [...] that gesture, without any words or any action, should have explained the completeness of the desire.'[101] The scene, which Christina Klein identifies as 'the culmination of the sexual tension that has been building up,' opens with Miss Anna introducing 'the polka as a ritual of Western courtship, an initiation into the Western sexual and, by implication, political order': 'the King, transfixed, looks at her with desire and joins in as she sings about dancing with a lover' and the two begin to dance together from a polite distance. The dynamics then shift as the King,

> looking her straight in the eye and with his hand rigidly outstretched in an unmistakably phallic gesture, takes her in a firm, close embrace around the waist; they look at each other intently, their breasts heave, and when the music erupts they begin to dance and whirl around the room. The number is intensely erotic: Anna wears a low-cut gown that, for the first time, displays her in a sexual manner, while the King wears a loose costume that exposes his hairless chest and bare feet; their dancing brings their bodies into close and active contact, [with the King performing] his love for Anna in Western liberal and romantic rather than Oriental despotic form.[102]

With a wild waltz/polka standing in for a sexual exchange, with hand gestures suggestive of penile intent, with partly exposed expanses of skin standing in for more straightforward corporeal contact, and with music erupting to convey an erotic climax, the scene is both explicit and extensively euphemistic in how it uses bodily gestures, dance movements, and musical rhythm to convey sexual desire. The scene is followed by one where the king, enraged by the attempted escape of Tuptim, the young female slave brought to him as a gift, tears off his top with the intent of

Figure 4.2 An invitation to dance, followed by planned flagellation

flagellating her with a bullwhip. As the horrified Miss Anna exclaims, 'you *are* a barbarian,' the king stops in his tracks, throws his whip down, runs off, and soon dies.

It is indeed a recurrent development for Brynner's characters to die in the narrative closure, hence resolving the issue of sexual desire and romantic longing once and for all – especially when it crosses geopolitical or racial boundaries, as in *The Journey*, *Kings of the Sun*, and *Invitation to a Gunfighter*. The endings of *Anastasia*, *The Brothers Karamazov*, and even *The Sound and the Fury* promise coupledom while in *The Buccaneer* and *Solomon and Sheba* the romantic couples go their separate ways due to circumstance. In *Flight from Ashiya*, Brynner's Japanese-Polish-American character romances an Algerian woman during World War II, with tragic consequences. His character, later a laconic sea rescuer, remains traumatized after having 'accidentally demolished his winsome Moslem lover along with a bridge.'[103]

Ever since his interviews promoting *Port of New York*, Brynner expressed his aversion towards romantic parts. Arguing that onscreen male lovers were embarrassing to watch, he further identified men suffering from love as silly, most unattractive, and potentially unmasculine.[104] As his fame began to solidify, Brynner spoke of the unease of being labeled a romantic heartthrob and argued that what made the role of King Mongkut so attractive was him having 'a hundred wives, but not one love scene.'[105] In 1958, he reiterated this distaste for romantic leads that had made the careers of many (that of Tyrone Power, the original king in *Solomon and Sheba*, included) and addressed his initial hesitation in taking on the role of the King:

> I was afraid I'd have to play a lover, and to me that was a horrible idea. I played a few lovers in my time, and to me they are monsters. Writers must despise such characters or they wouldn't write them so abominably. Young male lovers are creeps, even venomous toads. I refer to characters who are publicly unhappy and are even destroyed when their love is unreciprocated. I can understand begging a woman to love you, but to be miserable if she doesn't I do not understand. It's not only unmanly, it's ridiculous. If you base your life on whether a woman is going to love you or not, you are better off dead.
>
> I read it and the character of the king carried me away. He was irresistible. There was nothing mawkish about *his* love life.[106]

This foregrounding of masculine autonomy and freedom over romantic submission was well aligned with the individualistic ethos that Brynner expressed throughout his career. It further aligned the actor and the characters that he preferred to play, and which he was best known for. Befitting the logic of reiteration that cuts through Brynner's star image, the actor himself repeated his dislike for romantic parts in combination with his fondness for the role of the King with nearly identical wordings well into the 1980s.[107] As Brynner eschewed romance as unmanly, mawkish, and boring, press accounts of his sex appeal and virile sexual agency abounded, as did screen appearances showcasing his bodily assets.

Showing off

From the 1950s studio epics to his late work, Brynner's onscreen performances featured more bare-chested appearances than historical accuracy or narrative logic, no matter how fragile, would have warranted. There is a topless shaving scene (*The Brothers Karamazov*) and a chain of towel-only sauna scenes (*The Double Man*). His characters freely appear topless both when fighting and without particular motivation, beyond the primitivism that these displays communicated. His chest was often

Figure 4.3 Brynner topless in *The Brothers Karamazov* (1958), *Kings of the Sun* (1963), *The Long Duel* (1967) and *The File of the Golden Goose* (1969).

shaved (e.g., *The Ten Commandments*, *The King and I*, *Kings of the Sun*) so as 'to facilitate the applications of oils and make-up to enhance its musculature.'[108] Makeup was further central to his diverse performances of ethnicity and accentuated exoticness, as Brynner's face and body were accordingly tinted in hues of brown.

At the beginning of their collaboration, producer Marvin Mirisch was quoted arguing that 'Yul Brynner in a starch shirt is a person no one wants see': consequently, as a journalist pointed out, the characters he was set out to play 'could hardly be described as wearing shirts at all.'[109] *Kings of the Sun* (1963) was one such film. According to critics, he wore 'almost nothing all': 'Brynner's body gets a big play. Often his head is chopped off in a shadow in order to focus at length on his pectoral endowments. Beefcake, as a matter of fact, disproportionally abounds.'[110] This remark is apt enough, given how the camera repeatedly lingers on Brynner's face and scantily clad, bronze-colored body. His limited wardrobe for the film reportedly cost a total of fifteen dollars.[111]

In *Kings of the Sun*, Brynner played Native American chief against the Greek-American George Chakiris's son of a Mayan ruler. In its review, *The Times of India* used the actors' names when describing the plot, performing what, in a contemporary perspective, reads as an inadvertent deconstruction of the ethnic casting policy – inadvertent in the sense that this was standard practice in film journalism internationally:

> George Chakiris, King of the Mayans, flees from his homeland to prepare for another day when he can return to face his traditional enemy, Leo Gordon. The new home is assailed by Yul Brynner and his North American tribes. Their feuds are soon settled and a friendship develops, to be disturbed by both gents falling for blue-eyed Shirley Ann Field [English actor playing Ixchel, daughter of a Mayan chief]. [...] Yul Brynner has a great time strutting and sulking as Black Eagle. Chakiris, a method actor, does his share of rough stuff but puts the onus of acting on his facial muscles. Miss Field, the bone of contention, is sombrely decorative.[112]

Rich in body-paint and decorative costumes complete with bright feathers and gems, *The Kings of the Sun* was characterized by American critics as 'a treat for the eye,' as 'painstakingly authentic in its recreation of early Mayan culture,' and as 'pictorially extravagant, historically simplified and melodramatically passionate' escapist fun where Brynner 'steals the show with his sinewy authority, masculinity and cat-like grace.'[113] His character's entrance is dramatic: Chief Black Eagle is first seen peering at the newly arrived Mayans behind branches in extreme close-up focusing on his eyes, then dashing behind another tree for an alternative perspective and athletically running to the shore to examine their boats with his equally bewildered men. Wearing a feather-decorated ponytail on his otherwise hairless head, leather pants, and leather decorations, Black Eagle is next depicted as the centrepiece of a tribal meeting, his skin brown, oily, and glistening, gravely pondering as to the meaning of the strange newcomers. A man of smooth movement, physical prowess, combat, authority, and gravitas, Black Eagle is not one to smile, nor does his character gain much depth during the remainder of the film that gears up to a final, spectacular battle scene where he is to make the ultimate sacrifice.

A reviewer for *Toronto Daily Star* identified Brynner as one of the film's few highlights as someone who 'looks and sounds and moves, as always, like some barely-humanized panther not of our time.'[114] Other reviewers similarly appreciated his 'Tarzan-like' performance as 'a Red Indian chieftain, a part into which he clearly puts a great deal of imagination, and a tremendous physical highlight' as something to 'attract the ladies.'[115] A snarkier critic described Brynner acting 'with his stomach muscles' in 'a coat of dark greasepaint and a loincloth.'[116] 'The pigtailed Brynner makes a whooping, whopping wild man indeed, a leaping spider of a fellow,' wrote the *Los Angeles Times*, acknowledging the film's spectacular aspects but complaining about its stock characters (such as Brynner's 'noble savage') and formulaic script.[117] Even as critics pointed out the film's contrived dialogue, its artificiality, and 'universe of convention,' little attention was paid to its extensive use of brownface, as this remained a norm in early 1960s Hollywood.¹¹⁸

Captured and injured by the Mayans – and, unbeknownst to him, prepped for human sacrifice – Black Eagle is seen lying on his back in a hut, tied to the ground in a crucifix position on a bed of straw, pulling at his restraints. As a Mayan princess (Field) arrives to attend to him, Black Eagle continues to resists, near-naked in body paint except for a minimal leather loincloth. Soft light falls on his Christ-like, glistening, and muscular body as it is displayed from different angles in an otherwise darkened room. As the angelically white-clad woman kneels next to him, touching his hand and then cupping his face, Black Eagle tries to pull away. Changing tactics, she sponge-feeds him some water and then straddles the writhing man who moves to, fro, and sideways, the scene gathering an air of copulation. Release only arrives as she cuts his restraints and the two eye each other with startled intensity. As she begins to gently attend to his wounded hip in a posture suggestive of fellatio, he strokes her hair and then grips her by the back of the neck. After a brief moment of tension, he eases back and she caresses his cheek. No words have been exchanged; merely grunts.

Exploring Brynner's star image in 2019, I argued that, with the exception of this particular scene, and despite his evident potential peplum prowess, his was not a body to be thrown into a gladiator pit, lashed with a whip, or sold to slavery, as happened to his *Ten Commandments* co-star Charlton Heston (who went on to play the title role in *Ben-Hur*). Rather, his off-white characters were more likely to be rulers ordering and overseeing such operations. In *Taras Bulba*, it was

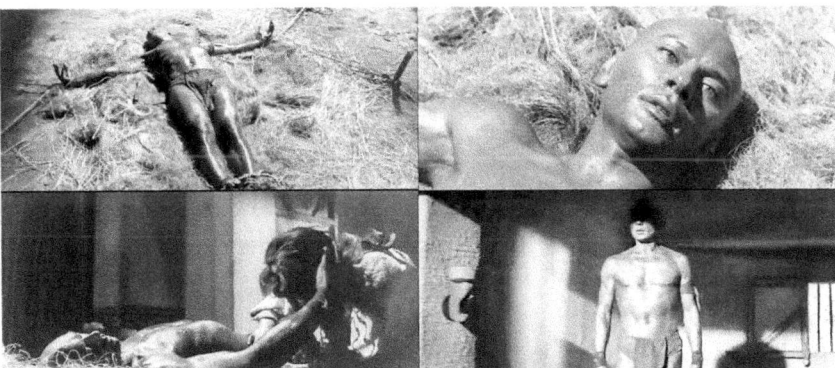

Figure 4.4   Chief Black Eagle, detained

the son, played by Tony Curtis of *Spartacus* fame (and previously as the imported slave of Kirk Douglas' Scandinavian warrior in *The Vikings*), and not the father, played by Brynner, who suffered flagellation at the hands of the Polish clergy.[119] While correct on the basis of his assembled screen work, this need not have been the case – and, had Brynner been the one to decide, it certainly would not have been.

In 1957, Brynner's company Alciona bought rights to Arthur Koestler's novel, *The Gladiators*, with the aim of producing it as part of the UA pact: the Hollywood blacklisted Abraham Polonsky was recruited to write the screenplay under a pseudonym.[120] It was announced in *Los Angeles Times*, *Hollywood Reporter*, and *Variety* that Brynner would play the Thracian gladiator, slave leader Spartacus, that Anthony Quinn was to co-star, and Martin Ritt to direct: UA advertised the forthcoming attraction in the press with a drawn likeness of the topless Brynner in gladiator guise.[121] Plans were well underway to start shooting in Italy (or perhaps Argentina) late in 1958 and, in order to economize, Brynner made a deal with the producer of *Solomon and Sheba* for reusing its costumes and chariots for his own film; Sophia Loren was briefly rumored to be the female lead.[122] Covering the prospective production, *Picturegoer* enthused over Brynner's easy fit for the part:

> The professional killer he will portray habitually fought naked. Not even the prodigious Brynner can be expected to get that far into the spirit of the thing. But at least the gladiator rôle will once again free him from what he considers the tyranny of wigs.[123]

Published in 1939, *The Gladiators* is, by and large, the same narrative as Howard Fast's 1951 novel, *The Spartacus*, for which Douglas's Bryna Productions brought the rights (once Alciona's project was already common Hollywood knowledge) and which Stanley Kubrick directed for 1960 release.[124] The two productions obviously rivalled each other and, despite talks of the productions partnering up to make a single movie, this plan evaporated and a court battle began over rights to the film's title, with Alciona winning sole use to *Spartacus and the Gladiators*, Bryna appealing, losing the appeal, and Brynner eventually giving them rights to *Spartacus* as a 'gesture of goodwill.'[125] Independent of the actual level of goodwill, in their minute analysis of the case Henry MacAdam and Duncan Cooper illustrate that – partly due to Brynner's work with the UNHCR (see Chapter 6), his other film roles, and his interest in making *The Magnificent Seven* – *The Gladiators* lagged behind in schedule,

Spartacus got ahead and, after its notable success, there was little point in going through with a rival project.[126]

For even as this may not come across as obvious, Brynner's star image was akin to those of American actors known for rough masculine roles and muscular bodies: Douglas, Heston, Quinn, and Burt Lancaster whose film careers were established before Brynner's ascendence to fame and which lasted longer than his. Such associations were explicit in both casting rumors (discussed in Chapter 2) and in joint on-screen appearances.[127] After their feud over their respective gladiator projects, Douglas and Brynner appeared together in *Cast a Giant Shadow* and *The Light at the Edge of the World*. Brynner was Heston's co-star in *The Ten Commandments* and *The Buccaneer*, and while he never collaborated with Lancaster, a fellow veteran circus performer, the two were friends and Brynner did publicity shots for *The Train* (John Frankenheimer, 1964) that he starred in.[128] Writing on the early 1980s stage revival of *The King and I*, a journalist described 'Brynner's at turns fierce and mischievous facial grimaces, his intriguing and expression-enhancing bald head [...] and his rock-solid physique' having made him 'the perfect choice for major "heavy" parts in Biblical epics and exotic adventure films'.[129] Brynner's physique made him an organic fit for the same calibre and style of roles that Douglas, Heston, and Lancaster played: his accent, needless perhaps to say, did not.

All these actors' oeuvres belong largely to genres which, in Ina Rae Hark's words, feature men in conflict with other men: 'Westerns, epics, swashbucklers, science fiction, sword and sorcery, war dramas, gangster and cop movies'.[130] Within these genres, the 1950s witnessed a notable range of leading men taking off their shirts and, on occasion, the additional pants in order to showcase their muscular, agile, and athletic bodies.[131] In doing so, they played characters covering a range of nationalities and ethnicities: Douglas was cast as an Italian race-car driver in *The Racers* (Henry Hathaway, 1955), as a Nordic warrior in *The Vikings* (Richard Fleischer, 1958) and, of course, as a Roman slave gladiator in *Spartacus*. Meanwhile, Heston played Moses in *The Ten Commandments*, a Judaic prince turned gladiator slave in *Ben-Hur* (William Wyler, 1959), and a Castilian warlord in *El Cid* (Anthony Mann, 1961). Lancaster was an Italian archer hero in *The Flame and the Arrow* (Jacques Tourneur, 1950), a Native American warrior Massai in *Apache* (Robert Aldrich, 1954), and the possibly Italian Captain Vallo in *The Crimson Pirate* (Robert Siodmak, 1956).

Unlike Brynner's, their star images were not constrained by, or limited to such casting options but moved seemingly smoothly between roles as American heroes, biblical figures, Nordic and Latin characters. Here, the Mexican American Anthony Quinn formed an exception. Starting his career at the birth of the Production Code, Quinn played a great range of ethnic roles over his long career. Perhaps best known for starring in *Zorba the Greek* (Michael Cacoyannis, 1964), his performances included (but were not limited to) Native American for example in *The Plainsman* (Cecil B. DeMille, 1936), *They Died with Their Boots On* (Raoul Walsh, 1941), and *Seminole* (Budd Boetticher, 1953), Chinese in *Island of Lost Men* (Kurt Neumann, 1939), Oriental King Kiang in *East of Sumatra* (Budd Boetticher, 1953), Bedouin Arab sheik in *Lawrence of Arabia* (David Lean, 1962), emperor Kublai Khan in *La fabuleuse aventure de Marco Polo* (Denys de La Patellière and Noël Howard, 1965 – a role that Brynner had turned down), and Inuk in *The Savage Innocents* (Nicholas Ray, 1960). Like Brynner, Quinn was typecast, and subsequently specialized in masculine, foreign, and exotic roles, but the two are hard to compare in terms of their physical presence and overall star image. Quinn's box-office magnetism was compared to Brynner's, yet he never reached quite the same star status.[132]

Given his star image rooted in physical prowess, it is not surprising for Brynner to have been interested in the Spartacus narrative – any more than it was for Quinn to be interested in a co-lead and for Douglas to take on a production project of his own. Gladiator films are textbook illustrations of Hollywood films centring on the exposed muscular white male body in genres of action and suspense, and in scenes of combat, torture, and humiliation that provide motivation for both the action and displays of male flesh.[133] Such scenes have offered visual gratification to viewers of diverse gender identifications and sexual orientations throughout film history. This has afforded a solution to what Mercer identifies as the enigma of male sex symbol's desirability – 'a puzzle that has to be worked out or made sense of in some kind of way.'[134] Such working out has involved the sexualization of male bodies as indices of masculinity and as markers of virility in the guise of violence (and occasionally humor), as well as heterosexualization, or the warding off of queer connotations arising from their display.

No threat, harm, violence, or humor was nevertheless required to justify scenes reveling in Brynner's corporeal assets. No pretexts were required for showing off his body as modes of undress were part and parcel of his exotic, primitive, and Orientalist roles. Since Brynner's 'Mongolian' star image was associated with these from the outset, gratuitous bodily displays continued. Such displays, as well as their occasional setting within the historical epic, all rang true of the aesthetics of peplum while failing to be confined to it.[135] Brynner's star image was distinct both in terms of his bodily aesthetic and the types of roles that he was repeatedly cast in, and identified with, and which formed the large bulk of his film work. In order to further map this out, the following chapter addresses Brynner's pan-ethnic roles in a topological vein, moving from his Russian displays to his French-American, 'Cajun,' Arab, Israeli, Indian, and German appearances in films, none of which were box office successes and which partly illustrate his stardom's downward trajectory from the 1950s to the 1970s.

Notes

1. *Top Spot Magazine*, 6 June 1959.
2. *Cosmopolitan*, May 1957, 35.
3. *Collier's*, June 1956, 34.
4. *Screenland*, May 1957, 53; *Hush-Hush*, July 1957; *The Austin Statesman*, 7 July 1958; *St. Petersburg Times*, 31 March 1957.
5. *Daily News*, 30 March 1957.
6. In the biographical film *Yul Brynner: The Man Who Was King*, 1995.
7. *The Washington Post*, 2 September 1956.
8. *Photoplay*, February 1957, 109.
9. *San Francisco Examiner*, 13 April 1976; *Saturday Evening Post*, 22 November 1958, 82; *The National Tatler*, 26 May 1974; Leonowens 1873, 238.
10. *Afternoon Plus*, 1979.
11. Capua 2006, 1.
12. *The Calgary Herald*, 22 January 1958.
13. *The Manchester Guardian*, 20 March 1959.
14. *The Jerusalem Post*, 31 May 1965.
15. *The National Tatler*, 26 May 1974.
16. *Life*, 29 June 1959.
17. *The Montreal Gazette*, 5 January 1957.
18. *Top Spot Magazine*, 6 June 1959; *Hush-Hush*, July 1957; *Newsweek*, 19 May 1958; or, 'Bald Box-Office King,' *Cosmopolitan*, May 1957.
19. *Hush-Hush*, July 1957, 34.
20. Here, examples are simply too abundant to list. See e.g., *The Jerusalem Post*, 19 June 1958; *Toronto Star*, 12 March 1957, 3.
21. *Picturegoer*, 12 March 1960; *Picturegoer*, 4 May 1957; *The Times of India*, 19 April 1969; *The Bennington Evening Banner*, 13 November 1956.

22. For select (Australian) examples, see *Australian Women's Weekly*, 30 September 1970; *Australian Women's Weekly*, 23 May 1973; *Canberra Times*, 10 March 1986.
23. *Life*, 18 March 1957; *Picturegoer*, 8 November 1958; *Australian Women's Weekly*, 29 April 1959; *NY Herald Tribune*, 30 December 1958; *San Francisco Examiner*, 23 February 1958.
24. *Ajan sävel* 7, 1957.
25. *Ajan sävel* 20, 1958.
26. *Ajan sävel* 48, 1961.
27. *Ajan sävel* 12, 1963.
28. *Picturegoer*, 21 February 1959.
29. *USA Today*, 24 January 1994.
30. *NY Herald Tribune*, 20 January 1957.
31. *Photoplay*, February 1957, 110.
32. *NY Herald Tribune*, 24 April 1958; repeated in *Picturegoer*, 31 January 1959, 14, and, to an extent, in *Seventeen*, October 1962, 172.
33. Wiseman 1957, 200.
34. *LA Times*, 30 July 1956; *Picture Show*, 8 December 1957, 4; *Picture Show*, 7 September 1957, 4.
35. *Screenland*, May 1957, 53, 70; *Screenland*, January 1960, 60.
36. *Picture Show*, 7 September 1957, 4; *Screenland*, January 1960, 68; *The Chattanooga Times*, January 19 1958.
37. *Redbook*, May 1957, 31; paraphrased in, e.g., *Picturegoer*, 17 January 1959.
38. *The Washington Post*, 30 July 1978. For its part, *The Vancouver Sun*, 9 October 1979, rehashes details of not only Brynner's appetite but also his baldness, general vigor, 'Asiatic cheekbones', and exotic family background.
39. *Cosmopolitan*, July 1957; the fan's reference was to *Cosmopolitan*, May 1957.
40. Collected digests of US gossip columns were published, for example, in the Australian *Truth*. Examples of Hopper and Parsons operating as sources are abundant: for just two examples, see *Elokuva-aitta* 16, 1957; *Elokuva-aitta* 17, 1957.
41. *Elokuva-aitta* 23, 1956a, 11; cf. *Picturegoer*, 15 September, 1956a; *Picturegoer*, 15 September, 1956b.
42. *Ajan sävel* 48, 1961; cf. *Picturegoer*, 17 January 1959; *Picturegoer*, 24 January 1959: *Picturegoer*, 31 January 1959. It was a specific quality of Hollywood gossip in Finnish papers to be ephemeral, even factually erroneous, to the degree of suggesting that facts were not a particular priority. For example, in 1960, Brynner was reported to be part of 'a certain humanitarian organisation': 'The story doesn't tell how the movie hero Brynner got caught up in this work but there's no doubt as to him having considerable merits in the field since he's become the chairman of the entire organization, or president, as they say in America. A film has also been made on this charity organisation, the lead part played by – Yul Brynner.' *Ajan sävel* 45, 1960.' As discussed in Chapter 6, the anonymous organization in question was the United Nations: Brynner was an appointed special consultant for the UNHCR (hardly its president). The film in question was the CBS Special Report, *Rescue with Yul Brynner* (1960).

Finnish film magazines freely appropriated content from international fan magazines and exhibited little interest in contextualizing the news and gossip items

they printed. In this context, mentions of films in the making – such as *Winter Coffee* shot in London in 1960 – emerged out of the blue, unconnected to Brynner's actual projects while a photo of Brynner, Maria Schell, and Claire Bloom on the set of the 1958 *The Brothers Karamazov* served to illustrate a 'reunion' among dear friends when filming *The Journey*. *Elokuva-aitta* 7, 1960; *Elokuva-aitta* 9, 1958.
43. *Picturegoer* was a key source for Finnish film and fan magazines, probably due to its easier accessibility as a British rather than American publication: among other sources, it was also appropriated for a Portuguese fan magazine special issue on Yul Brynner, *Álbum dos Aristas* 4, 1957. At the same time, articles did of course also circulate by more straightforward syndicated means, as in *Collier's*, June 1956 article appearing also e.g., in *Australian Women's Weekly*, 19 September 1956.
44. *Elokuva-aitta* 23, 1958.
45. *Collier's*, June 1956, 34.
46. *Picturegoer*, 31 January 1959 and 30 January 1960; *Screenland*, May 1957, 50, 53 and January 1960, 60.
47. *Screenland*, January 1960, 60.
48. *Collier's*, June 1956, 34–5.
49. *Photoplay*, February, 1957.
50. Cohan 1997, 151.
51. *Newsweek*, 19 May 1958, 102.
52. *Behind the Scenes*, 28 March 1957, 19.
53. Ibid., 56.
54. Ibid.
55. While the theme is too broad to tackle here, suffice to say that the gendered and sexual dynamics of late studio-era Hollywood are key to all this. In a system entirely run by men (albeit not all straight), few female actors held the kind of leverage to make decisions over their careers, and 'fixers' working for the studios neatly covered traces of transgression and sexual violence. Male stars could easily get away with rape (consider, for example, Natalie Wood's sister recently identifying Kirk Douglas as the then teenage star's violent rapist; *Variety*, 4 November, 2021).
56. *Cosmopolitan*, May 1957, 37.
57. E.g., *Modern Screen*, December 1958; *Daily News*, 10 August 1958; *The SF Examiner*, 29 November 1959; *Screenland*, January 1960; *The Washington Post*, 3 February 1960; *Picturegoer*, January 30 1960; *Elokuva-aitta* 20, 1958; *Elokuva-aitta* 7, 1960.
58. *The Washington Post*, 28 May 1959; *Screenland*, January 1960; *Picturegoer*, 31 January 1959; *Elokuva-aitta* 24, 1957.
59. On Hedda Hopper's early vitriol, see Robbins 1987, 62–3.
60. This balance was starkly different from the aggressive probing that he encountered in some European countries, shooting *The Journey* in Vienna being particularly confrontational and scandal-heavy. *Daily News*, 10 August 1958; Robbins 1987, 78.
61. Clarke 2000, 233–4; Brynner 1989, 42–4; Bret 2008, 189. According to a biographer, he sent Crawford 'an authored photograph of himself, stark naked but for his stage makeup,' Capua 2006, 46–7.
62. *LA Times*, 15 June 1951; *The Hollywood Reporter*, 25 June 1951; *Daily Telegraph*, 17 June 1951; *Photoplay*, February 1952, 72; *The Calgary Herald*, 11 September 1951; see also *Truth*, 1 July 1951; *Daily Telegraph*, 1 July 1951.

63. *Daily Mail*, 27 December 1999; *South China Morning Post*, 25 February 1990; Capua 2006, 83; Brynner 1989, 89–90, 95.
64. Bloom 1996, 104–7; on Novak rumors, see also *The Hollywood Reporter*, 3 December 1957.
65. *The Hollywood Reporter*, 19 June 1951; see also *The Hollywood Reporter*, 12 June 1951.
66. Yet rumors there were: e.g., *Truth*, 19 August 1951a; *Truth*, 19 August 1951b; *NY Herald Tribune*, 2 August 1956.
67. Brynner 2006, 151; similar timeframe is proposed in *Daily News*, 30 March 1957.
68. Riva 1993, 613–14.
69. Lerman 2007, 106.
70. *Daily Mail Online*, 30 April, 2009
71. To be precise, German donuts filled with apricot jam. Lerman 2007, 107.
72. Ibid., 106.
73. He further writes of the two attending Brynner's 'drab' 1986 memorial together, joking that they should retitle themselves 'The Had and the Hadn't,' as Lerman argued having turned down Brynner's sexual advances himself. See Ibid., 541.
74. Brynner 1989, 29; also *Saturday Evening Post*, November 22 1958, 84.
75. Thurlow 2011, 128, 130.
76. Levine 2001, 113, 121–2, 397n72. The biography is based on interviews with Puig.
77. Consider, for example, the continuing contestation over Cary Grant's sexuality, including his cohabitation with Randolph Scott, see Eyman 2020, 9.
78. E.g., MacDowall 2009; Monro et al. 2017.
79. *The New York Times*, 24 September 1993.
80. See *The Advocate*, 8 July 1997; *Gay Times*, October 1998; advert in *The Advocate*, 26 January 1993.
81. *Le Courrier Australien*, 18 January 1957; *Le Monde*, 11 May 1957.
82. Capua 2006, 16.
83. The correspondence between Beaton and Peter Watson has a prominent role in Clark and Dronfield 2015.
84. Plummer 2015, 14, 81.
85. Ibid., 61–2.
86. Brynner and Cocteau have also been rumored to have been lovers at some point, *The Telegraph*, 9 July 2020.
87. See Riva 1993.
88. *LA Times*, 15 June 1955.
89. Gallagher 2014, 112.
90. Scheibel 2013, 5.
91. Mercer 2013, 86.
92. *LA Times*, 1 April 1975.
93. *Saturday Evening Post*, 22 November 1958.
94. *The Washington Post*, 14 December 1974.
95. On Mansfield's life and celebrity, see Golden 2021.

96. Brynner and Mansfield were both US representatives at the 1958 Cannes Film Festival where *The Brothers Karamazov* was met with boos while Mansfield basked in extended public attention: they were also at one point eyed for the same film, yet it is impossible to estimate the degree of their mutual familiarity. Golden 2021, 133–4. As discussed in Chapter 3, the planned film was *The New Adventures of Tartarino* in 1958. Mansfield died in 1967 at the age of 34.
97. This argument is developed at length in Paasonen et al. 2021.
98. Jordan 2009, 155–6; Watts 2003.
99. *Picturegoer*, 2 March 1957b.
100. *LA Times*, 18 December 1956.
101. *Photoplay*, February 1957, 110.
102. Klein 2003, 208–9, 211.
103. *The Washington Post*, 8 August 1964; *South China Morning Post*, 4 December 1964.
104. *The Boston Globe*, 25 November 1949.
105. *Screenland*, May 1957; *LA Times*, 30 November 1955.
106. *Saturday Evening Post*, 22 November 1958, 82, emphasis in the original.
107. Consider, for example, a 1981 interview with Elliot Norton: 'I'd played mostly young lovers and I hated them. As a rule they're the worst parts in the world [. . .] they're [. . .] you take the classical, Armand Duval in Camille – he's a venomous toad! – you know, he's just an abominable young man! He's a dreadful part and I'm sure the author detested him, as he wrote him, because he couldn't have written worse, you know, even grammatically he's impossible. And that's the classical lover.' *Elliot Norton Reviews*, 1981.
108. Williams 2009, 46.
109. *The Calgary Herald*, 24 June 1961.
110. *The Washington Post*, 19 December 1963; *Variety*, 18 December 1963.
111. *The Austin Statesman*, 3 February 1963. This is a questionable claim, given the multi-colored feather cape he wore as an object of pending Mayan human sacrifice.
112. *The Times of India*, 24 September 1964.
113. *Boxoffice*, 16 December 1963; *The Independent Exhibitors Film Bulletin*, 23 December 1963; *Variety*, 18 December 1963.
114. *Toronto Daily Star*, 20 December 1963.
115. *South China Morning Post*, 26 September 1964; *Boxoffice*, 16 December 1963.
116. *The Globe and Mail*, 20 December 1963.
117. *LA Times*, 19 December 1963; also *Toronto Daily Star*, 20 December 1963.
118. *Monthly Film Bulletin* 1964; *Le Monde*, 23 January 1964.
119. Paasonen 2019, 252.
120. Plans varied so that, as pointed out in Chapter 2, Quinn was also eyed as director. *The NY Times*, 17 October 1957; *The Independent Film Journal*, 26 October 1957. Polonsky's screenplay, never filmed, has recently been published. See Polonsky 2020.
121. MacAdam and Cooper 2020, 80–2, 85–6, 102–3; see also *Variety*, 4 June 1958.
122. *The Hollywood Reporter*, 22 May 1958; *The Hollywood Reporter*, 20 June 1958; *The Austin Statesman*, 19 February 1959; *The Hollywood Reporter*, 20 February 1959; MacAdam and Cooper 2020, 147–8.
123. *Picturegoer*, 17 January 1959.

124. *Variety*, 21 May 1958.
125. MacAdam and Cooper 2020, 116–32; 149–51, 159–64; *The Hollywood Reporter*, 21 August 1958; *The Hollywood Reporter*, 25 August 1958; *Variety*, 27 August 1958; *The Hollywood Reporter*, 27 October 1958. The battle, however, extended from 1957 to 1963: for a detailed timeline, see MacAdam and Cooper 2020, 361–90.
126. MacAdam and Cooper 2020, 111–12, 134–6, 165–7, 235–6, 274.
127. According to rumors, Quinn was eyed as stand-in for Brynner's *The King and I* stage run during his filming plans, but Quinn turned down the offer. Hannan 2015, Kindle edition.
128. *LA Times*, 17 October 1963.
129. *Philadelphia Daily News*, 25 June 1981, 19.
130. Hark 1993, 151.
131. Neale 1983; Cohan 1997; Williams 2009; Fouz-Hernández 2011.
132. *Good Housekeeping*, February 1960, 69.
133. Hark 1993, 151.
134. Mercer 2013, 88.
135. On the body aesthetics of peplum, see Dyer 1997, 165–9.

Chapter 5

Strong, silent, ethnic types

Despite the range of ethnicities and nationalities that Brynner played during his career, his roles were largely variations of a type. Typecasting was, on the one hand, an external constraint. As Brynner stated, 'I'm not exactly a clean-cut All-American type. [...] And so [...] I play a lot of strange characters in a lot of strange lands.'[1] On the other hand, this was a plan of action that he knowingly operated by repeatedly taking on roles of bastards with a heart of gold. Within these, one recurring character type was that of an idealistic leader and/or warrior resisting tyrannical forms of governance; another being that of a tyrannical governor and/or warrior serving tyrannical forms of governance.

This chapter examines Brynner's ethnic characters from Russian military men and Cossacks to 'Cajun' gunslingers, Arab and Indian freedom fighters, and German army officers from the 1950s to the 1970s. Focusing on the characters' introduction scenes in particular, and exploring reviews of his performances, it maps out the types that Brynner's pan-ethnic star persona became associated with and inquires after recurrent elements in his performance style.

Playing Russian

As already discussed in Chapter 2, many of the first roles that Brynner was rumored to take on following his Broadway breakthrough were Russian ones. He played multiple Russian characters throughout his career, both speaking and singing in Russian onscreen, yet his star image did not become associated with, or reduced to these. His career took off in a highly polarized political Cold War context where being identified as Russian would, in all likelihood, have severely limited his casting options. With the execution of the Rosenbergs for Soviet espionage in 1953, the McCarthy hearings of 1954, and the extensive blacklisting of left-leaning Hollywood professionals, roles available to Russian actors were largely limited to historical and emigrant parts on the one hand, and to communist villains, military types and spies, on the other. As Harlow Robinson points out, similar to other outsider groups, Russians were depicted throughout the Cold War through political and ethnic stereotyping designed to support dominant US worldviews.[2]

In a cultural context permeated by anticommunism, anti-Bolshevism in particular, the role of the opportunistic White General Sergei Pavlovich Bounine in *Anastasia* (1956) was a safe one for Brynner to play, as was that of Dimitri in *The Brothers Karamazov* (1958), set as it was in the previous century. Major Surov in *The Journey* (1959) was a little riskier – however, the Major is prone to philosophical musings as to who counts as enemy, eventually has doubts about the political system he serves, and dies while giving freedom to a wounded Hungarian resister, so that he does not amount to a full-on enemy figure.

Brynner's Russians were characteristically stylized. Directed by the Russian-born Anatole Litvak, *Anastasia* and *The Journey* – as different as the two films are – are both narratives of displacement, Brynner's Bounine and Surov being variations of a type. Bounine first enters the film to greet champagne-drinking patrons at his Parisian nightclub as they enjoy a floorshow of spinning dance and Romani music. Stiff-backed and courteous, he is dressed in a black Cossack-style tunic with a silver knife at his belt. In the following scene he is called to see Bergman's Anna Anderson, Anastasia-to-be, brusquely questioning her and later pulling her away from attempted suicide on the banks of the Seine. Referred to as 'General' and 'Your Excellency,' Bounine is established as a social force to be reckoned with: a man of authority and determination with a clearly displayed ruthless streak.

In *Anastasia*'s critical, highly positive reception, Brynner's Pygmalion-like Bounine was somewhat overshadowed by Bergman's comeback Hollywood performance resulting in her second Academy Award.[3] *The New York Times* saw his performance as being best 'when he is browbeating the girl, displaying his Slavic perseverance, and least impressive when he is itching with love': the newspaper further noted that he 'appears oddly youthful for a former Russian general, some ten years out of circulation, but he sure has the visor for the role.'[4] Early critiques of Brynner's acting style and 'disturbing mannerisms' also emerged: 'Yul Brynner more or less repeats the manner of his performance in *The King and I*'; 'Brynner scowls and stalks through the role like a robot, never changing expression until the final scene, when a glint of love sneaks into those cold brown eyes.'[5]

In *The Journey*, Major Surov makes an entrance twice: he first appears briefly in a cloud of cigarette smoke, dressed in black leather, at Budapest airport where stranded international passengers await flights out following the Soviet invasion, to no avail. His second entrance is on horseback, similarly dressed, among Soviet soldiers and tanks in a small town at the Austrian border, speaking Russian as the man in charge of the travelers who are now trying to get across by bus. Described by a Hungarian server as a 'very good Russian. Drink like fish, sing like devil and brain like knife,' Surov is a man prone to debate who exhibits keen aesthetic sensibilities, is kind to children, and fluent in English. 'Tractors and Marxism are not the only things a Russian cares for,' he proposes: 'There's always time for music. And when there's music, we sit down and listen, and we feel sad, which is the best way of feeling good.'

Surov – 'virile, volcanic, a man of conflict' – drinks vodka through his dinners: his party trick is to down his shot without using hands, to bite the glass into pieces and chew on the bits with bloody lips.[6] Both Bounine and Surov are hard, authoritarian military men capable of violence who break into song when in festive mood. Their relations with Bergman's Anastasia-in-the-making and Deborah Kerr's Lady Ashmore move in registers of interest, dominance, and sexual desire with an undercurrent of menace. Their Russian masculinity is of the brusque and autocratic sort, yet steeped in melancholy, romantic tones.

An active military man, Major Surov goes about in uniform, protected against the cold by black leather or a black fur winter coat with padded shoulders which, with some poetic license, gestures toward Sergei Eisenstein's *Ivan the Terrible* (*Ivan Groznyy*, 1944). Bounine also prefers black: suits, occasional tuxedos, stylized Russian-style shirts, and Cossack-influenced jackets. Like Surov, he completes his look with shiny black riding boots. In order to communicate underlying savagery, both casually handle riding crops when engaged in social exchange, bending, flexing, and waving them to dramatic effect – despite Bounine being a Russian Roma nightclub owner in central Paris, anno 1928, and Surov, stationed in 1956 Hungary, having access to a military jeep as a means of transport. These crops echo the much more impressive bull whips wielded by Brynner in *The King and I* and *The Ten Commandments* to demonstrate authoritarian masculine control. Born of 'commanding,' 'powerful and muscular,' 'good, hard acting,' critics characterized Surov as 'naive, cruel, erratic and sentimental – a strange character who should fascinate women and impress men.'[7]

Figure 5.1 Riding crops in *Anastasia* and *The Journey*

Reviewers mainly applauded Brynner for humanizing the Russian Commander – 'capricious, sentimental, cruel, eager for love [...] bright as a precocious child and just as unsophisticated,' 'a man of sensitivity and romantic taste' – even as they also found his ultimate self-sacrifice poorly motivated and the film's romance puerile to the point of 'risking the laughter of the most sentimental of midinettes.'[8] Brynner's casting in both roles was seen as a good fit, not least since the actor was starting to be recognized as 'the most dominant cinema star of the moment.'[9] 'He is the sort of Russian you would expect to see Yul Brynner play – and since Mr. Brynner does play him, the circumstances are suitable, indeed. [...] Mr Brynner plays a stern, sweeping, striding Soviet officer with bewilderment and pity in his eyes,' wrote *The New York Times*.[10] *The Hollywood Reporter* similarly accredited much of Surov's appeal to Brynner's 'dynamic magnetism', describing his character as a 'magnificent barbarian, whether he is eating a vodka glass or soothing his hormones by galloping through the night on a black stallion.'[11]

Much of these characterizations would equally apply to Brynner's breakthrough role as King Mongkut counter to Kerr's Miss Anna – a character depicted in broadly Orientalist terms as both child-like and tyrannical. Picking up on the connection, *Picturegoer* identified *The Journey* as 'The King and I for the modern times' and eschewed the film's geopolitical theme in favor of the electric pitting of 'Deborah's brave English ladylike reserve against the Mongol flamboyance of Brynner.'[12] *The King and I* also functioned as a template for making sense of General Bounine: for *The Observer*, 'the colour, the gauds, the clamour and Yul Brynner's mesmeric personality suggest that *Anastasia* might almost be called *The Grand Duchess and I*.'[13]

As is customary with star vehicles, Brynner's exotic masculine persona was seen to intermesh with the roles he took on while also carrying traces of previous performances so as to build a continuum. Here, Bounine's or Surov's Russianness mattered as much, or little, as King Mongkut's nationality in that they all stood for exotic, alien masculinity of the kind that characterized Brynner's star image from the outset, and throughout. And, given how critics commended his handling of Russian dialogue in *The Journey* as authentic-sounding, and noted that 'without his Mongolian appearance [...] Yul would look very much like an American playing Russian,' it appears that he did not, either at this point or at a later date, become particularly fixed along Slavic lines.[14]

'Gambler, sinner and great lover'

The 1958 Fyodor Dostoevsky adaptation, *The Brothers Karamazov*, was deeply embedded in studio imaginaries of exotic Russia. With an international cast featuring Brynner as the volatile Dimitri, William Shatner as his younger monk brother, Alexey, and the Austrian Maria Schell as Grushenka (a role that Marilyn Monroe had long pursued[15]), and also including Claire Bloom, Albert Salmi, and Lee J. Cobb, the film catered stylized, melodramatic and emotionally intense nineteenth century Russia in full Metrocolor. Brynner singing Russian Roma songs – the ones he had once performed in Paris – operated as something of an accent gesturing towards the kind of cultural authenticity that the film did not aim to deliver. Within its artificial displays, no actor communicated Russianness more than any other, even though Brynner's Dimitri, 'excitingly haughty and intense, with the virility of a whiplash and the eventual humility of a monk' is the central character encapsulating the film's overall libidinal and dramatic mood.[16]

Dimitri is first seen in a rowdy party scene complete with a vodka-drinking dancing bear as his monk brother comes to bring him money from their father. A fellow officer calls Dimitri a thief for not repaying his gambling debts and attacks him, only to be wrestled to the ground. Quickly thus established as reckless, cavalier, and strongly masculine, Dimitri leaves, saying goodbyes to the men and the bear alike, and is next seen topless shaving his face and skull, displaying his athletic torso in a medium shot. As the film progresses and Dimitri begins to convey more complex emotions, the camera lingers on his figure, and on his face in particular, lit in chiaroscuro. The chosen form of display involves degrees of posturing so that, according to a critic, 'Brynner changes from one noble stance to another.'[17] 'With his carved Slavonic features and fanatically burning eyes, he gives a wonderful interpretation of the accepted Russian preoccupation with living – whether it be gambling, loving, dancing with wine and song, or indulging in orgies of misery,' a Hong Kong based reviewer wrote. Although yearning for 'a little for the old Yul Brynner of *The King and I*, with his delighted "et-cet-e-ra" and gleeful puzzlement' she identified the performance as 'an artistic triumph.'[18] *The Hollywood Reporter* agreed, and then some:

> Brynner's Dimitri is the soul of Dostoyevsky's narrative made manifest in the flesh. Often, without dialogue, he makes us see and feel the extremes of virtue and sin present in the character. During an orgy, he radiates the magnetic evil of a Lucifer. In his final humility, he makes you feel the gigantic importance of a saint. The compelling sex appeal when he takes possession of his woman has scarcely been equaled since Valentino played *The Sheik*. But Brynner is more than a vivid personality. He is an actor whose craftsmanship is guided by rare intelligence. This is the most subtle acting the theatre can give us – here the sensitive brain of the interpreter equals that of the creator. The measure of its brilliance will be found in the authoritative quiet strength which Brynner lends to other players in scenes where the focal point is not his.[19]

'In Brynner's Dimitri,' the paper continued, the younger generation of viewers can 'feel, vicariously, the fulfilment of their own drive to live up all that life has to offer,' the film's 'wild emotionalism' giving them 'the charge of a jazz jam session.' As a variation of the bastard with a heart of gold trope, Dimitri is brash, impulsive, heavy-drinking, and manly – 'gambler, sinner and great lover'[20] – yet harbors a romantic soul as the narrative unfolds in sumptuous studio settings complete with trick riding, sleighrides, displays of sexual desire, violence, and vengeance. Richard Brooks's screenplay transformed Dostoyevsky's complex novel of tortuous family relations into a straightforward narrative, foregrounding the visual splendor 'of the Russian outdoors, its dark and shadowy forests, its colorful skating ponds and village squares, as well as its gloom-filled rooms' in 'wildly orgiastic scenes' depicting 'lusty, bawdy, loving hating kind of life' where the 'luscious Grushenka' is 'stolen by Dimitri from his sensual father!'[21]

Many critics praised the film a masterpiece, its 'rich and ornate' production resembling a 'Byzantine basilica,' its 'bold treatment of crude, unbridled passion' where 'a landscape of greed, lust and murder' comes to life 'with throbbing urgency,' lauding its characters as 'gems of histrionic art, flawless and scintillating creatures by top-drawer Thespians.'[22] European reviewers were, in the main, less generous pointing out the film's many shortcomings, from the 'detestable' color intended to highlight the intensity of the action to the film's simultaneous lack of passion, 'inordinately foolish' dialogue, and happy Hollywood ending.[23] It seems that many of the film's qualities lauded in the US media – the film's intensity and its overall take on Dostoevsky's story – were found lacking elsewhere. At the 1958 Cannes Film festival, audience famously booed the film and snubbed Brynner and Bloom as they turned to take a bow: 'Many of the fans stood up in their seats and shook their fists. Cries of "ridiculous," "absurd" and "shameful" could be plainly heard.'[24] Since Brynner had been flown in on a military plane under Washington orders to divert positive press attention away from the Soviet delegates promoting Mikhail Kalazatov's *The Cranes Are Flying* (*Letyat zhuravli*, 1957), the end-result was doubly anticlimactic.[25]

Flamboyant Cossacks

Brynner's lavish Slavic displays continued in *Taras Bulba* (1962), freely adapted from Nikolai Gogol's novella, where he took on the titular Cossack role. Shot in Argentina, this was an epic narrative – or, in less flattering terms, a 'mammoth,' 'frenetic horse opera,' with a reported 10,000 mounts[26] – of father (Brynner) and son (Tony Curtis) battling against Polish occupation in sixteenth century Ukraine, the father ultimately killing the son for betraying the ancestral cause. We first see Taras Bulba as he emerges victorious from battle against the Turks and is appointed as the unwilling Cossack representative to meet with the Poles. Dressed in red and ochre, Taras walks over with a swagger, a sneer on his face and an exposed sabre in his hand, refuses to enter the Polish tent, and laughs at the prospect of free Cossacks being integrated into their army. As the Cossacks are outfought and in retreat, they dramatically cut off their now forbidden scalp locks, swearing revenge.

Figure 5.2 The statuesque, butch Taras Bulba

The scene introduces Taras Bulba as a fearless macho man of honor and principle, as well as the focus of attention and action, and this is what he remains throughout the film. The epitome of alpha masculine ferocity, bravado, and virility, Bulba is something of a comic book character composed of angular movements, furrowed brows, and stiff poses. Similar stylized artifice applied to the film's overall historical re-enactment. Brynner 'hasn't progressed much from the thespic position he was in when he played the King of Siam,' a critic complained, expressing equally little enthusiasm towards the film's supply of 'splendidly unsanitary barbaric types, striding about with hands on hips and showing off gleaming capped choppers in wolfish grins.'[27] Another continued that the Cossacks 'are shown in true story-book guise, almost child-like in their high spirits, always singing, brawling, or dancing, or being thrown up in blankets in the rough and tumble of an excited crowd.'[28] A third reviewer largely shared the sentiment:

> What it is, mostly, is about a million Cossacks and Poles racing around the steppes (really the Argentine pampas, where it was filmed) hacking away at each other. When they stop for a breather, they pass time by leaping into the air and touching their toes and tossing each other around in blankets a la St. Paul's winter carnival.
> This might not sound like sheer enchantment, but actually it's pretty entertaining stuff. Thanks for this are due Brynner, who persuades me that he really could lord it over all these idiotically tough and energetic Cossacks.[29]

Brynner's Bulba is tanned (and heavily made-up), bare-chested and totally butch. His aging in the course of the film is mainly made evident through gray streaks inserted in his eyebrows and moustache. Curtis's Andriy Bulba is similarly ageless yet also of somewhat bizarre age, given that the actor was only five years younger than Brynner. Larger than life, Taras Bulba is a striking presence who, despite the actor's height or Curtis's nominal star billing, dominates the scenes he appears in. Brynner's performance was partly praised for pulling out all stops as the 'truly vigorous and authentic' fiery Cossack who 'drinks, dances, struts and fights with equal gusto' played in 'lusty, forceful fashion' befitting the actor's star image.[30] Some saw it as overdone to the point of hammy, with him posturing through the story.[31] In yet other critical responses, praise and critique were difficult to tell apart:

> As Taras Bulba, Brynner is a snarling lion of a man for whom sword play, curses, feats of strength, honor, cavalry charges and heavy

> drinking are essential facets of virility. And he is so convinced of a rendezvous with destiny that he announces, with swaggering finality, that he will one day be the subject of a legend. What a guy![32]

This role, the preparation for which arguably took fifteen weeks, was of exceptional interest and ambition for Brynner, so that the film's ultimate failure – for which he blamed editing irrespective of timing or emphasis – came as a personal blow.[33] The flamboyant largesse of his Taras Bulba, a 'howling sword-swinging barbarian' of statuesque posing, brooding, and menacing looks is nevertheless theatrical and pathos-filled in ways that seem to exceed any editing choices made.[34]

Brynner's other Cossack character was notably different. While equally ostentatious, Captain Stoloff of the European co-production, *Romance of a Horsethief* (1971), was more ornate and markedly less the stuff of legend. Exiled from St. Petersburg for 'loving well' to run a Russian garrison in a small Jewish border village in Poland, Stoloff attempts to make it his own kingdom, in 1904 during the Russo-Japanese war in Manchuria. We first see him facing away from the camera in a bedroom, standing on two chairs with his hands and legs apart, wearing black leather riding boots and looking into a mirror in the process of having his new custom-made Cossack uniform fitted. Stoloff then bends his knees, moves now to the left, then to the right in order to test the fit. Focused, he spins around and redoes the movement for the tailor, whom he refers to as a 'little Jew.' Next, a horse is brought into the room: mounting it, Stoloff energetically dashes out for some trick riding.

The scene sets the tone for the film which shares some of the exaggerated, tongue-in-cheek aesthetics of Brynner's later Westerns, *Adiós, Sabata* (1970) and *Catlow* (1971) made around the same time. Its plot revolves broadly around the villagers' resistance to Imperial Russia taking possession of their horses for the war effort against Japan. It is nevertheless the individual characters that easily overshadow the plot: Eli Wallach's horse thief, Kifke, Jane Birkin's freedom-loving, Paris-educated Naomi of revolutionary ideas, and Brynner's flamboyant Captain Vladimir Nikolaevich Stoloff of the Cossack regiment, played with stylized expressions and large gestures.

Hard-drinking, harassingly womanizing, and prone to impromptu recitals of poetry, Captain is a man of luxury unhappily stuck in the village of Malava of 'swine and geese' who presides over imperial festivities seated on something resembling a thrown. This man of luxury speaks English intercepted with Russian that easily spills over to French, not least when

Figure 5.3 Bounine and Stoloff in Cossack fashions

he longingly recalls the joys of Paris past. When merry, he expresses his feelings through whistling and twirling motions even as choleric rage constantly simmers just under the surface, and rapidly bursts. Channelling Surov, Stoloff bites his champagne glass apart in violent melancholy when toasting the town in a wardrobe partly copied from Bounine's night club fashions. Like Surov, he is a leading figure in a place revolting against the powers that he serves and symbolizes, yet is designed to evoke less empathy.

Romance of a Horsethief was applauded primarily for being the director Abraham Polonsky's second film after his long blacklisting as 'anti-American' in 1951. Critics drew parallels to the 'lively wisdom' of Jean Renoir's comedies, with *Le Monde* dedicating an entire review to the film's 'astonishing beauty' and elaborating on Polonsky's poetic skill as auteur.[35] Others, however, identified the film as a 'mess' and questioned the historical accuracy of its lightly comical depiction of Jewish-Cossack relations.[36] Polonsky – himself of Russian Jewish origin – defined the film as a nostalgic fairy tale set in times preceding the Holocaust.[37] As befits a folk tale, Brynner plays a caricature in a narrative largely consisting of types: his is an aggregate type, put together from a range of his earlier roles as Russians, Cossacks, tyrannical rulers of diverse lands, and uniformed officers barking orders.

Within the overall campy artifice of *Romance of a Horsethief*, all characters were types, so that the actors' national or ethnic origins hardly mattered a great deal: as *The New York Times* noted, 'Almost everybody speaks with an accent, and almost nobody's accent conforms to anybody else's. Thus Jane Birkin's beautiful Polish revolutionary is British, Eli Wallach's Polish horsethief is Upper West Side and Yul Brynner's Russian Cossack captain is Hollywood.'[38] By 1971, Brynner operated with an established, albeit faded star image unlikely to change through further ethnic typecasting, so that critics saw him as delivering 'the same glowering stiff-backed portrayal we have come to expect of him' in 'his familiar role as a dashing Cossack officer,' playing 'to the hilt a part that fits him like a glove' as 'a proud swashbuckler': 'Yul Brynner pretty much plays Yul Brynner.'[39]

Brynner's other Slavic roles included the massive international coproduction, *Battle of Neretva* (1969), where he re-emerged as Vlado, a swaggering, butch accordion-playing Yugoslav Partisan explosions specialist in a decisive battle of 1943 under the command of Tito. Given Brynner's overall star persona and his socializing with the president during the shoot, it is easy to understand why a journalist thought he was playing Tito himself.[40] Despite the film's lavish use of extras – a group of 200,000, reportedly the entire Yugoslav army – and an international cast of stars including Orson Welles, the film was broadly panned as dull, hard to follow, waxwork-like in its performances, and monotonous as a historical reconstruction.[41]

In the star-studded cast of the spy thriller *Le Serpent / Night Flight from Moscow* (1973) also featuring Henry Fonda, Philippe Noiret, and Dirk Bogarde, Brynner played the laconic Colonel Vlassov who pretends to defect to the West with a list of double agents in order to disturb the precarious geopolitical balance of the Cold War. According to a critic, Brynner, as the deceptive high-ranking KGB official, 'glowers nicely, displays his worryingly pointed ears, and delivers his testimony in a satisfying Vladivostok bass.'[42] Another agreed, arguing that the actor had found his stride as 'the enigmatic, powerful, and slightly sinister Russian Agent' while, for a third, his performance was 'paper-thin.'[43] Since Brynner had played American agents in the British spy films *The Double Man* (1967) and *The File of the Golden Goose* (1969), his Vlassov was, at this point, continuation of a generic theme (see also Chapter 7). With characterisations of him playing the part as 'a combination Siamese king and cowboy robot – two of his past move roles, as it happens', it was not Brynner's presumed Russian identity that was at stake (this most likely being of little interest at this point in his career), but rather his overall expressive range.[44]

Off-white Americans

In its trademark foreignness, Brynner's star image had some resemblance to that of the Egyptian-born Omar Sharif who transitioned from Middle Eastern film stardom to Hollywood and European co-productions, starting with his appearance as Sherif Ali in *Lawrence of Arabia* (1962). While Brynner, as Rameses II, was the Pharaoh of Egypt, Sharif played Russian in *Doctor Zhivago* (David Lean, 1965) and *The Tamarind Seed* (Blake Edwards, 1974), and while Brynner sometimes envisioned himself as the direct descendant of the mythic Mongol ruler, Sharif was cast in the title role of *Genghis Khan* (Henry Levin, 1965). Sharif appeared in range of parts similar to those that Brynner played: the King of Armenia in *The Fall of the Roman Empire* (Anthony Mann, 1964), a German major in *The Night of the Generals* (Anatole Litvak, 1967), the Crown Prince of Austria in *Mayerling* (Terence Young, 1968), a Mexican outlaw in *Mackenna's Gold* (J. Lee Thompson, 1969), a guerrilla leader in *Che!* (Richard Fleischer, 1969), an Afghan in *The Horsemen* (John Frankenheimer, 1971), and an Arab prince in *Ashanti* (Richard Fleischer, 1979) – partly with the same directors. At the same time, Sharif, unlike Brynner, was not averse to romantic roles, but rather specialized in them instead.

There was little commonality in the two actors' performance styles or physical aesthetics – Sharif's overall style being suave, while he sported a notable amount of dark hair and, throughout most of his career, a moustache. Their star images nevertheless shared malleably exotic, masculine, and cosmopolitan traits that resulted in them being cast as foreign others within a broad racialized spectrum. Now portraying this ethnicity and then another, the onscreen bodies of both Brynner and Sharif functioned as artificial, fantastic, and highly unstable signifiers of 'cultural uniqueness of nations and ethnicities.'[45] Of the two, it was Brynner who was the more muscular and macho, yet the roles of both moved broadly across nationalities and social strata, from the royal to the outlaw, his accent – like Sharif's – barring him access to most available Hollywood roles.

Consider, for example, Brynner's casting as Jason Compson in the 1959 *The Sound and the Fury*, a role that Laurence Olivier was first rumored to take on, and which Brynner played with hair (depending on sources, either a hairpiece or his very own).[46] Based on William Faulkner's novel, *The Sound and the Fury* is a theatrical melodrama of family tensions and conflicts. A background story introducing Compson's French roots was added to explain Brynner's accent, which presented something of a challenge in a film set in the American South. This obviously did little to alleviate the fact that his accent was Russian rather than French in ways further contributing to the film's DeLuxe-colored artifice. As his 1960 comedies, *Surprise Package* and *Once More, with Feeling!* (discussed in Chapter 8) further illustrate, Brynner's diction could sound awkward with faster dialogue, this being one possible reason for his frequent appearances in strong and silent parts.

Some critics, echoing those of his 1956 breakthrough films, lauded Brynner's 'energetic' and 'powerful acting' as 'every inch the household tyrant' and 'a fierce domineering personality.'[47] The character is certainly authoritarian, and is first presented as a violent bully barking and brooding by a doorway, then dragging his step-niece Quentin (Joanne Woodward) over to scold her. As she bursts into tears in the comforting arms of the Black housekeeper, Dilsey (Ethel Waters), Jason looms in the foreground with a grim expression identical to that of Rameses plotting revenge on Moses. A reviewer's appreciation of Brynner's subtle shading of character 'with maximum skill' is not altogether self-evident, Jason being a one-tone character of barks, furrowed brows, enraged and mocking glances.[48]

The film failed to impress critics largely panning 'the churlishly Slavic Mr. Brynner' as 'the most incongruous Southern rotter we've ever seen.'[49] For one reviewer, 'a hennaed wig and a Southern drawl' proved to be too much for the actor to take on.[50] Another was willing to accept his 'phony Cajun accent' but drew the line at Margaret Leighton (who played Caddy Compson, Quentin's estranged mother) wavering 'from Oxford British to Los Angeles American to Piccadilly Circus Cockney' and declared foreign accents a general distraction in what was essentially an American family melodrama.[51] Equally concerned with Leighton's 'Mississippi-West End accent,' yet another critic wondered whether the film was in fact a parody and classified the screenplay as a 'pilfering outrage.'[52] For its part, the

British press marveled at the number of Hollywood clichés – 'insanity, disease, inertia, livers pickled in alcohol and promiscuous whoring and wenching, with a spot of incest on the side' – of decayed families in the Deep South on simultaneous display.[53]

The film poster has Jason standing above Quentin's bed with a partly opened shirt, hands on hips in a fashion familiar from Brynner's other 1950s film roles – this having been established as his trademark pose (see Chapter 8). There is no such scene in the film, where Jason appears fully clothed throughout: the most skin he bares is his arms with sleeves rolled up while at work. The aesthetic choice was similar to the poster of *The Buccaneer* that featured Brynner's drawn, muscular, and topless likeness wielding both a sword and a gun, despite him swashbuckling through the film respectably, albeit flashily clothed. In both cases, poster design tapped into Brynner's broader star image of exposed chests and forceful masculinity in order to ramp up the films' audience appeal. Despite garnering relatively broad media attention, *The Sound and the Fury* was no box office magnet. Subsequent offers for drama films failed to arrive and Brynner continued to specialize in domineering personalities in genre fiction.

Dandy Creole

Of Brynner's films, the 1964 *Invitation to a Gunfighter* is the one to touch on racial politics at any length. Its executive producer was Stanley Kramer who had previously produced and directed *The Defiant Ones* (1958) and who went on to make *Guess Who's Coming to Dinner* (1967), both dealing with racial dynamics in the contemporary US. In *Invitation to a Gunfighter*, Brynner played Jules Gaspard d'Estaing, 'a mysterious, dandified creole' gunman from New Orleans burdened by his family background and Civil War-era racial ideology in a layer of makeup not dissimilar to that which he had worn in *Kings of the Sun* the year before.[54]

A man of refined tastes and laconic countenance, d'Estaing stops by at a small New Mexico town and takes on a job as hired gun, enticed by the sight of an attractive woman and accounts of local injustice combined. Stepping out from a carriage, observing his surroundings, listening in and figuring things out, he is very much positioned as the outsider. Son of a Black slave and a wealthy French-speaking man, d'Estaing is a gunfighter due to both pleasure and limited prospects: 'There was a wide range of choice for the son of a quadroon slave; piano-player in a fancy house, backroom gladiator for white gentlemen betters.' Stylishly dressed in black and sporting sparkling-clean white ruffled shirts, puffing on cigars, and playing the occasional harpsicord with skill while singing lullabies in French, he educates the townsfolk in properly pronouncing his name: 'Jules, soft g, silent s; Gaspard, silent d; d'Estaing, just a touch of diphthong.'

Figure 5.4 Jules Gaspard d'Estaing

An agent of entropy, d'Estaing plays by his own rules, exhibiting stone-faced masculine bravado, a keen sense of moral justice, and an acute aesthetic eye extending to presenting potential dress fabrics to townswomen. Regularly shot in dramatic chiaroscuro with light and shadow playing on his face, d'Estaing channels the volatile Dimitri Karamazov more than he does Chris Adams of *The Magnificent Seven*, even as these two characters share the same black-hatted elite sharp-shooting skills. In the film's climax, d'Estaing gets drunk in a Mexican saloon and runs amok across the white part of town, abandoning the killing task he had been paid to do and dying while taking revenge on the rotten small town powers-that-be instead. This self-sacrificial move resonates with those concluding *Kings of the Sun* and *The Journey*; its overall psychological motivation remains equally flimsy.

In the United States, the film was critiqued for staginess and Brynner – Yul as Jules – for playing himself in an 'appropriately wooden' performance: 'Brynner's stolid Slavic face and bald pate, both heavily bronzed for Creole effect, and those piercing eyes stabbing through the shadows provoke considerable snickering, though that hospital-white ruffled shirt may also be to blame.'[55] Some reviewers considered the film's generic clichés rather enjoyable so that, for 'sheer sinister, sexy, screen villainy, Yul Brynner emerges as daddy-of-them-all' as the arrogant, suave, cat-like and soft-spoken gunman.[56] Reception was more positive abroad, with *The Times of India* identifying it as a 'thinking man's Western,' the British trade paper *Kinematographer Weekly* applauding Brynner's 'theatrical flourish,' and *Le Monde* chiming in on the film's psychological merits and Brynner's symbolic hero investing it with 'a force, a truth, a complexity that frees it from habitual clichés.'[57]

In a particularly inspired review, *Sight and Sound* identified the film's studio backgrounds as communicating a sense of the town as 'claustrophobically closed on its problems [...] where the Mexican inhabitants are strictly segregated, the Southerner who fought for slavery is the only person who treats them as equals, and the gunfighter who still intends to kill him turns out to be a son of a slave from New Orleans.' Within this complex social context, Brynner's gunfighter of elegant quirks is 'overplaying in a cat and mouse game throughout, driving his hosts to hysteria by gambits such as winning a poker hand with five kings.'[58] The same reviewer continued to address the nuance of Brynner's performance in BFI's *Monthly Film Bulletin*: 'the conventional image of the gunfighter, an impassive and chilling figure in black from head to toe' gathers ambiguity as the film progresses, there eventually being 'a touch of Lucifer about him.'[59]

There is much offbeat to a film addressing racial segregation and discrimination through a leading brownface role and impassive, victimized Mexican side characters. Should one follow some of the European reviewers, d'Estaing is less a full-bodied, rounded character than a symbolic hero serving as a catalyst for action facilitating the romantic coupling of the former Confederate soldier and the female protagonist. According to this line of interpretation, the film's main character is something of an instrument, or an actant, in the social network of others. Contracting the all-round exotic A-list actor to play the part was possibly a means of distancing the plot very much rooted in the US context and rendering it more abstract, or allegorical, a depiction. To approach the issue generously, it would not then matter who played this abstract, Luciferesque figure. At the same time, the fact remains that Sidney Poitier and Harry Belafonte were the only major Black male film stars of the period. Brynner was part of a Hollywood logic where off-white actors were applicable to play virtually any ethnic roles for which Black actors were not considered, or at least not chosen: freedom of mobility within ethnic spectrums thus spoke of unilateral privilege.[60]

Noble poses

In *Escape from Zahrain* (1962) Brynner played Sharif, an Arab freedom fighter imprisoned by a despotic Sheik in a fictitious oil-rich country somewhere in the Middle East (the film was shot in the Mojave Desert). The film opens with student supporters helping Sharif escape in the midst of prison transport and, for the rest of the film, he drives and treks across the desert toward freedom in the British Protectorate, Aden, together with three fellow prisoners, a student, and a kidnapped nurse (Laila, played by Madlyn Rhue). *Escape from Zahrain* reunited Brynner with Sal Mineo who played Crown Prince to his King Mongkut on Broadway, the two becoming friends.[61] Mineo, of Sicilian-American origin, had previously played the Native American White Bull in Disney's *Tonka* (Lewis R. Foster, 1958) and a pro-Zionist militant in *Exodus* (Otto Preminger, 1960). Here, he was cast as Ahmed, the student masterminding Sharif's escape. For authentic flair, Paramount recruited '57 young Arabians' for the riot scene setting off the action.[62]

Brynner plays Sharif with brooding looks and fixed stares befitting the leader of a cause much larger than himself, frequently folding his arms to communicate both dominance and frustration. Sharif is the quintessential strong, silent type of 'fierce gravity and single-minded determination' who 'scarcely ever relaxes his guard, mental or physical' so as to express emotion.[63] As part of the downward spiral of Brynner's 1960s films, *Escape from Zahrain* was characterized by critics as nonsensical, cartoonish, unconcerned with the 'niceties of character and nuances of motive,' and sporting a range of dull stereotypes.[64] *The New York Times* labeled Sharif as 'patently absurd' while *The Hollywood Reporter* regretted that 'Brynner is allowed only to be tight-lipped and mysterious, with no indication of his ideological or patriotic motivations.'[65] Adding to the disappointment, reviewers noted that Brynner wore a headdress throughout the film so as to deprive viewers the sight of his bald pate.[66] Playing up his 'Arab headdress' was, however, also offered as an 'exploitip' for exhibitors to highlight and thus lure audience interest.[67]

In yet another variation of the strong and silent type, Brynner played a heroic, self-sacrificing US Air Rescue Service officer of American-Japanese origins 'with a Polish mother, presumably to explain his Slavic appearance and accent' in the 1964 *Flight from Ashiya*.[68] Taking place on a mission to rescue Japanese citizens lost at sea in a typhoon, the film unfolds in three flashbacks detailing the leading characters' respective traumas connected to war, unsuccessful missions, and the deaths of their

Figure 5.5 Brynner as Arab, Japanese-Polish-American, Israeli, and German (*Escape from Zahrain, Flight from Ashiya, Cast a Giant Shadow* and *Triple Cross*)

beloveds. Sergeant Mike Takashima's personal trauma is revealed as he is about to drown somewhere in the North China Sea. This involved the death of Leila (Danièle Gaubert) whom he met while recuperating from a wound in Algeria during WWII. Despite the two not having a common language, they plan a future together during their quick romance until she, running after him, gets blown up on a bridge exploded by his crew. Literally overcoming the pull of trauma to tug him under, Takashima resurfaces and, having saved the people in need, closes the film holding a rescued Japanese boy in his arms as the two plan to eat large quantities of sukiyaki together. Opening to poor reviews describing it as melodramatic and 'consistently bad,' the film garnered relatively little attention.[69] At this point, it was Brynner who held top billing, even though his co-star George Chakiris was also an Academy Award winner (with *West Side Story*).

Complaints of Brynner hiding his baldness with headwear were repeated with the 1967 film, *The Long Duel*, where the subtly bronzed Brynner played Sultan, the leader of an Indian nomadic tribe turned outlaw by colonial circumstance. After the arrest of his people, Sultan both evades and avenges the British among whom the policeman, Young (Trevor Howard), forms a rare exception in advocating less bloody forms of governance. The narrative focuses largely on the confrontation and the gradual establishment of mutual respect between the two men, with Sultan eventually dying and leaving his son for Young, now identified as a friend, to raise. Throughout the film, the camera makes extensive use of Brynner's trademark grim stare as he is seen posing against arid mountain landscapes on a white horse, elegantly adorned in headdresses of varying hues of browns, yellows, whites, pale blues, and grays which he does not remove even when stripping topless in order for the 'dancing girl' Champa (Virginia North) to attend to his wounds. The actor's body operates as a decorative element signifying exoticness, even as the performance itself was rather similar to his stoic Chris Adams in *The Magnificent Seven* (see Chapter 7).

It is, in fact, the camera rather than Brynner's body that often does the moving: while the actor stands, sits on a horse, or merely gazes about him with pensive, stern expressions, the camera zooms in, closer and closer, all the way to close-up. The same technique was used in *The File of the Golden Goose* the following year (and beyond) to capture the brooding thoughts of Brynner's protagonists: while the actor's facial expression remained more or less the same, the camera moving from medium shot to extreme close-up did the necessary communicating. Much of this is standard fare

Strong, silent, ethnic types   127

Figure 5.6   Zooming in (*The Long Duel* and *The File of the Golden Goose*)

in that close-ups are used in film's key moments, 'separated out from the action and interaction of a scene, and not seen by other characters but only by us, thus disclosing for us the star's face, the intimate, transparent window to the soul.'⁷⁰ I argue that there is, nevertheless, something specific to Brynner's positioning as a man-statue around whom the action revolves, and whom the camera seeks, throughout his film work.

Although shot in Spain, *The Long Duel* was praised for its 'authentic shots,' however, reviewers largely saw it as not living up to its promotional poster's promise to showcase 'The blazing passions of a land ... its proud warriors ... its exotic women ... bursting aflame in revolt!'⁷¹ The film was critiqued for a clumsy use of backdrops, wooden direction, and uninventive use of genre clichés: 'the dialogue [...] seems to have been written by a computer fed a programme of execrable films on the same theme.'⁷² Brynner's role as a 'noble savage' was further characterized as meaty yet palling due to his 'usual impassive expression' and lack of humor: 'Brynner, as unrelentingly a scowler as ever, plays Sultan, a nomadic combination of Robin Hood and rapacious renegade.'⁷³ The *Los Angeles Times* saw Brynner still playing King Mongkut in *Escape from Zahrain*, whereas *The Globe and Mail* identified Sultan as 'one of his inscrutable Oriental characters' and the actor as having 'lost the fire that made him star originally. He is much too close-shaven, well-groomed and carefully tailored to be anyone other than Yul Brynner in costume.'⁷⁴ In the late

1960s, Brynner was still very much associated with the breakthrough role that made him an international star. At the same time, his particular standard type had grown clearly recognizable, and complaints of him merely playing himself began to steadily accumulate.

A military man

Brynner's range of military characters – stiff-backed men of authority and command of the kind that formed the backbone of his star image – extended beyond the parts of Russian officers. The pro-Zionist 1966 *Cast a Giant Shadow*, starring Kirk Douglas as the curt Colonel Mickey Marcus fighting for independent Israel in 1948, featured Brynner as Asher Gonen, an underground Haganah commanding officer – along with appearances from Frank Sinatra, John Wayne, and Angie Dickinson.[75] In the even more star-studded *The Poppy is Also a Flower* of the same vintage Brynner played an equally small part as the Iranian Colonel Salem, fighting the opium trade in collaboration with the United Nations. Dressed in a beige uniform of appropriate decorations, or in traditional garb with riding boots, Salem was a man of few facial expressions, all of them as determined and grim as Gonen's. These military characters largely lacked personal depth, appearing onscreen only briefly to fill a mission and narrative function.

There was a degree more interiority to his German types. The 1965 *Morituri* – released in Britain as *The Saboteur* – is an action film set in World War II, and Brynner's gruff sea captain, Mueller, a variation of a uniform-wearing authority type clouded in perpetual cigarette smoke. A heavy smoker since his early teens, at one point consuming five packs a day, Brynner used cigars and cigarettes as props near-permanently lodged in his fingers (eventually dying of lung cancer at the age of 65 despite having given up the habit at 50: see Chapter 9).[76] A German merchant sea captain with a liking for drink, Muller is transporting a cargo of rubber from Tokyo to Bordeaux for the war effort. Being forced to work with a crew of prisoners against his principles, his fuming dismay is made explicit in his introductory scene where he storms uninvited into German military headquarters to express his opinion. Muller is firmly in command onboard – 'I am the master of this ship. You are under my authority here' – yet also a humanist resistant to the antisemitic Third Reich rule. In a climactic scene after discovering that his son has been decorated for sinking an allied hospital ship, Muller trashes his quarters in drunken, sad rage.

Like so many of Brynner's other films, *Morituri* features many men: the only female character, Esther Levi (Janet Margolin), appears fifty minutes into the action. A survivor of Gestapo gang rape with a murdered family, she is subsequently shot herself. In a much larger role, and with star billing, Marlon Brando plays a German pacifist who is recruited to work for the allied disguising as a high-ranking SS officer. Critics interpreted his emulated Teutonic accent as both tongue-in-cheek and credibly authentic.[77] The same did not apply to Brynner – and could not have. Despite his linguistic prowess, Brynner played no accents whatsoever beyond his own since his first film. With the exception of actually shifting languages from English to French or Russian, as was the case in several of his films, whether Arab, Irani, Israeli, Indian, Cajun, German, Egyptian, or Siamese, his characters all spoke the same.

Triple Cross (1966) featured Brynner's more flamboyant take on the German trope as Colonel Baron von Grunen. Attired in a gray uniform and shiny black boots complete with a slight limp, monocle, cigarette holder, and an iron cross or two, von Grunen is a 'brooding romantic German aristocrat who is really a pacificist,' broadly gesturing toward Erich von Stroheim's Major von Rauffenstein of *La grande illusion* (Jean Renoir, 1937).[78] A piano-playing, hand-kissing, decadent party-hosting afficionado of quality drink and fine antiques, von Grunen comes with little biographical detail, motivation, character development, or expressive range beyond the stock character that he represents. His barks, sharp glances, menace, and veneer of aristocratic sophistication – combined with his self-designed death – reverberate with Brynner's roles past and future as yet another variation of the bastard with a heart of gold trope, this time a Nazi officer involved in an assassination plot against the Führer. Von Grunen is first seen half an hour into the film, as the British protagonist (Christopher Plummer) is being trained as a German spy in a salon of a French manor house doubling as Third Reich secret mission office. He enters the salon which is decorated with red roses, Oriental carpets, objets d'art, a classic portrait, and a large piano to his colleagues' 'heil Hitler,' to which he responds with nothing more than a sigh and a small gesture of the hand. Von Grunen is a piano-playing pacifist who, much like von Rauffenstein, is caught in politics not of his own choosing.

The New York Times saw Brynner's stylized performance rich in references befitting a film that offered 'splendid fun' as 'a spoof of all the spy movies made in the last twenty years or so' where the actors 'have an immense amount of quiet hilarity with the stereotype roles in which they have been cast'.[79] Most critics nevertheless had little patience with the film's predictabilities and character types, which one saw as assuming 'the porous consistency of tripe.'[80] The film's self-referential camp sensibilities – which fully extended to Romy Schneider's elegant, leather-clad Countess steeped in Nazi espionage plots – were thus unequally noted, and appreciated, even as such campy artifice grew manifest in Brynner's film catalog of the late 1960s and 1970s.

Universal stories?

Writing in 1962, a film journalist argued that Brynner 'is inclined to look and sound the same in each successive film,' even as 'his dominant and forceful personality' can infuse his performance with 'excitement, and a passion for life.'[81] To reiterate, as variations of a type, his characters were infused with moral fibre, fearless in the face of battle and sacrifice. They were, of course, types also due to the similarities in Brynner's performance style and screen presence, as he repeated the same gestures and poses. There was, however, also thematic similarity to his pan-ethnic gallery of types struggling for freedom from oppression or caught up in transforming times: this was already the case with the puzzled King Mongkut.

There is Surov, unsuccessfully challenging his unwilling international guests to debate divisions between friends and enemies on the different sides of the Iron Curtain, Bounine caught between imperial nostalgia and contemporary cosmopolitan life, and the equally nostalgic Stoloff implanted in a rural village where he has few friends. Taras Bulba acts according to his anti-Polish principles even when this means killing his beloved son, while Captain Muller, torn between his dislike for Nazis and his love of fatherland and military son, tries to help the young imprisoned Jewish woman onboard his ship and turns to the bottle. The disillusioned von Grunen has a similar dislike for the system he serves. The Creole gunslinger d'Estaing, scarred and shaped by racism, sets out to destroy the local status quo, while Jason Compton tries to secure a dignified life for his dysfunctional, once prominent family. Sharif resists the local corrupt 'Zahraini' regime feeding American oil capitalism, Sultan fights the oppression of British colonialists, and Mike Takashima communicates racial tolerance and common respect. All these characters establish friendships – and the occasional love – with people cast as their enemies, Sultan handing over his only son to the man who has been tasked with hunting him down.

A journalist's characterization of Brynner as 'American cinema's Cold War-era ambassador from everywhere, slipping in and out of nationalities and representing the Hollywood worldview' is apt up to a point, with the caveat that no such singular worldview existed.[82] Rather, Brynner's film work was, at least up until the final years, embedded in liberal Hollywood humanism embracing difference, diversity, and shared human values in combination with melodramatic templates, routinely discriminatory casting policies, and easy stereotyping.

Interviewed in 1965 on his humanitarian efforts with the United Nations, which form the foci of the following chapter, Brynner argued that actors were exceptionally well attuned to the plight of others: 'In our business there is more genuine generosity and compassion for other human beings than in any other. This is because actors, as artists, deal with the human soul and dreams. We are merchants of illusions.'[83] There is much that could be deciphered from this quote in terms of Brynner's heavily fabricated star image, yet the point I want to make has to do with his take on cosmopolitan ethics and the work of filmmaking as a commitment to advancing equal rights and solidarity across national or ethnic lines.[84] This is a connection that Brynner had made already in a 1959 article titled 'The Eggman' illustrated with three photos of the actor's head (as well as one of him standing bare-chested, legs apart, and with hands on hips in *The King and I*) where he was quoted arguing for a cosmopolitan commitment to the thespian craft:

> He honestly believes that any actor, or actress, has a reason for being – to portray to all men, everywhere, the basic idea that 'all men are brothers.' Along those lines he says [...] 'There is a responsibility on us film people to present human beings, real human beings, like those all over the world.'[85]

Brynner further elaborated in 1966: 'There is a responsibility involved in film making because its impact on people carries even more weight than a dictatorship – more than laws.'[86] Befitting Brynner's cosmopolitanism – his unwillingness to be pinned down in terms of origins, first language, nationality, or ethnic identity – he identified cinema as an important and effective form of global, even universal, communication.[87] It did not matter whether he appeared in American films or international productions, Brynner continued to argue: his career choice had simply been 'to play parts that have universal appeal and meaning in movies that would reach the widest audience possible' as he understood the importance of popular cinema in people's everyday lives across the world.[88] According to this line of thought, Brynner playing a broad array of ethnic parts translated as an exercise in universalist human solidarity, rather than one of cultural appropriation. Or, to be more precise, the issue of cultural appropriation connected to the ethics and politics of representation simply did not emerge as a concern. This, I propose, was very much a matter of cultural context, considering Hollywood's racist representational practices and casting policies, as well as Brynner's positioning within them. In order to make further sense of the actor's ethical commitments to diversity and equality, the following chapters extend to post-World War II ideologies of cosmopolitanism, and his work with the UNHRC.

Notes

1. *St. Petersburg Times*, 17 April 1961.
2. Robinson 2007, 6.
3. E.g., *Australian Women's Weekly*, 24 October 1956; *Variety*, 19 December 1956; *South China Morning Post*, 11 February 1957; *Picturegoer*, 2 March 1957; *The Tatler*, 6 March 1957; *The Sketch*, 13 March 1957.
4. *The NY Times*, 14 December 1956; *Le Courrier Australien*, 10 May 1957.
5. *NY Herald Tribune*, 14 December 1956; *South China Morning Post*, 11 February 1957; *Monthly Film Bulletin* 1957.
6. *Seventeen*, February 1959. Unsurprisingly, some critics identified the gesture as unintentionally comic, and the character as an 'ultra-stereotype Russian.' *Monthly Film Bulletin* 1958; *Tribune*, 3 September 1980.
7. *Monthly Film Bulletin* 1959a; *The Tatler*, 1 April 1959, 33; *The Observer*, 22 March 1959: *LA Times*, 19 February 1959.
8. *Variety*, 4, February 4 1959; *The NY Times*, 20 February 1959; *LA Times*, 8 February 1959; *NY Herald Tribune*, 22 February 1959; *South China Morning Post*, 27 April 1959; *Le Monde*, 20 April 1959. For similar critiques, see also *The Washington Post*, 20 February 1959; *The Independent Exhibitors Film Bulletin*, 16 February 1959; *SF Examiner*, 23 February 1959.
9. *Top Spot*, 18 April 1959; *The Globe and Mail*, 28 March 1959.
10. *The NY Times*, 20 February 1959.
11. *The Hollywood Reporter*, 2 February 1959.
12. *Picturegoer*, 21 March 1959; the connection was, unsurprisingly enough, also raised in e.g., *The Washington Post*, 20 February 1959; *Australian Women's Weeekly*, 4 March 1959; *Picture Show*, 21 March 1959; *The Vancouver Sun*, 23 April 1959.

13. *The Observer*, 24 February 1957.
14. *The Globe and Mail*, 28 March 1959; *Australian Women's Weekly*, 24 June 1959.
15. *SF Examiner*, 12 January 1958; *SF Examiner*, 16 March 1958; *Picturegoer*, 19 July 1958.
16. *The NY Times*, 21 February 1958. In fact, Brynner's American accent was picked up as a distraction, *Australian Women's Weekly*, 16 July 1958.
17. *Monthly Film Bulletin* 1958.
18. *South China Morning Post*, 5 June 1958.
19. *The Hollywood Reporter*, 19 February 1958, 15.
20. Advert in *Variety*, 26 February 1958.
21. *The Independent Film Journal*, 1 March 1958; *The Tatler*, 29 October 1958; *LA Times*, 17 February 1958; advert in *Variety*, 26 February 1958.
22. *Variety*, 19 February 1958; *The Independent Exhibitors Film Bulletin*, 17 February 1958; *The Times of India*, 31 July 1958; see also *Redbook*, February 1958; *Seventeen*, February 1958; *Modern Screen*, May 1958; *Harrison's Reports*, 22 February 1958; *Daily News*, 30 March 1958.
23. *Le Monde*, 13 May 1958; *Le Monde*, 4 June 1958; *Sight and Sound*, Summer 1958; *Monthly Film Bulletin* 1958; *The Observer*, 29 June 1958; *The Guardian*, 16 September 1958; *Picturegoer*, 19 July 1958; *The Tatler*, 9 July 1958; *The Washington Post*, 13 May 1958.
24. *NY Herald Tribune*, 13 May 1958b; *Playboy*, May 1960, 72; *Toronto Daily Star*, 12 May 1958. It should nevertheless be noted that booing at Cannes was hardly exceptional: in 1960, the audience booed Federico Fellini's *La Dolce Vita* as it won the Palme d'Or award, *Elokuva-aitta* 11, 1960.
25. *NY Herald Tribune*, 13 May 1958a; *The Austin Statesman*, 12 May 1958; see also Golden 2021, 133.
26. *The NY Times*, 26 December 1962; *The Times of India*, 19 December 1963; *Minneapolis Tribune*, 20 January 1962; *SF Examiner*, 16 December 1962; *SF Examiner*, 22 December 1962. On the lavish scale of the production, see also *The NY Times*, 24 December 1961.
27. *The Montreal Gazette*, 19 January 1963.
28. *South China Morning Post*, 12 February 1963.
29. *Minneapolis Tribune*, 20 January 1962.
30. *Boxoffice*, 10 December 1962; *The Independent Exhibitors Film Bulletin*, 10 December 1962; *South China Morning Post*, 9 February 1963.
31. *The Times of India*, 19 December 1963.
32. *SF Examiner*, 22 December 1962.
33. *Seventeen*, October 1962, 172; Brynner 1989, 144–5; Brynner 2006, Kindle edition; Brynner in *Les mille et une vies de Yul Brynner*, 2019.
34. *The NY Times*, 26 December 1962.
35. *The NY Times*, 19 August 1971; *LA Times*, 15 September 1971; *Monthly Film Bulletin* 1977a; *Le Monde*, 14 August 1971; *Minneapolis Tribune*, 29 July 1971.
36. *Toronto Daily Star*, 20 October 1971; *The Montreal Gazette*, 16 October 1971.
37. *Sight and Sound*, Spring 1971.
38. *The NY Times*, 19 August 1971.
39. *SF Examiner*, 17 September 1971; *The Independent Film Journal*, 5 August 1971; *The LA Times*, 15 September 1971; *Minneapolis Tribune*, 29 July 1971.

40. *The Korea Times*, 9 March 1969.
41. E.g., *The Montreal Gazette*, 17 April 1969; *The Calgary Herald*, 2 May 1969; *The Calgary Herald*, 20 March 1971; *Toronto Daily Star*, 22 February 1971; *Le Monde*, 25 August 1970.
42. *The Observer*, 2 February 1974.
43. *St. Petersburg Times*, 19 July 1974; *The Toronto Star*, 22 January 1974.
44. *The Washington Post*, 26 November 1973.
45. Regev 2007, 125.
46. *Chicago Daily Tribune*, 23 October 1956; *The Washington Post*, 10 October 1985.
47. *NY Herald Tribune*, 19 April 1959; *The Independent Exhibitors Film Bulletin*, 16 March 1959; *Variety*, 4 February 1959b.
48. *Variety*, 4 February 1959b.
49. *Le Monde*, 6 June 1959; *The NY Times*, 28 March 1959.
50. *Monthly Film Bulletin* 1959d.
51. *NY Herald Tribune*, 28 March 1959; on coaching the accents, see *Woman's Day*, November 1958, 12.
52. *The Washington Post*, 27 March 1959
53. *The Observer*, 29 March 1959; *The Tatler*, 8 April 1959; *Picturegoer*, 18 April 1959. Another British fan magazine featured a promotional four-page summary of the film, complete with a large advert, suggesting its interest to a teen audience: *Picture Show*, 2 May 1959.
54. *The NY Times*, 28 October 1964.
55. *South China Morning Post*, 2 June 1965; *LA Times*, 24 October 1964.
56. *Boxoffice*, 26 October 1964; *Motion Picture Exhibitor*, 21 October 1964; *Variety*, 21 October 1964; see also *The Guardian*, 14 May 1965; *Le Monde*, 27 January 1965.
57. *The Times of India*, 8 September 1966; *Kinematograph Weekly*, 20 May 1965; *Le Monde*, 27 January 1965.
58. *Sight and Sound*, Summer 1965.
59. *Monthly Film Bulletin* 1965, 105.
60. Shohat 1995, 171.
61. See Mineo's essay, 'The King and Me,' in *Photoplay*, October 1957.
62. *The Hollywood Reporter*, 20 July 1961.
63. *South China Morning Post*, 17 December 1962; *The Globe and Mail*, 18 June 1962.
64. *The NY Times*, 12 July 1962; *Monthly Film Bulletin* 1962; *Elokuva-aitta* 1, 1963; *The Guardian*, 30 June 1962.
65. *The NY Times*, 12 July 1962; *The Hollywood Reporter*, 29 May 1962.
66. *The Pittsburgh Press*, 2 June 1962; *The NY Times*, 12 July 1962; *The Globe and Mail*, 18 June 1962.
67. *Boxoffice*, 4 June 1962.
68. *South China Morning Post*, 4 December 1964.
69. *The Washington Post*, 8 August 1964; *The NY Times*, 23 April 1964; *Daily News*, 23 April 1964.
70. Dyer 2004, 10.
71. *Boxoffice*, 2 October 1967.
72. *Monthly Film Bulletin* 1967a.

73. *South China Morning Post*, 30 November 1967; *Variety*, 2 August 1967; *The NY Times*, 2 November 1967.
74. *LA Times*, 14 June 1962; *The Globe and Mail*, 12 October 1967.
75. See *Boxoffice*, 4 April 1966; *Le Monde*, 23 January 1967; *Monthly Film Bulletin* 1966.
76. See also Brynner 1989, 215, 227.
77. *Variety*, 28 July, 1965; *The Globe and Mail*, 4 August 1965; *South China Morning Post*, 1 February 1966.
78. *Variety*, 21 December 1966.
79. *The NY Times*, 20 July 1967.
80. *The Globe and Mail*, 23 August 1967; *The Guardian*, 23 June 1967.
81. *Toronto Daily Star*, 22 December 1962.
82. *Bidoun*, Fall 2005.
83. *LA Times*, 15 December 1965.
84. E.g., *Radioscopie*, 1974.
85. *Top Spot Magazine*, 6 June 1959.
86. *The Montreal Gazette*, 12 September 1966.
87. *Pour le cinéma*, 2 March 1973; *Pour le cinéma*, 11 September 1980.
88. *LA Times*, 15 December 1965.

Chapter 6

Cosmopolitan commitments

> On screen Yul Brynner conquers women with his unique brand of bald-pate virility and men with a flourish of swordplay or a quickly-drawn pistol. Off screen he cuts the same dashing figure, a well-cut double-breasted navy blue blazer and grey flannels setting off the acrobat's physique he still retains at 45. [...] In addition to the screen swashbuckler, the doctor of philosophy (Northwestern, '54 – Master's and Bachelor's in science and philosophy from the Sorbonne), the drinking companion of Akira Kurosawa and Toshiro Mifune, the connoisseur of Viennese Biedermeier architecture, the prize-winning star of Broadway musicals, the pioneer director in television, the ex-cabaret singer and guitarist, the former circus acrobat, the one-time backstage electrician, carpenter and wig-maker (the latest item said with a smile) and the Academy Award winner, there is the special consultant to the United Nations High Commissioner for Refugees.
>
> – Kevin Thomas, *Los Angeles Times*

In 1959, named World Refugee Year, Brynner was appointed as special consultant for the United Nations' High Commissioner for Refugees. The unsalaried – or rather, $1-a-year – position involved visiting refugee camps in Europe and the Middle East to do photography, radio, television, and film work in order to bring attention to the experiences and plight of refugees worldwide. At this point, Brynner was having something of a sabbatical from film work after earning $1 million from *Solomon and Sheba*, his first marriage having recently disintegrated and him having relocated back to Europe. The ambivalence that Brynner voiced about his film career and loss of privacy early on found an outlet in lending his fame to a humanitarian cause, while also broadening his star image – otherwise steeped in exotic macho magnetism – towards the issues of human rights and cosmopolitan ethics of care.[1] As journalists put it, Brynner's work with the UNHCR made it possible to see him as more than a 'cranial gimmick,' rebranding him as 'a humanitarian with a sense of humor, a poet with a flourish' instead.[2]

Brynner's work with the UNHCR continued till the end of his life, paving the way for the organization's many later collaborations with film stars. In the late 1970s, he also became an internationally recognized advocate for the rights of Romani people, lobbying the UN in particular.[3] While Brynner's humanitarian work may, at first glance, seem like an ill fit in terms of his exoticized star image, this chapter suggests that cosmopolitanism provides a sense of coherence between his film work and other public roles. In what follows, I inquire after the forms and functions of cosmopolitanism in Brynner's stardom, moving between post-World War II values and ideologies pertaining to human rights, to his affiliation with the Romani. Not least when considering the pan-ethnic range of roles that Brynner played during his career, this self-adopted affiliation evokes questions concerning cultural appropriation, its ethics, stakes, and politics.

In considering these, I argue that, as a modern commitment to 'thinking and feeling globally,' cosmopolitan ideology grounded in liberal humanism and resistant to nationalism and patriotism allows for considering these roles beyond straightforward critiques of representation.[4] While such critiques are of value, this route of argument risks flattening out contextual nuances and ambiguities on possibly anachronistic terms. Brynner's cosmopolitanism was individualistic in both foregrounding his nomadic origins as an issue of personal brand building and in focusing on individuals when advancing the rights of displaced people, yet came with ethical and political commitments exceeding such foci. Broadening into a discussion of Brynner's luxury jet-set lifestyle, this chapter further explores cosmopolitanism in terms of aesthetics – style, fashion, and flair – connected to masculinity, mobility, and social privilege. Much of this, I suggest, is rife with ambiguity.

Cosmopolitan solidarity

Brynner's work with the UNHCR allowed for him to hone his skills as a photographer and a radio and television professional. His attempts to combine humanitarian work with star status date back to 1951–1952 when he was co-chairman of the fourteen-hour charity telecast, 'Celebrity Parade for Cerebral Palsy,' collecting funds for work on CP in the Greater New York area with the aid of a hundred guests from the fields of film, stage, television, and professional sports.[5] Brynner's appointment with the UNHCR resulted in multiple media outcomes, including the star-rich radio show, 'Pattern of Our Lives' (1959) where Bing Crosby, Doris Day,

Kim Novak, Rhonda Fleming, Joseph Schildkraut, and Peter Ustinov narrated stories based on the true-life experiences of refugees (all with eventual happy endings).[6]

In addition, Brynner narrated the thirty-minute documentary, *Mission to No-Man's Land* (1960), exploring the conditions of refugee children in Eastern European camps produced by the BBC for the UNHCR, did radio reports for the BBC, and a radio appeal simultaneously broadcast in Austria, Belgium, France, Italy, Luxembourg, Monaco, Netherlands, and Switzerland.[7] He also hosted the one-hour CBS special television report, *Rescue, with Yul Brynner* (1960), which won the special award for a current affairs program at the 1961 Monte Carlo International Television Festival.[8] The same year, he published the book, *Bring Forth the Children: A Journey to the Forgotten People of Europe and the Middle East* amply illustrated with black and white documentary photographs taken together with his fellow Magnum photographer Inge Morath, to some critical acclaim.[9] The book, the sales of which went to the UNHCR, involved Brynner detailing life in refugee camps in Austria, Germany, Jordan, Jerusalem, and Gaza as well as the UN's practical efforts, both past and present, to improve the living conditions of displaced people.

Although encountering Hungarian refugees in Vienna when making *The Journey* with Anatole Litvak in 1958, it was not until visiting a camp, Brynner explains, that he became committed to the cause.[10] The specifics remain opaque: according to his son, it was a fascination with stamp collecting, and the desire to acquire special UN stamps, that ignited the collaboration.[11] Brynner himself claimed that his appreciation for the UN sparked his interest in the stamps and that the UNHCR approached him in 1959 'to assist in the making of a documentary film and to give some advice about the postage stamps that were to be issued during World Refugee Day.'[12] In more streamlined narrations, *The Journey* came to mark the moment when Brynner realized the volume of people remaining in refugee camps since World War II.[13] As he explained in an interview more than a decade later:

> People who've lived in a state of complete despair without respect to either their own lives or the lives of others, who haven't been part of anything and who can never be part of anything. [...] It's an environment of despair. To start with, there's nothing to do. And nothing can create more despair than to be in a sordid environment where nobody wants you, waiting from one day to another, and waiting for all the documents; when will the documents arrive, and your papers haven't been made yet. No, you haven't yet been

> accepted, this country doesn't want any part of you, others don't want you. To be the one that nobody wants, being without anything to do all day, waiting for something, completely destroys a human being.[14]

This articulation is quintessentially cosmopolitan in taking a critical stance toward national tactics of governance that delimit the freedom of individuals to live, move, and be. As a political notion, cosmopolitanism involves the promotion of a global community premised on universal values: while building on the Enlightenment thought, it gained political momentum after the two world wars, the founding of United Nations in 1945 serving as a key development.[15] Historically, such community-building has been informed by awareness of corporeal vulnerability and the moral imperative to offer humanitarian support for those at risk on the basis of solidarity.[16] Cosmopolitanism's values, as Martin Held points out:

> espouse the idea that human beings are, in a fundamental sense, equal, and that they deserve equal political treatment; that is, treatment based upon the equal care and consideration of their agency, irrespective of the community in which they were born or brought up.[17]

In making general ethical claims concerning human value and individual rights irrespective of nationality, location, or citizenship status, cosmopolitanism is anti-nationalistic by definition, entering the terrain of international law. This ethos cuts through the UN's Declaration of Human Rights, ratified in 1948.

Brynner's 1960 CBS report, *Rescue*, detailed the 'dismal hopelessness' of extended displacement in conditions detrimental to people's mental and physical wellbeing. The report implanted Brynner as its centrepiece and UN mouthpiece who, directly addressing the viewer with an unblinking stare, narrated both the conditions of everyday life at the camps and the personal stories of the people at its focus. These stories included that of a symphony orchestra, formerly based in Budapest, displaced in the course of the 1956 Hungarian uprising, which found a new homebase in a purpose-built concert hall in Marl, Germany. None of the musicians were interviewed for the report; when the mayor made his speech at the concert hall's inaugural event, it was Brynner who delivered the translation. After Brynner's own brief speech, the orchestra accompanied his stern recital of the preamble to the 1945 Charter of United Nations reaffirming 'faith in fundamental human rights, in the dignity and worth of the human person, in the equal rights of men and women and of nations large and small.'

Another key focus of the report was on the Ukranian-born Naumoff family who, after being released from a German labor camp, had spent fifteen years at Central European refugee camps and were just about to relocate to Winnipeg. Brynner narrated the family's experiences, thoughts, fears, and feelings, the only diegetic sounds being their faint murmur over dinner and the song, laughter, and clapping of fellow camp-dwellers as the actor entertained their farewell party with a guitar and Russian songs. As the older Naumoffs looked on with stiff, expressionless faces, the actor explained that they did not even know how to dance, or laugh. The report then followed the family as they left the camp near Lintz, giving voice to a Canadian government representative explaining immigration practices in German (with Brynner's voice-over translation). Voice was literally allowed for agents of cosmopolitan hospitality while the refugees themselves were heard speaking only when tearily inquiring about their future.[18] It was only over footage of their flight to Canada when Nina Naumoff, the family's teenage daughter, regained a voice through her basic mastery of English, recounting her initial feelings of fear. It was Nina, introduced as 'an Anne Frank of the Cold War,' who became the report's special focus, hers being a happy ending as the family habituated to their new life, all smiles as Nina practiced her accordion. By evoking the tragic figure of Anne Frank, whose posthumously published diary had recently been made into an Oscar-winning feature film (*The Diary of Anne Frank*, George Stevens, 1959), the report suggested that both the UN and individual donors, such as its viewers, facilitated Nina, and others like her, to live and thrive – that happy endings were, in fact, a possibility.

Against these happy endings, the other half of *Rescue* outlined the global scale of the refugee crises from South Europe to North Africa, India, Pakistan, South Korea, South Vietnam, Hong Kong, and the Middle East. Brynner was seen entertaining displaced children in Jordan, singing in English as they clapped their hands with varying degrees of enthusiasm. As its title, *Rescue*, indicated, the report operated with a clear distinction between those in need of help and those able to help them, centring Brynner throughout. Speaking with the CBS journalist Edward R. Murrow in a no-man's-land in divided Jerusalem about his motivation for doing the program, Brynner explained that we cannot turn our backs on people who are:

> rotting away and who have been rotting away in camps for ten, fifteen years through no fault of theirs. And you cannot turn your back on the fact that there are children who are born in these camps. You can't turn your back on a new race of people that we're allowing to be created, the race of camp-dwellers.

Moving from sub-par refugee accommodations to interviews with Jordan's King Hussein and Israel's prime minister Golda Meir, the report mapped out the different stakes and deadlocks of the crisis, distributing voice unequally as it went along. Refugees have no official voice, Brynner stated, and *Rescue* did little to amplify individual ones. 'But perhaps they have a different kind of voice in the Philarmonia Hungarica,' he continued, 'an orchestra of refugees whose very flight from Hungary was a symbol, whose every performance is a protest, a voice for the millions who have lost their voice, but not their right to be heard.' Positioned here as a voice for the globally displaced, Philarmonica Hungarica was established in 1957 through support of American foundations – mainly Rockefeller and Ford. The orchestra was soon established as a West Germany-based soft anti-Soviet instrument of the Cold War, symbolizing freedom through art.[19] This emphasis was hardly surprising in a CBS program sponsored by Philip Morris.

Brynner then read lines from Leviticus on the necessity of loving strangers in one's land, emphasizing the importance of migrants for the United States; the orchestra's music swelled to an emotional high; the report came to a close. Brynner's static, grave narrations found a faint echo with his performance as doorkeeper to Hell in *The Testament of Orpheus* the same year. Similarly stationary, shot in black and white, the doorkeeper repeats the request for Jean Cocteau to wait, wait, and wait some more. In *Rescue*, the camp-dweller's endless waiting translates as loss of agency and sense of future in what qualifies as a living hell: in *The Testament*, hell is that which presently awaits.

Bring Forth the Children

Brynner generally identified his work with the UNHCR as originating from his concern for children and nationless young people living or born in camps without even necessarily knowing which country they were in due to constant relocations.[20] This focus was pronounced in the title of *Bring Forth the Children*, which cast children as figures of hope in contrast to older generations who, after decades spent on camps, had difficulties imagining, let alone having, a different kind of future. Dictated in one afternoon, the book was motivated by refugee children's living conditions and the violent outcomes that these might later have.[21] Its overall content and foci directly overlap with that of *Rescue* zooming in on the lives and faces of children against the broader, violent backdrop of post-WWII global politics.

In a designed affective address, the textual vignettes accompanying the book's documentary photography focus on the expressions and experiences of displaced children in an Austrian camp before broadening into descriptions of the hopes and fears of family members and displaced people of different ages. When addressing the Palestinian refugee crisis in Jordan, Jerusalem, and Gaza, the perspective grows more general, seldom dwelling on individuals except for local leaders voicing critique toward both the UN and the US for not facilitating their repatriation. Unlike in the TV special, there is nevertheless little attempt to balance things with an Israeli perspective. Rather, the book relies on the affective punch delivered by photos of Palestinian children shot from the other side of barbed wire fences, combined with accounts of their dire conditions.

Since the book was aimed at the US market with the purpose of increasing both awareness of the refugee crisis and to fuel charitable desires, a focus on children, the appeal to the rights of individuals, as well as the possibility and freedom of individual agency over the inequalities of global politics was understandable. The book further tried to appeal to its readers' attention and will to donate money for the cause, a point also repeated and hence amplified in the book's reviews.[22] Like *Rescue*, the book was aligned with the overall liberal cosmopolitan ethos of the UN and the interconnected necessity for UNHCR representatives to gauge politics. Even so, the inclusion of Palestinians in the account of a global humanitarian crisis seems to have been exceptional by US standards, with *Variety* reporting that:

> He realistically renders the bitterness of the dispossessed Arabs, driven from Israel by war, without getting into politics. [...] The anguish of the Arabs is no less acute than of the Latvians, Lithuanians, and other 'stateless' people of Europe who just get enough rations to live on, and no more.[23]

Brynner's demonstrated concern for the Palestinians did not, of course, stop him from taking on the role of a Naganah commanding officer in the melodramatic *Cast a Giant Shadow* (1966) set in the Arab-Israel war that set off the Palestinian displacements to start with.

In addition to advancing general awareness of the scale of the refugee crisis and helping to raise funds for solving it, Brynner's discoveries of slave labor at German and Austrian camps resulted in a Washington hearing with the Secretary of State featuring the actor as a UN representative.[24] In 1961, Brynner became special consultant to the United States Department of State on refugee affairs, and President Kennedy appointed him as a member of the advisory group for UN's Food for Peace program and the Freedom from Hunger Campaign for developing public awareness on global hunger.[25] Brynner's cosmopolitan commitments to equal human rights earned him an honorary doctorate in Humane Letters at Wilmington College – making him an actual PhD title holder – the same year.[26] These efforts significantly broadened the actor's public image, even as his breaking away from the film star mold was also approached with some suspicion: 'It is sufficiently remarkable to have a player of Brynner's stature exhibit this kind of humanitarism [*sic*], whatever the ego-drive of his personal yen as a sideline pro in photography.'[27]

In its attachment to universal values and shared commonness, cosmopolitanism has been critiqued for playing down and effacing social hierarchies and power differentials connected to race, ethnicity, and gender, so as to contribute to different kinds of vulnerabilities.[28] In particular, there are tensions in how ethical commitments to hospitality map onto humanitarian efforts to affectively mobilize cosmopolitan solidarity – as in the visual iconography of suffering intended to evoke pity that risks erasing the agency of those in pain.[29] Both *Bring Forth the Children* and *Rescue* show how, while aiming to reinstate the value of individuals, cosmopolitan humanitarianism can contribute to the logic of othering. Lilie Chouliaraki conceptualizes cosmopolitan solidarity as suspended 'between common humanity and de-humanization' where the acknowledgement of human vulnerability comes embedded in dynamics of distance and privilege that may result in casting those assisted, or merely pitied, as less-than.[30] There is further the risk of humanitarianism becoming refigured as 'self-centred consumerism' in the shape of aid charity of the kind that Brynner's initiatives paved the way for, so that extant global relations of power become reproduced rather than challenged.[31] Considering the post-World War II context of long-term displaced people, such concerns would nevertheless have been overshadowed by the importance of advancing refugee rights and overall awareness of their acuteness in a context where public interest remained scarce.

Bring Forth the Children presents an early example of affective mobilisation through the visuality of suffering, its key aim being to bring in donations from the American public with the aid of Brynner's visuals, narrations, and fame. As such, the book came embedded in specific power differentials by default. Presenting the refugees as victims of circumstance, and steering clear of global politics connected to the Soviet invasion of the Baltic states or armed conflicts involving Israel, the book nevertheless did not perform quite the kind of effacement of historical context that Chouliaraki associates with humanitarian visuals of suffering. Its documentary black-and-white photography is starkly unsentimental: there is much less attempt at artistic composition than at conveying the circumstantial grimness of life in the camps.

In *Bring Forth the Children*, Brynner explains that, since his teens, he had made it a point to visit an orphanage or a children's hospital on Christmas Eve, 'either to entertain or simply be with the children and give them some attention.'[32] Even as concern for children's wellbeing is perhaps the most popular and widely accepted of humanitarian causes, this focus may seem like something of a gap in a star image of someone identified with macho bravado.[33] In the press, Brynner's fondness for children was to be established as something of a trope through accounts of him bringing Christmas presents to the children of a Rhodes orphanage when filming *Surprise Package*, distributing candy at refugee camps, hosting and donating to orphans when filming in Japan, and giving out free tickets to children when he was just a young circus performer.[34] Characteristically, Brynner blended fact and fiction, as in mentioning his work in Asian orphanages 'years before he started his show business career' when discussing his commitment to his activities with the UNHCR.[35]

Brynner first became a father at the age of 26 with the birth of Rock (born Yul Jr.) and, despite his reluctance to discuss his family life in public, he regularly addressed the importance of fatherhood.[36] As the years went by, and as Brynner's marriages ended and new ones began, he became father to Lark, in 1960, and to Victoria, in 1962. In 1974 and 1975, he adopted two Vietnamese war orphans, Mia and Melody, together with his then wife, Jacqueline Thion de la Chaume. The same decade, he began collaborating with the Swiss organization, Land of Men, caring for children damaged by malnutrition.[37]

Cosmopolitan mobilities

The narrative tactics of both *Rescue* and *Bring Forth the Children* foreground individuals struggling with conditions on which they can have barely any impact. As such, they offered a means of humanizing refugees largely addressed as a mass through statistical means: to make them relatable and equal as individuals.[38] While Brynner wrote of his feelings and personal encounters in refugee camps, he drew no parallels between his own history of displacement and migration and those of the people he conversed with. In other words, the tone was intimate only to a degree. In the introduction, Brynner writes of encountering displaced Russians in 1940 when 'traveling in North China' – the year when he visited his father, a displaced Swiss citizen from the Far East Russian Republic, in Beijing and Shanghai.[39] This was also the same year that Brynner and his mother emigrated to New York due to the impending German occupation of France. The displacements experienced by Brynner and his family were certainly dissimilar to those of people living in camps, yet his own positioning as traveler enabled boundary work where similarities were coined on the abstracted level of individual value and human rights, not on the level of forced migration. Meanwhile, Inge Morath, his Austrian-born friend and collaborator in *Bring Forth the Children*, identified as a refugee.[40]

It was only the random journalist that drew connections between Brynner's 'odyssey' with the UNHCR and his own life as 'a wayfarer' for whom 'family circumstances, war, and careers of an acrobat and actor' have occasioned world travel: 'Born of Russian parents who fled to Japan after the Communist revolution, Brynner had to make his way in the world much as the stateless persons the UN helps.'[41] Such connections were understandably hard to draw due to Brynner's own contingent, unreliable autobiographical narrations. On some occasions, he simply labeled associations between his nomadic origins and his affinity with men without countries as presumptuous, identifying the issue as one of thespian sensitivity toward difference instead, so that his profession (or even his professional calling), rather than his origins, came to explain his humanitarian interests.[42]

Within the framework of cosmopolitan solidarity rooted in pity, Brynner, as one of the best-known male movie stars of the era turned UNHCR delegate, was understandably positioned as an outside giver 'from above.' At the same time, his humanitarian work went well beyond tokenistic Hollywood charity – the documentary work on camps alone preoccupying him for a good year. Brynner's personal detachment from the experiences of refugees was markedly different from Audrey Hepburn's – close friends with his second wife, Doris Kleiner, and godmother to their daughter Victoria – who worked as UNICEF Goodwill Ambassador from the late 1980s, starting with a mission to Ethiopia. Hepburn's personal experiences of malnutrition as a teenager during the 1944–1945 'Dutch Hunger Winter' in German-occupied Netherlands were directly relevant as she was a recipient of food aid from UNICEF (founded directly after the war in 1946), and she credited the organization with saving her life.[43]

Such relating through personal experience does not presume sameness between the humanitarian and those in dire need of aid: rather, it showcases contextual vulnerability owing to global politics as much as to structural inequalities. Yet personal vulnerability was not something that Brynner was keen to showcase, even in retrospect. Not only would such disclosures have gone against his star image projecting masculine strength and virile dominance: they would also have required autobiographical detail of the kind that he was manifestly unwilling to distribute. As traveler, Brynner positioned himself as one with the freedom of mobility, as opposed to those locked away, immobilized, and forgotten in camps. On the one hand, this meant reiterating inequalities inherent in liberal modern cosmopolitanism which, while engaged with common humanity and universal rights, is less preoccupied with relations and hierarchies of privilege.[44] On the other hand, this meant acknowledging actual differentials in social privilege as matters of ethical gravity. Brynner certainly was an experienced traveler, given not only his formative, mobile years but equally his film work that took him to location shoots across the world from Argentina to Japan, and the journeying that he did with the UNHCR, to the point of him being identified as Hollywood's 'travelingest' star.[45]

In contrast to displaced people with no viable forms of citizenship, Brynner was, by birth, a holder of a Swiss passport securing legitimate passage from Far East Russia to China, France, and the United States, and later had a UN passport. This Swiss affiliation, handed down from his grandfather on patrilinear terms, was not based on national identification, let alone familiarity with the country, which Brynner did not visit or live in until he was an adult.[46] Brynner was aligned with the cosmopolitan logic whereby 'citizens of the world' have no need for either nationality nor for 'an identity based upon the lived vicissitudes of expatriation, but for what we might call the voluntary assumption of "dispatriation".'[47]

Unbound by national origins yet secure enough with the appropriate documents, able to choose his places of residence and to eventually enjoy considerable wealth, Brynner subscribed to, and promoted, an articulation of cosmopolitanism as an ethical commitment to equal rights while also embodying cosmopolitan style and flair bound up in privilege.

Brynner's collaboration with the UN extended to film work beyond radio and television. In 1966, he starred in *The Poppy is Also a Flower* (also distributed as *Operation Opium* and *Danger Grows Wild*), 'the most star-studded film ever,' also featuring Omar Sharif, Rita Hayworth, Eli Wallach, Senta Berger, Angie Dickinson, Marcello Mastroianni, and Trevor Howard, among others: Brynner was in fact identified as the driving force behind the enterprise.[48] All actors volunteered their labor so that each received a symbolic compensation of one US dollar.[49] Based on a concept by Ian Fleming, directed by Terence Young, mainly shot by Henri Alekan, narrated by Grace, the Princess of Monaco, and funded by the Xerox Corporation for UN's Children's Emergency Fund, the film nevertheless failed to fulfill its potential. In the United States, it was a television film and never made it to the cinemas outside festivals and special screenings.[50] The film, which critics panned as 'a uniquely unthrilling thriller about drug peddling' with inconceivably banal dialogue, tracked the attempts of narcotics agents employed by the UN to tackle the opium trade on the Afghanistan-Iran border and drug exports to Europe.[51] Brynner's Iranian Colonel Salem got relatively little screen time, most of which was spent on horseback, stylishly clad in local fashions: his part of the film was shot on location in Iran. While the project never took off, Brynner was also cast in a UN film on the India-Pakistan conflict.[52]

Adopted family?

In 1967, Brynner recorded an album of twelve Russian Romani songs together with Aliosha Dimitrievitch, titled *The Gypsy and I*. In its rather uninspired play off on *The King and I*, the album's title involves a degree of ambiguity: who is the gypsy, and who the 'I'? As Miss Anna was the 'I' to Brynner's King Mongkut, and as Brynner is the first name on the record sleeve, he would seem to occupy the first person in relation to Dimitrievitch's gypsy here rhetorically taking the king's place. And, given Dimitrievitch's high-profile career as interpreter of Russian Romani music, it would only be fair for Brynner to play the symbolic second guitar, even if occupying the foreground in the album's promotion and doing the vocals.[53]

As Brynner and Dimitrievitch performed on *The Ed Sullivan Show*, it was only the actor's name that appeared in the titles and it was his presence, complete with a moustache grown for the role of Pancho Villa in *Villa Rides*, that the camera lingered on.[54] It would be easy to cast *The Gypsy and I* as an example of cultural appropriation and exoticism of the kind that has run rife in connection with 'Gypsy' music to date.[55] The easy rapport between Brynner and Dimitrievitch nevertheless suggests something else – not least since the two had first performed together in 1933 when Brynner was a month shy of thirteen. His sister Vera had joined the Dimitrievitches to sing Russian folksongs in a Montmartre restaurant, and, after introducing his younger brother, Brynner became something like an adjunct family member and learned enough of the Romany language to communicate – even though they all spoke Russian.[56] The Dimitrievitches had left St. Petersburg via Vladivistok and Harbin after the revolution, ending up in Paris's Cirque Bouglione after touring Asia and North Africa.[57] It was no coincidence that Maroussia Dimitrievitch starred among the Russian Romani entertainers performing in the Parisian nightclub owned by *Anastasia*'s former White General Bounine. Neither was it a coincidence that Brynner joined in the performance with his seven-string guitar and baritone voice. The family was also present on the soundtrack of *The Brothers Karamazov*.[58]

It can be argued that *The Gypsy and I* was comparable to the duo's 1930s Paris nightclub performances as an ethnic show where the authenticity of their displays of 'Gypsyness' was a matter of stage impression. Taking a more generous route of interpretation, Brynner and Dimitrievitch's joint performance entailed cosmopolitan musical bonding detached from essentializing notions of origin and authenticity. Following Jocelyne Guilbault, cosmopolitan musical bonding can be understood as an affective practice 'not defined either through the borders of nation-states nor tied to a national vocabulary, such as nation-building, multiculturalism, and national identities': as such, it entails 'an ethical embrace of difference.'[59] This perspective foregrounds affective bonding across differences through playing and listening as ongoing 'worlding' that establishes and nurtures relationships and affinities with individuals, groups, and soundings, 'the aesthetics they convey, the ethical values they enact, the political positioning they stand for, or the ideas they

Figure 6.1 Brynner with Maroussia and Aliosha Dimitrievitch (in *Anastasia*, 1956, and *The Ed Sullivan Show*, 1967.)

communicate.'⁶⁰ The record both boosted Brynner's exotic star image and simultaneously offered Dimitrievitch an international platform. Even as the record was primarily targeted at mainstream American and European audiences, it had impact among European Romani musicians since Russian Romani music was not broadly recorded in, let alone exported from the Soviet Union, and hence in limited supply.⁶¹

There is little reason to doubt Brynner's affective alliance with Russian Romani music that he played since his early teens and which he integrated to many of his film performances. There is equally little reason to doubt his affective alliance with the Romani, this worlding also involving political advocacy. In the early 1970s, Brynner was reported to support a school for Romani children in England, speaking of the importance of being able to retain one's culture and language.⁶² In 1978, Brynner was appointed Honorary President of the Second World Romani Congress in Geneva and closed the event by reading the seven-point bill of rights composed by the representatives. The congress drove for the recognition of Romani as national minorities entitled to citizenship rights in their countries of residence, for advancing their equal human rights through recognition by non-governmental organizations, and for affiliating the newly founded International Romany Union with UN's Commission for Human Rights and the Economic and Social Council.[63]

While Brynner's advocacy for the Romani shared the same goal as his work with the UNHCR in advancing the rights of underprivileged people, its roots and motivations were somewhat dissimilar. Contra Brynner's absence of personal affiliation with the experiences of displaced people, his commitment to the Romani cause was positioned as an issue of roots and heritage. These Romani origins became a 'foundational fiction' of sorts, in that his felt affinity became, through the force of repetitive performative reiterations, framed as an issue of ancestral sensibility.[64] Or, as Constance Towers put it, 'he really considered himself this gypsy and that he came from this mysterious, this romantic, dark world of the wandering, nomadic gypsy, and somehow he believed it so strongly that you wanted to believe it too.'[65] According to his son, Brynner's Romani identification involved a distinction from *gadje*, the non-Romani: 'The gaje [*sic*] could never be trusted to speak the truth; that is why the Gypsies always tease the gaje.'[66] It is this unruly, teasing playfulness that came to characterize Brynner's differing and romantic tales of origin as something akin to trickster sensibility.

Brynner's Romani identification involved many a paradox, not least since his romantic uses of 'gypsyness' in building his star image ran against the political ends that he advocated for. While wanting to 'strip away some of the picturesque myths about Romanies' and to focus on minority rights instead, the Second World Romani Congress deployed Brynner, 'a man who embodies that myth' as its figurehead symbolizing 'one of the few ways for gypsies to escape poverty and harassment.'[67] Brynner's Romani affiliation evokes the inevitable question of the ethical and political ramifications of members of non-disadvantaged social groups misappropriating marginalized and underprivileged cultures. To the extent that appropriated 'Gypsyness' broadly denotes 'the exotic, the authentic, and the marginal,' it invested Brynner with the same qualities in ways instrumental to his self-fashioning.[68] Brynner's narrations of Romani identity were a tangle of fabulated romanticism, felt kinship, and political alliance. These narrations, combined with the overall extent of ethnic drag in his onscreen work, mean that the issue of cultural appropriation is forever present when considering his star image. It can easily be argued that such appropriation was the very stuff that made up and sustained his star persona, and that it has since contributed to Brynner's partial disappearance from public memory – just as the epics he starred in have grown quaint, or even obsolete, in their displays of exotic otherness.

For Brynner, lending his public visibility to the Romani meant taking the place of Romani as his activities were based on claims of ethnic belonging. Somewhat puzzlingly, the Associated Press saw the actor's previous roles as 'a make-believe Russian nobleman, pirate, hired gun from Texas, Yugoslav freedom fighter and three kinds of king – Israeli, Egyptian and Siamese' making him a natural leader for the ten million Romani represented at the Second World Congress. In other words, for AP, Brynner's Hollywood career operated as on-the-job-training for a Romani rights spokesperson, suggesting that his own origins mattered little in comparison to his ability to move across ethnic spectrums.[69]

The Romani were hugely affected by the ethnic purges of the Third Reich, and Brynner's embrace of both Jewish and Romani origins (the former through fourth-generation ties, the latter as a felt affinity) meant self-alignment with two peoples intensely hurt by World War II. To date, the Romani remain socioeconomically marginalized in Eastern Europe, and well beyond, and while they represent something of a cosmopolitan population irreverent of national boundaries, they have largely been excluded from conceptualizations of cosmopolitanism focusing on differently privileged, and hence differently mobile, communities and commercial cultures.[70] As virtually the only international film star ethnically identifying as Romani from the 1950s to the 1980s, Brynner formed a rare exception.[71] Among Romani activists, his participation in advancing their rights seems to have been embraced and, given that he spoke some of the language and played the music, his claims of origin were apparently accepted as a fact. In news articles of Brynner as a 'Gypsy spokesman' at the time of the Second World Congress, he described himself as 'Rom in my soul and Rom through my mother, the Rom have accepted me like no other people.'[72] In some interviews, he expanded this heritage to both maternal and paternal sides of his family.[73] At other times, he argued that his advocacy was more that of an ally and based on his formative experiences with the Dimitrievitches: 'It isn't that I personally experienced a lot of discrimination; it's just that I've seen a lot of discrimination against gypsies.'[74] As was routinely the case with Brynner's narratives of origin, things did not remain fixed for long.

The year after the Second World Congress, Brynner wrote a piece for *The New York Times* detailing the advancements made, such as the UN Human Rights Commission calling for countries to accord equal rights to the Romani, while also pointing out the work yet to be done: 'At present, we are a stateless people with few citizenship rights in our host countries. We see northern India, or Punjab, as our homeland. [...] The rights of equality we want are no more than those already enjoyed by others.'[75] Written by someone who had always had a citizenship (occasionally doubly so) and who was not ethnically Romani, this declaration, independent of its political intentions, remains preposterous.

Brynner's son suggests that his felt affiliation stemmed from a perfect resonance between Romani worldview and 'Yul's repeated experiences as refugee,' yet Brynner never had refugee status, even as he was repeatedly a displaced migrant and excluded from considerable family wealth when young.[76] It is the case, as Ella Shohat argues, that, independent of social positioning, 'one's ancestral community does not necessarily dictate one's identifications and affiliations' so that the question is not merely that of 'what one is or where one is coming from, but also of what one desires to be, where one wants to go and with whom one wants to go there.'[77] With Brynner, the 'self-made mystery man,' such mobility was extensive, and Romani one of the things that he wanted to be.[78] Felt resonances and factual early poverty aside, he nevertheless enjoyed the kind of mobility – both geographical and social – inaccessible to many Romani at the time. Even as Cold War Hollywood was averse to many things Russian, beyond spending a night in a Baton Rouge 'coloreds' jail in the early 1940s, Brynner did not particularly suffer from social discrimination, becoming a luminary of the international jet-set instead.[79] Some of this disparity is evident in an archival excerpt included in the 2019 documentary *Les mille et une vies de Yul Brynner* of the actor visiting a French Romani camp in a Rolls Royce to speak of the importance of education and the possibility of preserving one's culture and heritage – a contact with one's origins.

Cosmopolitan tastes

References to Brynner's Romani heritage emerged once again in his co-authored 1983 *Yul Brynner Cookbook: Food Fit for the King and You*, where he claimed to have spent several of his 'teenage years traveling through France with a gypsy troupe' (which he did not, as the Dimitrievitches were Paris-based) before describing a fantastically romantic feast:⁸⁰

> *'Patshiv'* in the Gypsy language, Romany, means ceremonial celebration. Among the requirements for an ideal patshiv are a warm summer night with cooling breezes, a grassy meadow with a sweetwater brook for a border, crackling campfires with a huge reserve of cut firewood, and a squad of violin and guitar players with nimble fingers – not to mention the lavish amount of food. The aromas of rich hunter's steak and wild goose seasoned with sage, thyme, and marjoram waft through the air.
>
> [...] As the evening wears on, someone will hum the melody of a folk song, and, before you know it, everyone will join in, and the campfires will be surrounded by whirling dancers. A storyteller will be moved to speak of her ancestors, and new legends will be born before the night retreats from the sun. Dawn will finally make an entrance accompanied by the echoes of an epic song composed just for the guest of honor. You'll fall asleep believing that the romantic view of a gypsy's life isn't so far from the truth.⁸¹

The scene described is highly cinematic, especially if the film in question were a Hollywood production of the 1950s or early 1960s reminiscent of the folksy choreographies of *Taras Bulba*, complete with whirling dancers, storytellers, and a squad of ethnically passable (or brown-faced) musicians. Realism is clearly not the chosen genre in how the fantastic camp fire scene conflates romantic imagination with claimed truth about the culture in question. Brynner's account further folds back on itself by commenting on its romantic hues composed for the reader – the 'you' of the American book market, the imaginary guest of honor in the textual vignette – to enjoy and consume.

Divided into sections on Russian, Japanese, Gypsy, Swiss, Chinese, French, and Thai cuisine, the cookbook sets out to cover Brynner's diverse places of origin, residence, and affiliation, comprising a culinary biography of sorts. According to the introduction, 'he possesses one of the greatest of all gifts: a natural facility with languages that easily allows him to be at home anywhere. (Brynner speaks eleven languages, including Russian, Chinese, Romany, Japanese, French, and English.)'⁸² The introduction then plunges into closer descriptions of Gypsy, Mongolian, and Swiss cuisines identified as part of his ancestry, with citations from Brynner describing the Mongolian style of roasting an unskinned sheep with hot rocks inserted in its intestinal cavity. 'But what else influences Brynner's culinary tastes? Ah, here is a man who has tried everything, who has lived in Paris and Peking and New York, who has journeyed throughout Europe, America, and Asia.'[83]

The book comes complete with glossaries and sections where Brynner describes, or is written to describe, culinary conventions based on personal experience, from the Japanese preference for harmony and visual display, to Russian vodka-serving habits. Although it remains unclear whether Brynner ever visited Thailand, there is also a section on the country's food. Each of the book's sections opens with these brief introductions addressing Brynner's affiliation with the food cultures in question – his travels, palates, and origins included. Showcasing understanding of their principles, nuances, and social codes, these intros occasionally broaden into socio-historical sketches. These contextual vignettes, as well as their ample insider recommendations for dishes and drinks to try, are lodged in Brynner's experiences and memories: 'I have worked and traveled all over the world,' he states:

> Of all the places I've been the country that captured my heart more than any other was France. I love the combination of gracious cosmopolitan elegance and ageless charm of gentle rural beauty that I have found in Normandy, the province where I maintain my real home.[84]

The cosmopolitanism that Brynner performed – in this book and beyond – was not that of a more or less seasoned tourist. Rather, it was suggestive of deeper mastery of cultural nuance based on extensive social connections and diverse roots facilitating instinctual insight into the intricacies of manner, habit, sensibility, and style. Writing on culinary tourism, Lucy M. Long points out that ethnic foods become defined as such only in relation to a dominant culture – which, in the context of *Food for the King and You*, was that of mainstream America. Asking who gets to be an authority in defining cuisines and writing the recipes, she further argues that, construed in these terms,

> 'ethnic food' is more than just foreign or international food. It reflects a social status of being Other, and of existing within another larger, more dominant culture. It is the foodways of a cultural heritage perceived as not belonging to the mainstream culture.[85]

Befitting Brynner's pan-ethnic star image premised on his positioning as an ethnic other (in opaque terms), the cookbook performs discursive mastery over a range of regional cuisines framed on ethnic terms so as to narrate them to the American reader. Here, Europe and Asia are similarly exotic in the degrees to which their cultural details become translated. As the book was written for a domestic market, its regional range excludes the United States even as this was long Brynner's country of residence and work: in doing so, it covers that which is foreign and exotic yet approachable enough through accessible recipes (most likely composed by co-author Susan Reed) to be enjoyed at home.

All in all, the book's structuring logic illuminates the more general strands of Brynner's star image as a fabricated, cosmopolitan composite designed to dazzle and seduce the US consumer market. This image had, at this point, been in the making for over three decades. In all this, authenticity operated as a condiment more than a commitment. Consider, for example, the first recipe in the opening section focused on Russia: 'Avocado with caviar' inclusive of chopped eggs and lettuce, served in the style of a 1970s prawn cocktail. Featuring avocado – hardly a traditional food staple in Russia – and listing the luxury preference for Beluga caviar, the recipe is an unorthodox mix gesturing towards the high life in a context of targeted mass consumption. It is hard to resist drawing a broader analogy to Brynner's star image as one combining ethnic remix with the mastery of cross-cultural nuance for an audience of primarily American film viewers, magazine readers, and theatregoers. A penchant for luxury was a recurrent feature in Brynner's interviews, as in the 1958 quote: 'What drives me is not compulsion [...] It's more because of something someone once said of me, "Yul was born with an extra quart of champagne in his blood".'[86] And since his love of champagne and caviar – 'all the right wines, all the right sauces' – was established early on, it was something of a compulsory gesture in a book claiming to showcase the actor's tastes.[87]

Refined, expensive tastes

Probably the most obvious aspect of Brynner's cosmopolitan star image had to do with his overall aesthetic, flair, and style, as articulated through preferences for fine dining, Italian and French designer clothing, high society, and luxury cars. His habit of touring with an abundance of clothing made the news as early as 1954, and newspaper and magazine articles continued to report on his style for decades thereafter.[88] Hence, a bald head appearing from a 'sleek black limousine,' the man, dressed 'in all black Balenciaga' imperiously declaring, 'we will eat Japanese'; an actor sporting a golden computer watch, and a hairless man 'smartly turned out in a French-style suit with split lapels and side vents' at an ambassadorial reception dressed in a pink stripe shirt and loafers decorated with gold chains.[89] In his memoirs, George Sanders, who played Brynner's warring brother in *Solomon and Sheba*, reminisced that Brynner, 'inspired no doubt by the grandeur of his role,' arrived on set with an entourage of seven:

> The function of one member of this retinue appeared to consist of placing already lighted cigarettes in Brynner's outstretched fingers. Another was permanently occupied in shaving his skull with an electric razor whenever the suspicion of a shadow darkened that noble head. While these services were being rendered unto him, Brynner sat in sphinx-like silence and splendor wearing black leather suits or white leather suits, of which he had half a dozen each, confected for him by the firm of Dior.[90]

The glaring gap between this narration pertaining to the production of the 1959 film and the travels to refugee camps that Brynner started the same year with minimal luggage in his role with the UNHCR, sleeping in cots is, I suggest, a matter of perspective. The ambiguities of Brynner's star persona mean that both narrations are equally accurate. As Rock Brynner explains:

> His extensive personal wardrobe included custom-built shoe trees for his custom-made John Lobb shoes, and a dozen black leather Gucci suitcases. He kept his collection of Havana cigars in the humidor rooms of Dunhills in several cities. And while shooting *Anastasia* in Paris, he had purchased the new Mercedes 300 SL sports car, best remembered for its gull-wing doors.[91]

Brynner collected 'precious Cartier and Audemars Piguet watches' and had 'his shirts made to measure and his suits in London.'[92] Good friends with Frank Sinatra, Brynner was part of Hollywood's jet-set. He was invited to galas organized by Princess Grace and Prince Rainier of Monaco, set off on a sailboat to Nassau with Aristotle Onassis, and cooked ad-hoc caviar omelettes at Christina Onassis's house together with the Andy Warhol Factory fixture, Richard Dupont.[93] His personal photography documented much of the social circle, including leisure time spent with DeMille, Cocteau, Sinatra, Mia Farrow, the Chaplins, the Guinnesses, Elizabeth Taylor, and Richard Burton, as well as select aristocrats.[94]

With his marriages to Doris Kleiner (1960–1967) and Jacqueline Thion de la Chaume (1971–1981), Brynner entered European high society, relocating to Paris, Lausanne, and the sixteenth-century fifty-acre Manoir de Criqueboeuf in Normandy where he raised pigeons and wild duck, collected modern art from Picasso to Paul Cezanne, Amedeo Modigliani, Bernard Buffet, and Alexander Calder, and enjoyed exclusive vintage wines, and where he also kept penguins.[95] As a journalist covering the television premiere of the 1972 *Anna and the King* enthused, 'It is said Brynner lives like a king in France, moving between country manor and city, raising rare birds, employing the best.'[96] His house was close to Deauville, a seaside race course and casino resort favored by socialites where Brynner had gone as a teenager with his mother and sister, where he had worked as a teen lifeguard, and where he had long enjoyed casual gambling.[97]

A former model and fashion house executive, Doris Brynner was a regular figure in society columns covering designer fashion, dressing only in Balenciaga, and later working for Valentino and Dior.[98] Thion de la Chaume, aristocrat, socialite, and former fashion editor for the French *Vogue*, was similarly friends with a range of top fashion designers. In a lifestyle interview, she casually described the couple's domestic habit of changing from jeans to more formal dinner wear – for example, Brynner donning his trademark black for a pink Karl Lagerfeld silk shirt.[99] Associated with 'dandyishly-cut suits – all roped shoulders, generous lapels and jetted hacking pockets – [that] emphasised his imposing figure and urbane air,' Brynner was featured in international listings of best dressed celebrities.[100] An 'internationalist and social lion,' he was eventually remembered as someone 'as much at home in the drawing rooms of the capitals of Europe as in New York and Beverly Hills.'[101]

For Marlon Brando, Brynner's *Morituri* co-star, this desire 'to hang out at chic places and be seen with fashionable people' separated him from more serious actors prioritising their art, suggesting – at this point quite accurately – that Brynner was more invested in the money that he could make.[102] He was, from early on, specific and demanding with contracts, and his level of requirements grew on a par with his fame and status.[103] When shooting *Morituri*, for example, Brynner insisted on traveling between the mainland and the set on Catalina Island by helicopter, as opposed to a regular boat.[104] During the filming of *The Flight from Ashiya* in Japan, he reportedly brought over 'his $8,000 air-conditioned dressing room trailer,' hence introducing locals to Hollywood luxury.[105]

News items further detailed Brynner keeping a private French chef on sets, installing an electric rotisserie in his studio dressing room in order to make his lunch, dining in the best restaurants, flying from London to Paris 'to sit for hours in out-of-the-way bistros with his friends, eating wonderful French food, drinking fine French wines' and then taking a private jet the other way to have lunch, visit his tailor and bootmaker, and return again 'to dine in Paris with President Pompidou.'[106]

While intermeshing with cosmopolitanism as an ethical commitment to equal human rights and solidarity independent of national boundaries, cosmopolitan style 'as attitude, stance, posture, and consciousness' is more ephemeral in referring to sophistication and elegance in the vein hinted at by the *Cosmopolitan* magazine (launched in 1886 and reimagined as a women's lifestyle magazine in 1965).[107] In such a commercial articulation, cosmopolitanism stands for stylistic self-expression which, while being highly dependent on socioeconomic constraints, is equally an issue of individualism.[108]

Brynner's particular brand of cosmopolitanism wove ephemeral origins together with nomadic tendencies, opaque ethnicity, and keen, expensive consumer preferences and aesthetic sensibilities expressed through photography, art, and design. As such, it was irrevocably connected to social class, wealth, and masculinity. Even though Brynner was a self-made man, and at times tangibly poor, he came from both socioeconomic privilege and cultural capital. In his star image of vaguely international origins, French connections and broad language skills met exceptionalism characteristic of movie stardom marking individuals as outstanding personalities.

Cosmopolitan mobilities

In 1975, Brynner became honorary chairman of the Emergency Committee to Save the Babies founded to facilitate the adoption of Vietnamese war orphans and raised funds for medical supplies.[109] Through his collaboration with the UN, Brynner had visited Vietnamese orphanages, adopting a 4-month-old child, Mia, the previous year.[110] As the Brynners were expecting their second adopted child, Melody, to arrive in 1975, the plane carrying her and other orphans crashed near Saigon. Travel logistics being challenging during the last stages of the war, Brynner contacted *Playboy* publisher Hugh Hefner who sent his private

DC-9 plane, Big Bunny, complete with a seven-foot circular bed, to airlift the children who, according to *The Washington Post*, 'were carried down the ramp from the jet by Playboy bunnies, nurses and agency representatives.'[111] Once the mission was accomplished, Brynner helped set up a special unit in Boston's Children's Hospital for the orphans' needs.[112] Back home, the fashion designer Karl Lagerfeld became godfather to both Mia and Melody Brynner.[113] Meanwhile, Brynner was godfather to Mia Farrow and André Previn's daughter Daisy (Summer Song), also adopted from Vietnam.[114]

International adoptions from Asia and Europe were one consequence of US post-World War II military influence, so that the 'figure of the white parent to the non-white child' came to operate 'as a trope for representing the ostensibly "natural" relations of hierarchy and domination.'[115] Taking into consideration Brynner's advocacy for the rights of misplaced people, and for those of children in particular, it would nevertheless be reductive to identify his adoptions as simply symbolic of global relations of power and dominance. While power differentials were certainly present in Brynner's privileged forms of mobility, public visibility, and agency, there was much ambiguity to his positioning in terms of ethnicity and nationality. Brynner himself critiqued transplanting children into a different country or culture, yet argued that airlifts and international adoptions were, under the conditions, an act of 'human brotherhood': 'If a child has been totally abandoned, then it is not immoral to consider yourself his human brother or father.'[116]

All in all, Brynner's cosmopolitanism bridging his humanitarian efforts, screen roles, self-identifications, consumer preferences, and overall style was framed in terms of what Rebecca L. Walkowitz identifies as a 'planetary humanism' approach characteristic of post-war sentiment rooted in 'epistemological privilege, views from above or from the center that assume a consistent distinction between who is seeing and who is seen.'[117] As a subject position, Brynner's cosmopolitanism involved the capacity to move between, and to cross, geographical and cultural boundaries with apparent ease, as well as to occupy a range of positions without being bound to any single one of them – the ones connected to national origins included. According to Brynner's agent, Guy McElwaine:

> His gypsy background, which he was very proud of, gave him an incredible sense of belonging to wherever he was. Whenever he was in America, he was American. And when he was in France where he lived for years, he was French. And when he was in China, in Japan, in the Far East, he was Asian.[118]

The flexibility of his ethnic casting then found direct correlation in the international mobility of the actor himself. Brynner regularly played aloof men of the world with sophisticated tastes in dress, art, and cuisine in ways concurrent with his public image of a cosmopolitan polyglot gourmand womaniser with a penchant for designer clothing. In Brynner's paradoxical brand of cosmopolitanism, a taste for the good life met humanitarian work among refugees, orphans, and the homeless, for which he was also awarded.[119] This cosmopolitanism was rife with contradiction, moving from universalist liberalism to displays of solidarity, charity, ethnic impersonation and appropriation, as well as the parading of mobility and privilege in the shape of cultural knowledge and international jet-set lifestyle. These contradictions all came together in the incident of the Big Bunny.

Encompassing constant, easy mobility, broad mastery of and affective affinity with global cultures, Brynner outlined an effortless kind of cosmopolitanism that was not continuous or easy to pair with his elaborate, stylized onscreen performances as brash Cossacks and impervious alien rulers that do not convey much nuanced insight into the cultural settings they claim to depict. There is characteristic, drag-like excess to many of Brynner's ethnic performances that dates them in unfavorable ways, so that the antiquated air of his historical epics, combined with the flamboyance of his performances, are unlikely to invite much contemporary recognition of cinematic artistry. While I return to the issue through the analytical lens of camp in Chapter 8 examining stylizations and repetitions in Brynner's film work, the following chapter first explores a range of his roles that have thus far hardly been touched upon: those of violent gunslingers, assassins, spies, and killer robots.

Notes

1. *Radioscopie*, 1974.
2. *Philadelphia Daily News*, 18 November 1960.
3. *The NY Times*, 4 June 1978.
4. Walkowitz 2006, 5.
5. *Motion Picture Daily*, 30 November 1951; *St. Petersburg Times*, 2 January 1952; *Variety*, 10 December 1952.
6. *Patterns of Our Lives*, January 1 1959.
7. *The NY Times*, 4 December 1960; *The Guardian*, 29 December 1959.
8. *NY Herald Tribune*, 4 December 1960a; *NY Herald Tribune*, 4 December 1960b; *LA Times*, 22 January 1961.

9. Brynner 1960; *Tampa Bay Times*, 11 December 1960; *NY Herald Tribune*, 1 January 1961; *LA Times*, 29 January 1961.
10. Brynner 1960, 2.
11. Brynner 1989, 122.
12. *NY Herald Tribune*, 18 May 1959; Brynner 1960, 3.
13. *Philadelphia Daily News*, 18 November 1960.
14. *Radioscopie*, 1974.
15. Braidotti 2012, 1; Walkowitz 2006, 3.
16. Chouliaraki 2012, 77.
17. Held 2012, 29.
18. On the ethics of hospitality and cosmopolitanism, see Derrida 2005, 16–17.
19. Berghahn 2001, 188–9.
20. Le Régional, 13 October 1960.
21. *Radioscopie* 1974.
22. E.g., *St. Petersburg Times*, 11 December 1960.
23. *Variety*, 30 November 1960.
24. *The Washington Post*, 9 February 1960. Fundraising projects included star-studded musical albums and banquets, the sales of which went to the UNHCR. *Le Courrier Australien*, 16 November 1962; *The Montreal Gazette*, 1 March 1963; *Boxoffice*, 4 March 1963; *The Washington Post*, 20 May 1963.
25. *The Hollywood Reporter*, 19 January 1961; *The Record*, 24 January 1961; *The Washington Post*, 7 May 1961; *Boxoffice*, 11 September 1961.
26. *Wilmington News*, 27 April 1961; *The Hollywood Reporter*, 28 April 1961.
27. *Variety*, 30 November 1960.
28. Dayal 2019, 6–7; cf. Braidotti 2012.
29. Chouliaraki 2012, 78.
30. Ibid.
31. Ibid., 78–9.
32. Brynner 1960, 3.
33. Brynner's roles were largely void of parental hues – just as they only occasionally extended to romance, even as he played the occasionally father: King Mongkut, after all, sports a small army of offspring; Rameses plunges into deep, vengeful grief with the loss of his only son; the plot of *Taras Bulba* is structured on the relationship of father and son, the former finally killing the latter; Sultan of *The Long Duel* is a committed father; the CIA agent Dan Slater of *The Double Man* seeks vengeance on the death of his estranged son and, in an offbeat variation of the theme, Jason Compson of *The Sound and the Fury* becomes romantically involved with a step-niece he raised.
34. *The Times of India*, 10 January 1960; *Variety*, 21 October 1959; *The Hollywood Reporter*, 19 September 1962; *The Boston Sunday Globe*, 4 December 1960.
35. *The Austin Statesman*, 16 February 1960.
36. E.g., *Australian Women's Weekly*, 16 April 1975; *SF Examiner*, 12 December 1982a, 45.
37. *The Guardian*, 23 March 1974.
38. *Australian Jewish News*, 23 December 1960. One can, of course, ask to what extent the selective tactics of allocating voice in *Rescue* align with the aim of equality.

39. Brynner 1960, 2; Brynner 2006, Kindle edition.
40. In Brynner 1996, 50.
41. *The Washington Post*, 4 December 1960; *The Kansas City Sun*, 23 July 1961.
42. *LA Times*, 15 December 1965.
43. Hemenway 2019.
44. Nava 2002.
45. *The Austin Statesman*, 13 May 1963.
46. As Rock Brynner explains, 'male descendants of any Swiss father are automatically Swiss wherever they are born for the next four generations. This only operates along the male line, described frankly under the law as 'paternal privilege': the right of a Swiss father to pass his nationality down to his sons, his grandsons, and even his great-grandsons.' Brynner 2006, Kindle edition.
47. Wollen 1994, 189.
48. *The Guardian*, 12 May 1966.
49. *Le Monde*, 28 September 1965a.
50. *LA Times*, 15 December 1965.
51. *The Guardian*, 1 November 1966; *Monthly Film Bulletin* 1967b.
52. *Le Monde*, 28 September 1965b.
53. Brynner did not play the guitar on the album and he was not, in fact, the first in his family to do such a recording as his sister had released an LP *Vera Brynner: Russian Gypsy Folk Songs*, in 1958. *Toronto Daily Star*, 14 March 1959.
54. *The Ed Sullivan Show*, 17 September 1967.
55. Silverman 2015; Szeman 2019.
56. Brynner 2006, Kindle edition.
57. *Harpers and Queen*, December 1981, 226.
58. As Brynner explained, 'We recorded in Europe some gypsy songs done by a group of Russian gypsies with whom I worked in Paris during my night club years. These are worked, and beautifully, into the score.' *SF Examiner*, 23 February 1958.
59. Guilbault 2017, 102, 103, 135.
60. Ibid., 101.
61. *Helsingin Sanomat*, 1 May, 2010.
62. *The Austin Statesman*, 12 September 1971.
63. *SF Examiner*, 12 April 1978, *The Times of India*, 11 April 1978; *South China Morning Post*, 19 May 1978.
64. On foundational fictions, see Koivunen 2003.
65. *Yul Brynner: The Man Who Was King*, 1995.
66. Brynner 2006, Kindle edition.
67. *South China Morning Post*, 21 April 1978; see also *The Guardian*, 12 April 1978.
68. Silverman 2012, 266.
69. *The Korea Times*, 20 August 1978.
70. For an extended discussion on the Romani and cosmopolitanism, see Rövid 2011.
71. *The Observer*, 3 November 1968.
72. *Le Monde*, 15 April 1978.
73. *SF Examiner*, 12 April 1978.
74. *Ashbury Park Press*, 23 August 1978.
75. *The NY Times*, 3 June 1978.

76. Brynner 2006, Kindle edition.
77. Shohat 1995, 168.
78. *Redbook*, May 1957.
79. On the prison visit, see Brynner 2006, Kindle edition.
80. Brynner and Reed 1983, 55.
81. Ibid., 56–7.
82. Ibid., xiv.
83. Ibid., xv.
84. Ibid., 137.
85. Long 2018.
86. *Saturday Evening Post*, 22 November 1958, 81.
87. *Behind the Scenes*, 28 March 1957, 54; *NY Herald Tribune*, 12 June 1958.
88. *Los Angeles Times*, 7 June 1954.
89. *The Washington Post*, 14 December 1974; *The Guardian*, 23 March 1974; *The Washington Post*, 13 November 1969.
90. Sanders 1960, 57.
91. Brynner 2006, Kindle edition.
92. Tonchi 2010, 9; see also *Town & Country*, September 1976, 149.
93. *The Washington Post*, 13 June 1962; *LA Times*, 17 February 1964; *Out*, 1 June, 2012.
94. See Brynner 1996; Brynner and Pages 2010a; Brynner and Pages 2010d.
95. *Harper's Bazaar*, December 1967; *The Guardian*, 23 March 1974; *The Washington Post*, 2 August 1962; *Town & Country*, June 1970; *The NY Times*, 6 May 1988; *Orlando Sentinel*, 4 December 1992; Brynner 1989, 151; on the penguins, see *LA Times*, 10 August 1975; *Harper's Bazaar*, February 2012.
96. *The Journal News*, 13 August 1972.
97. *LA Times*, 26 July 1956; *Elokuva-aitta* 19, 1959; *The Vancouver Sun*, 24 June 1960; *Elokuva-aitta* 9, 1961; *Town & Country*, August 1976.
98. *Life*, 25 April 1960; *The Montreal Gazette*, 24 September 1968; *The Washington Post*, 30 July 1964; *Vogue*, 1 May 1964; *Harpers & Queen*, December 1988, 130.
99. *The Washington Post*, 11 January 1971.
100. *The Rake*, November 2015; *Esquire*, 30 August 2013; *The Washington Post*, 11 January 1971; *The Globe and Mail*, 12 January 1971; also *Australian Women's Weekly*, 13 March 1974.
101. *The Indianapolis News*, 10 October 1985.
102. In Capua 2006, 110.
103. *The Washington Post*, 15 May 1957.
104. *The Washington Post*, 11 September 1964.
105. *The NY Times*, 14 October 1962.
106. *LA Times*, 15 April 1975; *LA Times*, 10 August 1975; *Screenland*, January 1960, 68; *Daily News*, 26 August 1956; *Philadelphia Daily News*, 6 February 1971.
107. Walkowitz 2006, 2.
108. Cf. Machin and Van Leeuwen 2005.
109. *The Washington Post*, 7 April 1975, C1.
110. *SF Examiner*, 26 January 1975. Brynner was also reported to have supported an orphanage in South Vietnam, *Los Angeles Times*, 7 April 1975.

111. *The Washington Post*, 10 April 1975, A17.
112. *LA Times*, 15 April 1975.
113. *The Washington Post*, 4 May 1979.
114. *The Washington Post*, 14 December 1974. Brynner was also godfather to Jane Birkin and Serge Gainsbourg's daughter Charlotte; Capua 2006, 138. Victoria Brynner's other godmother (in addition to Audrey Hepburn) was Elizabeth Taylor. *Yahoo Entertainment*, 30 August, 2016.
115. Klein 2003, 175.
116. *The Calgary Herald*, 24 April 1975; *The Austin Statesman*, 27 April 1975.
117. Walkowitz 2006, 2.
118. *Yul Brynner: The Man Who Was King*, 1995.
119. *The Austin Statesman*, 27 April 1975; *SF Examiner*, 21 January 1983. In 1980, Brynner was the first recipient of the Sheltering Arms Children's Service (SACS) Service Award. *Variety*, 5 November 1980.

Chapter 7

Man, beast, machine

From the 1950s, Brynner's star image was associated with authoritarian masculine roles to the point of him having 'virtually shaped the contemporary macho persona in his own brooding image.'[1] Even when his roles were not action-packed, popular imagination surrounding his figure established the actor, with little (if any) evidence, as a martial arts expert: 'Everybody knows that Yul Brynner speaks eleven languages. That he is an expert chef. That he is a world traveller. But what most fans don't know is that he's also a ju-jitsu champion!' Starting with this declaration in 1957, the fan magazine *Modern Screen* went on to narrate a lesson that Brynner allegedly gave to 'a wise-guy' Marine for doubting his authentic Oriental origins (as marked by martial arts prowess): the setting of the story was that of a party around the time of Brynner's immigration to the United States. Challenged by the Marine to a ju-jitsu session, it was said that Brynner held the man 'in an excruciatingly painful arm-lock,' then threw and slammed him down on the mat hard enough to break the man's wrist. In the punchline, Brynner revealed that his forte was actually judo.[2] This fabricated piece supported Brynner's enigmatic Oriental alpha male persona, even though it was not until later that his film roles expanded towards action.

A current of more or less pronounced violence runs through Brynner's film work, from the murderous Paul Vicola of *Port of New York* to the whip-waving King Mongkut wishing to flagellate an escapee slave, perhaps to death, to the tyrannical Rameses and many characters since – hired guns, military men, and freedom fighters included. Even in his more subdued role as Jason Compson in *The Sound and the Fury*, 'Mr. Brynner as a rasping tyrant spends a great deal of valuable time merely shouting and slapping at Joanne Woodward,' losing 'none of his characteristic menace.'[3]

As the Hollywood studio era came to a close, as Brynner's stardom began to fade, and as his roles grew less flamboyant in their ethnic displays, sets, and scale, he remained cast in masculine roles – some more playful than others – that were increasingly rife with violence. Previously dancing and moving with the confidence and grace of a former Cirque d'hiver acrobat, Brynner's body was now growing stiff, exhibited the occasional limp, and often grabbed a gun in many of its onscreen appearances. This chapter focuses on Brynner's spy thrillers, Westerns, action, and science fiction roles of the 1960s and 1970s in terms of their masculine displays and gender dynamics. Many of these were European co-productions, popular genre films with international casts and target audiences extending beyond those of national cinemas: in these, Brynner generally stood for an American.[4] The chapter addresses the impact of aging on his star image built on physical presence and allure, and further probes debates on screen violence since the 1960s. Some of Brynner's later bastard characters continued to have hearts of gold. Others failed to have any hearts whatsoever, them being diabolical monsters or robots.

Alpha-male spies

The opening credits of the 1967 spy thriller *The Double Man* feast on Brynner's face with extreme close ups of his lips, cheeks, eyes, and brow displayed in hues of black, red, blue, orange, and green dissolving into one another, and occasionally doubling for added effect. The establishing shot is of a Soviet military bunker in divided Berlin, anchoring the action in Cold War politics. The first sight of Brynner is a grim-faced black-and-white photograph in Soviet hands: 'when will this fantasy be ready?,' a voice asks.[5] The original mold of the fantasy himself, named Dan Slater, is then seen grimly stalking down the corridor of a CIA office, having just been notified of his estranged teenage son's death in a skiing accident on the Austrian Alps. Flying over just in time for the funeral, Slater expresses emotion by slightly opening his lips for an exhale, then returns to his hardened, suspicious glum countenance, exhibiting 'unflinching ferocity' throughout the rest of the film.[6]

There are a great many close-ups in the film, some of them displaying two Brynners at once – the original Slater and his psycho-biologically manufactured KGB double, Kalmar, designed to replace him – bathed in chiaroscuro as the conspiracy plan is being unpacked or as people are trying to tell the two men apart. Slater is a man of few words and stony comportment with a gun readily at hand, a type that Brynner played from the 1960 *Magnificent Seven* till the 1976 *Death Rage*. Even as his acting in these roles was void of the more flamboyant hues (à la King Mongkut or

Captain Stoloff), it was no less intense. Consider, for example, a scene where Slater sits gagged in the back seat of a car between two of his Soviet captors. A ski mask hides Slater's face except for his eyes communicating acute fury as the scene's focal point. 'Hollywood's apostle of the bald pate plays an American CIA man whose steely visage is as cold as the gun metal rod he carries,' a critic noted: 'Not once does he smile in this one.'[7] This type, according to reviewers, was a natural fit: 'it is also worth seeing for Brynner's typical performance. The actor radiates such personal dynamism that almost anything he does, even when it is ridiculous, is compelling.'[8]

Figure 7.1 Brynner shot in chiaroscuro in *The Brothers Karamazov*, *Invitation to a Gunfighter*, and *The Double Man*

His female co-star, Britt Ekland, played the part of a private secretary, eye-witness, and potential conspirator in one of the film's few female roles. As *The New York Times* pointed out, in one scene her character 'gets knocked about a bit too brutally and Mr. Brynner is too viciously scratched in return. But the plotting is tight and Mr. Brynner looks exotic and stony enough to keep one's mind off the title.'[9] *Daily News* chimed in, describing Ekland as 'looking fetching and being beaten up by one of the Yul Brynners, the bad one, I think.'[10] For its part, *The Calgary Herald* identified the scene as a reason for seeing the film, describing it in keen detail:

> he slaps her around, back-hands her, mauls her about, twisting her arm and finally ripping off her dress. Britt retaliates by raking his cheek with her fingernails, leaving a claw-like gouging mark. [...] Fury overcomes him and he wants to kill her, seeing his revenge for his son's death in her fragile figure. [...] It's best to see it, since the story is told in the visual medium.[11]

Such scenes were not uncommon in Brynner's films of the 1960s and 1970s where young women were routinely slapped about, assaulted, raped, and killed – and it would seem that they held certain appeal among critics and audiences. Despite the attack and heavy web of suspicion that coats the plot of *The Double Man*, Ekland's Gina Ericson has a heart of gold and, in the final closure, she enters a departing train carriage together with Slater as it (symbolically enough) heads for a tunnel.

The heavy-smoking, glum Dan Slater arguably reappeared as the American Secret Service agent, Pete Novak, in *The File of the Golden Goose* (1969) chasing counterfeiters in London while also avenging the death of his (ex) girlfriend. Both characters were incapable of balancing romantic relationships or family intimacy with their professional lives, and their work was the reason for their loved ones to end up being killed. The plots of both films are motivated by avenging the blood of innocents that has inadvertently landed on the male protagonists' hands. *The File of the Golden Goose* opens with a scene of a boy and a dog playing on a beach near Naples only to discover a young, dead female sex worker, attired in white lingerie, washed ashore: in terms of narrative, the point is not her demise but the counterfeit one-hundred-dollar bill that she had received for her services, and which she is still holding.

In the first shot of Pete Novak he is seen returning from a date with Ann Marlow (played by Hilary Dwyer, twenty-five years his junior) whom he scolds for being 'such a baby' before severing their connection due to her inability to not ask questions about his super-secret line of work. As he walks her to the door, drive-by shooters aiming at him gun her down, leaving Novak, in his dark suit, to realize the loss of his young beloved (clad in scanty yet virginal-cum-sacrificial white). 'There's not much to know about Pete Novak,' the film's poster explains: 'they killed his girl and now he sleeps with his gun!' In his next scene, Novak, now black-hatted, is playing pool as if visually commenting on the endless references to the actor's head being 'as bald as a billiard ball.'

As similar as these two silent, butch, and steely characters were, the latter film received a much chillier reception. Once more commenting on the cinematic sight of Brynner's 'shiny, bald pate,' critics panned it as the only shimmer in the film.[12] 'To a sourly cynical expression, Mr. Brynner simply adds super-muscularity, while flanked by [...] criminal stereotypes,' a reviewer complained.[13] Others characterized him impassively 'stalking through' the film 'with the animation of a computerised robot,' 'steelyeyed, tightlipped,' as if predicting his role as *Westworld*'s robot gunslinger in four years' time.'[14] Novak was indeed a glum man of unblinking fierce stares surrounded by a perpetual cloud of cigarette smoke.

In a montage sequence set to a jazzy score, Novak heads to the saunas of Soho, London, in order to track down a potential suspect, earlier characterized as 'a queer queer.' Moving from one establishment to another, the appropriately disrobed Novak carefully checks out their male patrons. In one sauna, sights of male nudity, demurely shot from behind in a steamy shower, give way to Brynner's baldness while another man is seen rubbing his hairy chest. In another, men congregate in a well-lit downstairs space (dressed in towels), one of them awkwardly touching his back with a bath whisk void of leaves to a self-flagellating effect. In a third, Novak receives a brisk, slappy back massage from a tattooed fellow. While wandering around in a fourth, this one with more of an Oriental theme and female servers, he finally lays his eyes on the man, Harrison (campily played by Charles Grey), all naked in a cubicle with a masseuse.

The film has no actual female characters beyond the very quickly slain love interest, a mobster girl (Jan Rossini) whom Novak slaps about and ties down, and, as something of an afterthought, a female leader of the counterfeit gang (Adrienne Corri) who enters the film at its climax. Whisking her aside with ease, Novak then takes down the escaping gangsters' helicopter with an automated gun to final, satisfying, pyrotechnic effect.

Brynner never was the typical romantic hero, yet his earlier films featured central female characters – the 'I' in *The King and I* being Anna Leonowens, *Anastasia* being named after Ingrid Bergman's part, Deborah Kerr carrying much of *The Journey*, and Kay Kendall most of *Once More, with Feeling!* Few of Brynner's later films would pass the Bechdel test asking whether two female characters converse with one another over other topics than men. Most of his Westerns, spy dramas, and action films are, in fact, so sparsely populated by women that there are no scenes where two women could converse about any topics whatsoever. Featured female characters were romantic or sexual interests, sex workers, or combinations thereof. Their narrative focus was occasionally low enough for reviewers to suggest that these parts could just as well have been edited out.[15]

As the loosening of film censorship, in combination with Brynner's work on European co-productions, allowed for increasing displays of female nudity, these women came to occupy a highlighted role as eye-candy, as in the scantily clad women – both dancing, sauna-working, and dead – in *The File of the Golden Goose*. These dynamics did not go unnoticed, with reviewers pointing out the visual credentials and 'proffered bosom interest' catered by *Catlow*'s female Mexican 'tiger-cat' and 'spit-fire' characters (mainly Daliah Lavi's Rosita), or by the 'buxom whore' (Lainie Kazan's Estusha) of *Romance of a Horsethief*, 'lusty mistress, proprietress of the local bordello. In the film's most comic moment Miss Kazan attempts to distract Brynner with a song (and a generous display of her formidable cleavage).'[16] Gertrude Lawrence was twenty-two years Brynner's senior when the two subtly romanced onstage in *The King and I*: by now, these age dynamics had firmly flipped, female leads being systematically two decades younger than Brynner. The overall gender dynamics had much to do with the established conventions and intended audiences of genre films: Westerns, action films, and spy thrillers that all 'focus on men in conflict with other men.'[17] This makes these dynamics no less noticeable, or remarkable.

Black-hatted men (and Villa)

Of Brynner's Westerns, *The Magnificent Seven* (1960) was the first, and the most successful. In an adaptation of *Seven Samurai*, he played Chris Adams, a Texan hired gun who assembles a group of seven to protect a poor Mexican town against a gang of marauding bandits. 'Americanizing a familiar and formal Oriental theme seems to be the first conscious formalizing of the Western as a classic movie form,' a critic remarked.¹⁸ It was fitting for one of Hollywood's most Orientalist stars to be a key engine behind the enterprise, his own ambiguous presence gesturing towards both east and west as 'Chris, apparently Americano but with a faint aura of the Orient still about him.'¹⁹ 'I went into this part with a clear head,' Brynner himself pointed out: 'I realize my looks limit the roles I can play, but I felt this part was safe since the story was set in Mexico and I am again a "foreigner".'²⁰ Although characterized as 'slightly Central European,' Brynner's pack leader was also considered a suitably 'handsome, laconic, steel-nerved Cajun' with 'femme appeal' as a variation of the 'silent, immobile type' who 'keeps his hat on, plays it cool and rumbles volcano-style.'²¹ His was a 'philosophical, hardened gunslinger' who was 'cool and pantherlike in movement, sparing of speech.'²²

Chris Adams is introduced as a butch man either unconcerned with racial segregation or resistant to it. A hearse drives up the main street of a small Western town, then stops. A traveling corset salesman (Val Avery) has seen a man get shot in the middle of the street and wants him properly buried after witnessing people merely pass him by. The undertaker (Whit Bissell), however, cannot perform the rite. Adams appears at the sidelines in a black hat and a dark gray shirt, with cigars tucked in his front pocket, and leans in to listen. The problem, the undertaker explains, is that the deceased 'Old Sam was an Indian' and many in the town object to his body being mixed in the same soil with white corpses. Due to racial segregation, he is considered 'unfit' to be buried on Boot Hill, despite there being 'nothing up there but murderers, cutthroats and derelict old barflies.' This could, however, happen, should someone be willing to drive the hearse up the hill with the risk of being gunned down themselves.

'Oh, hell,' Adams says with a low, gravelly voice, 'if that's all that's holding things up, I'll drive the rig,' walks over and climbs on. Among the onlookers, a young man – Steve McQueen's Vin Tanner – asks for a gun from another bystander who happily obliges.²³ Tanner then walks to the hearse and, rather than taking aim at Adams, climbs on: the two start ahead, sharing their experiences of action drying up across the West as they ride up the hill. Onlookers follow with varying degrees of interest and the men continue, shooting those who try to take them down: once at the graveyard, volunteers step up to carry the casket as the theme music swells. Properly impressed by the performance, the Mexican villagers seeking defence from a murdering bandit gang led by Calvera (Eli Wallach, in a heavy coat of makeup), know just who their preferred hired gun might be.

Figure 7.2 Chris Adams, and *Westworld* robot

The opening scene is one of deadpan nerves-of-steel, balls-of-lead macho bravado where a man may blink when the tip of his cigar gets shot off – but not much – and where men measure and admire each other's gunmanship as their primary form of social relating. This is not a film where characters grow, where additional depth is created through flashbacks, or where action needs much motivating: it is simply the action that defines and motivates the characters. The taciturn Adams is a black-clad surface for masculine fantasies of resolution, grit, and gut who, for reasons poorly explained, decides to fight for the villagers even when their case seems doomed, and even though there is no money involved. He is possibly a man with a strong moral compass; possibly none.

Despite the film's eventual fame, it was not a unanimous hit among American critics – in fact it was initially something of a flop – and grew into a notable box office success only with its international releases.[24] The film's reception was mixed, with some describing it as a failure: 'juvenile,' 'tedious,' 'dismal,' 'Bushido to bushwhackers' with 'explosive outbursts of the most intense violence.'[25] Others welcomed the adaptation for its simplicity and rhythm.[26] For its part, *The New York Times* dubbed the film 'a pallid, pretentious and overlong reflection of the Japanese original' (even though the film was more than an hour shorter than *Seven Samurai*) and refused to accept Brynner as a plausible cowboy.[27] This speaks of the difficulties involved in Brynner breaking away from his career mold to date so as to move into the quintessentially American genre, yet this was a transition that he eventually managed, and mastered. Kurosawa's film remains a canonized favorite among art cinema audiences. For its part, Sturges's version is currently considered a classic Western, spawning sequels and remakes.

If *Magnificent Seven* received mixed reviews, the ones for the sequel, *Return of the Seven* (1966), were straightforwardly negative, with critics highlighting both the film's degree of violence and overall lack of interest.[28] The plot of *The Magnificent Seven* involved a group of Americans rescuing Mexicans. In the sequel, the group saves Mexicans from slave labour:

> [S]o self-sufficient are the seven [...] that the natives aren't even permitted to load their guns during the attacks. Brynner's Chris is a bald Baden-Powell who says 'hell' too much. He rides taller than tall, bringing hope to one and all, including a priest. He is, in short, a bore.[29]

The first shot of Adams is at a bullring where he is leaning on a fence in a pose near-identical to the one in his introductory scene in *The Magnificent Seven*, wearing the same clothes. We first see him from the waist down, as the camera follows a man (Jordan Christopher's Manuel) crawling on the ground among the spectators. As the man looks up, both he and the viewers see Chris Adams smoking a cigar, ignoring the crawling. At this point, there was no need to introduce the character's previously established persona, yet the chosen perspective literally establishes him as one to look up to. Described by reviewers as 'strutting around like the cock-of-the-walk,' Brynner's character – like the rest of the film – was now, however, accused of being too over-the-top in its machismo:[30]

> [S]waggering through this all is the black-shirted, booted, hatted, spurred, and belted King of Siam. Brynner's walk deserves an essay in itself so suffice to say here that it promises tigerish action which never materialises. Radiating menace (remember, Brynner has read the script and knows just how bad it is) the feared gunman who once led *The Magnificent Seven* then compiles his group of seven to take on some 260 enemies.[31]

The *South China Morning Post* simply recommended the film for 'the western fan who enjoys mass slaughter.'[32] This unenthusiastic reception did not hinder the production of Brynner's next Western, *Villa Rides* (1968). This was Brynner's only realized biopic: Pancho Villa being a man of fame, the issue was not so much explaining or motivating the character but rather interpreting him. The film's opening aerial shot was accompanied by the text: 'This film is dedicated to PANCHO VILLA an ardent patriot, a beloved tyrant who lived larger than life. His personal magnetism, his simple uncluttered idealism, made him a hero in his time.' This already suggests much of how the interpretation comes about – that is, the degree to which Brynner's Villa channels the performer's star image, and vice versa. Villa is first seen attending to his horse's hoof and then leading his men to shoot down enemy soldiers busy hanging his supporters. Describing the Mexican soil as both his wife and mistress, Villa broods, sneers, and leads his men with panache. His dark wig, moustache, and black attire aside, there is an echo of King Mongkut to Brynner's Villa who stubbornly demands to fly a plane solo with only the most rudimentary guidance and who dictates a message with the staccato gestures and emphasis of the Siamese ruler.

Reviewers paid little attention to Brynner's fit for the part – this being only a notch more surprising than the lack of such discussion in connection with *Viva Zapata!* (Elia Kazan, 1952) starring Marlon Brando in the title role as Villa's fellow revolutionary ally and Mexican national hero. According to a review, 'Brynner struts less in the title role,' depicting Villa as a 'sophisticated human being, but an exciting and inspiring one just the same.'[33] Others were less kind, arguing that 'Yul Brynner's characterization of Villa is most unsympathetic. He portrays the rebel leader as a paranoid and sadistic agitator with none of the enobling heroic dimensions of a patriot.'[34] His Villa, 'bloodthirsty' and of 'brutal vigor,' had 'no redeeming feature to counteract the bloody carnage which director Buzz Kulik's merciless camera examines in precise and graphic detail.'[35] While Charles Bronson's 'super violent,' 'ambidexterous and trigger-happy aide' was singled out for injecting 'liveliness and humour into the sordid business of guerrilla warfare,' the film was classified as a 'shoot-'em-up adventure' not calling 'for sensitive character or dramatic development.'[36]

These three Westerns, despite their mutual differences, were fairly straightforward genre films depicting Brynner as a group (or revolutionary army) leader facing, and conquering, a superior enemy: in this, they were not too distant from his Taras Bulba. There was, nevertheless, a distinct transformation in the roles he played thereafter. With the exception of the macho characters in *The File of the Golden Goose* and *Battle of Neretva* (both released in 1969), his roles grew increasingly artificial, flamboyant, and even campy.

In-your-face

Much of this was evident in Brynner's return to Westerns in the Italian *Adíos, Sabata* (1970). The film's plot revolves around a wagon of gold that Brynner's dandy hired gun is paid to help steal for the republican forces from the occupying Austrians during the short reign of Emperor Maximilian I in 1860s Mexico, and various acts of deceit. *Adíos, Sabata* is the second part of the 'Sabata trilogy,' Spaghetti Westerns directed by Gianfranco Parolini, and the only one starring Brynner rather than Lee van Cleef. The three films are – understandably – stylistically similar in focusing on the main characters' astonishing prowess as gunmen and featuring much shooting and explosions in the Wild West, complete with saloon-brothels. Brynner's gunslinger is nevertheless much more flamboyant than van Cleef's: in contrast to the latter's black suits and neat shirts, he struts through the film in fringed black suede, the shirt semi-open to display a chest decorated with a large medallion. The Schubert-piano-playing Sabata exudes a degree of glam sophistication similar to Jules Gaspard d'Estaing of *Invitation to a Gunfighter*, while his impassive countenance is similar to the Westworld robot that Brynner was about to portray.

Like *The Magnificent Seven*, the film opens with white-clad Mexican peasants facing nasty trouble. In the first scene, a priest complains of there being 'too much violence in the world' to the children of a small town pestered by an armed gang. One of the children hurries over to ask for help from their friend, Sabata, who is introduced as something akin to God's right hand. The next scene features an Austrian firing squad gunning down Mexican villagers. Sabata himself first appears in the third scene set at the Texas Bountyhunters Agency, calmly stepping up to a pile of wooden planks, his right hand resting on a gun and the left holding a gun belt that hangs across his chest. Dressed all in black except for a reddish shawl casually thrown over his shoulder, Sabata stands on the elevation, the fringes on his sleeves gently waving in the wind, ready for a face-off with the marauding gang.

A literal cockfight then ensues as Sabata fires at a weathercock placed at the centre of the yard. His opponent reciprocates and the two wait for the metal rooster to stop spinning as their cue to start a shootout.[37] In order to display his superiority and blasé attitude, Sabata removes the ammunition from his decorative harmonica gun and casually lifts it to his shoulder. As in *The Long Duel*, Brynner stands immobile as the camera zooms closer and closer to his face, his expression revealing little beyond a small, knowing smirk. As the action starts, he sticks in a side-fed magazine, shoots his three antagonists with ample ammunition, then takes out and lights a cigar placed in the very last chamber (for additional display of panache, he shoots down a fence so that one of his enemies ends up lying on the ground; another is gunned into a coffin, which is then shot shut). The scene ends with Sabata handing over a purse of coins to the white-clad Mexican child admiring his handiwork.

Sabata is next seen playing the saloon piano to classy effect, hardly blinking an eye when an Austrian throws a dagger through his sheet music. When the man challenges him to a gunfight, Sabata sits down, leisurely lifts up his legs and, as the man draws, kills him with a small flip of his foot resting close enough to the gun to make it go off, losing none of his lethal accuracy. The overall style is, in short, fantastic. Sabata is a stiff-walking man of swagger, purposeful motion, supreme gunmanship, ingenious trap tricks, and the occasional one-liner who rides a dark, shiny horse. All this befits a film of deliberate comic book sensibility that is populated by blonde evil Austrians, innocent suffering Mexicans, and a colorful group of mercenaries, many a killing and hardly any blood to be spotted, where extras fall 'off roofs in graceful death-falls.'[38] The film's sole accredited female role is that of a nameless saloon dancer with no actual lines to deliver (played by Nieves Navarro García as Susan Scott) under whose skirts the camera peeps as she twirls on a table.

The film was no hit among critics. 'The laconic Brynner, astride a prancing sable stallion and wearing a grim expression and black gunslinger's outfit he affected 'way back in *The Magnificent Seven* simply gets a lot of exercise this time. There is little that's magnificent in *Adios, Sabata* other than the scenery, which obviously isn't man made.'[39] Paying little attention to the differences between Chris Adams's dark gray and black denim and Sabata's flamboyant fringes, this *New York Times* reviewer continued to characterize the film as 'mostly shooting and gore,' joining others concerned with its degree of violence. The body count of *Adíos, Sabata* – one critic counting some ninety in total – became a specific point of conversation, so that the film's 'vague trite plot' was

Figure 7.3 Sabata, a gunslinger with flair

seen as a mere excuse for showcasing killings 'for the sake of portraying slaughter.'[40] 'There's no skimping on means of execution, either,' another critic complained, calculating a sharp 116 deaths:

> Firing squads, Gatling guns, nitroglycerin explosions, and derringer hidden in boots all get their turn, and for those with special tastes, one man is crushed behind a door, another gets a broadside from the guns in a model ship, and a third has a gargantuan sack of grain dropped on his unsuspecting head, while a trio of lads are felled by ping pong ball-sized lumps of lead that one of the characters, a churlish mute, propels with his feet. Yes, his feet.
> Standing tall in the midst of all this carnage is Yul Brynner, clothed in fetching black fringed leather pants, matching decollete shirt, plus a hat which never comes off and an optional red and black blanket that can be draped negligently over either shoulder. It's what all mass murderers are wearing this year.[41]

There seems to have been little contextual appreciation among reviewers for Spaghetti Westerns as variations of genre fiction operating with their own, fantastic logic – or for *Adiós, Sabata*'s particular tongue-in-cheek aesthetics in particular. Accusing contemporary Westerns for feasting on 'pointless display of Italianate violence,' the *Los Angeles Times* made the 1971 *Catlow*'s relative lack of gore and light-hearted mode points of modest acclaim.[42] This mode is evident from the very start: *Catlow* opens to credits and a herd of cows kicking up clouds of dust to an upbeat banjo score. A man appears on horseback in a straw cowboy hat, clad in blue denim and a brown leather vest, his nose and mouth covered with a scarf. As he pulls down the scarf, Brynner's Jed Catlow greets viewers with a pearly, satisfied smile. The effect is upbeat inasmuch as it is offbeat for those familiar with Brynner's introduction scenes to date – for even the hard-partying Dimitri of *The Brothers Karamazov* had an air of decadent menace about him. The fully denim-clad Catlow, however, just comes across as a happy, working man (even if he is stealing the cattle in question, and seldom parts with his gun).

When Catlow next appears, it is after we have seen a Marshal (Richard Crenna) attacked by a Native American fighter (whom he then kills). Laughing, Catlow scolds the man: 'Ben Cowan. When are you gonna learn? That badge is only a target for trouble.' As it turns out, the Marshal was on his way to arrest Catlow, his old buddy. Released the year after *Adiós, Sabata*, *Catlow* was equally, if differently, tongue-in-cheek in style and the film's plot similarly revolves around stolen gold. It nevertheless has the specific tone of a buddy movie that Brynner moves through with flashing smiles, jovial grins, and the occasional 'howdy.' His means of playing a happy-go-lucky character, a reviewer complained, 'is to crease his visage into a grimace and to periodically emit hearty bellows of laughter.'[43] According to another, Brynner 'grins and sprawls his way through the role of *Catlow*, relying more on personal charm than acting.'[44] It is no wonder that *The New York Times* identified the end-product as 'somewhat too aggressively agreeable':

> With everybody pretty much a protagonist, major antagonisms are pushed to one side, reserved for occasional Indians, who do most of the film's dying, and for a hired killer (Leonard Nimoy), who also dies, but whose main function is to reveal the cruel scars of an action that would otherwise be no more than happy highjinks with deadly weapons.[45]

For *The Guardian*, Brynner, 'pate as shiny as ever and looking remarkably as if time has stood still in his part of a devil-may-care maverick cattleman' gave a satisfying performance, turning in 'a formidable amount of the old roguish charm while belting the daylights out of his sluttish girl friend (Daliah Lavi) and shooting attackers through the sole of his boot.'[46] Lavi's Rosita is one of large gestures, semi-hysterical fits, scheming, and romantic adoration for Catlow. In an eventual confrontation, she attacks him with a knife and kicks him in the groin for comic effect; he punches her in the face in return. The film's other memorable moments include a fight scene with the hired killer, Miller (Leonard Nimoy) who, surprised whilst bathing, battles in the nude, and Catlow's emergent stubble beard. There is an unsettling, even creepy undertone to Brynner's joking maverick cowboy's grins, smirks, and smiles, given how he used similar gestures to convey ill intent (for example, in *The Light at the Edge of the World* and *Westworld*, discussed below).

Figure 7.4 Evil and jovial grins (*The Light at the Edge of the World* and *Catlow*)

Particularly nasty pieces of work

Sabata's combination of flamboyance and readiness to kill was akin to Brynner's roles in *The Light at the Edge of the World* (1971) and *Fuzz* (1972), both combining a taste for luxury with menacing presence and murderous intent. An especially elaborate and nasty combination of opulence and murder came together in the former. Based on a Jules Verne Story, the Spanish-French-Italian co-production cast Kirk Douglas's lighthouse keeper, Denton, against a group of wrecker pirates lead by Brynner's 'vicious but sybaritic captain' Jonathan Kongre.[47] Kongre first emerges from his ship's hold some twenty minutes into the film, his bald head appearing first and a decorative black coat soon following after. The music is menacing; Kongre is holding a black riding crop. At this point, viewers have already witnessed his crew disemboweling Fernando Rey's lighthouse keeper. In the following shot, Kongre is shown reclining in a dinghy, dressed in black all the way to his shiny leather boots, a bare-chested minion rowing him ashore as a young, Black, male servant stands at the helm in courtly clothing. Next, a whinnying white Arabian horse is lifted onto a raft to accompany him. There is little doubt as to Kongre being both exotic and evil from the outset: the question is rather one of scales of ill-intent, which turn out to be expansive, drastic, and imaginative.

When Denton and Kongre eventually meet, the former has been thrown to the floor and the latter looks on impassively, framed by a crystal wine carafe and gilded antiquities. 'Allow me to introduce myself,' Kongre says, channeling the Rolling Stones's 'Sympathy for the Devil': 'I'm Jonathan Kongre. Your Captain.' As Denton gets up, we see more of the room hastily decorated with black fabrics, classic paintings, and antiques, and also featuring a group of pirates partially clothed in silks, pelts, ornaments, and military pieces. In the middle of a stone dining table lies an offering of pineapple, bananas, grapes, oranges, and pears on a silver bowl, made remarkable by virtue of the location being close to Tierra del Fuego.

'Do I detect an American accent?' Kongre asks with a low voice: 'How very agreeable. I used to have dealings with your countrymen during the happy days of the slave trade. Most profitable. Most revealing about human nature,' as the young, Black server (slave?) offers coated lobster. After witnessing the gutting of his pet monkey, Denton is hung upside down from the lighthouse and then dragged over to meet Kongre's handsome horse, now sporting a golden headpiece complete with a sharp unicorn horn. When Denton is let loose from his noose, Kongre

Figure 7.5 The diabolical Captain Kongre

begins a hunt with the intent of piercing him with said horn. The fur-clad Kongre is next seen leading his men to misdirect a ship in order to loot it and slaughter the passengers. As this then transpires, the only female passenger (and the film's only female character, Arabella Ponsonby, played by Samantha Eggar) salvaged from the shipwreck gets not only humiliated but raped and killed by the pirate crew. The *Minneapolis Tribune* was unimpressed:

> Its kind would get an Oscar from a Motion Picture Academy of athletic vampire bats. It's touch and go whether the blood outflows the action or the action outjumps the blood. Belly-stabbing leads the various techniques, but hand amputation, immolation, hoisting upside down, rending and a neat bullet in the forehead all play their parts.[48]

This was despite MGM having cut out 15 to 20 minutes of the film in order to keep it from getting an X-rating – which, according to another critic, it would have well deserved for dwelling on 'floating drowned victims and the ripping of skin with boating hooks, etc.'[49] *The Guardian* dryly pointed out that, despite the edits, the outcome 'appears to be violent enough as it is, though we now see precious little of the pet monkeys stabbed, humans tortured and the female lead being gang-banged. The blood is out, the intimations are still there.'[50] Wondering whether the edits had caused the film to disintegrate, *Monthly Film Bulletin* continued: 'As it now stands, the action is grotesquely unconvincing, lurching erratically through a series of aimless chases and killings and tortures without ever getting anywhere.'[51]

These views were shared by an appalled 27-year-old viewer who, in a letter to the *Los Angeles Times*, complained about the sights he had just witnessed: 'I [...] thought I had seen just about every type of violence in movies. Then the shock came when I attended the showing of the film *The Light at the Edge of the World*, incredibly so.' He then went on to describe the scenes depicted, from disembowelment to a 'stomach cut open, heart pierced with a lance and head cut off,' a female survivor 'stripped nude, then raped and murdered by the pirates after she has witnessed a companion's hand amputated and the knife-torture of a wrecked ship's officer,' a surviving crew member's chest being cut open 'and the flesh pulled with a hook from his body.' All this, the viewer protested, in a GP-rated film 'playing opposite *Pinocchio* in Glendale!'[52]

The following year, Brynner played a rather similar character, albeit one now residing in contemporary Boston. In the Burt Reynolds and Raquel Welch vehicle, *Fuzz*, Brynner's mysterious 'Deaf Man,' Sordo, is a master criminal running an extortion and bomb racket. As Sordo first appears onscreen, he is sitting in an armchair by a fireplace with his back to the camera, surrounded by gilded antique furniture and statuettes. It is his left hand that we initially see, sporting both a gold signet ring and a golden wristwatch as he reaches for a jar of Beluga caviar on a sidetable. Meanwhile, his Black female assistant, Rochelle (Tamara Dobson, soon of *Cleopatra Jones* fame) – whom he characterizes as 'a marvellous empty-headed bitch' – keys a harpsichord in the background for sophisticated mood. As minions arrive to bring batteries for his hearing aid, the Deaf Man stands up, holding one of them by the necktie and setting the tone for his character defined by vehemence. As with Kongre, there is no motivation for the character beyond his consistently evil streak, greed, and love of luxury. These, again, can be seen as motivated through Orientalist tropes of frivolity and exoticism 'that marginalize the Other as spectacle through disguise.'[53] Like Kongre, Sordo has a lust for both material things, cruelty, and sex within unequal gendered power dynamics.

In the narrative closure, this champagne-sipping antagonist, mastermind of an extortion-murder plan against the Boston powers-that-be, clad in a dapper three-piece suit, is shot and set on fire before falling into the sea. In one of the film's many plotlines, young men target and kill homeless men by setting them on fire. Two days after *Fuzz's* television screening, the *Los Angeles Times* reported young men pouring gasoline on a woman and setting her aflame in Boston. Despite racial tensions playing a part in the incident, the blame was firmly planted on the film – and on 'other films making sport of nauseating violence' for inspiring the act.[54] This public contention over screen violence, which built up to the 'video nasties' debates of the following decade, marked the reception of much of Brynner's 1970s film work, as was already evident in the reviews for *Adiós, Sabata* and *The Light at the Edge of the World* critical of their degrees of gore.

To be precise, such complaints had emerged already a decade prior. The 1962 *Taras Bulba* was critiqued for violence and being a 'bloodbath,' *The New York Times* identifying it as a 'brazen display of slaughterous clashes between cossacks and Polish cavalry' and *The Guardian* arguing that its lack of acting and directing skill were compensated with 'bubonic plague, whipping scenes, boiling oil, filicide, threats of castration, hands being chopped off and a "U" certificate.'[55] Further critiques complained of bloodlust and 'screen massacre' involving 'scenes of physical violence (wrestling bouts, sword fights, cavalry charges, whippings, and plague)'; 'The greater part of the film is taken up with violence (to prepare you for which a gentleman has his right arm lopped off in the first reel).'[56] The *Toronto Daily Star* saw the film as symptomatic of a broader Hollywood 'flagellant syndrome':

> No pre-World War II spectacle has been free, if memory serves, from the lash – and in *Taras Bulba* it's laid out with a will on at least three occasions, once most savagely. [...] The floggings appear largely superfluous, dragged in for the sheer joy of showing what cord thudding into flesh looks like in Eastmancolor and echoes like in stereophonic sound.[57]

For its part, the British trade paper, *Kinematograph Weekly*, lamented screen violence and the plot of *The File of the Golden Goose* before its premiere (on the basis of the press fact sheet). 'The synopsis reveals a drowning, a shooting, a running-over, a knifing and drug-taking' – plus characters 'who would "slaughter their grandmothers at the drop of a cigar butt",' the magazine puzzled, referencing its own earlier prediction of an increase in film violence and arguing that the recent assassination of Senator Robert Kennedy should have been enough to curb the disturbing trend.[58]

Interviewed during the making of the 1973 *Westworld* on violence being possibly overdone in contemporary films 'to the point that we are getting used to it and are no longer impressed,' Brynner responded by addressing its diverse qualities. 'I think that violence has to be treated in a certain manner,' he started, arguing that 'very starkly realistic violence is unwelcome and, in fact, unpleasant as well as uninteresting.' As for worthwhile screen violence, this was of the inner and more indirect kind: 'violence by implication and emotions, violence in thoughts,' he suggested, was more frightening.[59] Meanwhile, such subtlety was not always apparent in Brynner's own film work.

Repetitions

Some of the repetitions across Brynner's roles resulted from typecasting and others from his performance style; yet others were spotted by critics as intertextual references involving more or less intentional play. This was certainly the case with Brynner's role as robot in *Westworld* that he played as a variation of his previous black-hatted gunslinger parts as Chris Adams of *The Magnificent Seven* and *The Return of the Seven*. If Adams was characterized as a 'deadly efficient, humane killer,' his machine doppelganger was 'mechanized death personified.'[60] The intertextual connection between the two characters was obvious, including their identical clothing (black hat, dark gray shirt, black jeans, black boots) now fitted on a robotic body.

Westworld is set in Delos – a theme park simulating life in Imperial Rome, a Medieval European court, and 1880s American West, respectively. Tickets cost $1000 per day, and Delos caters to the wishes of its wealthy patrons. Its vision of the American West is very much a facsimile of a Hollywood film set complete with humanoid robots performing the roles of saloon keepers, gunslingers, and brothel workers. 'A movie about movies,' it shows 'people living out their movie fantasies in an amusement park.'[61] The film was written and directed by Michael Crichton, and its narrative warning against the power of science and technology not only predates but very much resembles the 1993 *Jurassic Park* based on the author's later novel.

Having arrived in Delos, visitors are 'soon bedding whores and challenging gunmen with the best of them, aware that the most dangerous bar brawl won't harm a hair on their well protected heads. The robots, Brynner's gunslinger included, are always on the losing side.'[62] Brynner's robot first makes its entrance as two fresh male arrivals enjoy their whiskeys in a saloon. Brynner's black-hatted machine appears next to them. 'Sloppy with your drink,' it starts in the classic style of a Western troublemaker, as one of the men coughs up his whiskey; 'He needs his mama.' As the man thus addressed finally replies, he is met with a literal steely gaze: 'You say something boy?' A perfect replica of a Western bad guy, the unblinking robot is asking for it, and very soon meets its fate when gunned down in a duel. All fixed and reassembled, the robot – stiff-backed, steely-eyed, and determined – briskly reappears the next day at the men's hotel room door, only to be shot down anew (and to fall through the second-story window for additional cinematic effect).

In what Gaïd Girard sees as playing with both the generic conventions of the American Western and the straight, white male dominance of 1970s cinema, Westworld patrons have a grand old expensive time drinking, having sex with, partaking in bar fights with, and killing robots of perfect human likeness while delivering clichéd movie lines in the process ('he won't trouble you anymore'; 'you wanna try me?').[63] Within all this, Brynner's robot has no depth or purpose beyond what is programed into it – to perform a function in a theme park so that paying guests get the pleasure of eliminating him. The status quo does not, however, hold as the robots begin to suffer from a general system malfunction spreading in viral ways: now it becomes their single purpose to kill the patrons instead. Described as an opponent impossible to beat, always a step ahead ('There's nothing you can do. If he's after you he'll get you. You haven't got a chance'), the robot stalks the remaining protagonist (Richard Benjamin) as relentlessly as a machine might, all the way to their final showdown.

The robot's mechanical motions and upright posture can be seen as commenting on the degree to which Brynner had repeated such gestures and poses, with only minor adjustments to his emotionally stumped and technically superior gunslingers, over two decades. A more accurate point would be that Brynner's stylized presence afforded *Westworld* with much of its appeal precisely due to this reverb. For Crichton, he was something of a perfect cast: 'If anyone really built a place like Westworld, they probably would make the gunfighter robot in the image of Yul Brynner.'[64] Critics agreed, arguing that the actor had 'truly found his forte' in his 'appropriately wooden' performance in a robot role fitting 'him like a glove':

'Brynner, who has been behaving increasingly like a robot in his recent roles, finally has the opportunity to give a persuasive performance.'[65] If, in *Return of the Seven*, critics saw the 'Old Stoneface' beating 'every previous record of utter impassivity' to the effect of 'the leaden balloon for tedium,' in *Westworld* his lack of expression contributed to much of the character's menace and made Brynner dominate the scenes he appeared in.[66] With 'eyes glowing with an uncanny metallic shine' and 'as cold and inhuman as the circuitry and plastic he is made of,' he was identified as 'the cinema's most memorable clockwork monster since Brigitte Helm' of *Metropolis* (Fritz Lang, 1927).[67]

Despite mixed reviews and content warnings pertaining to violence, *Westworld* was a box office success.[68] It was followed by the 1976 *Futureworld* where Brynner made a brief cameo. Although being on the screen for only a few minutes, he was visibly present in the film's promotion as a starring actor whose face graces the covers of the film's DVD and BluRay releases to date, in ways pointing to his promotional star status over the film's actual male lead, Peter Fonda. *Le Monde* identified Brynner as 'somewhat parodying himself' in both films, yet it was the latter where self-referentiality and oddity particularly intermeshed.[69]

In *Futureworld*, Brynner's killer robot does not re-emerge rebuilt in the amusement park itself but rather in the female protagonist's (Blythe Danner) dream – and, given the advanced state of the film's futuristic 1985 technology, dreams can now be videotaped and played back for

Figure 7.6 A fantasy sex robot

all to witness.⁷⁰ Fixing its eyes of metal shimmer on her, a slight smile playing on its lips, the robot is both a figure of predatory menace and, as the scene proceeds, an object of her sexual desire – its metallic eyes now implying a different kind of intent as the two fall into embrace. At the same time, the robot's perpetually open eyes and awkward pose point to inorganic, uncanny, and disturbing artifice. The altered state of reality afforded by the dream sequence balances the threat of death with sensuous bliss, and menace with desire, transforming the killer machine into something of a sex robot. In doing so, the scene brings together the elements of physical force, strangeness, and sex appeal that were elementary to Brynner's star image. 'Brynner has performed like a robot for most of his movie career,' a reviewer could not but argue: 'it is a chance to report that in *Futureworld* he is almost human, compared to just about everybody else, that is.'⁷¹

Age, sex, and violence

While not completely void of humor and lightness, Brynner's later film roles were premised on the recognizably hard, masculine edge of his star image. This similarly applied to Kirk Douglas, Burt Lancaster, and Charlton Heston whose films grew more violent by the 1970s, following a trend set by the likes of Charles Bronson and Clint Eastwood. Of these three, Heston perhaps most notably ventured into the hairy and sweaty terrain in dystopian science-fiction and action in postapocalyptic films such as *The Planet of the Apes* (Franklin J. Schaffner, 1968), *The Omega Man* (Boris Sagal, 1971), and *Soylent Green* (Richard Fleischer, 1973). The latter shared a double bill with *Westworld* in many an American film theatre.⁷²

Brynner's 1975 *The Ultimate Warrior* was set in postapocalyptic New York where '[p]lague, privation and pestilence have reduced civilization to the survival of the fittest. Roaming the streets like dog-packs, scavengers kill and loot the unwary or enfeebled.'⁷³ His urban warrior, Carson, is recruited to help a vegetable-growing commune, led by Max von Sydow's Baron, in their fight against a violent, pillaging gang. The film's trailer opens with the huge mushroom cloud of a nuclear explosion. A voice-over declares, 'after the ultimate war comes the ultimate warrior,' as a fade transition reveals a topless Brynner standing as still as a man-statue.

Figure 7.7 Carson, a man-statue

This statuesque pose is from Carson's introductory scene where the warrior stands immobile with a leather belt tight at his waist, his muscles tensed, standing on an elevation nonverbally advertising his physical wares: he is first seen through the lens of Baron's binoculars as he eyes the display on offer. As Baron and his men go to make their offer to the man, the warrior is shown from behind, starting with his bald head as the camera pans down to his back, his waist (a knife tucked into his belt), and underneath his crotch – the men are seen approaching from between his legs, gathering at his feet. As they glance at Carson from below, Brynner, despite his modest height, towers as a monument of masculine force that others depend on for their survival. He listens to the offer with his eyes closed, both impassive and tense, only slowly opening them once the men have turned to leave. When we first see his body move, it takes on and defeats a band of goons who have attacked Baron's men.

Sarcastic reviewers characterized Carson as 'an unhappy blend of Superman, samurai, and *Dollar* Western hero' and 'an inarticulate Super-thug'; 'in spite of being absolutely uninventive in battle – he always kills with the same Shakespearean uppercut of the dagger – Yul defends his master's tomatoes impressively.'[74] Identified as 'an uninspiring flop,' the film was broadly critiqued for its degrees of violence, carnage, and murder (including a scene where Carson cuts off his own arm), and it was banned for these reasons in several countries – Finland, my own country of residence, included.[75]

The reception of Brynner's very last film, the Italian 1976 *Con la rabbia aglo occhi/Death Rage*, where he played a retired mob hitman – a legend in his trade – avenging the death of his younger brother, was similarly unenthusiastic.[76] The first scene with Brynner opens to mellow, semi-funky music, and the camera panning the New York City skyline; the shot ends with a car arriving under the Manhattan Bridge, a man steps out. A man in a black cap and leather coat is fishing on the East River: this is the retired killer Peter Marciani, already highly spoken of. It is only when he turns to look at the visitor that his face is shown, on it a grim, pensive expression. As the visitor standing against the sun starts to speak of the death of his brother, Marciani blinks in apparent confusion, his eyesight becoming muddled in red as the soundtrack gains an electronic, computerized feel to further communicate the trauma involved. As he is told the city and name of his brother's killer, Marciani, now in close-up, responds with a slight grimace, his facial register steely. Opening credits begin, with Brynner's name listed first in red before the film's title. Next, the location is established as Naples. As the camera moves from close-up to mid shot, Marciani is seen clad in business attire, all in black in a dapper suit and turtleneck sweater.

Marciani first catches sight of the film's (only) female character, and his love-interest, the strip-tease artiste Annie (Barbara Bouchet), as she performs at a club to a sultry saxophone number. As viewers, we are positioned to watch him watch her and, as her show progresses, the camera creeps ever closer to Marciani whose expression now communicates startled, acute attraction. By the time she goes topless, his expression is one of predatory determination and as the show ends with full nudity, his lips are parted. As Marciani next meets Annie at a market, she is instantly attracted to the stranger some two decades her senior: in the following scene of the two together, she is naked in his bathrobed arms. Champagne is served on the bed and kissing ensues. After the brief interruption of an enemy acid attack, Marciani is topless and, it is suggested, also fully exposed. The scene bears little resemblance to the subdued gesturing of desire in *Anastasia* or *The King and I*, just as the expanse of exposed female flesh is a far cry from the controlled displays of nudity under the Production Code.

The film's English title, *Death Rage*, played on *Death Wish* (Michael Winner, 1974), the film that made Charles Bronson – supporting actor in *The Magnificent Seven* and *Villa Rides* – a major action star even as it evoked much controversy due to its violence and embrace of vigilante justice.[77]

Figure 7.8 Marciani at a strip show

Despite there being little connection between the films, *Death Rage* was advertised as 'The second chapter of the big city vigilante! BRONSON started it – BRYNNER finishes it!'[78] It was not therefore surprising for most critics to compare the two films, some approaching *Death Rage* as sequel to the 'urban bloodbath,' with a 'corpse rate of about one every five minutes.'[79] Others failed to see a connection, identifying the film simply as a mafia-vengeance picture where Martin Balsam's police character 'tries rather ineffectively to prevent Brynner from shooting half the population of Naples' and where 'Barbara Bouchet wanders around naked with Brynner between shootings.'[80] In addition to the film's violence, Brynner's performance style once again became a source of complaint: 'Presumably Marciani is a human being, but Brynner portrays him with exactly the same stony glare and reptilian repose the actor displayed four years ago while depicting a gunslinger in *Westworld*. That gunslinger was a robot.'[81]

Brynner's final films bring into focus the dilemma of aging for an actor whose star image was built and dependent on physical performance and desirability. At the age of 50, Brynner made the list of male celebrities whom *Cosmopolitan* readers next wanted to see naked, following Burt Reynolds's highly successful centerfold. According to editor Helen Gurley Brown, Brynner 'they want to see bald all over.'[82] Around the time of fighting topless through much of *The Ultimate Warrior* and shooting *Death Rage*, Brynner also starred as a 'lusty, flamboyant adventurer' in the title role of the ill-fated stage musical, *The Odyssey*.[83] Despite being a success among audiences, the play did not charm the critics and, renamed *Home Sweet Homer*, folded in 1976 on the night of its Broadway premiere.[84] 'As Odysseys,' a review wrote, Brynner 'variously pops or narrows his eyes, churns out the machismo and sings rather flat,' another describing a scene where he emerged 'from the seas naked except for the protection offered by a hastily plucked branch.'[85] In short, stylized bodily displays remained Brynner's staple throughout his career, even as their reception began to grow mixed. In their lengthy review of *The Ultimate Warrior*, *The Advocate* (at the time catering to a gay male rather than broader LGBTQ+ readership) addressed Brynner's physical presence in detail:

> Yul Brynner appears in a burst of light, a tough, silent man who looks as if he could slay dragons with his bare hands, build a city in a day, and then ravage all the coeds at Vassar (if Vassar had still existed) without a second thought. As portrayed in the movie, he is indeed the ultimate warrior: bare-chested, aggressive, afraid of nothing – a kind of bald, latter-day Marlboro Man who stirs up fantasies of any kind in men and women alike. [...]

> In person he is a rather short, thickset man who, in the bright light of the day, looks old and tired, scarred from days of decadence, brothels and opium dens. But onscreen – and even onstage in his touring *Odyssey* – he is a man among men, a tall, ageless, supergiant of power.[86]

Exploring a similar friction between Brynner in person – 'rather wrinkled, average-sized,' with a limp – and his sex appeal onstage in *The Odyssey*, another journalist pondered about the alchemy of sex appeal: 'Yul can still set a female heart aflutter. [. . .] Because it's not only good looks and brawn that make a male sex symbol. There is something intangible. Call it charm, call it charisma – Brynner exudes it.'[87]

In a piece not too subtly titled 'Brynner Is Just Too Old for This Kind of Thing,' a Canadian reviewer critiquing *Death Rage* as 'preposterous' was particularly struck by the actor's wrinkled appearance and his character's 'instant love affair, complete with nudity, with a gorgeous blond stripper' where the 'only thing puckered' was his skin. 'Characters like Brynner, with only gimmicks to rely on, have to grow old less than gracefully,' he continued.[88] A fellow critic, unilaterally panning the film (and Brynner's talents), described these love scenes as 'ludicrous, but mercifully brief' and the close-ups as 'particularly grotesque.'[89] These dismayed voices were not the only ones seemingly disturbed by close-ups of Brynner's topless body: 'Put him alongside an undressed female – and Barbara Bouchet is a natural, au naturel – and he freezes with embarrassment. It's the sort of demand that should never be made of a middleaged actor whose selling point is mystery.'[90] 'The movie is so bad it would be rejected at an amateur night for 8 mm movies made by retarded camels,' yet another witty critic exclaimed.[91]

Displays of Brynner's body, athletic as it remained for someone in their mid-fifties, had at this point grown unpalatable to many a reviewer, as close-ups and large screens made its aging hard to miss. Brynner's heavy smoking had had its effect on his skin but age differences among male and female leads being standard film fare in Hollywood, and beyond (consider, for example, Roger Moore's Bond films), the targeting of his looks was nevertheless noteworthy.

Reviewers struggling with Brynner's final cinematic displays had at least seen these two films which were not reviewed by many major newspapers, so that his onscreen career may seem to have ended ahead of time. As Brynner died in 1985, the listing of Brynner's stage and film work compiled by the Associated Press for syndicated use simply left out both *The Ultimate Warrior* and *Death Rage*.⁹² While I will return to posthumous forms of remembrance in Chapter 9, more remains to be said of both Brynner's performance style and the stylization and excess of his onscreen appearances. Zooming in on Brynner's onscreen presence, the following chapter examines its recurrent features, limitations, and camp qualities.

Notes

1. *Philadelphia Daily News*, 25 June 1981, 19.
2. *Modern Screen*, June 1957.
3. *The NY Times*, 28 March 1959; *Good Housekeeping*, March 1959.
4. On European co-productions, see Bergfelder 2000.
5. The beginning is similar to *Port of New York* that starts with a contemplation of a book spread featuring a large photo of Brynner's Vicola, so that the character becomes established as a centerpiece before the actor's onscreen appearance.
6. *Kinematograph Weekly*, 8 April 1967, 11.
7. *The Boston Globe*, 8 May 1968.
8. *South China Morning Post*, 9 August 1967; see also *LA Times*, 22 May 1968.
9. *The NY Times*, 2 May 1968.
10. *Daily News*, 2 May 1968.
11. *The Calgary Herald*, 22 October 1966.
12. *The NY Times*, 3 October 1969; *The Boston Globe*, 16 October 1969.
13. *The NY Times*, 3 October 1969.
14. *SF Examiner*, 18 October 1969; *Toronto Daily Star*, 1 December 1969.
15. This was the case with *Catlow*, see *Daily News*, 21 October 1971.
16. *The Calgary Herald*, 15 January 1972; *The Boston Globe*, 18 November 1971; *The Vancouver Sun*, 27 January 1972; *SF Examiner*, 17 September 1971; *LA Times*, 15 September 1971.
17. Hark 1993, 151.
18. *NY Herald Tribune*, 24 November 1960.
19. *LA Times*, 30 October 1960.
20. *The Austin Statesman*, 2 May 1960.
21. *Sight and Sound*, Spring 1961; *LA Times*, 25 November 1960; *The Washington Post*, 14 October 1960. Brynner keeping his hat on was enough to inspire news items addressing the dilemma, e.g. *The Calgary Herald*, 21 October 1960.
22. *Harrison Reports*, 8 October 1960; *South China Morning Post*, 21 June 1961.
23. There is a heavy cloud of gossip surrounding McQueen and Brynner with stories of onset clashes and rivalry, e.g., *SF Examiner*, 2 November 1960; *The Globe and the Mail*, 18 May 1984. Rock Brynner denies such claims, arguing that the rift only happened, on Brynner's part, when McQueen did not agree to reprise his role in *Return of the Seven* contrary to a previous understanding, see Brynner 1989, 132, 207. Brian Hannan, in his detailed analysis on the making

of the film, argues that the rivalry was on McQueen's part, see Hannan 2015, Kindle edition.
24. For detailed analysis of the film's box office success, see Hannan 2015.
25. *The Hollywood Reporter*, 5 October 1960; *The Globe and Mail*, 26 October 1960; *LA Times*, 30 October 1960.
26. *Variety*, 5 October 1960; *The Guardian*, 15 April 1961; *Arlington Heights Herald*, 27 October 1960.
27. *The NY Times*, 24 November 1960; see also *Monthly Film Bulletin* 1961.
28. *South China Morning Post*, 20 March 1968.
29. *The Washington Post*, 27 October 1966.
30. *The Times of India*, 7 November 1968.
31. *South China Morning Post*, 20 March 1968.
32. *South China Morning Post*, 17 March 1968.
33. *The Times of India*, 20 February 1969.
34. *SF Examiner*, 20 June 1968.
35. Ibid.
36. *The Washington Post*, 13 June 1969; *The Times of India*, 20 February 1969; *The NY Times*, 18 July 1968.
37. The scene has similarities to the one in *Taras Bulba* where Tony Curtis's son is fixing the weathercock on the family's straw-roofed house, then glides down and takes on his very butch father for the first time, unavoidably losing. In a later tavern scene, Taras Bulba's sons are fondly referred to as 'little cocks' to further underline the connotation.
38. *Monthly Film Bulletin* 1973a.
39. *The NY Times*, 23 September 1971.
40. *LA Times*, 16 September 1971; see also *Daily News*, 23 September 1971.
41. *The Washington Post*, 21 August 1971.
42. *LA Times*, 4 November 1971.
43. *The Calgary Herald*, 15 January 1972.
44. *St. Petersburg Times*, 11 November 1971.
45. *The NY Times*, 21 October 1971.
46. *The Guardian*, 15 June 1972.
47. *The NY Times*, 17 July 1971. The film was produced by Douglas's own company (Bryna) and was hence designed as a vehicle for the star: its financing involved twenty-three different deals, see *Sight and Sound*, Fall 1970, 174.
48. *Minneapolis Tribune*, 29 July 1971.
49. *Monthly Film Bulletin* 1973b; *St. Petersburg Times*, 22 June 19, 1971.
50. *The Guardian*, 21 December 1972.
51. *Monthly Film Bulletin* 1973b.
52. *LA Times*, 29 August 1971.
53. Järvinen 2020, 82. Järvinen is building on Achille Mbembe's (2017) analysis of racist logic.
54. *LA Times*, 12 October 1973.
55. *The Montreal Gazette*, 19 January 1963; *The NY Times*, 26 December 1962; *The Guardian*, 5 April 1963.
56. *Australian Women's Weekly*, 19 June 1963; *Monthly Film Bulletin* 1963; *The Tatler*, 24 April 1963.

57. *Toronto Daily Star*, 21 December 1963.
58. *Kinematograph Weekly*, 3 August 1968.
59. *Photoplay*, 23 August 1973, 37.
60. *Kinematograph Weekly*, 17 December 1966, 158; *St. Petersburg Times*, 22 November 1973.
61. *The Washington Post*, 26 September 1973; see also *Monthly Film Bulletin* 1974.
62. *The Guardian*, 14 March 1974.
63. Girard 2018.
64. In *The Daily Telegraph*, 18 July 2020.
65. *South China Morning Post*, 15 May 1977; *SF Examiner*, 28 July 1976; *The Calgary Herald*, 26 November 1973; also *Canberra Times*, 8 May 1974.
66. *South China Morning Post*, 20 March 1968.
67. *Monthly Film Bulletin* 1974; *Boxoffice*, 19 November 1973.
68. *The NY Times*, 22 October 1973; *LA Times*, 24 October 1973; *Cosmopolitan*, February 1974.
69. *Le Monde*, 11 October 1985.
70. *The Austin Statesman*, 23 July 1976.
71. *The Vancouver Sun*, 9 September 1976.
72. *Boxoffice*, 22 December 1975.
73. *St. Petersburg Times*, 15 December 1975.
74. *Monthly Film Bulletin* 1976; *The Observer*, 4 April 1976.
75. *South China Morning Post*, 23 November 1975; *St. Petersburg Times*, 15 December 1975.
76. E.g., *Monthly Film Bulletin* 1977b.
77. See Talbot 2006.
78. E.g., *Boxoffice*, 9 January 1978.
79. *The Ottawa Citizen*, 6 December 1977.
80. *The Globe and Mail*, 14 November 1977.
81. *Toronto Daily Star*, 15 November 1977.
82. *LA Times*, 14 May 1972.
83. *Australian Women's Weekly*, 16 April 1975, 17.
84. *The Washington Post*, 30 January 1975; *The Washington Post*, 7 January 1976.
85. *The Toronto Star*, 27 February 1975; *The Washington Post*, 11 October 1985a.
86. *The Advocate*, 3 December 1975.
87. *Courier–Post*, 29 January 1975.
88. *Edmonton Journal*, 30 November 1977.
89. *St. Petersburg Times*, 11 December 1978.
90. *The Ottawa Citizen*, 6 December 1977.
91. *Ottawa Journal*, 5 December 1977.
92. *St. Petersburg Times*, 11 October 1985.

Chapter 8

Performance style, posturing, and camp

'Flamboyance' was a term frequently associated with Brynner's performances: others included 'strut' and 'swagger.' This vocabulary dates back to his breakthrough in *The King and I*: 'As the semibarbaric King, Yul Brynner struts and frets with [...] virile swagger'; 'striking-looking Yul Brynner [...] plays it flamboyantly and aggressively and even "hams" a little, but he injects terrific vitality into the picture.'[1] The degree of stylization, and indeed hyperbole, involved in many of his onscreen performances was such that, from a contemporary perspective, they can come across as somewhat hammy. This impression is easily supported by the overall artifice of studio-era Hollywood, the overblown hues of Technicolor, and the lavishly designed sets of freely re-imagined historical ships, villages, and abodes where his characters sulked, schemed, and ruled against a backdrop of extras – sometimes hordes of them – building pyramids, fighting decisive battles, and serving up courtly entertainment.

Onscreen, Brynner's body was rigid yet moved with sudden grace, occasionally bursting into song and dance. The accentuated masculinity of his performances remained unaffected by ornate accessories and the occasionally liberal application of makeup which he sported all the way up to *Adiós, Sabata* of 1970. Despite *Newsweek*'s 1958 declaration that Brynner should simply stick to exotic roles – 'He could never get away with being the John Wayne/Cooper cowboy; light comedy is definitely out' – his work expanded across genres from historical and biblical epics to comedies, drama, spy films, Westerns, action, fantasy and sci-fi while nevertheless retaining a readily identifiable – even idiosyncratic – screen presence throughout.[2] This chapter explores Brynner's performance style in terms of its recurrent features, and by zooming in on its embrace of artifice and excess. Starting with a discussion of Brynner's gestural registers and acting techniques in the context of Hollywood's transforming notions of dramatic craft and skill, it moves to considering their limitations through his rather unsuccessful comedy roles, and explores the presence and meanings of camp in his later film work in particular. Throughout, my interest lies in repetitions as the stuff that makes characteristic performance styles.

Acting versus presence

Over the years, critics recurrently suggested that Brynner's idiosyncratic look was more interesting, or magnetic, than his professional skill, so that he was 'more of a personality than an actor.'[3] In 1958, the fan magazine *Picturegoer* complained of Brynner having repeated the same performance in *The King and I*, *The Ten Commandments*, *Anastasia*, and *The Brothers Karamazov*, in roles rife with 'brooding glances and animal vitality': this risked reducing him to an 'exotic personality' making 'a career out of a polished cranium.'[4] The following year, the same critic continued with the suggestion that Brynner had won his Academy Award for his personality rather than for his acting.[5] Similarly reporting on the award, *Elokuva-aitta* characterized Brynner as 'undeniably one of the most interesting actors produced by Hollywood in recent years,' yet one who 'so far has absolutely caused more sensation and attention with his smooth-shaven head than with his acting skill.'[6] The magazine had previously raised the issue in connection with *The King and I* ('Just on the basis of this film I can't say whether Brynner has anything else to give to film art than his hairless head: as the king of Siam his acting is based more on effects than skill') and *Anastasia* ('Yul Brynner with his bald head boasts dynamically').[7] The issue would get picked up again with *The Brothers Karamazov* ('Even Yul Brynner, in the role of the fierce Dimitri, manages to get more out of himself as an actor than previously') and *Once More, with Feeling!* ('Yul Brynner as the self-centred conductor prone to explosive tantrums is not good enough an actor to offer Key Kendall the kind of collaboration she would've needed. Brynner is just always towering, dour, and dull').[8]

Brynner's performance style ranged from the markedly theatrical in *The King and I* to the more simplified in *The Magnificent Seven* and *The Double Man*. Covering a range of genres, characters, and aesthetics, and spanning from the mid-1950s to the mid-1970s, his performances built on idiosyncratic bodily stances, gestures, and motions, characterized by 'direct movement and almost rigidly upright posture.'[9] This posture partly owed to the vertebra that he fractured while shooting a trick Cossack-style riding scene for *The Brothers Karamazov*, which he completed wearing a steel brace and continued to wear when shooting *The Journey*.[10] Combined with the earlier circus injury, this had a life-long, occasionally debilitating, impact even though stiffness would, in time, also become a question of aging.

Criticism of Brynner's acting skills was voiced throughout his career, even though reviews tended to be mixed. In most US press, Brynner's film performances of 1956–1959 were received with praise. As the years progressed, it nevertheless became obvious that his screen presence – the mere spectacle of the actor himself – risked eclipsing the nuances of character building and displays of emotional complexity, to the extent that film scripts afforded this. By early 1960s, some of his films were already framed as unintentionally comic: 'It is awfully hard to take seriously anything about *Kings of the Sun*, and even the names of the characters have a way of evoking laughter,' a Canadian critic noted.[11] A Hong Kong-based writer further elaborated:

> Yul Brynner is the only redeeming feature of this most odd picture. As the wild barbarian he gives a magnificent display of over-acting. With an ingenious little pigtail attached to his bald pate, his splendid torso oiled and bronzed, he writhes and snaps magnificently when chained hand and foot to a bed of grass, and only allows himself to be pacified by the gentle ministrations of Shirley Ann Field.
>
> He is the only member of cast to whom the allotted dialogue seems appropriate; and his manner and primitive expressions of adoration are a trifle reminiscent of his famous impersonation of The King of Siam.'[12]

Brynner's performance style recycled, and was arguably built on mannerisms such as recurrent poses and intense gazes, as introduced in his breakthrough role. Pointing to the latter, George Sanders (his co-star in *Solomon and Sheba*) argued that Brynner 'has one very intense expression which he uses all the time on the screen, and one intense expression is more valuable to a film star than a dozen faces.'[13] This expression involving grim, brooding gazes and hard stares was central to launching Brynner's film career and to establishing his specific star brand. Variations of the expression repeated in his later film roles, and were in extensive use onstage as he reprised the role of King Mongkut in 1976. His star image was built on playing 'characters who were Larger Than Life, more powerful than ordinary mortals' and he did so largely by tapping into displays of anger in order to express masculine dominance.[14]

By the 1960s, Brynner's corporeal aesthetic nevertheless began to fit poorly with the newly fashionably 'wiry, untoned, hairy, and sweaty physiques' of New Hollywood.[15] This was not merely a question of age (although it was also that) but also one extending to his overall aesthetic. As 'gritty, character-driven verité' came into fashion, 'the larger-than-life fare in which Brynner thrived was out (with his brooding expressions and sinuous movements, one could almost make a case for him being the last silent-movie star).'[16] In acting, more naturalistic styles and simplified gestural registers grew standard while major studios, pressed for money due to low ticket prices and increasing competition from television, cut down on star publicity and largely shifted to funding independent films.[17] Lavish productions gave way to smaller budgets, the artifice of studio sets was replaced with location shoots, the hue-saturated spectacle of wide-screen Technicolor was supplanted by 35mm Eastman Kodak, and the end of the Production Code enabled the exploration of previously unacceptable sexual, subcultural, and anti-establishment themes while also tangibly impacting casting options pertaining to ethnicity. It would have been difficult to imagine Brynner starring in a film such as *Kings of the Sun*, had it been made a decade later – although, most likely, it would not have been made at all.

With the mainstreaming of method acting since the 1950s, film performance was increasingly framed as a craft and effort resulting from the actor's identification with, and immersion in the role. Whereas in classic Hollywood unique star personalities were seen to radiate their glow on film, inside-out, method acting risked the 'collapse between the distinction between star and character' as actors dug inwards for psychological authenticity in something of a reversed process of 'outside-in.'[18] In the course of this, the perceived continuity between actors and roles that made star personae in the studio era was being reframed, even if it did not become fully undone as such. This, of course, did not mean that such personae ceased to matter as constructs exceeding the cinematic frame: actors continued to be cast according to what they were imagined to do best in terms of type and film genre.

Brynner was never a friend of the Method.[19] Throughout his life, Brynner emphasized the influence of his early acting mentor, Michael Chekhov, who had developed his own techniques based on bodily imagination, affective atmospheres, sensation, and tempo. His main principles were unpacked in the 1953 book *To the Actor*, for which Brynner wrote a brief preface.[20] Whereas method acting involves tapping into actors' own memories and building characters through an introspective process, Chekhov highlighted the role of the imagination instead, inviting actors to experiment and use their creative intuition when building characters so as to 'wear another body' and become someone else:[21]

> Step by step, you begin to move, speak and feel in accord with it; that is to say, your character now dwells within you (or, if you prefer, you dwell within it). [...]
>
> How strongly you express the qualities of your imaginary body while acting will depend on the type of play and on your own taste and desire. But in any case, your whole being, psychologically and physically, will be changed – I would not hesitate to say even possessed – by the character. When really taken on and exercised, the imaginary body stirs the actor's will and feelings; it harmonizes them with the characteristic speech and movements, it transforms the actor into another person![22]

Chekhov's acting techniques moved from the outside in, as it were, so that physical comportment helped the actor to arrive not merely at the right gestures but at something akin to internal transformation: Brynner arguing in 1984 that, on stage, King Mongkut took him over could well be seen as resulting from the repetition of such transformations over a number of years (see also Chapter 9).[23] The techniques for achieving this were based on a balance between physique and psychology so that an actor could become flexible, and receptive enough, to accommodate – or to be taken over by – forever new strangers to play, irrespective of genre. It then followed that an actor should not limit themselves to any particular kinds or types of roles but should rather approach each one as a fresh challenge.[24] The exercises towards this were highly concrete, many of them involving the quest of wearing and becoming a character through playful means.

Observation nevertheless remained at the heart of things: 'try to penetrate the psychology of different nations; try to define their specific characteristics, their psychological features, interests, their arts. Make clear the main differences that distinguish these nations from one another.'[25] This advice to identify and emulate something akin to national temperament bordered on the logic of stereotype, even as it also entailed a call to acquaint oneself with cultural nuance in a vein broadly gesturing towards cosmopolitan sensibilities. Chekhov's teachings were formative to how Brynner approached and practiced his craft. This logic of imagining and becoming other also helps to contextualize his claims that actors, in portraying 'all men,' develop universal compassion towards others as part of their trade (see Chapter 5).[26]

Given the centrality of physical expression to his techniques, Chekhov further highlighted the importance of characterization as attention to features or gestures specific to the part played – 'a typical movement, a characteristic manner of speech, a recurrent habit, a certain way of laughing, walking or wearing a suit, an odd way of holding the hands, or a singular inclination of the head, and so forth' – allowing for finishing touches.[27] It is easy to map repetitions in such gestures across Brynner's work adding up to his star presence. His acting was much less concerned with delivering lines is a certain way – in fact, many of his films had few lines for him to deliver. There is a strong sense of his acting style solidifying fairly early on so that the characters he came to play were variations of a theme rather than independent quests: while much of this is obviously an issue of typecasting, it also extends beyond this in how Brynner's characters shared the same traits, gestures, poses, and mannerisms, so that it became hard to tell where the actor ended and the role began, or vice versa. At the very least, Chekhov's foregrounding of physical being – taking on the gestures of a character, imagining how their body would comport itself – was key to how Brynner fashioned his roles.

Striking a pose

Brynner's performance style was rarely subtle yet quickly recognizable: it blended acting into appearing and the role into presence largely since much of his characteristic expression occurred through bodily stances, gestures, and motions. Physical technique and movement vocabulary are standard features of any actor's skillset, yet his style was more intense than most. And, of course, Brynner's body was much more than a mere instrument: as discussed in the preceding chapters, it was key to his star image, from his instantly recognizable baldness to his regularly bared muscular body displayed topless up to his very last onscreen performance (and additional stage work).

Across Brynner's roles, an idiosyncratic stance expressive of phallic authority repeats: hands on hips, legs apart, head held up, muscles tensed, as introduced to exude royal authority, masculinity, and control on stage in *The King and I*. In accordance with Chekhov's techniques pertaining to characterization through gestures, movements, and mannerisms, the

Figure 8.1 Striking poses in *The King and I*, *The Ten Commandments*, and *Taras Bulba*

pose made its way to the musical's film version to convey the aggressive, intense, and authoritative personae of the Siamese king. Dressed in a blue silk jacket with rich gold trimming, the King stands with his legs apart, hands on hips, brows furrowed as a shirtless living statue. In gold-embroidered red silks, he reclines, sings, and then strikes the pose again, his chest bared. In pale, brown silk with elaborate golden embroidery he thus poses, argumentative, chest once more exposed. In full royal red and gold regalia complete with a cap and golden slippers he proudly stands, his firm stare and flexed muscles balancing the potentially feminizing effect of his ornamental, Orientalist garb.[28] And when the King eventually dances, he does so with exaggerated, aggressive stomping energy that leaves Miss Anna quite breathless.

In a 1981 interview, Elliot Norton asked Brynner whether this pose – 'arms akimbo, legs astride' – had been his own concoction. Answering in the affirmative, Brynner first explained it through his initial inexperience: 'I was not an actor, when we started. I really had very little experience in acting. I'd done *Lute Song*, it's the only time I'd played a principal character.' He then continued to reiterate his fondness for the role as the first one he enjoyed playing:

> Because I transcended completely my own being and became somebody else, you know, portrayed somebody else that I could admire and try to understand more and more. And that's why this particular work will go on forever; it takes forever to find out everything about somebody, and I'm going to try to do that with the king.[29]

The interview did little to explain the origins of the pose beyond the lack of professional experience, yet it strongly echoes Chekhov's teachings on becoming someone else so that, momentarily, one unbecomes one's own self. The degree to which Brynner accomplished this is, of course, a different matter. His 'becoming-Mongkut' was nevertheless premised on this specific pose which, through repetitions, became his star trademark. Often involving semi-toplessness or at least expanses of bare chest on display, the pose meandered through Brynner's onscreen performances as a reverberation of sorts, weaving in and out of his subsequent roles – sometimes, as in *Anastasia* or *Once More, with Feeling!*, fleetingly taken within a scene and, at other times, as in *Taras Bulba*, recurring throughout the film as a staccato accent suggestive of mannerism. Addressing his work with Brynner in the 1965 *Morituri*, Marlon Brando mentioned a joke on-set, 'I wonder what Yul would look like if he ever put his legs together' due to his 'constantly striking the magisterial pose he used in *The King and I*, with his legs separated, planted firmly on the ground, and his hands on his hips.'[30] The pose accompanied Brynner's performances as kings, captains, military men, revolutionary leaders, and macho fighters from one decade to the next. In a 1981 review of the Broadway revival of *The King and I*, a journalist describes the stance with flair:

> With his feet dramatically parted, his trunk thrust forward, his elbows pointed to either side, and his head and shoulders cocked gently but proudly to the rear, he looks like a practitioner of some ancient and devastating form of Oriental wrestling, never witnessed by Western eyes, which he is ready to demonstrate to anyone or anything reckless enough to question his territorial imperative.[31]

In his discussion of male sex symbols, John Mercer argues that each has a 'defining performance, emblematic moment, or (and probably most importantly) an iconic image that 'symbolises sex-symbol status.'[32] In the case of Brynner, it may just be this very pose, combined with his defining role as King Mongkut, that symbolize his star image and the sex symbol status associated with it. As a stylized display of masculine assertiveness, the pose solidified Brynner as a statue of flesh which, as vibrant, virile, and agile as it may have been, often stood stationary as the world literally moved around it.

Consider, for example, a scene from *The Ten Commandments* following a conflict with his father, the Pharaoh, and his brother Moses, where Rameses stands stiffly still in the pose as other characters gesture, and as the camera moves closer. Brynner's statuesque stillness against the fluttering background accentuates Rameses' visual and narrative centrality. As he begins to move and speak of his plans and lust for power, Rameses does so rigidly, keeping his hands to his hips and without altering any of his grimly pouting facial register. Across the film's scenes, key characters similarly remain largely immobile except for select dramatic motion, while an entire choreography of quivering, pulsating flesh takes place among the film's extras erecting a city out of sand in the Pharaoh's honor.

In contrast to such extras who, following Will Straw, function as 'graphic detail or as expressive human body,' stars are cinematic centerpieces and highlights.[33] As background, extras and supporting actors afford stars with much of their extraordinary presence in how they move, at what or whom they look, and how they react to lead actors' presence within the frame.[34] The issue is one of 'scales of presence' where extras, as filmic ornament, become dissolved 'within a film's broader organization of graphic lines and shapes' as 'part of the rippling of graphic information outwards from a scene's central characters.'[35] Whereas extras are, by definition, the stuff of the background as bodies filling and moving in space, creating

Performance style, posturing, and camp

Figure 8.2 Yul Brynner: the centerpiece. Clockwise from top left: *The King and I, Surprise Package, Taras Bulba, Kings of the Sun, Solomon and Sheba, The Ten Commandments, Invitation to a Gunfighter, The Buccaneer*, and *Anastasia*

atmosphere and feel – and, on occasion, giving rise to mass ornaments such as those seen in *The Ten Commandments, Taras Bulba*, and *Solomon and Sheba* – star performers are very much the stuff of foreground. Theirs is not the part of long shots: their features are feasted upon in close-ups. It is not their position to appear at the edge of the frame for a fleeting moment, rather cameras linger on their presence in the centre of the frame. Brynner's frequently exposed and lavishly adorned body was showcased as a noteworthy sight, towards which attention meandered and upon which it fixated.

Consider another scene where Rameses has recently discovered Heston's Moses being the son of Hebrew slaves, rather than an Egyptian prince of royal blood and serious contender for the crown, as previously presumed. Standing by the throne at the side of his father, the still-ruling pharaoh, Rameses prepares for his moment of triumph as guards bring in the shackled Moses. Approaching the throne, Moses occupies the visual foreground, topless and in chains, his tall, muscular body glistening with perspiration. Out of the two, Heston's body is the more exposed and bulkier, yet visual attention travels towards Brynner's Rameses, notably shorter and of smaller frame, dressed in an elaborate, shiny gold-plated skirt, golden armbands, and an ornate headpiece, his other foot up on the stairs for an impression of additional height and authority. Both men stand still with their legs apart, muscles tensed: Brynner's motions stiffen as he whisks their mutual love-interest Nefertiri (Anne Baxter) aside. This angularity and force of movement, combined with his grim facial expression and the near immobility of his erect body, conveys masculinity and authority independent of the make-up, heavy body ornaments, and extravagantly decorated couture.

Heston, born in Wilmette, Illinois, was as unlikely an Israelite prophet as the Siberian-born Brynner an Egyptian prince. Alternatively, this made perfect sense in a pious American film of the Cold War-era where 'Heston depicts Moses as a Westerner rather than as a Semite, especially when compared to Brynner's more Oriental features.'[36] Despite Heston's alpha masculinity and muscular body, his trademark husky Americanness lacked explicit sex appeal in ways befitting a religious leader of prophetic standing; his was also a markedly stiff form of acting with a limited affective range.[37] Meanwhile, within this Hollywood imaginary, Brynner, according to Steve Cohan, represented 'pagan idolatry, racial Otherness, and imperial tyranny,' which became coded as Asian so that Egypt's royal court was 'as "Oriental" as, say, that of nineteenth-century Siam.'[38]

The juxtaposition of Moses and Rameses involves two distinctly different styles of masculinity. As the film's hero, Moses represents the ideal (as self-sacrificing, robust, just, and morally principled) of which Rameses, as the anti-hero, clearly falls short (him being vengeful, stubborn, ambitious, and greedy). If, in Brynner's 'physique there is more the grace of a dancer à la Nurejev than the thrill of fear that you feel in the strapping figure of Charlton Heston,' Rameses is by far the more ominous of the two.[39] The issue, in short, is that of stylized presence, the centrality of which was equally manifest in Brynner's later film work.

Performance style, posturing, and camp   207

Figure 8.3 Rameses, Nefertiri, and Moses in chains

Large gestures

Most directors either did not wish, or were unable, to reign in Brynner's gestural register. J. Lee Thompson, who directed Brynner in *Taras Bulba* and *Kings of the Sun*, described him as 'an open-air actor who needs a great expanse, a big tour de force. He is a marvelous Tara and a fine actor, but should never play comedy.'[40] In both these films, Thompson literally gave much open space and air for what critics identified as Brynner's strutting and 'absurd posturing,' possibly ignoring the fact that a 'big tour de force' is not necessarily synonymous with grandiose gesticulation.[41] Thompson nevertheless had a point in his assessment of Brynner's comic skills.

While broadly lauded for his semi-comic role as King Mongkut and mentioned for his sense of humor by colleagues,[42] Brynner was not an accomplished comedian due to limitations of both timing and enunciation. These were evident in his 1960 comedies *Once More, with Feeling!* and *Surprise Package*, both directed by Stanley Donen of MGM musical fame. In the first of these, he played the egocentric and combustible, world-renown orchestra conductor, Victor Fabian, possibly in order to depart from the formula around which his star image had been shaped to date in exotic roles and historical spectacles. His co-star was Kay Kendall who died of leukemia shortly before the film's premiere: consequently, reviews largely focused on the loss of the British comedian and the quality of her 'zaniest, brittlest' of performances carrying both Brynner and the film, the plot of which was identified 'as flimsy as a stripteaser's costume.'[43]

Victor Fabian was a generously scripted comedy role, 'an egomaniac symphony orchestra conductor with a passion for music rivalled only by his passion for himself.'[44] The film's plot revolves around Fabian's harp-playing wife Dolly (Kendall) wanting to leave him and his cheating ways for a quieter life with a new nuclear scientist husband, yet being unable to get a respectable divorce since the two had never been married to start with. Fabian then tries to woo her back in order to maintain balance within his orchestra and private life by promising to marry and divorce her as a generous gesture, and ultimately succeeds. The film opens with a series of visual puns: shots of portraits of the great conductor executed in styles ranging from the more realistic to the high modernist emulating the styles of George Rouault and Marc Chagall.[45] Within these portraits, Fabian is seen majestically swinging his baton, his hands raised and arms

Figure 8.4 Visual gags in *Once More, with Feeling!*

spread, surrounded by his orchestra. As the maestro is finally seen in the flesh, he is reclining on a sofa below one of his looming portraits, listening to his own recording of Wagner's 'Ride of the Valkyries' at high volume while browsing through a pile of other albums, the covers of which are all decorated with his own likeness. Not only is Fabian's professional status instantly established but so is his grandiose, possibly narcissistic personality. Slapstick comedy is then amply served throughout the film on the level of visual composition as Fabian broods and strikes identical poses to those of the portraits around him, lies down on his bed modeled after a gondola, and appears in a secret wedding ceremony wearing a mullet wig.

Brynner plays Fabian of explosive temper and monomaniacal self-centerdness with great gusto and gestures communicating energy, temper, and determination. According to the trade paper *The Independent Exhibitors Film Bulletin*:

> He seems very much at home strutting peacock fashion around his alter ego's home complete with mazes of stereo equipment, beds resembling Viking ships and a collection of oil portraits done in the style of the great masters, and he is the artistic genius personified ripping shirts off and smashing violins across the heads of bumbling orchestra members, including the upper echelon of Festival Orchestra Boards or going into tongue-in-cheek trances before he is to perform.[46]

Some critics considered this Brynner's best role since *The King and I* and *Anastasia*, and him offering viewers 'alloyed delight' by acting 'with vigor and tongue in cheek.'[47] His heavy-handed, off-sync comic timing, however, rubbed some reviewers the wrong way, as he was criticized for 'grimacing and bouncing about like a broken kite'.[48] Brynner's 'arrogant extravagance' was further seen to be at variance with Kendall's more satirical style, his accent conspiring 'to rob some of the dialogue of its clarity'.[49]

Brynner's lack of comic talent became something of a unanimous critical conclusion at the release of *Surprise Package* later the same year: Brynner, 'whatever his other talents, is not a comedian'; his 'line-punching,' heavy-handed, stomping performance style did not elegant comedy make.[50] The film opens with Nico Marsh, soon introduced as 'America's Greek gambling czar,' signing piles of papers in his mansion before rushing off to meet his associates and collect a cut of the illicit earnings. The men eagerly cluster around Marsh to light a cigar that he is purposefully holding: there is no doubt as to who is the man in charge, and to whom attention and respect are paid. Brusque, bossy, and short-tempered, Marsh is just about to be deported to a small Greek island, his ancestral homeland. Once on the island, Marsh aims to get some of his money back whereas his men send over his girlfriend Gabby – played by Mitzi Gaynor in the tightest of clothing – instead. To highlight Nico Marsh's flashy, jumpy mobster qualities, Brynner, puffing on cigars, is consistently clad in black except for a white tie and hat band (until the last scene where the color schema becomes reversed so as to suggest a new life). The character's barking, aggressive manner is akin to virtually all Brynner's films roles to this point.

Critics deemed his mobster 'a caricature of a foreign-born denizen of the State-side underworld' although one also found this 'animalistic illiterate of the Neanderthal tradition' quite hilarious.[51] It was Noël Coward in the role of the peasant-girl-harem keeper and exiled King Pavel the Serene of Anatolia who was seen to steal the film – according to many reviewers, merely by playing himself.[52] Riffing off Brynner's kingly fame, Pavel details the pitfalls of being a king with a plummy posh accent, with Marsh explaining in accented American English that he is merely an excitable guy, too big for the island: large parts of the plot revolve around attempts to steal Pavel's crown.

While the shortcomings of *Surprise Package* were partly associated with the quality of its script, Brynner's lack of comic timing, 'harshly arrogant playing,' and mumbling delivery of fast dialogue – already evident in *Once More, with Feeling!* – were seen to do the film the most harm.[53] According to a critic, the role simply was not suitable for Brynner – 'or is he merely muffling his lines?', she wondered, continuing to note that these were 'delivered with the weight of a concrete mixer.'[54] Another critic's opinion came fully formed:

> I'm very likely to go into a decline after the disappointment of seeing Yul Brynner in *Surprise Package*. Like most women I'm an ardent fan but please, please I beg film producers don't put him into a comedy part like this again. [...] I can no more happily visualise Yul Brynner as a sort of comedy Al Capone than fly. He just doesn't fit.[55]

The film makes for odd contemporary viewing, from the clumsily executed 'ancient' Greek statue props to Nico Marsh's bullying ways towards his 'squirrel-brained' girlfriend – a former Vegas showgirl described by a critic as a 'dumb dancer.'[56] Although sexism certainly was no rarity in films of the era, there is a particularly acidic edge to *Surprise Package*. Right after Gabby's arrival on the island, Marsh throws her violently down on the beach in a gesture which, while seemingly abusive, saves the lives of both as they are suddenly shot at from a passing boat. Later, a similar move repeats as someone tries to kill Gabby at the ruins of a temple. Marsh's aggressive, barking bluntness is in line with Brynner's broader resistance to romantic roles yet it unavoidably gives the relationship a rather abrasive tone. Adding to the film's gender dynamic, in virtually all his scenes, Coward's king delivers ample sexist commentary on his subservient, young, and bikini-clad female entourage, highlighting their semi-savage and illiterate ways while enjoying their intimate favors.[57]

Both Victor Fabian and Nico Marsh repeated the gestural registers of King Mongkut in far less successful ways. Even though it is possible to identify Marsh as something of a half-brother to Brynner's later macho undercover character in *The File of the Golden Goose*, there was limited similarity to their respective performance styles. *Once More, with Feeling!* and *Surprise Package* were released the same year as *The Magnificent Seven*, which involved a distinctly different performance lacking in stomping motions and dramatic posturing: while Chris Adam certainly postured, his was a figure of stillness, minimal motion and speech.

Brynner largely gave up comedy roles after 1960, returning to similar gestures only in the 1971 *Catlow* and, partly, in *The Madwoman of Chaillot* of 1969. The latter film, based on a satire by Jean Giraudoux and starring Katharine Hepburn, was set in contemporary times yet featured 'the madwoman' and her friends clad in fin-de-siècle finery. Meanwhile, Brynner's evil Chairman led a conspiracy of tapping into oil under central Paris and destroying much of the city in the process. The film is something of a fairytale so that its theatrical acting amplifies the overall feel of stylized artifice.

The Chairman is first seen emerging from a chauffeured luxury car by the Chaillot metro station together with The General (Paul Henreid): The Chairman wears a dapper dark suit and the General is in full military attire as they enter a café to meet with fellow co-conspirators (The Reverend, The Commissar, and The Broker, played by John Gavin, Oskar Homolka, and Charles Boyer). The Chairman then introduces his character by loudly complaining about the poor quality of service before venturing into his own poor background: 'my mother spent most of her life bent over a washtub in order to send me to a good school. I'll always be grateful to her, of course, but you know, I just can't remember her face.' A little later, he apologizes to his company for peddlers and beggars having turned the café into a circus (in a seeming allusion to Brynner's own Parisian circus career) and laments the disturbance:

> They come here, in Chaillot, in the very citadel of management and they have the audacity to be with us with their raffish individualism, with the right of the voiceless to sing, the dumb to make speech, the unemployed to juggle!

The Chairman's grin is pearly-shiny: he expresses excitement and menace combined with facial gestures large and small. Some critics identified these as brilliant, others as authentically chilling, and yet others as overacting.[58] To capture the gestures, the camera worked with close-ups and extreme close-ups of Brynner's face as The Chairman further recounted once having torpedoed a ship which he had insured for three times its value, killing all onboard. As The Chairman and his co-conspirators eventually go down in a tar pit opening up in Hepburn's 'Mad Woman' Countess's vast basement, and never re-emerge, it is only poetic justice that gets served. The Chairman, like all the film's characters, is decidedly a type, yet one which Brynner plays with notable levity, communicating a sense of fun.

The Madwoman of Chaillot was released the same year as *The Picasso Summer* was finished: the latter film was shelved, only shown on television in 1972 and released on DVD as late as 2010. Based on a story by Ray Bradbury, it was originally offered to François Truffaut and was eventually directed by Serge Bourguignon and produced by CSC (co-founded by Bill Cosby). Starring Albert Finney and Yvette Mimieux as a couple setting

Figure 8.5 The evil Chairman

off from San Francisco to search for Pablo Picasso in Southern Spain, the film features Brynner's friend and matador celebrity, Luis Miguel Dominguín, as well as a brief cameo by Doris Kleiner. Meanwhile, planned and pre-agreed cameos by Picasso and Brynner are nowhere to be seen. Dominguín, Picasso, and Brynner were all friends (also with Jean Cocteau, all three doing cameos for his 1960 *Le testament d'Orphée*). The apparent reason for Picasso and Brynner dropping out was Dominguín's affair with Kleiner: their cameos were shot in 1967 during the making of *Villa Rides*, the year the Brynners divorced.[59] These cameo connections signal both towards Brynner's position within the European cosmopolitan jet-set and the degree to which his screen performances were, at this point, about presence and appearing rather than character acting.

Full-on camp

In 1969, Brynner made a short cameo drag appearance as a nightclub torch singer in *The Magic Christian*. The scene opens with a champagne-drinking Roman Polanski turning his head to look at an approaching woman who has already fixed her gaze on him. The nightclub space is of futuristic 1960s design: the lighting makes the ceiling appear purple while simultaneously tinting the performers' faces in funky hues of green. Leaning next to Polanski on the bar, the woman softly inquires, 'do you want to buy a girl a drink, big boy?' A cocktail soon arrives and

Figure 8.6 An alluring torch singer

she remains at his side – a towering presence glamorously made up in a blonde wig, large crystal diamanté necklace, and pale-yellow silky dress. Daintily sipping on her cocktail and still centring her seductive attentions on Polanski, she coos, 'here's looking at you, mister' by way of a toast.

Exhaling cigarette smoke, the woman then looks firmly at Polanski as she begins a rendition of 'Mad About the Boy' to (nondiegetic) piano accompaniment. Softly touching Polanski's nose with a gloved hand, she focuses her eyes at a distance while immersing herself in the increasingly emotional performance. Moving behind Polanski and stroking his arm, she sits to face the camera, her expressions at turns happily mesmerized, coy, wistful, and melancholy. Leaning against the bar (singing 'Lord knows I'm not a school-girl / in the flurry of her first affair'), she toys with her hair and necklace and begins to eye a raptured older man next to her. Holding his shoulder, she then turns dramatically to the left and right to deliver the song's climax. Singing the final note, the woman then lifts her hand to her forehead in a studied, stylized gesture of despair. Here, her dramatically pained expression stills into a macho stare: as she tugs off her wig with one determined motion, the adoring eyes of the men around her shift into expressions of horror when witnessing the acute, undeniable baldness beneath. As the man whose arm the singer is still holding exclaims, 'Oh, no!', and she replies with 'Oh, yes!' and an additional nod, it is clear that the actress Miriam Karlin's voice work has been replaced with Brynner's own recognizable baritone: end of cameo.

One critic interpreted the character as 'hooker' and another as a Marlene Dietrich impersonation – yet it is not self-evidently either.[60] Christopher R. Brown points out that 'Mad About the Boy' 'references the erotic appeal of male stardom ("on the silver screen / he melts my foolish heart in every single scene") to women, but also to men.' Written by Noël Coward 'as a love song to another man,' it comes steeped in queer connotations.[61] To make things a little meta: dramatically singing of love for a boy on a screen whilst cross-dressing, Brynner can be seen to serenade his own erotic star appeal.

Operating in a decidedly different gestural register than Brynner's other roles the same year – as the jovial but very butch Yugoslav partisan in *Battle of Neretva*, and as the hard-edged, gruff American agent in *The File of the Golden Goose* – this playful take on masculine star image remains the most drastic instance of flexibility in the actor's performance styles. The scene succeeds not only due to its achievements in dress, makeup, and lip-sync, but also because of the drastic rift separating Brynner's customary poses, gestures, motions, and expressions from the torch singer's smooth, soft yet a little heavy body language as she leans on the bar, fondles her hair, focuses her eyes on, and casually caresses the male patrons. It also brings to the foreground the humor that ripples through Brynner's onscreen appearances in the form of smirks, amused looks, and over-the-top gestures.

I suggest that, all in all, Brynner's film performances were characterized by the kind of flaunting that lies at the heart of the French term, *se camper*, upon which the very notion of camp is based. By the late 1960s, camp sensibility had become rooted in popular culture – film included – beyond the urban gay cultures from which the term emerged.[62] Susan Sontag's 1964 essay, 'Notes on "Camp"' had done some of this mainstreaming. Addressing camp as both an attitude and a sensibility, Sontag outlined it as an anti-serious tactic of drawing quotation marks around cultural objects in a gesture both ironically detached and loving, so that camp became 'a mode of enjoyment, of appreciation' that 'relishes, rather than judges.'[63]

This mainstreaming also involved a gesture of depoliticization that shifted camp from a specifically form of queer critique to a notion descriptive of the pleasures of pop culture among diverse audiences.[64] Within all this, camp became reframed less as a queer undoing or refusal than as an ironic appreciation of cultural objects so that the term could be conflated with 'rhetorical and performative strategies such as irony, satire, burlesque, and travesty.'[65] Camp also became identified as a tactic of cultural production encouraging 'outlandish plotting, baroque visual design, corny dialogue, and wooden acting' – of which *The Magic Christian* serves as prime example.[66]

This Peter Sellers and Ringo Starr vehicle can be broadly interpreted as commenting on the logics of capitalist accumulation, and unfolds as series of more or less absurd scenes where Sellers' aristocratic billionaire plays people and burns money on the side. The film is rich in cameos, brief credited appearances, and celebrity lookalikes and takes place largely on the ocean-liner after which it is named. Featuring, among other characters, Raquel Welch's 'Priestess of the Whip' and her female slaves and male bodybuilder nightclub entertainers clad in golden underwear presenting their wares to a diversely interested crowd, the film offers a somewhat belabored form of camp where queer elements operate as amusing accents and backdrops for the antics of its main (straight male) stars.

At this point in his career, being positioned as an object of desire – male or female, queer, straight, or other – was hardly a novelty to Brynner, aged 49. With the exception of a handful of commercially unsuccessful comedies and dramas, his roles had revolved around demonstrations of masculine authority performed within the gestural registers of butch bravado. And while Brynner's only onscreen cross-dressing scene may be in *The Magic Christian*, his work was certainly rich in instances of ethnic drag where the main prop was the actor's own body. In one film after another, Brynner was positioned as an object to behold – even as an animal force both fascinating and fearsome in his unpredictability, dominance, and violence. Meanwhile, his cosmopolitan, decidedly alien figure occupied a compromised position in the registers of whiteness in ways that aided its ornamental, sexualized display while also limiting its scope of available roles. As Hollywood film culture transformed, as different body aesthetics got pushed to the fore, and as Brynner himself aged, these options grew even more limited. I argue that they also grew increasingly self-reflexive, as in the cameo just addressed.

More flamboyant strutting

Steve Cohan suggests that Brynner's performance in *The Ten Commandments* was already deliberately camp: 'the star's delivery of his lines; the suggestive positioning of his relaxed body in relation to Heston's stiffer one; his manipulation of props, like his horsewhip, against his body' served to 'accentuate the transgressive edge to his screen presence.'[67] I propose that such knowing and enjoyed campiness cuts through much of Brynner's film work, being particularly evident in his posing as Captain Stoloff, Sabata, Captain Kongre, The Chairman, Sordo, and Westworld robot.[68] The deliberate artifice and stylized excess of these roles, as different as they are, communicates a sense of amused enjoyment, even glee. None of these roles were concerned with authenticity or credibility tied to notions of realism: rather, they are types played with flamboyant flair and limited gestures defining the characters whose inner motivations remain a mystery. Their surroundings are not those of lavish studio settings radiating artifice since much of the action takes place outdoors (on location in Yugoslavia, Italy, Spain, France, Boston, and the Mojave Desert, respectively). Artifice is, nevertheless, the stuff that these characters are made of as they reference not merely Brynner's previous roles (Stoloff harks back to *Anastasia*'s Bounine while all his later Western parts retain a connection to Chris Adams of *The Magnificent Seven*) but also the broader catalog of Hollywood villains, exotic types, and genre clichés.

As discussed in Chapter 7, *The Light at the Edge of the World* and *Adíos, Sabata* were broadly critiqued for their degrees of violence, acting mannerisms, and casts of comic book-like characters. One critic characterized *The Light at the Edge of the World*, with its 'dim protagonists' and pirates resembling a rock band, as 'the most inept dramatization of a Jules Verne work made yet,' arguing that Brynner's 'evil scowl and sneer have become petrified' so that his performance comes across as 'weary and sadly funny.'[69] Another hinted at the pirates' overall queerness, with Kongre wearing his 'fur lined kaftan [. . .] like a Mongol chieftain' while surrounded by 'paintings, silverware and fine wines captured by wild, motley crew almost as weird as their glowering captain.'[70]

Some reviewers simply settled for framing the film through the lens of camp: 'The film undoubtedly manages its darkling, brooding atmosphere well [. . .] and appears to be something of a camp joke. Someone tells me that the lighthouse is a phallic symbol, and certainly the homosexual overtones are clear enough.'⁷¹ An ironic campy angle of interpretation was also manifest among viewers:

> Taking charge of the island, Yul Brynner looks into camera, talking to an unseen person, and says, in his *The King and I* accent, 'Let me introduce myself.' That did it. The audience howled with laughter and resumed the hilarity every time he opened his mouth.⁷²

Critics described Brynner's exotic pirate captain, leader of 'gaudy barbarians,' as hilarious, 'intentionally or otherwise': 'he carries on like some despotic eastern potentate – the King of Siam, maybe – in elaborate robes amidst fancy plundered trappings and with an incipient drag queen (Jean-Claude Drouot) as his chief aide.'⁷³

Harry M. Benshoff associates the 1960s ironic mode of 'turning the terrible into something grotesquely amusing' with a gap between traditional Hollywood film-making and the era's countercultural sensibilities that rendered camp evident in a range of genre films, from Biblical epics to science fiction, peplum, and beyond.⁷⁴ It does not, indeed, require a massive interpretative leap to identify Kongre – a man of sophisticated culinary tastes in environments of makeshift opulence complete with a royal servant on a remote barren rock of an island – as a full-on camp villain. The character is both cartoonish and, as may be obvious, highly intertextual in how it taps into Brynner's previous film work (in referencing the opulent lifestyle of *The Buccaneer*'s gallant, heroic 'pirate king' Jean Lafitte in particular). It is further fair to suggest that action scenes where men start their face-off by first shooting at a weathercock, and then staring at its spinning while glancing at one another, or where a lavishly clad marauder pirate hunts down a man with a horse equipped with a unicorn horn, were not performed entirely straight to begin with.⁷⁵

When Captain Kongre first meets Arabella, the film's sole female character posing as an aristocrat, he flashes a toothy, menacing grin and extends his hand, stating, 'A lady. May I offer you my arm? Ms. Ponsonby.' The gesture ironically references King Mongkut's invitation to Miss Anna in 'Shall We Dance,' made even more explicit by Samantha Eggar, here Arabella, co-starring with Brynner in the television series, *Anna and the King*, the following year. Kongre is then seen seated on his throne of pearl inlay, with a rug of panther pelts at his feet, as he presents Arabella with her presumed aunt's cut-off hand (severed because of the valuable rings) and addresses her with dress options: 'What is your colour? Cerise?

Apricot? Virginal white. Ah, how delightful it is to talk of such delicate matters.' The scene echoes one in *Invitation to a Gunfighter* where the dandy, menacing yet alluring Jules Gaspard d'Estaing exhibits flashy salesmanship in order to offer a widowed lady something 'more gay' by way of fabrics. Meanwhile, *The Light at the Edge of the World* took camp to another level with its cross-dressing, partying pirates.

Brynner's flamboyant characters can be interpreted as being both inadvertently and intentionally camp: I do not, however, find it particularly productive to simply nail them down in these terms so as to reduce them to a singular interpretative framework. There is playfulness and knowing over-the-topness to much of his film work which critics largely either overlooked or alternatively criticized for the lack of dramatic insight. Brynner's performances speak of in-depth familiarity with genre conventions and many of them exhibit joy taken in playing with these.

It then follows that the gunslinger Chris Adams is a condensing of previous hired Western guns: black-hatted, impassive, unhesitant in pulling his gun, and sparing of words to the point of not saying much at all. Brynner's more dandified, piano and harpsicord-playing gunslingers in *Invitation to a Gunfighter* and *Adíos, Sabata* added an elegant foreign frisson to the type, whereas the *Westworld* robot stripped the character to the bare minimum. Brynner's Cossacks, monocle-bearing Nazi officers, Asian, American, and European freedom fighters and Oriental kings were all types, yet this is not to say that they were merely flat.

Following novelist E. M. Forster's vintage definition, the roundness of fictional characters is a matter of credibility and degrees of complexity: it involves the character having orientation, interests, and social connections – in short, having personality of the kind that flat characters resembling caricatures lack.[76] Personality, or consistency, is achieved through repetition, so that formal patterns are 'endlessly repeated, beneath the apparent changes in a character's behaviour.'[77] Such repetitions dot and pattern Brynner's individual roles and create continuities between them. Just as the lens of realism is not the most apt for analysing the films he starred in, given their generic and often fantastically stylized features, it falls equally short in considering Brynner's presence and overall performance style. Repetitions remained key to Brynner's star image as his screen career folded and he moved back to the stage, basically performing the same role for the last nine years of his life. This repetition had much to do with how he became subsequently remembered, this being the topic of the following, final chapter.

Notes

1. *Cosmopolitan*, July 1956; *Argus*, 24 December 1956.
2. *Newsweek*, 19 May 1958, 103.
3. *Cosmopolitan*, June 1963, 15–16; the extract is a quote from Inger Stevens who played Lafitte's romantic interest in *The Buccaneer*. *Woman's Day*, January 1959, 12.
4. *Picturegoer*, 5 July 1958.
5. *Picturegoer*, 16 May 1959.
6. *Elokuva-aitta* 8, 1957, 5.
7. *Elokuva-aitta* 23, 1956b; *Elokuva-aitta* 5, 1957.
8. *Elokuva-aitta* 20, 1958; *Elokuva-aitta* 18, 1960.
9. Baron 2008, 15.
10. *NY Herald Tribune*, 20 June 1957; *Picture Show*, 12 October 1957; *Saturday Evening Post*, 22 November 1958.
11. *The Globe and Mail*, 20 December 1963.
12. *South China Morning Post*, 28 September 1964.
13. Sanders 1960, 57.
14. Brynner 1989, 84.
15. Brown 2012.
16. *The Rake*, November 2015.
17. E.g., Boddy 1985; Grant 2008; Jordan 2009, 167.
18. Baron 2004, 83–94; Palmer 2010a, 4.
19. E.g., *The Manchester Guardian*, 20 March 1959.
20. Chekhov 2014, 115–18; see also *Saturday Evening Post*, 22 November 1958, 85.
21. Chekhov 2014, 73.
22. Ibid.
23. *The Jerusalem Post*, 23 December 1984.
24. Chekhov 2014, 108.
25. Ibid., 13.
26. *Top Spot*, 6 June 1959; *LA Times*, 15 December 1965.
27. Chekhov 2014, 77.
28. Studlar 1989, 26.
29. *Elliot Norton Reviews*, 1981.
30. In Capua 2006, 110.
31. *The Washington Post*, 20 February 1981.
32. Mercer 2013, 87.
33. Straw 2011, 125.
34. Drake 2006, 92–3.
35. Straw 2011, 125.
36. Shaw 2007, 122; this dynamic is also discussed in Cohan 1997.
37. On Heston's star image, see Palmer 2010b.
38. Cohan 1997, 124.
39. Tonchi 2010, 9.
40. *LA Times*, 11 November 1962.
41. *The Guardian*, 5 April 1963.

42. E.g., Danny Kaye in *Picture Show*, 28 September 1957, 4.
43. *Picture Show*, 2 April 1960; *Sight and Sound*, Spring 1960; *Harrison's Reports*, 6 January 1960; *The Independent Exhibitors Film Bulletin*, 15 February 1960; *Elokuva-aitta* 18, 1960; *The Times of India*, 9 June 1960; *Toronto Daily Star*, 4 April 1960; *The Globe and Mail*, 2 April 1960; *South China Morning Post*, 29 July 1960; *Picturegoer*, 9 April 1960b.
44. *The Times of India*, 9 June 1960.
45. Some of the artwork was featured in *The Washington Post*, 7 February 1960.
46. *The Independent Exhibitors Film Bulletin*, 15 February 1960.
47. *Variety*, 10 February 1960a; *Daily News*, 12 February 1960; *The Hollywood Reporter*, 5 February 1960; see also *Australian Women's Weekly*, 15 June 1960.
48. *NY Herald Tribune*, 12 February 1960.
49. *Monthly Film Bulletin* 1960a.
50. *The Hollywood Reporter*, 11 October 1960; *Australian Women's Weekly*, 26 October 1960; *LA Times*, 28 October 1960; *The Tatler*, 5 October 1960; *The Washington Post*, 28 October 1960; *South China Morning Post*, 16 December 1960.
51. *Variety*, 12 October 1960; *Motion Picture Daily*, 11 October 1960.
52. *The Tatler*, 5 October 1960; *Harrison's Reports*, 15 October 1960; *Motion Picture Exhibitor*, 12 October 1960: *Motion Picture Daily*, 11 October 1960; *The Hollywood Reporter*, 11 October 1960.
53. *Monthly Film Bulletin* 1960b; *NY Herald Tribune*, 15 October 1960.
54. *South China Morning Post*, 16 December 1960.
55. *Picture Show*, 24 September 1960; *South China Morning Post*, 16 December 1960.
56. *Motion Picture Exhibitor*, 12 October 1960.
57. The black-and-white, flopping *Surprise Package* premiered at the same time as Kirk Douglas's Super Technirama 70mm spectacle *Spartacus*, the latter garnering both favorable critical attention and having much box office appeal. Given the bitter rivalry between the two actor's respective gladiator projects (see Chapter 4), this temporal coincidence may have highlighted the fact of Brynner's defeat.
58. *The Observer*, 2 November 1969; *Monthly Film Bulletin* 1969; *SF Examiner*, 30 October 1969.
59. *Variety*, 4 October 1967; *Variety*, 8 November 1967; *The Independent Film Journal*, 20 January 1968; *Variety*, 10 January 1968; Lindbergs 2019; Capua 2006, 125.
60. *Los Angeles Advocate*, 1 April 1970; *The Guardian*, 12 December 1969.
61. Brown 2012, 356.
62. On queer cultures and politics of camp, see e.g., Newton 1972; Bergman 1993; Frank 1993; Meyer 1996; Cleto 1999.
63. Sontag 1999, 54–5, 65.
64. Mathijs and Sexton 2011, 86.
65. Meyer 1996, 7.
66. Benshoff 2008, 150.
67. Cohan 1997, 154.
68. This is not an outrageous claim to make, given that the issue was raised by reviewers, as in the *Canberra Times*, 8 May 1974 discussing *Westworld*'s 'low-camp humour.'
69. *The Globe and Mail*, 30 July 1971.
70. *The NY Times*, 17 July 1971.

71. *The Guardian*, 21 December 1972.
72. *Daily News*, 17 July 1971.
73. *LA Times*, 12 August 1971.
74. Benshoff 2008, 151, 153.
75. There is a remarkable photograph of Brynner visiting Federico Fellini on the set of his *Clowns* in full Sabata costume, the two posing with a selection of the film's fully made-up clowns. Brynner smiles brightly at the camera while Fellini studies him with bemusement suggesting for this sight to be the most bizarre of all. See Brynner and Pages 2010d, 212.
76. Forster 1927, 103–4.
77. Dyer 1979, 108.

Chapter 9

An afterlife – et cetera, et cetera, et cetera

Brynner died on October 10, 1985, the same day as Orson Welles so that the two were reminisced about as something of a Hollywood double bill, occasionally joined by Rock Hudson who had died the week prior.[1] Covering the event of Brynner's death, *The Washington Post* characterized him as an actor internationally known 'for his shaved head.'[2] The accompanying illustration was from *The King and I*, bringing together two key strands of the actor's star image.

Exploring star image in a posthumous perspective, this concluding chapter first returns to Brynner's association with his kingly role by focusing on the stage revivals of *The King and I*, 1976–1985, solidifying the link. This is followed by a discussion on the forms and diverse technologies of remembrance: obituaries, posthumously aired infomercials, biographies, statues, and contemporary products of vernacular digital culture. Focusing on both repetitions and variations, the chapter asks what remains of film stardom after an actor's demise.

A king on repeat

Promoting the new Broadway run of *The King and I* in 1977, Brynner emphasized the play's contemporary feel and factual timeliness in comparison with the time of its initial premiere:

> Oscar Hammerstein […] had certain ideas about human rights. He touched on many things, such as the right of a woman to have her condition respected. The play has stood still, but the world around it has moved. The values were there all the time, but they were then an intellectual concept. Today, human rights are a part of everyday life.[3]

Brynner recurrently argued that the different revival and tour productions were in fact nothing less than novel productions – less facsimiles than re-imaginings staged for a changed social context where equal human rights were no longer a novel invention.[4] Even as it may seem odd to argue that a musical play written in the 1950s, set in a nineteenth century Siamese court was, in fact, ahead of its time, Brynner framed it in metonymic terms as a spectacle tackling modern human rights, cosmopolitan notions of equality, and culture clashes between East and West.[5] This cosmopolitan metonymy was particularly focused on a scene where King Mongkut's children walk in to greet their father:

> The presentation of the children has to do with the respect that we must always keep for the individual human being of any age, of any colour, of any breed, of any religion. The individual must be respected for his individuality. [...] What does the word individual mean? It means that he's unique as a human being. I believe that every human being is absolutely unique: there's nobody like you; there's nobody like me and there'll never be two beings that are exactly alike.[6]

Here Brynner reiterated his belief in the fundamental solitude of individuals – as in his oft-repeated maxim: 'In the realest sense you live your life alone: in essence you are born, live and die alone. If you can learn to live with yourself, the relations you acquire with other people, be they close or casual, are gravy.'[7] This mantra involved an emphasis on the importance of ego, even selfishness, as necessary professional tools for actors – or for anyone else.[8] Brynner's individualistic stance, according to which people are not defined by their origins as much as through their beliefs and actions, may even seem similar to the contemporaneous individualistic philosophy of the Russian-born Ayn Rand. Brynner's brand of liberal individualism was nevertheless clearly distinct in not cancelling out altruism or structures of support, such as those facilitated by the UNHCR: as argued above, his perspective was aligned with modern cosmopolitan values on which the notion of human rights is based. By framing *The King and I* through the lens of liberal cosmopolitanism of the kind that he had espoused throughout his career, Brynner invested the play with both personal and social importance. And by arguing that he had only recently discovered the play's more complex dynamics, he framed the task of mediating the role of King Mongkut as something akin to his life's work.[9]

Some critics agreed, arguing that the 'new, refreshing, sumptuous and stunning' staging was more appropriate than during its premiere in 1951. The clash between Miss Anna and the King, in particular, was seen as 'a page right out of women's lib' while aging seemed to have only improved Brynner's performance:

> It is a musical that deals with human values. As for Yul Brynner, who first stomped the stage as the brash king when he was in his early thirties, this lithe, lean, statuesque actor is much more mature in his mid-fifties. Brynner NOW is the King of Siam.[10]

Brynner supported the assessment by pointing out that he no longer was 'all arrogance' like in his younger days but now understood human frailty.[11] According to historical records, King Mongkut died of malaria in 1868, at the age of 63. Played by a thirty-something, muscular, and physically fit Brynner who had, till the death scene, projected high energy throughout the show (and film), the King did not quite seem ready to fade away. In the revivals, Brynner had matured for the role and while emotional realism may not be the first quality to be associated with the Orientalist musical fantasy, this at least lent more credibility to the narrative closure. As Christina Klein dryly notes, 'Yul Brynner spent the rest of his life playing the leader of a developing nation who welcomes the West into his country and willingly dies rather than impede the process of modernization.'[12]

For some reviewers, the issue was that of peak performance: 'Nothing beats seeing this unique actor at his best in his best role, and that's what's happening on Broadway.'[13] While pointing out Brynner's limited vocal range and facial registers, *The New York Times* simultaneously argued for their expressive power:

> Yul Brynner is a great actor – or at the very least a great acting presence – not because of what he does but because of what he is. He strides on a stage caught in the inimitable spotlight of his person. He gestures, gesticulates, and moves with the certainty of an automaton and the grace of a dancer. Often he is very still, his body seemingly carved out of time [...]. He is a Ghengis Khan in Savile Row suit and a Maserati.[14]

There are at least two ways to interpret the review's opening lines: that the actor, in the course of years of repetition, has internalized his best-known role to the degree that it has become a second skin, or that the performance primarily involves the actor taking pleasure in showcasing himself. Independent of which interpretation one opts for, the gap between the performance and the actor seems to have here closed up, if not disappeared. Such conflation was far from novel since Brynner's film work had been continuously compared with his breakthrough role, the identification with which had also been seen to shape his very personality since the 1950s.[15]

Brynner's portrayal of King Mongkut is representative of an iconic performance where star image is not subordinate to the demands of characterization but the opposite occurs, or where the two become hard to tell apart.[16] Or, as *The Hollywood Reporter* praising Brynner's 'enigmatic, Asiatic prideful glare' put it, the play involved the actor living 'his alter ego before our eyes.'[17] His stage performance was, especially after years of revivals, occasionally criticised for the lack of subtlety and delicacy, its every gesture 'rendered with child-like extravagance.'[18] It is nevertheless obvious that this was very much a show with a singular star and point of attention, and that it was Brynner whose particular brand of stage magnetism mobilized the paying audience.[19] Or, to rephrase, the play was a means for Brynner to capitalize on his star image once his film career had come to an end. 'What is it about Yul Brynner?', *The Washington Post* pondered as the show was entering its final run in 1985, pointing out that, 'despite lukewarm reviews, the lines outside the Broadway Theatre won't stop.' The answer was found in female fans 'gushing' about his magical appeal as if the actor was 'Prince rolled into John Travolta into . . .'[20] 'Despite the years,' another newspaper continued in its review of the terminally ill actor, 'Yul's impish charm and swift panther-like movements on stage are still capable of causing female hearts to beat faster.'[21]

Some critics were in a position to compare the revivals to the original show, commenting on Brynner's virtually unchanged looks, energy, and presence: 'He plants himself like a colossus, with everyone about swirling to the toss of his head, and when he dances he starts a whirlpool.'[22] Others pointed out that his performance was 'a pretty true copy of the original.'[23] Yet others approached him as something of a living relic, admiring the performance as an endurance test:

> It is a role he has played off and on for nearly a generation. As the theatrical profession measures time, this iron-man achievement is little short of miraculous. If we were talking about anthropology, it would be like having a Cro-Magnon man around to talk about bison paintings on the walls.[24]

Familiarity, in sum, was seen both as the show's forte and weakness: 'As a well-traveled production, it has the tameness of a domesticated cat. The spontaneity and ferocity of the tiger it once was are nowhere in sight.'[25] It is difficult to say whether this *Los Angeles Times* critique referred to the show's feline qualities, those of Brynner, or whether the two were at this point simply impossible to ply apart. By the time the show entered its last run, *The New York Times* characterized his stylized performance as 'ritualistic,' with 'the timelessness of Kabuki, not the self-parody of camp.' It further identified the sadness of the play's conclusion not involving the death of the King inasmuch as 'the inevitable passing of an archaic but entirely lovable tradition of Broadway showmanship':

> Yul Brynner's performance in *The King and I* – the longest-running theatrical star of our time – can no longer be regarded as a feat of acting or even endurance. After thirty-odd years of on-and-off barnstorming in the Richard Rodgers–Oscar Hammerstein classic, Mr. Brynner is, quite simply, The King. The man and the role have long since merged into a fixed image that is as much part of our collective consciousness as the Statue of Liberty. One doesn't go to Mr. Brynner's 'farewell engagement' to search for any fresh interpretative angles – heaven forbid! One goes to bow.[26]

Covering the show's 4,625th, and final, performance on 30 June 1985, the paper similarly addressed the merging of the actor and the character, to which Brynner first brought 'his special brand of animal magnetism' as a young man. Despite now being unable to sing some of the numbers due to throat and ear infection (in fact, cancer) the allure of 'his muscular interpretations – his regal stomping and posturing, his scowl, the burning eyes under flaring brows – remained.'[27]

Goodbyes

At this point, Brynner was very much living with terminal lung cancer, preceded by a precancerous growth in his vocal cords when rehearsing the relaunched musical in 1976. Brynner died three months after his last performance, the curtain-call for which lasted a good fifty minutes, yet he did not mention cancer as the reason the show could no longer go on.[28] Rather, he contended that he was in full remission, and that it was his desire to satisfy a need for quality of life and to enjoy friends, arts, and culture in order to renew himself that motivated his retirement from the role – or, as multiple writers put it, made him 'abdicate.'[29]

All in all, the revivals were a remarkable financial success. Aided by print and television advertising campaigns, the show's last week alone grossed $605,546, breaking the all-time Broadway record. Brynner, who had been firmly in control of the productions, had a contract guaranteeing him half of the show's profits, as well as fifteen percent of weekly box office receipts, earning him an estimated $8 million for the role.[30] By the time the performances ended, Brynner had played to approximately 3.6 million theatergoers on Broadway since 1951 and to some 4.5 million while on tour; as early as 1979, the show had made him more money than his films combined.[31] His only unsuccessful rendering of the role was in the short-lived 1972 television series, *Anna and the King*, which failed to attract viewers despite high expectations, possibly by virtue of lacking in musical numbers and relying on situation comedy instead.[32] Even there, Brynner's lack of success was not of the financial sort as he made a reported $20,000 – the equivalent of around $130,000 today – for each half-hour episode.[33]

In the course of the revivals and touring productions, Brynner's high demands for comfort had become something of a standing object of wonder, dismay, and mockery: dressing rooms needed to be refitted according to his specifications – dark brown walls, Jacuzzis, and electric massage chairs included – while the actor himself invested in chauffeured Rolls-Royces.[34] The press largely labeled this as outlandish, diva-like posturing, yet Brynner argued that this was a mere necessity due to the time spent at theaters and the physical toll taken by up to eight weekly performances.[35] Adding to the identification of the actor with the role in the course of its repetitions, Brynner's demands were considered regal enough for the press to suspect that he had, indeed, confused the boundary between stage and real life. Commenting on the issue, Brynner expressed amazement at being labeled 'as a stern first cousin to all those glaring autocrats he's played on stage and screen' and being thus 'unfairly cast as an unfeeling ogre': 'We have to have some joy backstage if we're expected to bring joy in front of an audience, right?'[36] Returning to the question of the disappearing gap between the actor and the role in 1984, he further argued that identifying him with the role was plain silly:

> Life would not be liveable – and acting would not be feasible – if I came home from work and approached my wife as the King of Siam. I never identify with the king – except on stage. On stage, I portray the king; he takes me over.[37]

Yet it was, of course, precisely this role that he was identified with. At Brynner's death, Broadway dimmed the lights of its marquees in homage and, hailing the actor as the king of classic musicals and 'theatres's "king",' American obituaries associated, or even fused, him with his most famous role: 'If ever there was a role cast in heaven, it was Yul Brynner in "The King and I." With his elegant gestures, aristocratic features and erect, lion-like walk, he was *born* to play the king's part.'[38]

Mentions of panther-like grace, animal magnetism, and exotic erotic appeal of the sort that had dotted film reviews and journalistic accounts on Brynner for decades remained part of the posthumous repertoire: Mary Beth Peil – Miss Anna in the 1983–1985 *The King and I* production – recalled him, 'gliding into the light, erect, with the body of a sleek jungle cat,' despite being painfully infirm and in his mid-60s.[39] Feline metaphors were even deployed by Brynner's spokesman, according to whom, '[h]e faced death with a dignity and strength that astounded his doctors. He fought like a lion.'[40] To visually reiterate the kingly reverberation, obituaries used photos of him in full stage make-up as Mongkut while recapping the main details of his life (with varying degrees of accuracy and detail):

> Although he appeared in more than thirty movies and at least five Broadway productions, as far as the public was concerned, Yul Brynner had only one role in him. But it was a beaut: He was The King. [...] His presence sliced through the atmosphere and demanded, rather like the King himself, undivided attention. His elegantly bald head was his trademark, but his magnetism came from his burning eyes, the sharply arched eyebrows, the high cheekbones, the curiously pointed ears and an implicit sense of superiority that approached haughtiness, both onstage and off.[41]

Given the short timespan between Brynner's death and his last performance as King Mongkut, it was not surprising for obituaries to largely focus on this kingly legacy. This connection was most obvious in the United States and England where he had starred in the stage revivals. It was less so in regional contexts where Brynner's stardom remained that of a film star – one whose career had peaked a while back but who remained, nevertheless, recognizable. Predictably headlining its obituary as 'Actor Yul Brynner is dead: man with shaved head,' *Le Monde* listed a version of his origin tale and expansive language skills (here encompassing Mongolian, Japanese, and Hungarian, among others), along with his full film catalog, leaving his stage performances as something of a sideline. With *The King and I*, the paper wrote, 'Yul Brynner gained international fame in film. Cosmopolitan charm with an Asian touch, virile eroticism reinforced by a bald head.'[42] Somewhat paradoxically, given the fact of the star's fresh demise, the *South China Morning Post*'s obituary described him as an 'indestructible, iron man.'[43]

For the most part, Brynner's obituaries, to the degree that I have been able to assemble them, were either direct or slightly edited versions of material published by news agencies such as the Associated Press or Times-Post News Service (aka Los Angeles Times – Washington Post News Service). An obituary credited to the latter began with '[t]hough there were other Broadway and movie roles for Yul Brynner, it is doubtful that any successful actor has been so associated with a single character as was Brynner with the arrogant, bombastic King of Siam,' before moving to his birth and the death of his Gypsy mother on Sakhalin Island in 1917, as well as the main details of his career in which *The King and I* played the key part.[44] The recycling and remodification of syndicated content across continents highlighted the repetitions that had patterned, and structured, Brynner's star image for decades, thus to a degree solidifying them as an exotic kingly figure (through headlines such as 'Yul Brynner, Theatre's "King," Dies' and 'The King Yul Brynner Is Dead').[45] With further forms of remembrance, this image was to be both replicated and challenged.

When appearing in ABC's *Good Morning, America* in January 1985 to promote his farewell engagement as King Mongkut, Brynner taped a segment to be posthumously screened as an anti-smoking television infomercial for the American Cancer Society, first in the United States in February 1986 and then internationally.[46] The laconic infomercial opened with a black screen and white text reading 'YUL BRYNNER, 1920–1985,' and a grave voice-over bringing the issue home: 'Ladies and gentlemen, the late Yul Brynner.' The following thirty seconds featured a one-angle close-up of the talking Brynner, dressed in black turtleneck against a studio background. 'I really wanted to make a commercial when I discovered that I was that sick, and my time was so limited. I wanted to make a commercial that says, simply' – and here he turns to directly face the camera – 'now that I'm gone, I tell you, don't smoke, whatever you do. Just don't smoke.' As the screen fades back to black and the logo of the American Cancer Society appears, Brynner continues on voice-over: 'If I could take back that smoking, we wouldn't be talking about any cancer. I'm convinced of that.'

As a posthumous gesture identified as 'eerie' as though the actor were speaking 'from the grave,' the ad was dramatic just as it was visually striking, making use of Brynner's famous physical trademark, along with his recognizable low voice, now possibly made lower by the cancerous

An afterlife – et cetera, et cetera, et cetera **231**

Figure 9.1 Brynner's posthumous anti-smoking ad

growth.[47] His posthumous activities extended to the Yul Brynner Head and Neck Cancer Foundation (currently the Head and Neck Cancer Alliance) founded to educate the public on the health hazards of smoking.

Brynner had, at times, been highly candid about his health, perhaps most famously appearing in a CBS's *60 Minutes* with Mike Wallace in 1984 to talk about his illness which, at that time, he seemed to have overcome.[48] That this forthcoming approach was not a default is hardly surprising, given the actor's desire for privacy. Only the previous year, rumors of cancer treatment had been dismissed as medical care relating to his old circus injury, while Brynner canceling shows in Minneapolis was explained away as fatigue ('I am not ill. My health has never been better'). Even his final hospitalization was attributed to a 'mild case of bacterial meningitis.'[49] On his deathbed, Brynner insisted on being treated for a stroke rather than cancer.[50] Brynner's illness was partly easy to hide because he missed no shows during his initial radiation therapy treatment when *The King and I* played in Los Angeles – in fact, he missed very few performances whatsoever, even though he needed to skip individual numbers.[51] This was very much an effort to make the show go on.

Man-statue?

As a means of remembering public figures, obituaries are one established representational practice among others – biographies, biopics, portraits, and statues included. Of these, statues, as metal-cast or stone-carved physical productions of likeness, are undoubtedly among the most fixed, and certainly the most concrete. Versions of such likenesses, in the form of wax, emerged well before the actor's death. When Brynner's likeness was presented at the Movieland Wax Museum in the 1970s, it was as The King: the same applied to his figures at the Hollywood Wax Museum and Florida's Stars Hall of Fame wax museum.[52]

When Brynner was immortalized in a statue revealed in Vladivostok in front of his house of birth in 2012 with the inscription, 'Yul Brynner – king of theatre and film,' it was also in his iconic role as Mongkut, standing with his legs apart, hands on hips, head held haughtily high. Designed by the sculptor Alexey Bokiy, the statue is larger than life – albeit not monumentally so – at ten feet tall. The granite statue represents a materially permanent form of reminiscence through which Brynner becomes a visible, tangible form of public urban memory, despite the fact he hadn't lived in, nor even visited, the city of Vladivostok since the age of six. 'He stands,' a journalist writes, 'Social Realist hero-style, in a Mongkut-esque tunic and harem pants, shiny pate glinting in the evening sun. It's a singular figure, and one that – all his life – Brynner was proudly conscious of cutting.'[53]

In addition to being memorialized in statues of wax and stone, his trademark pose has continued to live on in less physical forms of remembrance, re-emerging, for example, in a 2013 *New York Times* article discussing how a person's posture can have an impact on others' moods and impressions. 'A consultant to aspiring politicians and business leaders' who was quoted in the article, advised people to spread their 'arms and legs to form an X like Yul Brynner in *The King and I* before any stressful situation': 'We've seen posing make a tremendous difference in people's presentation and performance [...] It gives you a boost of testosterone.'[54] While there is something a little grim in being thus posthumously positioned as a man-symbol conducive to testosterone boosts, this speaks of the overall function – and continuing appeal – of Brynner's characteristic pose as a means of communicating self-assured masculine dominance through stylized physical means.

The work of remembrance occurring in biographical accounts can contribute to such symbol (or statue) making, yet this has not exactly

Figure 9.2 Yul Brynner statue in Vladivostok. Photograph by Rock Brynner (Wikipedia, Creative Commons License 3.0).

been the case with Brynner. The first of his biographies, Jhan Robbins's *Yul Brynner: The Inscrutable King* appeared in 1987. The book opens with a preface detailing the author's theatrical encounter with the stage-ready King Mongkut during the first Broadway run of *The King and I*: 'I had been warned that Brynner was his own best press agent; that rarely had a self-created image received greater prominence or told more elaborate, spurious tales,' starting with three different accounts on his year of birth. Despite such initial resistant skepticism, Robbins soon describes the magnetism of the actor's 'naked skull, mesmerizing eyes, and flaming nostrils' working their magic:

> 'My true name is Taidge Khan, Jr.,' he said. 'The blood of Ghengis Khan flows through my veins ... My father was a leading adviser to the Czar ... I ran away from home at age thirteen to join the circus ... I have a Ph.D. from the Sorbonne ... The money I earn from acting helps support my destitute gypsy family.'[55]

The preface reads effectively as one of willing seduction. Diving deeper into this narrative web, Robbins tells of fellow journalists witnessing three versions of Brynner's origin stories within three minutes and giving in to their draw, then quickly following suit himself and inviting readers to join the ride: 'So let's enjoy.'[56] The biography draws on interviews with Brynner, his colleagues and friends, many of which appear to be repurposed from previous press sources. All in all, the book offers colorful details, some of arguable accuracy. Contributing to Brynner's self-representation as 'an exotic Oriental,' Robbins, for example, elaborates on his linguistic range expanding from Russian and French to Chinese, Mongolian, Romany Gypsy, and Korean, 'sprinkled with words and phrases of Yiddish, German, Greek, Italian, and Japanese.'[57] And, recounting Brynner's early days with the Chekhov Players, he quotes a fellow actor describing his dormitory room as decorated in the fashion of an 'Arab harem' and posing a veritable erotic honey trap for the visiting women.[58]

Robbins's narrations communicate a pleasure taken in storytelling matching some of the imagination and glee of Brynner himself. Many of the book's passages bear striking resemblance to magazine features and profiles published since the 1950s which, balancing fantasy with biographical fact while dwelling on Brynner's captivating, magnetic figure, helped to solidify the key constituents of his star image: once more, with feeling. In fact, some of these are repeated almost verbatim, so that female fans' and anonymous studio employees' descriptions of Brynner's appeal in *Newsweek* and *Photoplay* (see Chapter 4) – his 'brute strength,' 'subtly gentle tenderness,' commanding presence and gaze that takes 'you back centuries [...] as if a spell had suddenly been cast' – are now attributed to 'a former girlfriend.'[59]

The biography is built on the realization that, despite intentions, the factual details of Brynner's life were impossible to decipher since fantasy and fact had, by this point, become fused together.[60] The premise, approach, and aim were drastically different, even opposite, in Rock Brynner's *Yul: The Man Who Would Be King. A Memoir of Father and Son*, published two years later. This book was very much an attempt to set the record straight and to undo the man-statue, and to do so within a highly personal register where the narration of Brynner's career, marriages, and other social ties met analyses of his persona and recollections of the relation between son and father, both tight and tension-ridden. Rock Brynner himself has characterized the biography as a story 'of how the man became artist, how the artist became king, and sadly, how the king became slave to his own extravagance,' arguing that his father's extensive attachment to the role resulted in something of a tragic over-identification in his later years.[61] As its subtitle suggests, the book is to an extent about the son writing himself into his father's history: such a focus is equally manifest in the 2006 *Empire & Odyssey: The Brynners in Far East Russia and Beyond*, where Rock Brynner traces the life-stories of his great-grandfather, grandfather, and father, as well as that of his own.

The emphasis is to a degree similar in the books that Victoria Brynner edited of her father's photography, starting with the 1996 *Yul Brynner: Photographer* and continuing with the massive 2010 four-volume *Yul Brynner: A Photographic Journey* showcasing his work as both photographer and photographic model. Both book projects offer an overview of Brynner's photographic work while also zooming in especially on images of Victoria Brynner and her mother, Doris Kleiner (Rock Brynner's memoirs similarly foreground his mother, Virginia Gilmore, and the author himself, over other spouses and siblings). The 2010 photographic tribute explores Brynner's star image through its visuality and transformations, just as it presents documentation of his social circle, private life, and public photographic work. In other words, it comprises an analysis, or at least a mapping, of his persona through visual means.

Further biographical explorations include Michelangelo Capua's 2006 *Yul Brynner: A Biography*, which has the benefit of drawing on the two previous accounts of his life. Dutifully researched, it offers a straightforward telling of Brynner's life and career, spiced up with occasional salacious gossip.[62] In addition, Brynner has been memorialized audiovisually in two documentaries, the 1995 *Hollywood Biography* episode *Yul Brynner: The Man Who Was King*, and Benoît Gautier and Jean-Frédéric Thibault's 2019 *Les mille et une vies de Yul Brynner*, the former presenting his life-story through archival materials and interviews with family, friends, and colleagues and the latter being mainly composed of excerpts from Brynner's films and interviews. In charting 'the thousand and one lives of Yul Brynner,' it reiterates much of the actor's self-fabricated myth for posterity so as to reinforce his star image, even as it conflicts with some biographical facts. Beyond these long-play narratives, Brynner has been the occasional topic of articles re-presenting him as an exceptional vintage Hollywood character. In these, he has been framed as mean and egomaniac – yet possibly not entirely so – in ways also befitting King Mongkut.⁶³

A digital afterlife

'They forget old stars so easily these days, unless they see your old movies on TV,' Brynner lamented in 1975, explaining that his touring with *The Odyssey* was a means to 're-plant the seeds of remembrance in my fans.' This, he pointed out, was his reason for making at least three films every two years.⁶⁴ Around this time, Brynner's film career was about to end even though he would go on to energetically cultivate seeds of future remembrance with the stage revivals of *The King and I*. The issue, as identified by Brynner himself, was that of visibility connected to media circulation whereby the stars of years past rapidly disappear from popular awareness.

From a posthumous perspective, forms of remembrance are bound to cluster around the media products that stars have left behind: their screenings and lingering fame. As would be the case with any star, film work remains the primary form of Brynner's contemporary presence. Some of his films are hard to access and virtually forgotten, while others remain recognizable as classics, or at least films familiar enough from television replays. In addition, comparisons and reminiscence have emerged with remakes of Brynner's films. The 1999 *Anna and the King* starred Jodie Foster as Miss Anna, against Chow Yun-fat's King, replacing a Glasgow-born actress with one born in Los Angeles and a Vladivostok-born Mongkut with one of Hong Kong origins. When *The Hollywood Reporter* tweeted that Paramount Pictures had purchased the rights for a Rodgers and Hammerstein musical remake, users responded with comparisons between the 1956 film and the 1999 remake, further venturing into memories of first seeing Brynner onscreen: 'saw this movie when I was five, and I swear, when he slid his hand onto her waist, I swooned'; 'How on earth can they think they could improve on the original. Yul Brynner panther-like, oozing sex appeal and the frightfully English Deborah Kerr ... just wonderful'; 'Seeing them dance together might have been my sexual awakening, and I was only five.'⁶⁵

In the 2016 version of *The Magnificent Seven*, there was no Chris Adams. It was Denzel Washington's Sam Chisholm that led the pack instead, the actor's Blackness coding the character as standing even more strongly out from the white hegemony of the nineteenth century American South. And as *Westworld* was re-imagined as an HBO series, the first season premiering the same year, there was no exact replica of Brynner's gunslinger robot: in a reversal of roles, it is Ed Harris's frequent guest (Man in Black) who becomes the predator instead. In such remakes, echoes of Brynner remain even as changes within them speak of things transforming in how an Asian (albeit not Thai) actor becomes Mongkut; in how an African American star actor, rather than Brynner's brownface Cajun, leads the pack of gunslingers, and in how people, rather than the robots they build, are figured as monstrously inhuman.

Many, but certainly not all, Brynner's films remain available on DVD, subscription-based streaming services, and as YouTube uploads of questionable copyright status. YouTube further hosts archival clips ranging from Brynner's 1957 game-show appearance in *What's My Line* (the main punchline involving his baldness) to his Academy Award acceptance speech ('I hope this isn't a mistake because I won't give it back for anything in the world. Thank you very much.') and posthumous anti-smoking ad. There are diverse fan tributes and a remix composed of every time someone says 'Moses' in *The Ten Commandments*, the drag cameo from *The Magic Christian,* as well as the scene from *The File of the Golden Goose* where Brynner's character meanders through London's saunas, looking for his man. The result is a highly contingent mass of mediated remembrance that speaks of what people find worthy of sharing, for the purposes of titillation, appreciation, amusement, obscurity, and commentary alike, user comments being spaces for articulating memories and impressions of the actor.

Stills of Brynner's Rameses have found their way into contemporary circulation in the form of memes: from his pitying, bemused face combined with the caption 'Rameses watching you complain about just one plague' during the COVID-19 pandemic, to his staring, looming presence declaring 'so it shall be written, so it shall be done' by way of encouragement for doctoral students struggling with their thesis work. He also features in animated GIFs used as reactions to social media posts, to communicate and comment on moods, sentiments, and opinions. Crafted from video clips, GIFs are a means of both capturing an actor's iconic or idiosyncratic gestures, and for communicating mood and attitude in a more impersonal manner. Usually a few seconds long, they both highlight and decontextualize their source materials as excerpts pointing to specific,

Figure 9.3 Google Image search results for 'Yul Brynner animated GIF'

often gestural, detail, allowing for social media users to simultaneously perform affect and demonstrate cultural knowledge.⁶⁶ Brynner's physical presence was often the key attraction in his films while his performances were largely built on poses and gestures: GIFs foreground, isolate, and display these on looping, silent replay. In doing so, they both extend and alter the storage capacities of cinema as an archive of gestures and their transformations traceable across a performer's body of work.⁶⁷

While ending with such digital ephemera may seem like an anti-climax, I argue that it makes for an appropriate place to conclude. A star image is, after all, an impression created through repetitions over time – a performative achievement based on reiteration. Yul Brynner GIFs and YouTube clips can be understood as ripples of cinema history that encapsulate some his most recognizable gestures and scenes in a transformed social and technological context where much of his film work has been virtually forgotten due to its anachronistic notes. What remains and thrives in such vernacular circulation and repurposing is indicative of how film stars of years past continue to be identified, and perhaps appreciated, as well as how their likeness is brought back into social circulation. Star images are fragile in how they continue to be recognized and remembered: digital ephemera is one means of re-planting the seeds of remembrance.

So, there is Rameses, mockingly embracing Nefertiri and then sharply turning away from her, revealing his muscular back and dramatically swinging his blue cape in protest: ornamental, masculine, sassy, mocking, and proud. There, various gunslingers loop, dressed all in black and on the prowl, falling down and shooting to kill, some with robotic facial panels removed and smoking, communicating menace and lethal intent. And, there, the King of Siam gestures exaggeratedly, exhibits child-like astonishment, fumes in exasperation, engages in a frenzied polka-waltz, and snaps his fingers in a gesture of regal command. Et cetera, et cetera, et cetera.

Notes

1. E.g., in *The Guardian*, 11 October 1985; *SF Examiner*, 10 October 1985; *The Calgary Herald*, 11 October 1985; *South China Morning Post*, 13 October 1985; *The Daily Times*, 11 October 1985; *The Montreal Gazette*, 11 October 1985.
2. *The Washington Post*, 11 October 1985b.
3. *The NY Times*, 27 April 1977.
4. Ibid.; *GBH Archive*,1981; *Philadelphia Daily News*, 25 June 1981, 27. This point is also discussed in Chapter 6.
5. *Toronto Star*, 19 August 1984.
6. GBH Archives, 1981.
7. *Saturday Evening Post*, 22 November 1958.
8. *The Calgary Herald*, 13 September 1961.
9. This was explicitly suggested in e.g., Elliot Norton Reviews 1981.
10. *The Sydney Morning Herald*, 29 May 1977, 45.
11. *SF Examiner*, 12 December 1982a, 37; *Afternoon Plus*, 1979.
12. Klein 2003, 222.
13. *The Austin American Statesman*, 26 June 1977.
14. *The NY Times*, 3 May 1977.
15. E.g., *Good Housekeeping*, July 1955, 117; *Cosmopolitan*, October 1957, 20.
16. On iconic performances, see Drake 2006, 85–6.
17. *The Hollywood Reporter*, 9 January 1985.
18. *The Washington Post*, 20 February 1981.
19. *The Sydney Morning Herald*, 29 May 1977; *Cosmopolitan*, May 1978; *LA Times*, 10 November 1983; *The Hollywood Reporter*, 23 August 1983; *Daily News*, 8 January 1985.
20. *The Washington Post*, 22 January 1985.
21. *South China Morning Post*, 11 March 1985.
22. *The Washington Post*, 27 February 1981; *The Washington Post*, 30 July 1978.
23. *SF Examiner*, 12 December 1982b, 44.
24. *SF Examiner*, 12 December 1982a, 37.
25. *LA Times*, 22 August 1983, D2.
26. *The NY Times*, 8 January 1985.
27. *The NY Times*, 1 July 1985. For a summary of reviews for the final run, see *SF Examiner*, 9 January 1985.

28. *LA Times*, 1 July 1985.
29. E.g., *Daily Record*, 30 December 1984; *South China Morning Post*, 11 June 1985; *Variety*, 3 July 1985. Brynner was interested in alternative and experimental cures, from 'Tibetan applied acupuncture,' 'oriental medication,' and homeopathy to meditation, holistic diets, and vitamin treatments. For an early mention, see *Australian Women's Weekly*, 16 April 1975, 17.
30. *Variety*, 3 July 1985; *St. Petersburg Times*, 26 September 1977; already in 1979, Brynner was speculated to be the highest paid Broadway performer to date, *The Calgary Herald*, 30 March 1979.
31. *The NY Times*, 1 July 1985; *SF Examiner*, 15 July 1979.
32. *The Austin Statesman*, 22 September 1972; *The Montreal Gazette*, 24 October 1972; *The Journal News*, 13 August 1972; *LA Times*, 4 October 1972.
33. *LA Times*, 26 October 1971.
34. *The Observer*, 15 April 1979; *Variety*, 25 July 1979; *The Washington Post*, 28 July 1978.
35. *The Washington Post*, 30 July 1978; *The Washington Post*, 11 October 1985a; *SF Examiner*, 15 July 1979; *SF Examiner*, 12 December 1982a.
36. *The Toronto Star*, 12 December 1982.
37. *The Jerusalem Post*, 23 December 1984; also *Elliot Norton Reviews* 1981.
38. *The Washington Post*, 10 October 1985; *The NY Times*, 10 October 1985; *Daily News*, 11 October 1985, emphasis in the original.
39. *The NY Times*, 31 January 1986.
40. *LA Times*, October 10 1985, 3.
41. *The Washington Post*, 11 October 1985a.
42. *Le Monde*, 11 October 1985.
43. *South China Morning Post*, 13 October 1985.
44. E.g., *Calgary Herald*, 11 October 1985.
45. *The NY Times*, 10 October 1985; *South China Morning Post*, 11 October 1985. All this obviously means that obituaries were extremely similar. See also the *LA Times*, 10 October 1985; *The Times of India*, 11 October 1985; *The Times and Democrat*, 11 October 1985.
46. The infomercial was shown in several countries, e.g., Hong Kong, Japan, Israel, and, after some deliberation, Australia: *The NY Times*, 20 February 1986; *The NY Times*, 25 January, 2005; *South China Morning Post*, 20 April 1986; *The Age*, 19 June 1986.
47. *LA Times*, 20 February 1986.
48. *SF Examiner*, 15 December 1984; see also *Good Housekeeping*, November 1985.
49. *LA Times*, 10 November 1983; *St. Petersburg Times*, 11 September 1984; *St. Petersburg Times*, 28 September 1985; *The Korea Times*, 29 September 1985.
50. *South China Morning Post*, 25 February 1990.
51. *Daily Record*, 30 December 1984; *South China Morning Post*, 11 March 1985; *The Daily Times*, 11 October 1985; Brynner 1989, 237.
52. *The Globe and Mail*, 16 February 1980.
53. *The Rake*, Spring 2015.
54. *The New York Times*, 3 May, 2013.
55. Robbins 1987, ix–x.
56. Ibid., xi.

57. Ibid., 2.
58. Ibid., 16–17.
59. Ibid., 79.
60. Ibid., 151.
61. *South China Morning Post*, 25 February 1990; see also *The NY Times*, 12 November 1989.
62. These largely involve gossip on Brynner's sexual affairs, some of which were addressed in Chapter 4, extending to a purported pornographic film featuring the actor in an orgy with Sharon Tate, Peter Sellers, and Cass Elliott of The Mamas and the Papas, Capua 2006, 128. Tate, Sellers, Polanski, and Brynner were all friends. E.g., *Canberra Times*, 15 August 1969.
63. *The Telegraph*, 9 July, 2020; *The Daily Telegraph*, 18 July, 2020; *The Daily Telegraph*, 24 July, 2001.
64. *The Toronto Star*, 22 February 1975.
65. See https://twitter.com/THR/status/1360333701150699520
66. Milter and Highfield 2017, 3.
67. Straw 2011, 126.

References

Films and television shows

Adíos, Sabata / Indio Black. 1970. Gianfranco Parolini (dir.), Alberto Grimaldi (prod.). Italy: Produzioni Europee Associati.
Anastasia. 1956. Anatole Litvak (dir.), Buddy Adler (prod.). United States: 20th Century Fox.
Battle of Neretva. 1969. Veljko Bulajić (dir.), Steve Previn (prod.). Yugoslavia, Italy, West Germany, and United States: Bosna Film, Jadran Film, Kinema Sarajevo, Radna Zajednica Filma, Igor Film, Eichberg-Film and Commonwealth United Entertainment / American International Pictures.
Cast a Giant Shadow. 1966. Melville Shavelson (dir. & prod.). United States: Batjac Productions, The Mirisch Corporation and Lienroc Productions / United Artists.
Catlow. 1971. Sam Wanamaker (dir.), Euan Lloyd (prod.). United States and United Kingdom: MGM.
Con la rabbia agli occhi / Death Rage. 1976. Antonio Margheriti (dir.), Franco Caruso and Raymond R. Homer (prod.). Italy: Giovine Cinematografica / Euro International Films.
Escape from Zahrain. 1962. Ronald Neame (dir.), Francisco Day and Ronald Neame (prod.). United States: Paramount Pictures, CBS and Olive Films.
Flight from Ashiya. 1964. Michael Anderson (dir.), Harold Hecht (prod.). Japan and United States: Harold Hecht Productions / United Artists.
Futureworld. 1976. Richard T. Heffron (dir.), James T. Aubrey and Paul N. Lazarus III (prod.). United States: The Aubrey Company / American International Pictures.
Fuzz. 1972. Richard A. Colla (dir.), George Edwards, Jack Farren and Ed Feldman (prod.). United States: Filmways and Martin Ransohoff Productions / United Artists.
Invitation to a Gunfighter. 1964. Richard Wilson (dir. & prod.). United States: Hermes Productions and Stanley Kramer Productions / United Artists.
Kings of the Sun. 1963. J. Lee Thompson (dir.), Lewis J. Rachmil (prod.). United States: The Mirisch Corporation / United Artists.

Le Serpent / Night Flight from Moscow. 1973. Henri Verneuil (dir. & prod.). France, Italy & West Germany: Les Films de la Boétie, Euro International Film & Rialto Film / Pathfinder Pictures & AVCO Embassy Pictures.
Le testament d'Orphée / Testament of Orpheus. 1960. Jean Cocteau (dir.), Jean Thuillier (prod.). France: Les Editions Cinégraphiques.
Les mille et une vies de Yul Brynner. 2019. Benoît Gautier and Jean-Frédéric Thibault (dir.), Marc Lustigman and Noam Roubah (prod.). France: Arte France and Darjeering.
Morituri. 1965. Bernhard Wicki (dir.), Aaron Rosenberg (prod.). United States: 20th Century Fox.
Once More, with Feeling! 1960. Stanley Donen (dir. & prod). United Kingdom: Columbia Pictures.
Port of New York. 1949. László Benedek (dir.) Aubrey Schenck (prod.). United States: Samba Films and Contemporary Productions / Eagle-Lion Films.
Rescue, with Yul Brynner. 1960. Williams (dir.). United States: CBS Reports.
Return of the Seven. 1966. Burt Kennedy (dir.), Ted Richmond (prod.). United States and Spain: Mirisch Productions and CB Films / United Artists.
Romance of a Horsethief. 1971. Abraham Polonsky (dir.), Gene Gutowski (prod.). France, Italy & Yugoslavia: Jadran Film, International Film and Company Prima Cinematografica / Allied Artists.
Solomon and Sheba. 1959. King Vidor (dir.), Ted Richmond (prod.). United States: Edwin Small Productions / United Artists.
Studio One: Flowers from a Stranger. 1949. Paul Nickoll (dir.) Season 1, Episode 15. United States: CBS.
Surprise Package. 1960. Stanley Donen (dir.), Stanley Donen and Paul B. Radin (prod.). United States: Stanley Done Productions / Columbia Pictures.
Taras Bulba. 1962. J. Lee Thompson (dir.), Harold Hecht (prod.). United States: Harold Hecht Productions and Curtleigh Productions / United Artists.
The Brothers Karamazov. 1958. Richard Brooks (dir.), Pandro S. Berman (prod.). United States: MGM.
The Buccaneer. 1958. Anthony Quinn (dir.), Cecil B. DeMille and Henry Wilcoxon (prod.). United States: Paramount Pictures.
The Double Man. 1967. Franklin J. Schaffner (dir.), Hal E. Chester (prod.). United Kingdom: Albion Film Corporation / Warner Bros.
The File of the Golden Goose. 1969. Sam Wanamaker (dir.), David E. Rose and Edward Small (prod.). United Kingdom: Caralan Productions, Ltd. and Dador Productions / United Artists.
The Journey. 1959. Anatole Litvak (dir.). United States: Alby Pictures / MGM.
The King and I. 1956. Walter Lang (dir.), Charles Brackett (prod.). United States: 20th Century Fox.
The Long Duel. 1967. Ken Annakin (dir. & prod.). United Kingdom: London Independent Producers / Rank Organisation and Paramount Pictures.
The Light at the Edge of the World. 1971. Kevin Billington (dir.), Kirk Douglas, Alfredo Matas, Alexander Salkind, and Ilya Salkind (prod.). United States and Spain: The Bryna Company: National General Pictures.

The Madwoman of Chaillot. 1969. Bryan Forbes (dir.), Ely Landau and Anthony B. Unger (prod.). United States: Commonwealth United Entertainment / Warner Bros and Seven Arts.

The Magic Christian. 1969. Joseph McGrath (dir.), Denis O'Dell (prod.). United Kingdom: Grand Films, Ltd. / Commonwealth United Corporation.

The Magnificent Seven. 1960. John Sturges (dir. & prod.). United States: The Mirisch Corporation and Alpha Productions / United Artists.

The Poppy is Also a Flower / Operation Opium / Danger Grows Wild. 1966. Terence Young (dir.), Hassan Alavikia and Euan Lloyd (prod.). United States, France and Austria: ABC and Astral Films.

The Sound and the Fury. 1959. Martin Ritt (dir.), Jerry Wald (prod.). United States: 20th Century Fox.

The Ten Commandments. 1956. Cecil B. DeMille (dir. & prod.). United States: Paramount Pictures.

The Ultimate Warrior. 1975. Robert Clouse (dir.), Paul Heller and Paul Weintraub (prod.). United States: Warner Bros.

Triple Cross. 1966. Terence Young (dir.), Jacques-Paul Bertrand (prod.). United Kingdom and France: Cineurop Company / Warner Bros.

Villa Rides 1968. Buzz Kulik (dir.), Ted Richmond (prod.) United States: Paramount Pictures.

Westworld. 1973. Michael Crichton (dir.), Paul N. Lazarus III (prod.). United States: MGM.

Yul Brynner: The Man Who Was King. 1995. *Hollywood Biography* Season 1, Episode 8. Gene Feldman (dir.). United States: Janson Media.

Television and radio interviews

Afternoon Plus. 1979. Thames Television. https://www.youtube.com/watch?v=WXVdV-QEp0U

Be My Guest – Yul Brynner, 20 July 1972. BBC. https://www.bbc.co.uk/archive/be-my-guest-yul-brynner/zh736v4

Cinépanorama, 11 July 1959. https://www.ina.fr/ina-eclaire-actu/video/i00010205/yul-brynner-expose-ses-vues-sans-concession-a-pierre-dumayet

Elliot Norton Reviews. 1981. About Yul Brynner – The King and I. WGBH Boston.

GBH Archives. 1981. Elliot Norton interviews Yul Brynner, https://www.youtube.com/watch?v=xXNmP9bkGUY

Le Régional, 13 October 1960. https://www.youtube.com/watch?v=drJoHbkQeB4

Midi trente, 10 November 1972. ORTF. https://www.ina.fr/ina-eclaire-actu/video/i00018116/yul-brynner-en-francais-avec-henry-fonda

Pour le cinéma, 2 March 1973. https://www.ina.fr/ina-eclaire-actu/video/i00010229/yul-brynner-et-henry-fonda-au-sujet-de-leurs-roles-in-le-serpent

Pour le cinéma, 11 September 1980. https://www.ina.fr/ina-eclaire-actu/video/i00011425/yul-brynner-au-festival-du-cinema-americain-de-deauville-en-francais

Radioscopie. 1974. Jacques Chancel avec Yul Brynner. France inter. https://www.youtube.com/watch?v=LO83Kpi8EPE

Patterns of Our Lives, 1 January 1959. United Nations. https://www.unmultimedia.org/classics/asset/C730/C730/

The Ed Sullivan Show, 17 September 1967. https://www.youtube.com/watch?v=UFRueoqXctU

Magazine and newspaper articles

Ajan sävel 7, 1957. YUL BRYNNER. 12–13.
Ajan sävel 11, 1957. Kirjoittaisinko Hänelle?, 16.
Ajan sävel 20, 1958. Mitä pidät Yulista?, 8, 11.
Ajan sävel 46, 1958. Dmitri Karamazov ja Grushenka, 37.
Ajan sävel 11, 1959. Miten kirjoitan lempitähdelleni?, 16.
Ajan sävel 21, 1959. Deborah Kerr ja Yul Brynner MGM:n elokuvassa 'Kohtaus rajalla,' 23.
Ajan sävel 29, 1960. Back cover.
Ajan sävel 45, 1960. Hyväntekeväisyyttä, 35.
Ajan sävel 5, 1961. Ajan sävelen tähtikuvasto, 2.
Ajan sävel 48, 1961. Hän valehtelee niin herttaisesti..., 18–23.
Ajan sävel 12, 1963. Film Cat, Movies, 35.
Álbum dos Aristas 4, 1957. Yul Brynner: A Special Issue.
American Cinematographer, November 1956. Arthur Rowan. Cinematography Unsurpassed, 658–60, 680–3.
Argus, 24 December 1956. F. Keith Manzie. A Dazzling 'King,' 4.
Arlington Heights Herald, 27 October 1960. Jim Phillips. 'Magnificent Seven' Is Successful Film, 48.
Ashbury Park Press, 23 August 1978. Henry Gottlieb. Actor Yul Brynner Is Gypsy Spokesman, B7.
Australian Jewish News, 23 December 1960. Brynner's Report, 5.
Australian Jewish News, 22 December 1967. 'Ten Commandments,' 13.
Australian Jewish Times, 19 August 1960. Jerry Wald Reports from Hollywood, 5.
Australian Jewish Times, 10 October 1974. Peter Brown. Hollywood Film On David Ben-Gurion, 16.
Australian Women's Weekly, 19 September 1956. Joel Sayre. Brynner – He's Sensational!, 14–15, 20.
Australian Women's Weekly, 24 October 1956. New Bergman Film is Her Comeback Bid, 36.
Australian Women's Weekly, 3 April 1957. And All the World's Their Stage, 4.
Australian Women's Weekly, 16 July 1958. New Film Releases, 52.
Australian Women's Weeekly, 4 March 1959. Ainslie Baker. Brynner, Kerr, Together Again, 61.
Australian Women's Weekly, 29 April 1959. Ainslie Baker. Brynner Keeps His Hair On, 57.
Australian Women's Weekly, 24 June 1959. Ainslie Baker. New Releases, 52.
Australian Women's Weekly, 23 December 1959. Ainslie Baker. New Films, 42.
Australian Women's Weekly, 15 June 1960. Miriam Fowler. New Films, 58.

Australian Women's Weekly, 26 October 1960. Miriam Fowler. New Films, 75.
Australian Women's Weekly, 1 May 1963. Marilyn Monroe: The Whole Truth and Nothing but the Truth, 15, 52–3.
Australian Women's Weekly, 19 June 1963. Winifred Munday. Reviews of New Films, 15.
Australian Women's Weekly, 30 September 1970. Model with a Yul Brynner Hairstyle, 5.
Australian Women's Weekly, 28 February 1973. Nan Musgrove. Family Reunion When Yul Brynner Visits Sydney, 10.
Australian Women's Weekly, 23 December 1973. Round Robin Adair. Hair Today – Gone Tomorrow, 105.
Australian Women's Weekly, 13 March 1974. What People Are Wearing Overseas, 13.
Australian Women's Weekly, 16 April 1975. 'A Truly Beautiful Experience': Yul Brynner on Fatherhood at 54 . . ., 15, 17.
Behind the Scenes, 28 March 1957. John Martin. The Awful Truth About Yul Brynner, 18–19, 52, 54–6.
Beverley Times, 24 December 1958. The Films, 3.
Bidoun, Fall 2005. Brian Ackley. Yul Brynner: Hollywood's One Man Melting Pot. *Bidoun* 5: https://bidoun.org/issues/5-icons (accessed 10 March 2022).
Boxoffice, 3 December 1949. 'Port of New York,' 15.
Boxoffice, 16 February 1959. Velma West Sykes. The All-American Favorites of 1958, 19, 23.
Boxoffice, 11 September 1961. Yul Brynner to Capital, 12.
Boxoffice, 5 February 1962. William Herbert. Hollywood Report, 16.
Boxoffice, 4 June 1962. 'Escape from Zahrain,' 28.
Boxoffice, 10 December 1962. 'Taras Bulba,' 11.
Boxoffice, 4 March 1963. Brynner Presents U Thant with Record Album, E7.
Boxoffice, 16 December 1963. 'Kings of the Sun,' 19.
Boxoffice, 26 October 1964. 'Invitation to a Gunfighter,' 11.
Boxoffice, 4 April 1966. 'Cast a Giant Shadow,' 8.
Boxoffice, 2 October 1967. 'The Long Duel,' 11.
Boxoffice, 19 November 1973. 'Westworld,' 7.
Boxoffice, 5 May 1975. Yul Brynner Undecided About X-Rated Pictures, NE3.
Boxoffice, 22 December 1975. Hollywood Report, 15.
Boxoffice, 9 January 1978. From S.J. International Pictures, 12.
Broadcasting, 7 February 1949. Sunday Morning Video, 78.
Broadcasting, 22 August 1949. Production, 62.
Broadcasting, 28 August 1950. Block Sponsors, 69.
Broadcasting, 20 December 1957. Reports on TV Deal Premature – UA's Krim, 63.
Canberra Times, 15 August 1969. Director Weeps at Wife's Funeral, 6.
Canberra Times, 8 May 1974. Not-so Good Sci Fi, 17.
Canberra Times, 10 March 1986. Walter Reisender. Ready to Go for a Thrill of a Life Time . . . Hold on for the Downhill Ride, 15.
Chicago Daily Tribune, 23 October 1956. Hedda Hopper. 'The Sound and the Fury' may Star Olivier and Leigh, B4.
Christian Science Monitor, 27 December 1999. Justin Pritchard. Even Updated 'King and I' Banned in Thailand.
Collier's, 6 July 1956. Joel Sayre. Yul Brynner: Why Do Women Find Him Irresistible?, 32–6, 38.

Cosmopolitan, July 1956. Marshall Scott. Your Cosmopolitan Movie Guide, 44.
Cosmopolitan, August 1956. Marshall Scott. Your Cosmopolitan Movie Guide, 20–1.
Cosmopolitan, November 1956. Marshall Scott. Your Cosmopolitan Movie Guide, 30.
Cosmopolitan, May 1957. Jon Whitcomb. Bald Box-Office King, 34–7.
Cosmopolitan, July 1957. Our Readers Write: The Last Word, 134.
Cosmopolitan, October 1957. Amram Scheinfeld. Are You a Rejected Parent? Actor's Urges, and Sleepwalk Killers, 20–1.
Cosmopolitan, August 1959. Jon Whitcomb. Gina as Sheba, 12–15.
Cosmopolitan, June 1963. Hollis Alpert. Confessions of a Critic, 14–16, 18, 20.
Cosmopolitan, February 1974. Liz Smith. Cosmo Goes to the Movies, 24.
Cosmopolitan, May 1978. Helen Gurley Brown. Step into My Parlor, 16.
Courier-Post, 29 January 1975. Ron Avery. The Yul on the Elevator Is Something Else Onstage, 6.
Courier-Post, 13 October 1985. Angela Fox Dunn. A Man Who Would Be King, 15.
Daily Mail, 27 December 1999. Jane Kelly. I Turned Down Clark Gable and Ditched Sinatra, 13.
Daily Mail Online, 30 April 2009. Michael Thornton. The Rumbustious Life of Gertrude Lawrence, https://www.dailymail.co.uk/femail/article-1175140/The-rumbustious-life-Gertrude-Lawrence--Hollywoods-maneater.html (accessed 5 March 2022).
Daily News, 7 February 1946. John Chapman. 'Lute Song' Visually Magnificent but Selfconscious as to Drama, 41.
Daily News, 3 February 1950. Wanda Hale. 'Port of New York' Globe's Melodrama, 68.
Daily News, 13 May 1953. John Chapman. Mainly About Theatre, C15.
Daily News, 2 July 1956. Wanda Hale. The Perfect Musical on View at the Roxy, 41.
Daily News, 26 August 1956. Wanda Hale. Ingrid Tells Critic: This Is My Last Movie, B10.
Daily News, 30 March 1957. Jess Stearn. Bold, Bad and Bald, 12.
Daily News, 30 March 1958. Kate Cameron. 'Brothers Karamazov' Is Fascinating Film, 29.
Daily News, 10 August 1958. Russ Braley. It's Never Dull with Yul, 29.
Daily News, 12 February 1960. Kate Cameron. Gay Stage and Screen Shows at Music Hall, 44.
Daily News, 23 April 1964. Wanda Hale. Mediocre Melodrama Wastes Good Actors, 89.
Daily News, 2 May 1968. Wanda Hale. Plenty of Ski Action in a So-So Spy Yarn, 64.
Daily News, 17 July 1971. Wanda Hale. Another Tale from Jules Verne, C21.
Daily News, 23 September 1971. Kathleen Carroll. 'Adios, Sabata' Violent, Silly, C21.
Daily News, 21 October 1971. Kathleen Carroll. 'Catlow' Is Nice, Genial Horse Opera, 94.
Daily News, 8 January 1985. Douglas Watt. Long Live 'the King'!, 29.
Daily News, 11 October 1985. Death of a King, C17.
Daily Record, 30 December 1984. Michael Kuchwara. The King Is Hanging Up His Crown, B4.
Daily Telegraph, 19 May 1951. Strangely Enough, 1.
Daily Telegraph, 17 June 1951. Hedda Hopper's Hollywood, 38.
Daily Telegraph, 1 July 1951. Hedda Hopper's Hollywood, 46.
Edmonton Journal, 30 November 1977. Barry Westgate. Brynner is Just Too Old for This Kind of Thing, C2.

Elokuva-aitta 23, 1956a. Tom. Kaljupäinen Yul Brynner lumoaa naiset, 10–11.
Elokuva-aitta 23, 1956b. Kuningas ja minä, 28.
Elokuva-aitta 3, 1957. Elokuva-aitan tähti-kokoelma, 45.
Elokuva-aitta 5, 1957. Anastasia, 26.
Elokuva-aitta 6, 1957. Antreas Kälppäinen. Huomenna on mulle kulta uusi, 16–17.
Elokuva-aitta 8, 1957. Ingrid ja Yul saivat Oscarin, 5, 26.
Elokuva-aitta 16, 1957. Nalle Puh. Kurvamammasta probleemakuopukseen, 18–19.
Elokuva-aitta 17, 1957. Antreas Kälppäinen. Tutti Frutti, 16–17.
Elokuva-aitta 24, 1957. Antreas Kälppäinen. Kieltäydyn suutelemasta – suutelen sittenkin, 22–3.
Elokuva-aitta 9, 1958. Antreas Kälppäinen. Älkää sentään leikkikö rakkaudella, 22–3.
Elokuva-aitta 15, 1958. Sal Mineon kuvakokoelmasta, 14–15.
Elokuva-aitta 16, 1958. Kymmenen käskyä, 6–7.
Elokuva-aitta 20, 1958. Karamazovin veljekset, 32.
Elokuva-aitta 22, 1958. Antreas Kälppäinen. Sydämellä on oikkunsa, 24–5.
Elokuva-aitta 23, 1958. Heikki Eteläpää. Majuri Surov tapaa Lady Ashmoren, 8–9.
Elokuva-aitta 24, 1958a. Ovatko suosikkinne tässä joukossa?, 14–15.
Elokuva-aitta 24, 1958a, Antreas Kälppäinen. Muuttelevainen aina on nainen, 24–5.
Elokuva-aitta 15, 1959. Antreas Kälppäinen. Filmikesän touhuja, 18–19.
Elokuva-aitta 19, 1959. Antreas Kälppäinen. Kuinka paljon rakkautta..., 16–17.
Elokuva-aitta 7, 1960. Heikki Kajav. Salomo ja Saaban kuningatar, 25.
Elokuva-aitta 11, 1960. Aito Mäkinen. Vihellyskonsertti päätti loistavat elokuvakilpailut Cannes'issa, 4–7.
Elokuva-aitta 18, 1960. Raoul af Hällström. Vielä kerran, tunteella, 18–19.
Elokuva-aitta 9, 1961. Antreas Kälppäinen. Kalkutassa Gagnes... 22.
Elokuva-aitta 9, 1962. Yul Brynner kuvasi Anatole Litvakin, 22.
Elokuva-aitta 1, 1963. Pako Zahrainista, 40.
Esquire, 30 August 2013. Jake Gallagher. An Icon, A Detail: Yul Brynner's Roped Shoulders, https://www.esquire.com/style/mens-fashion/a24560/yul-brynner-roped-shoulders-0813/ (accessed 10 March 2022).
Film Bulletin, 23 December 1963. 'Kings of the Sun', 11.
Filmitähti 2, 1957. Kymmenen käskyä: kuvakertomus samannimisen Paramount-elokuvan mukaan, 5–23.
Gay Times, October 1998. Boxing Clever, 78.
Good Housekeeping, July 1955. Virginia Brynner. 'The King' and I, 52–5, 117–18, 121.
Good Housekeeping, March 1959. Ruth Halbert. Movies, 24.
Good Housekeeping, February 1960. Eleanor Harris. The Improbable Anthony Quinn, 68–9, 190–4.
Good Housekeeping, November 1985. Cindy Adams. The Strange Case of Yul Brynner's Cancer, 66, 68, 70–1.
Harper's Bazaar, April 1951. The King and I, 144.
Harper's Bazaar, December 1967. Rene Lecler. St Moritz! The Most Expensive Snow in the World, 32.
Harper's Bazaar, February 2012. Victoria Brynner, My Father, Yul Brynner, 90–1.
Harpers & Queen, December 1981. Charles Bricker. Russians in Paris, 222, 224, 226, 228, 230, 232, 234, 236, 238.

Harpers & Queen, December 1988. Simon Ausberg. Haute Culture, 128, 130, 134, 136.
Harrison's Reports, 22 February 1958. 'The Brothers Karamazov,' 32.
Harrison's Reports, 6 January 1960. 'Once More, with Feeling!' 23.
Harrison Reports, 8 October 1960. 'The Magnificent Seven,' 162.
Harrison's Reports, 15 October 15 1960. 'Surprise Package,' 166.
Helsingin Sanomat, 1 May 2010. Tommi Römpötti. Mustalaismusiikista tuli nyt klubien kuumetta, https://www.hs.fi/kulttuuri/art-2000004728087.html (accessed 10 March 2022).
Hush-Hush, July 1957. Leslie Paster. The Bald Facts about Yul Brynner's Secret Life, 32–4, 46.
Kinematograph Weekly, 20 May 1965. 'Invitation to a Gunfighter, 15.
Kinematograph Weekly, 17 December 1966. 'Return of the Seven,' 155, 158.
Kinematograph Weekly, 8 April 1967. 'The Double Man,' 10–11.
Kinematograph Weekly, 3 August 1968. Derek Todd. Violence Still An Easy Way Out?, 10–11.
Le Courrier Australien, 18 January 1957. Echos de l'ecran, 7.
Le Courrier Australien, 10 May 1957. Pierre Lambert. Le Cinema en France, 7.
Le Courrier Australien, 16 November 1962. Les plus grands vedettes du monde enregistrees sur microsillon au profit des refugies, 6.
Le Monde, 23 January 1957. Jean de Baroncelli. 'Le Roi et moi,' 12.
Le Monde, 11 May 1957. Michel Legris. Au drap d'or, 12.
Le Monde, 21 January 1958. Jean de Baroncelli. 'Les Dix Commandements,' 9.
Le Monde, 13 May 1958. Roger Régent. Quatre films dont: les 'Frères Karamazov' et des stars à gogo, 13.
Le Monde, 4 June 1958. Jean de Baroncelli. 'Les Frères Karamazov,' 13.
Le Monde, April 20 1959. Jean de Baroncelli. 'Le Voyage,' 15.
Le Monde, 19 December 1959. Les Nouveaux Films, 12.
Le Monde, 6 June,1959. 'Le Bruit et la fureur,' 12.
Le Monde, 23 January 1964. Yvonne Baby. 'Les Rois du Soleil,' 12.
Le Monde, 27 January 1965. Yvonne Baby. 'Le Mercenaire de minuit,' 11.
Le Monde, 28 September 1965a. Un film pour venir en aide a l'enfance déshértée, 20.
Le Monde, 28 September 1965b. Les Nations Unies commandent un film sur le conflit, 6.
Le Monde, 29 December 1965. Petites nouvelles, 10.
Le Monde, 23 January 1967. N.Z., 'L'ombre d'un géant,' 14.
Le Monde, 25 August 1970. Jean de Baroncelli. 'La Bataille de la Neretva,' 13.
Le Monde, 14 August 1971. Yvonne Baby. 'Le voleur de chevaux,' d'Abraham Polansky, 12.
Le Monde, 15 April 1978. Isabelle Vichniac. Les Tziganes veulent obtenir un statut consultative auprès de l'ONU, 14.
Le Monde, 11 October 1985. J.S. L'acteur Yul Brynner est mort, 21.
Life, 28 May 1956. The King, His Camera, and a Film Triumph, 109–14.
Life, 18 March 1957. Head of Hair for a Head of Skin, 140.
Life, 29 June 29 1959. A Fringe Benefit, 149.
Life, 25 April 1960. Brynner's Bride, 102.
Lincoln Journal and Star, 28 August 1949. CBS-TV Signs Brynner, B1.
London Life, 27 August 1966. What People Are Hating, 24–5.
Los Angeles Advocate, 1 April 1970. 'Magic Christian' Another Peter Sellers Disaster, 15.

Los Angeles Times, 7 December 1949. John L. Scott. Dope Smuggling Theme of New Screen Thriller, C10.
Los Angeles Times, 15 June 1951. Hedda Hopper. Anne Francis Will Get Starring Back, C6.
Los Angeles Times, 17 June 1951. Radie Harris. Yul Brynner Plans TV Stock Company, D2.
Los Angeles Times, 26 June 1951. Hedda Hopper. Three Stars Selected for Harding Original, C6.
Los Angeles Times, 9 June 1952. Hedda Hopper. Republic Will Costar MacMurray, Ralston, C3.
Los Angeles Times, 19 June 1952. Hedda Hopper. Hedda Tells Life Story in 'From Under My Hat', C10.
Los Angeles Times, 9 August 1952. Edwin Schallert. Audrey Hepburn Likely Brynner Costar, A9.
Los Angeles Times, 13 October 1952, Edwin Schallert. Cossack Theme Hovers for Brynner, 1, C9.
Los Angeles Times, 26 October 1952. Edwin Schallert. Films Attract Brynner as Newest Challenge, D9.
Los Angeles Times, 30 September 1952. Hedda Hopper. Prelle to Do 'Camille' in English and French, B6.
Los Angeles Times, 17 January 1953. Edwin Schallert. Vera Ellen Reported in Dramatic Role, A9.
Los Angeles Times, 9 February 1953. Hedda Hopper. Film Postponement Enriches Brynner, C8.
Los Angeles Times, 14 March 1953. Hedda Hopper. Burton, Simmons Set for Spy Drama, A10.
Los Angeles Times, 27 June 1953. Edwin Schallert. Kelly to Dance Sinbad with Cartoons, B7.
Los Angeles Times, 6 October 1953. Edwin Schallert. De Mille Selects Yul Brynner for Rameses, A21.
Los Angeles Times, 7 October 1953. Edwin Schallert. Mel Ferrer to Direct and Star for Bartley, B7.
Los Angeles Times, 11 October 1953. Edwin Schallert. Italian Film Men See Co-operation as Need in Crisis, D4.
Los Angeles Times, 30 October 1953. Philip K. Scheuer. 'Lust for Life' Artist Offered to Yul Brynner, C7.
Los Angeles Times, 11 March 1954. Hedda Hopper. 'Build-Up Boys' Will Be Andrews Picture, B10.
Los Angeles Times, 18 May 1954, Philip K. Scheuer. Yul Brynner, Coming to Play on Stage, Wants to Direct Film, Part D1 3.
Los Angeles Times Times, 21 May 1954. Hedda Hopper. 'King' Film Will Await Brynner in Year, B7.
Los Angeles Times, 28 May 1954. Yul Brynner By-passes Role of Holofernes, B6.
Los Angeles Times, 7 June 1954. Bert Bacharach. Stag Lines, A10.
Los Angeles Times, 19 June 1954. Edwin Schallert. Lo Jolla Festival Expands; Brynner Cited as 'Matador Star', A13.
Los Angeles Times, 3 June 1955. Hedda Hopper. Liz Will Ride High in Trio of Vehicles, C6.

Los Angeles Times, 15 June 1955. Hedda Hopper. Original Stars Will Play 'Guys and Dolls,' C10.
Los Angeles Times, 28 August 1955. Hedda Hopper. Yul Brynner Tires of Acting, D1, 4.
Los Angeles Times, 29 October 1955. Hedda Hopper. Brainwashing Story, 'Rack,' Leads Picket, B6.
Los Angeles Times, 30 November 1955. Hedda Hopper. 'Wedding Clock' Will Star Cagney, Wagner, C8.
Los Angeles Times, 5 April 1956. Hedda Hopper. Yul Brynner Will Star in 'Buccaneer,' C10.
Los Angeles Times, 2 June 1956. Hedda Hopper. Anna Kashifi to Star in '10,000 Bedrooms,' C8.
Los Angeles Times, 9 July 1956a. Hedda Hopper. Sheree North Will Star in 'Do Re Mi,' C6.
Los Angeles Times, 9 July 1956b. Edwin Schallert. Bill William Rounds Out Big Western Cast; Brynner Says No Stalin!, C7.
Los Angeles Times, 26 July 1956. Hedda Hopper. Gregory Peck Stars in 'Designing Woman,' B12.
Los Angeles Times, 30 July 1956. Hedda Hopper. Hugh Marlowe Will Star in 'Black Whip,' C8.
Los Angeles Times, 28 October 1956. Edwin Schallert. 'Commandments' Hits Epic Heights, D1, 4
Los Angeles Times, 15 November 1956. Hedda Hopper. Matador Will Star in Own Life Story, D14.
Los Angeles Times, 18 December 1956. Hedda Hopper. Metro After Fisher to Star in 'Jumbo,' A24.
Los Angeles Times, 22 January 1957. Hedda Hopper. Africa Calls Wayne for 'Rain in Kenya,' A22.
Los Angeles Times, 24 November 1957. Hedda Hopper. Irony Marks Yul's Career, E3.
Los Angeles Times, 17 February 1958. Hedda Hopper. Lee J. Cobb Signed for Two New Films, D8.
Los Angeles Times, 22 January 1958. Hedda Hopper. Brynner Considers Pear Buck Story, A16.
Los Angeles Times, 3 February 1958. Hedda Hopper. Brynner and Quinn to Do 'Gladiators', D8.
Los Angeles Times, 12 March 1958. Hedda Hopper. Quinn, Sophea Loren Form Own Company, C6.
Los Angeles Times, 16 May 1958. Hedda Hopper. Brynner Western from Japan Film, B8.
Los Angeles Times, 15 August 1958. Philip K. Scheurer. Fall-out Fishermen to Be Dramatized, B7.
Los Angeles Times, 17 November 1958. Hedda Hopper. Crosby May Act Priest Role Again, D8.
Los Angeles Times, 8 February 1959. Philip K. Scheuer. 'The Journey' Lifts the Iron Curtain, D1, 4.
Los Angeles Times, 19 February 1959. John L. Scott. 'Journey' Impressive and Thoughtful Film, C8.
Los Angeles Times, 2 November 1959. Hedda Hopper. Brynner Will Take 'Mad King' Role, D12.

Los Angeles Times, 27 March 1960. Yul Brynner Divorced in Juarez, Mex., A2.
Los Angeles Times, 28 October 1960. John L. Scott. Comedy Misfires in 'Surprise Package', C8.
Los Angeles Times, 30 October 1960. Philip K. Scheuer. Swords of Bushido Become Guns in 'Magnificent Seven,' D3.
Los Angeles Times, 25 November 1960. Charles Stinson. 'Magnificent Seven' Magnificent Western, D15.
Los Angeles Times, 22 January 1961. U.S. Wins Top Prizes in World TV Festival, A11.
Los Angeles Times, 29 January 1961. Marcia Cohen. Photos Add to Brynner Aid Appeal, C6.
Los Angeles Times, 6 July 1961. Hedda Hopper. Brynner Will Do 'Mound Builders,' A28.
Los Angeles Times, 14 June 1962. Philip K. Scheuer. Yul Brynner Takes 'Escape' Stoically, D9.
Los Angeles Times, 6 July 1962. Hedda Hopper. Jack Rumanian Trip Was a 'Wow!', D7.
Los Angeles Times, 11 November 1962. Hedda Hopper. Film Director's Velvet Glove Hides Tough, Firm Hand, A4, 5, 10.
Los Angeles Times, 26 September 1963. Hedda Hopper. Yul Brynner Stars in Second Western, D7.
Los Angeles Times, 17 October 1963. Hedda Hopper. Wilder Sets O'Toole as Sherlock Holmes, D10.
Los Angeles Times, 19 December 1963. Philip K. Scheuer. 'Kings of the Sun' Whooping Whopper, D11.
Los Angeles Times, 17 February 1964. Hedda Hopper. Wayne Will Play 'Harm's Way' Role, D16.
Los Angeles Times, 24 October 1964. Margaret Harford. 'Gunfighter' Is Moody Western, A18.
Los Angeles Times, 15 December 1965. Kevin Thomas. Yul Brynner's Favorite Role: Solving Plight of Refugees, E17.
Los Angeles Times, 2 December 1967. Movie Call Sheet, C9.
Los Angeles Times, 22 May 1968. Kevin Thomas. 'Kona', 'Double Man' Playing Citywide, D16.
Los Angeles Times, 9 December 1968. Joyce Haber. Having Her Own Seance at Home, D25.
Los Angeles Times, 12 August 1971. Kevin Thomas. Jules Verne's 'Light' Opens Citywide D15.
Los Angeles Times, 29 August 1971. William Wingfield. Letters: Looking on in Horror, D20.
Los Angeles Times, 15 September 1971. Kevin Thomas. Tell Them Brynner Is Here, D9.
Los Angeles Times, 16 September 1971. Kevin Thomas. 90 Bodies Bite the Dust in 'Sabata', D20.
Los Angeles Times, 26 October 1971. Joyce Haber. King and I Pilot Going First Class, D10.
Los Angeles Times, 4 November 1971. Kevin Thomas. Brynner in Nonviolent Western, D16.
Los Angeles Times, 14 May 1972. The Centerfold Competition Unfolds, 65.
Los Angeles Times, 4 October 1972. Cecil Smith. A TV Producer's Split-Level Mind, D13.

Los Angeles Times, 12 October 1973. Ernest B. Furgurson. It's a Weird Standard That Shrugs Off Violence, B7.
Los Angeles Times, 24 October 1973. Kevin Thomas. Acting Out Fantasy in 'Westworld', D11.
Los Angeles Times, 1 April 1975. Joyce Haber. No Sex Symbol, Says Yul Brynner, D6.
Los Angeles Times, 7 April 1975. Yul Brynner Overjoyed as His Orphan Arrives, A2.
Los Angeles Times, 15 April 1975. Joyce Harber. Glad Tidings and Great Joy for Yul, D10.
Los Angeles Times, 10 August 1975. Joyce Harber. Sensitive, Strong and Well In His Skin, 31.
Los Angeles Times, 22 August 1983. Sylvie Drake. 'King' Yul Brynner Still Ruling with Iron Hand, D1–2.
Los Angeles Times, 10 November 1983. Sylvie Drake. Taylor's Theatre Group: It's Curtains, D2.
Los Angeles Times, 1 July 1985. Jennings Parrott. Shall We Dance? Brynner Reaches the Last 'Et Cetera', A2.
Los Angeles Times, 10 October 1985. Michael Seiler. Yul Brynner Dies at 65: 30 Years in 'King and I', 3, 36.
Los Angeles Times, 20 February 1986, Yul Brynner's Posthumous Message, D21.
Los Angeles Times, 16 September 1989. Dan Sullivan. Critics Are a Royal Pain for Nureyev, 3.
Los Angeles Times, 10 October 1985. Michael Seiler. Yul Brynner Dies at 65: 30 Years in 'King and I,' 3, 36.
Meridien Record, 8 December 1945. 'Lute Song' With Mary Martin Opening Thurs., Company of 70, 5.
Minneapolis Tribune, 9 July 1951. Walter Winchell. King of Thailand Writes a Melody, 10.
Minneapolis Tribune, 20 January 1962. Ben Kern. 'Taras Bulba' Isn't Serious or Funny, F3.
Minneapolis Tribune, 25 June 1971. Ben Kern. Movie Reviews, D3.
Minneapolis Tribune, 29 July 1971. Will Jones. After Last Night, B14.
Modern Screen, October 1956. Florence Epstein. New Movies, 10.
Modern Screen, June 1957. When Yul Beat the U.S. Marine Corps, 31.
Modern Screen, May 1958. Florence Epstein. New Movies, 6.
Modern Screen, December 1958. Louella Parsons. That Brynner Rumor, 18.
Monthly Film Bulletin, index 1956. Penelope Houston. 'King and I, The,' 114.
Monthly Film Bulletin, index 1957. J.A.D.C. 'Anastasia,' 14.
Monthly Film Bulletin, index 1958. T.B. 'Brothers Karamazov, The,' 98–9.
Monthly Film Bulletin, index 1959a. D.H. 'Journey, The,' 56.
Monthly Film Bulletin, index 1959b. Robert Vas. 'Buccaneer, The,' 67.
Monthly Film Bulletin, index 1959c. L.G.S. 'Solomon and Sheba,' 148.
Monthly Film Bulletin, index 1959d. Peter John Dyer. 'Sound and the Fury, The,' 57.
Monthly Film Bulletin, index 1960a. Brenda Davies. 'Once More, with Feeling!,' 33.
Monthly Film Bulletin, index 1960b. 'Surprise Package,' 157.
Monthly Film Bulletin, index 1961. Peter John Dyer. 'Magnificent Seven, The,' 44–5.
Monthly Film Bulletin, index 1962. 'Escape from Zahrain,' 94.
Monthly Film Bulletin, index 1963. 'Taras Bulba,' 70.
Monthly Film Bulletin, index 1964. 'Kings of the Sun,' 57.
Monthly Film Bulletin, index 1965. Tom Milne. 'Invitation to a Gunfighter,' 104–5.

Monthly Film Bulletin, index. 1966. D.W. 'Cast a Giant Shadow,' 136.
Monthly Film Bulletin, index 1967a. 'The Long Duel,' 142.
Monthly Film Bulletin, index 1967b. 'Danger Grows Wild,' 9.
Monthly Film Bulletin, index 1969. Brenda Davies. 'Madwoman of Chaillot, The,' 233.
Monthly Film Bulletin, index 1973a. Tom Milne. 'Indio Black,' Sai Che Ti Dico: Se un Grand Figlio di . . ., 52.
Monthly Film Bulletin, index 1973b. Tom Milne. 'The Light at the Edge of the World,' 30.
Monthly Film Bulletin, index 1974. Philip Strick. 'Westworld,' 56.
Monthly Film Bulletin, index 1976. Richard Combs. 'The Ultimate Warrior,' 12.
Monthly Film Bulletin, index 1977a. Tom Milne. 'Romance of a Horse Thief,' 173.
Monthly Film Bulletin, index 1977b. Tim Pulleine. 'Con la rabbia agli occhi' ('Anger in His Eyes'), 191.
Motion Picture Daily, 30 November 1951. 100-Stars for UCP's 'Celebrity Parade,' 4.
Motion Picture Daily, 11 October 1960. William Werneth. 'Surprise Package,' 4.
Motion Picture Exhibitor, 27 November 1957. On the Other Side of the Camera, 19.
Motion Picture Exhibitor, 12 October 1960. 'Surprise Package,' 19.
Motion Picture Exhibitor, 21 October 1964. 'Invitation to a Gunfighter,' 25.
Motion Picture Herald, 30 June 1956. Feature Review: 'The King and I', 21.
Nepean Times, 19 April 1962. Writer's Success, 6.
Newsweek, 19 May 1958. Michael Mackay. Yul Brynner – Golden Egghead, 100–4.
New York Herald Tribune, 24 February 1946. Otis L. Guernsey Jr. The Playbill: Yul Brynner; Swiss Citizen Who Is Also Gypsy-Mongol, D1–2.
New York Herald Tribune, 3 February 1950. James S. Barstow Jr. 'Port of New York,' 14.
New York Herald Tribune, 30 March 1951. Otis L. Guernsey Jr. The theatres: 'The King and I,' 14.
New York Herald Tribune, 17 May 1951. Bert McCord. New of the Theater, 21.
New York Herald Tribune, 14 October 1952. Brynner to Play Russian in Film, 24.
New York Herald Tribune, 19 December 1955. Joe Hyams. This Is Hollywood, 13.
New York Herald Tribune, 11 March 1956. Louis Berg. The 'King' Takes Pictures, SM12.
New York Herald Tribune, 22 April 1956. Brynner Slated to Direct and Star in 'Buccaneer,' D4.
New York Herald Tribune, 29 June 1956. William K. Zinsser. Screen: 'The King and I,' 9.
New York Herald Tribune, 2 August 1956. Eugenia Shephard. Inside Fashion, 10.
New York Herald Tribune, 9 November 1956. Herbert Kupferberg. Screen: 'The Ten Commandments,' 17.
New York Herald Tribune, 14 December 1956. William K. Zinsser. 'Anastasia,' 13.
New York Herald Tribune, 20 January 1957. The Secret of Yul, G28.
New York Herald Tribune, 20 June 1957. Yul Brynner Is Hurt While on Horseback Ride, 5.
New York Herald Tribune, 7 February 1958. Joe Hyams. Yul Brynner Is Also a Skilled Photographer, 11.
New York Herald Tribune, 24 April 1958. Art Buchwald. Real Man on the Screen, A1.
New York Herald Tribune, 13 May 1958a. Brynner Sent by Washington, 5.
New York Herald Tribune, 13 May 1958b. 'Brothers Karamazov' Is Booed at Cannes, 5.
New York Herald Tribune, 12 June 1958. Joe Hyams. Yul Brynner; the Undefinable, 17.
New York Herald Tribune, 30 December 1958. Yul Brynner with Hair, 17.
New York Herald Tribune, 22 February 1959. Paul V. Beckley. Puzzle for a Red Soldier, D1, 4.

New York Herald Tribune, 28 March 1959. Paul V. Beckley. 'The Sound and the Fury,' 12.
New York Herald Tribune, 19 April 1959. Paul V. Beckley. William Faulkner's 'Sound and Fury,' D1.
New York Herald Tribune, 18 May 1959. Joe Hyams. Yul Brynner Makes His Hobbies Pay, 11.
New York Herald Tribune, 26 December 1959. Paul V. Beckley. 'Solomon and Sheba,' 4.
New York Herald Tribune, 12 February 1960. Paul V. Beckley. 'Once More, With Feeling!', 11.
New York Herald Tribune, 15 October 1960. Paul V. Beckley. 'Surprise Package,' 6.
New York Herald Tribune, 24 November 1960. Paul V. Beckley. 'The Magnificent Seven,' 18.
New York Herald Tribune, 4 December 1960a. Joe Hyams. Man on a Mission, 1, 3, 8.
New York Herald Tribune, 4 December 1960b. Ann W. Griffith. Yul Brynner's UN Tour Among Refugees, D23.
New York Herald Tribune, 1 January 1961. Mary Rosa. Young, Lost, Waiting, D23.
Orlando Sentinel, 4 December 1992. Yul Brynner's Wine Fetches a King's Ransom – $124,400, A2.
Ottawa Journal, 5 December 1977. Frank Daley. Junk Season at the Movies, 21.
Out, 1 February 1994. Bruce C. Steele. It's a Rapp, 34.
Out, 1 June 2012. Stephanie Theobald. Symposium: Wait 'til You Hear This!, 55–6.
Papua New Guinea Post, 1 September 1962. Double Excitement This Week, 21.
Pasadena Evening Post, 23 October 1923. Great Crowd Sees Film Preview, 1.
People, 5 April, 2019. Alexia Fernández. Anthony Rapp Says *King and I* Star Yul Brynner 'Punched Me in the Stomach Once,' https://people.com/movies/anthony-rapp-says-yul-brynner-punched-stomach/ (accessed 10 March 2022).
Philadelphia Daily News, 18 November 1960. Phyllis Batelle. Yul Brynner a Hard-Working UN Humanitarian, 26.
Philadelphia Daily News, 6 February 1971. Leonard Lyons. The Real Dayan's Disguise Stands Up, 22.
Philadelphia Daily News, 25 June 1981. Jonathan Takiff. How the King Was Crowned, 19, 27.
Philadelphia Inquirer, 13 August 1990. Karen Heller. Who Can Play a Role?, D1.
Photoplay, February 1952. Sheilah Graham. Believe It . . . Or not, 48–9, 72.
Photoplay, February 1957. Army Archerd. Who Needs Hair?, 64–5, 109–10.
Photoplay, October 1957. Sal Mineo. The King and Me, 53–4, 100–1.
Photoplay, 23 August 1973. Bert Reisfeld. Yul Brynner's Strange New Movie, 36–7, 47.
Picturegoer, 15 September 1956a. Can Hollywood Hold Brynner?, 7–8.
Picturegoer, 15 September 1956b. The Biggest Impact Since Brando, 16.
Picturegoer, 2 March 1957a. Bergman's Back – And Even Better, 16.
Picturegoer, 2 March 1957b. Love Without Kisses, 3.
Picturegoer, 4 May 1957. I'm Getting Tired of Oscar, 9.
Picturegoer, 8 June 1957. Your Favourite Stars, 5.
Picturegoer, 28 December 1957. Stop the Sneering – It's a Terrific Film, 20.
Picturegoer, 8 March 1958. Focus: Lifeline, 3.
Picturegoer, 5 July 1958. Elizabeth Forrest. Don't Let it Go into Your Head, 5.
Picturegoer, 19 July 1958. Monroe Gets the Last Laugh, 20.
Picturegoer, 8 November 1958. Around the Studios, 17.

Picturegoer, 17 January 1959. Peter Day. The Fantastic Yul Brynner, 8–9.
Picturegoer, 24 January 1959. Peter Day. Disaster on the Circus Trapeze: The Fantastic Yul Brynner, Part 2, 8–9.
Picturegoer, 31 January 1959. Peter Day. He's Scornful of His Appeal to Women: The Fantastic Yul Brynner, Part 3, 14–15.
Picturegoer, 21 February 1959. Cover image.
Picturegoer, 21 March 1959. Brynner and Kerr Make the Sparks Fly Again, 20.
Picturegoer, 18 April 1959. The South Still Intoxicates, 20.
Picturegoer, 9 May 1959. The Buccaneer, 11.
Picturegoer, 16 May 1959. Margaret Hinxma. Oh, Shirley, You Didn't Deserve It, 7.
Picturegoer, 31 October 1959. Picturegoer Parade: Solomon and Sheba, 11.
Picturegoer, 30 January 1960. Helen Hendricks. The Very Private Life of . . . Yul Brynner, 8–9.
Picturegoer, 12 March 1960. New Hair, 9.
Picturegoer, 9 April 1960a. Facts About Yul, 19.
Picturegoer, 9 April 1960b. The Gay Gifted Kay, 14.
Picture Show, 3 September 1955. Fay Filmer. Gossip, 3.
Picture Show, 21 July 1956. Fay Filmer. Gossip, 3.
Picture Show, 13 October 1956. 'The King and I,' 5–6, 10, 12.
Picture Show, 4 May 1957. The Life Story of Yul Brynner, 12.
Picture Show, 6 July 1957. Fay Filmer. Gossip, 3.
Picture Show, 7 September 1957. Fay Filmer. Gossip, 3–4.
Picture Show, 28 September 1957. Fay Filmer. Gossip, 3–4.
Picture Show, 12 October 1957. Fay Filmer. Gossip, 3.
Picture Show, 8 December 1957. Fay Filmer. Gossip, 3–4.
Picture Show, 21 March 1959. 'The Journey,' 3.
Picture Show, 2 May 1959. 'The Sound and the Fury,' 8, 12, 14–15.
Picture Show, 31 October 1959. 'Solomon and Sheba' . . . Well, It's Spectacular, 12–13.
Picture Show, 2 April 1960. Shirley Carrington. Wonderful, Wonderful Kay, 12.
Picture Show, 24 September 1960. Shirley Carrington. Surprise Package, 20.
Playboy, May 1960, C.B. Grenier. The Cannes Festival, 63–72, 86.
Playboy, January 1967. Arthur Knight and Hollis Alpert. The History of Sex in Cinema Part XIV: Sex Stars of the Fifties, 95–107.
Redbook, May 1957. Cameron Shipp. Self-Made Mystery Man, 30–3, 96–8.
Redbook, August 1957. Letters to the Editor, 12.
Redbook, February 1958. Picture of the Month, 2.
St. Louis Dispatch, 5 November 1946. Clarissa Start. In Play Out of a Distant Past, D3.
St. Petersburg Times, 13 December 1951. Leonard Lyons. Health Insurance Survey Soon to Get Truman Okay, 12.
St. Petersburg Times, 2 January 1952. Leonard Lyons. King of Siam Loses Voice but It's For a Good Cause, 16.
St. Petersburg Times, 31 December 1956. Louella O. Parsons. Hollywood's First Lady Forecast Movie Hit Parade of '57, 16.
St. Petersburg Times, 31 March 1957. Clyde Tussey. Yul Brynner – New Type Matinee Idol, B10.

St. Petersburg Times, 14 April 1957. Louella Parsons. Hakim to Do 'Rapture in My Rags', 34.

St. Petersburg Times, 7 May 1958. Louella O. Parsons. Ladd-Brynner Opus Twists History, B10.

St. Petersburg Times, 15 December 1958. New DeMille Spectacle, 'The Buccaneer,' Lusty Story of Jean Lafitte, D2.

St. Petersburg Times, 11 December 1960. Wilson Sullivan. Yul Brynner Among Children, 12.

St. Petersburg Times, 17 April 1961. Earl Wilson. Not Exactly the All-American Type, Yul Brynner Prefers Living Abroad, D10.

St. Petersburg Times, 22 June 1971. Charles Benbow. 'Light the Edge' Lacks Brightness, D2.

St. Petersburg Times, 11 November 1971. J. Oliver Prescott. Little New in 'Catlow', D1.

St. Petersburg Times, 22 November 1973. Dorothy Smiljanich. 'Westworld' a Nightmare World of Adventure, D3.

St. Petersburg Times, 19 July 1974. Dorothy Smiljanich. 'The Serpent' Gold Nugget for Spy Fans, D10.

St. Petersburg Times, 15 December 1975. Michael Marzella. 'Ulimate Warrior' Is All Bite and No Bark, D5.

St. Petersburg Times, 26 September 1977. William Glover. Yul Brynner: When He Plays the King of Siam His Wishes Are the Producers' Command, G2.

St. Petersburg Times, 11 December 1978. Roy Peter Clark. 'Death Rage' Should Be Bumped Off, D5.

St. Petersburg Times, 11 September 1984. Marilyn Beck. Fatigue, Not Health, Forces Brynner to Take a Break, D3.

St. Petersburg Times, 28 September 1985. Yul Brynner In Hospital, A3.

St. Petersburg Times, 11 October 1985. The Films and Plays of Brynner, A11.

San Francisco Examiner, 6 November 1952. Louella Parsons. Doris Day, Howard Keel to Be in New Musical Team, 17.

San Francisco Examiner, 25 October 1954. Louella O. Parsons. Yul Brynner Signed For 'King and I' Role, 27.

San Francisco Examiner, 2 July 1956. Louella Parsons. Yul Brynner to Star in 'Stalin's Secret Crimes,' 29.

San Francisco Examiner, 12 January 1958. Maria Schell and the Role Marilyn Wanted, 14.

San Francisco Examiner, 23 February 1958. Hortense Morton. 'The Brothers Karamazov': Yul Brynner and the Cast of Experts, 14.

San Francisco Examiner, 16 March 1958. Jackie Peterson. 'Brothers' – In Debt to Marilyn, 19.

San Francisco Examiner, 14 December 1958. Lydia Burman. Washington Burns, DeMille Fashion, 10.

San Francisco Examiner, 19 December 1958. Hortense Morton. Paramount Screens 'The Buccaneer' Starring Yul Brynner, B2.

San Francisco Examiner, 23 February 1959. Hortense Morton. Yul Brynner and Deborah Kerr Star in Iron Curtain Drama, B7.

San Francisco Examiner, 29 November 1959. Louella Parsons. Yul Brynner: Man of Mystery, 28.

San Francisco Examiner, 2 November 1960. Earl Wilson. The Reformation of Steve McQueen, B9.

San Francisco Examiner, 11 July 1962. Louella Parsons. Yul Brynner Has Dino in a Dither, 28.

San Francisco Examiner, 16 December 1962. Rick Setlowe. Blood on the Steppes: Yul Brynner in a Cossack Horse Opera, 2.

San Francisco Examiner, 22 December 1962. Stanley Eichelbaum. Excitement on Russia's Steppes, 13.

San Francisco Examiner, 20 June 1968. Jeanne Miller. Pancho Villa Rides and Rides and . . ., 28.

San Francisco Examiner, 20 September 1969. Gene Handsaker. Film Fortunes That Thrive Despite Flops, 10.

San Francisco Examiner, 18 October 1969. Jeanne Miller. Yul Plays Agent Baldly, 10.

San Francisco Examiner, 30 October 1969. Stanley Eichelbaum. A Star-Studded Asylum, 26.

San Francisco Examiner, 17 September 1971. Jeanne Miller. Sort of 'Fiddler on the Hoof,' 30.

San Francisco Examiner, 26 January 1975. Memo From John J. Miller, 30.

San Francisco Examiner, 13 April 1976. Mary Knoblauch. She Makes Stars Look Good, 24.

San Francisco Examiner, 28 July 1976. 'Futureworld' Robots Score Lively Hit, 24.

San Francisco Examiner, 12 April 1978. Gypsy Brynner Hits the Road for Soul-Mates, 15.

San Francisco Examiner, 15 July 1979. Roderick Mann. Yul Brynner Wants to Be King for Another Ten Years, at Least, 28.

San Francisco Examiner, 12 December 1982a. Marian Zailian. Yul Brynner Likes to Be the King of His Kingdom, 37, 44–5.

San Francisco Examiner, 12 December 1982b. Steven Winn. The Old Standbys and the Spanking New, 41–42.

San Francisco Examiner, 21 January 1983. David Johnston. Stars Help Mayor's Fund for Homeless, A15.

San Francisco Examiner, 15 December 1984. Kenneth R. Clark. Yul Brynner Talks of His Battle with Cancer, A10.

San Francisco Examiner, 9 January 1985. Yul's Triumphant 'Farewell Engagement', E12.

San Francisco Examiner, 10 October 1985. Yul Brynner, 'King of Siam,' Dies, A1, 20.

Saturday Evening Post, 22 November 1958. Peter Martin. I Call on Yul Brynner, 24–5, 81, 84–86.

Screenland, May 1957. Maxine Block. Egghead with Oomph, 50–3, 70–1.

Screenland, January 1960. Helen Hendricks. The Last Separation?, 34–5, 60, 68–9.

Seventeen, February 1958. Picture of the Month, 3.

Seventeen, December 1958. Edwin Miller. 'The Buccaneer,' 24.

Seventeen, February 1959. Picture of the Month, 3.

Seventeen, October 1962. Edwin Miller. Tony Curtis and Yul Brynner Among the Cossacks, 92–93, 172–73.

Showmen's Trade Review, 26 November 1949. 'Port of New York,' 23, 25.

Showmen's Trade Review, 31 December 1949. Adapt Boston Premiere Campaign For 'Port of New York' Key Runs, 21.

Sight and Sound, Winter 1957. Laurence Kitchin. 'The Ten Commandments,' 148–9.
Sight and Sound, Summer 1958. Richard Roud. 'Two Cents on The Rouble,' 245–6.
Sight and Sound, Spring 1960. Sam Kula. 'Once More, With Feeling!' 93.
Sight and Sound, Spring 1961. Penelope Houston. 'The Magnificent Seven,' 91–2.
Sight and Sound, Summer 1965. Tom Milne. Major Dundee and 'Invitation to a Gunfighter,' 144–5.
Sight and Sound, Fall 1970. The Crisis We Deserve, 172–8.
Sight and Sound, Spring 1971. Abraham Polonsky. Making Movies, 101.
South China Morning Post, 11 February 1957. Patrick Raymond. Brilliant Performance by Bergman, 4.
South China Morning Post, 24 December 1957. Brynner Productions, 20.
South China Morning Post, 5 June 1958. Jean Gordon. Compressing 'The Brothers Karamazov,' 4.
South China Morning Post, 27 April 1959. Jean Gordon. Yul Brynner Gives Skilful Portrayal, 4.
South China Morning Post, 20 October 1959. Jean Gordon. A Romantic Drama of US History, 4.
South China Morning Post, 29 July 1960. Elizabeth Fox. Kay Kendall Steals Nearly All Scenes, 4.
South China Morning Post, 16 December 1960. Elizabeth Fox. Yul Concrete and Souffle A La Coward, 4.
South China Morning Post, 21 June 1961. Jean Gordon. Magnificent Certainly Is the Word, 4.
South China Morning Post, 17 December 1962. Jean Gordon. An Unusual Story of Escape, 4.
South China Morning Post, 9 February 1963. Jean Gordon. Plenty of Good Film Fare, 4.
South China Morning Post, 12 February 1963. Jean Gordon. Loyalty and Love Among Cossacks, 4.
South China Morning Post, 5 December 1963. Catering for Catholic Tastes, 4.
South China Morning Post, 26 September 1964. Jean Gordon. All Kinds of Films In The Coming Week, 4.
South China Morning Post, 28 September 1964. Jean Gordon. A Kind of Mexican Western, 4.
South China Morning Post, 4 December 1964. Jean Gordon. Drama of Air-Sea Rescue, 4.
South China Morning Post, 2 June 1965. A Gunfighter Comes to Town, 4.
South China Morning Post, 1 February 1966. Gladiators of 20th Century, 4.
South China Morning Post, 9 August 1967. Yul Brynner In Double Trouble, 5.
South China Morning Post, 8 November 1967. Brynner and Kerr Return In 'King and I,' 5.
South China Morning Post, 30 November 1967. Two Promising Releases, 5.
South China Morning Post, 17 March 1968. Jack Moore. Lemmon and Falk Are at Their Best, 4.
South China Morning Post, 20 March 1968. They Shouldn't Have Bothered, 11.
South China Morning Post, 23 November 1975. For Survival Buffs, 19.
South China Morning Post, 15 May 1977. Flopworld, 16.
South China Morning Post, 21 April 1978. Peter Hulm. Gypsies Jump Into the 20th Century, 4.

South China Morning Post, 19 May 1978. Eric Bourne. Gypsies Want Their Place In the Sun, 4.
South China Morning Post, 11 March 1985. Iain McAsh. Long Live King, 34.
South China Morning Post, 18 March 1985. A Royal Pardon for Broadway, 7.
South China Morning Post, 11 June 1985. Yul Brynner Abdicates After 34 Years as King, 35.
South China Morning Post, 11 October 1985. The King Yul Brynner Is Dead, 4.
South China Morning Post, 13 October 1985. Requiem for Two Legends, 6.
South China Morning Post, 20 April 1986. Yul's Plea in Smoking Campaign, 1.
South China Morning Post, 25 February 1990. Sally Ogle Davis. The Truth About Yul, 51.
Studio Survey, August 28 1957. 1956–57 Laurel Award Winners: Topliner Male Stars, 40.
Sun, 9 April 1951. George Hart. Excellent Cast In an O'Neill Tragedy, 9.
Tampa Bay Times, 11 December 1960. Wilson Sullivan. Yul Brynner Among Children, 12.
The Advocate, 3 December 1975. Donald von Wiedenman. Films, 41.
The Advocate, 26 January 1993. Marketplace: Merchandise for Sale, 86.
The Advocate, 8 July 1997. Peter Galvin. In Focus: In the Buff, 65.
The Age, 19 June 1986. Bureaucracy Stops a Cancer Message, 41.
The Austin American Statesman, 26 June 1977. 'King and I' Revival Rare Experience, H6.
The Austin Statesman, 12 May 1958. Sending Star Via AF Craft Is Explained, 12.
The Austin Statesman, 7 July 1958. Inez Robb. Women's Hair Soon to Be Had in Store, 4.
The Austin Statesman, 19 February 1959. Economizing Film Folk Say 'Hold That Toga', B15.
The Austin Statesman, 16 February 1960. Robert Musel. Yul Brynner Aids Homeless of World, B14.
The Austin Statesman, 2 May 1960. Rick Du Brow. Yul Brynner To Become First Bald Western Hero, 7.
The Austin Statesman, 27 August 1960. Vernon Scott. Frank and Marilyn On Same Bill Is Proposed, 8.
The Austin Statesman, 3 February 1963. Yul Brynner Goes From Rich to Rag, E15.
The Austin Statesman, 13 May 1963. Bob Thomas, 3.
The Austin Statesman, 12 September 1971. Celebrity Soapbox: Yul Brynner on Gypsies, SM20.
The Austin Statesman, 2 July 1972. What in the World!, SM15.
The Austin Statesman, 22 September 1972. Yul Brynner Tries His Luck At a TV Series, 44.
The Austin Statesman, 27 April 1975. Babylift Supported By Actor, 21.
The Austin Statesman, 23 July 1976. Patrick Taggart. 'Futureworld' Much More Than Routine Science Fiction Movie, C8.
The Bennington Evening Banner, 13 November 1956. Yul Brynner's Bald Pate Stirs Men's Romantic Hopes, 9.
The Billboard, 10 March 1951. Sidney Golly. Rodgers-Hammerstein 'King' Needs Trimming from Stem, 3, 38.
The Billboard, 7 April 1951. Bob Francis. 'King' on Broadway Is Another Royal Rodgers-Hammerstein Smash, 3, 46.
The Boston Globe, 13 January 1946. Actor Born in Siberia Will Have Leading Role in 'Lute Song', 28.

The Boston Globe, 25 November 1949. Marjorie Adams. Nothing Sillier Than Suffering for Love, Says Movie Villain, 17.
The Boston Globe, 4 December 1960. Sheilah Graham. Brynner Explains His Bad Publicity and New Project, A8.
The Boston Globe, 8 May 1968. Edgar Driscoll Jr. Yul Brynner Scores in 'Double Man', 32.
The Boston Globe, 16 October 1969. Edgar Driscoll Jr. Yul Brynner 'Shines' in 'Golden Goose', 69.
The Boston Globe, 18 November 1971. Edgar Driscoll Jr. Brynner Keeps Pate Covered as 'Catlow', 40.
The Boston Globe, 11 October 1985. Jay Carr. Yul Brynner: 34 Years a King, 64.
The Brooklyn Citizen, 7 February 1946. Edgar Price. The Premiere, 10.
The Calgary Herald, 11 September 1951. Sheilah Graham. Hedy Lamarr Has Own Company in Mexico, 8.
The Calgary Herald, 20 July 1956. Bob Considine. On the Line, 11.
The Calgary Herald, 22 January 1958. Yul Brynner Sleeps Little but Has Frequent Meals, 15.
The Calgary Herald, 9 April 1959. Hedda Hopper. Hollywood, 60.
The Calgary Herald, 21 October 1960. Harold Heffernan. Cowboy Tradition Poses Problem for Yul Brynner in New Movie, 11.
The Calgary Herald, 24 June 1961. Modern Film Tycoons Live Forcefully, Lavishly, 6.
The Calgary Herald, 13 September 1961. Harold Heffernan. Egotism, Selfishness Major Needs for Acting Success, Says Brynner, 19.
The Calgary Herald, 22 October 1966. He-Men Stage Brawl, 7.
The Calgary Herald, 2 May 1969. Sally K. Brass. Entire Yugoslav Army Used in War Movie, 27.
The Calgary Herald, 20 March 1971. Clyde Gilmour. Battle of Neretva 'Dull' Film Despite Real Bravery, 29.
The Calgary Herald, 15 January 1972. Jamie Portman. New Yul Brynner Western Doesn't Really Make It, 54.
The Calgary Herald, 26 November 1973. Jamie Portman. Come to Westworld, Where Robots Are Supreme, 13.
The Calgary Herald, 24 April 1975. Yul Brynner Against 'Transplanting' Orphans, 15.
The Calgary Herald, 30 March 1979. James Bacon. Hollywood Close-Up, 42.
The Calgary Herald, 11 October 1985. The King and I a Love Affair with Brynner, E1.
The Chattanooga Times, 19 January 1958. Gene Handsaker. It Rhymes with Sinner, 20–1.
The Cincinnati Enquirer, 28 October 1950. Heavy Chore Faced by Yul Brynner, PD, 36.
The Daily Telegraph, 24 July, 2001. Skye Yates. King Yul Never Forget, 27.
The Daily Telegraph, 18 July 2020. The Story Behind . . . Yul Brynner's Egomania, 8.
The Daily Times, 11 October 1985. Jacques le Sourd. The Man Who Would Be King, C1.
The Globe and Mail, 30 March 1951. The King and I a Memorable Show, 10.
The Globe and Mail, 28 March 1959. Stan Helleur. The Journey Is Well Worth the Trip, 13.
The Globe and Mail, 28 December 1959. Frank Morriss. Solomon and Sheba a Dull, Uninspired Pageant, 4.
The Globe and Mail, 2 April 1960. Frank Morriss. Once More a Salute to Gay Comedienne, 13.

The Globe and Mail, 26 October 1960. Hugh Thompson. Magnificent? Magnificently Dull, 8.

The Globe and Mail, 18 June 1962. Frank Morriss. Zahrian Is a Movie from Which to Escape, 34.

The Globe and Mail, 20 December 1963. Frank Morriss. Bizarre Imaginings in a Bowl of Tripe, 11.

The Globe and Mail, 4 August 1965. Frank Morriss. Brando's Portrayal Comes Out Monotone, 11.

The Globe and Mail, 23 August 1967. Ralph Hicklin. 'Triple Cross': The Porous Consistency of Tripe, 10.

The Globe and Mail, 12 October 1967. Joan Fox. 'The Long Duel': Brynner vs. Howard in India, 14.

The Globe and Mail, 12 January 1971. Dislocated Hip Getting Off Taxi: Had Miniskirt Cut Off, Shipowner's Wife Makes Best-Dressed List, 9.

The Globe and Mail, 30 July 1971. Kaspars Dzeguze. Edge of the World very Bad Verne, 11.

The Globe and Mail, 14 November 1977. Robert Martin. Movies: As Junk, Film Fails, 13.

The Globe and Mail, 16 February 1980. Beverly Gray. Favorite Films Captured in Wax at Movieland, T6.

The Globe and the Mail, 18 May 1984. William F. Nolan. A Troubled Man of Action, E3.

The Globe and Mail, 18 March 1985. Thailand's Queen Meets Broadway's Musical King, M9.

The Globe and Mail, 11 October 1985. Ray Conlogue. A 'Clean-Cut Mongolian Boy', D9.

The Globe and Mail, 25 August 1989. Isabel Vincent. A Surprisingly Wooden King Nureyev Stiff in His Theatrical Debut, C9.

The Guardian, 16 September 1958. Manchester Cinemas: Dostoevsky – with Happy Ending, 5.

The Guardian, 29 December 1959. David Moreau. Nightfall in Skopje, 5.

The Guardian, 9 June 1960. Tennessee Williams Strains After the Symbols, 17.

The Guardian, 15 April 1961. Where East Meets West, 5.

The Guardian, 30 June 1962. At the Cinema, 5.

The Guardian, 5 April 1963. Richard Roud. Review: New Films in London, 9

The Guardian, 14 May 1965. Ian Wright. New Films, 13.

The Guardian, 12 May 1966. Hilde Spiel. Magnificent Sent-Off, 11.

The Guardian, 1 November 1966. Mainly for Addicts, 8.

The Guardian, 23 June 1967. Ian Wright. New Films, 9.

The Guardian, 12 December 1969. Richard Roud. Not for Kids, 8.

The Guardian, 15 June 1972. Derek Malcolm. One for the Road, 12.

The Guardian, 21 December 1972. Derek Malcolm. Fiddler on the Hoof, 8.

The Guardian, 14 March 1974. Derek Malcolm. Puke and Simple, 12.

The Guardian, 23 March 1974. Douglas Keay. Brynner in Doughville, 10.

The Guardian, 12 April 1978. The Gypsy Case Baldly Stated, 8.

The Guardian, 11 October 1985. Mystery Man of the Movies, 18.

The Hollywood Reporter, 23 November 1949. 'Port of New York' Poor, 3.

The Hollywood Reporter, 22 December 1950. Radio and TV Briefs, 11.

The Hollywood Reporter, 1 June 1951. Tales of Hoffman, 3.

The Hollywood Reporter, 12 June 1951. Radie Harris. Broadway Ballyhoo, 4.

The Hollywood Reporter, 19 June 1951. Radie Harris. Broadway Ballyhoo, 4.
The Hollywood Reporter, 25 June 1951. Rambling Reporter, 2.
The Hollywood Reporter, 17 July 1951. Jim Henaghan. Rambling Reporter, 2.
The Hollywood Reporter, 28 December 1951. Hartman Launching Drive for New Paramount Talent, 4.
The Hollywood Reporter, 8 August 1952. Wilder, Brynner Huddle, 6.
The Hollywood Reporter, 2 October 1952. Mike Connolly. Rambling Reporter, 2.
The Hollywood Reporter, 2 February 1953a. Paramount to Intensify Star-Building Program, 3.
The Hollywood Reporter, 2 February 1953b. Ratoff Rolls in Summer, 5.
The Hollywood Reporter, 10 February 1953. Radie Harris. Broadway Balyhoo, 4.
The Hollywood Reporter, 11 February 1953. Para. Still Trying For Brynner in '53, 2.
The Hollywood Reporter, 1 October 1953. Brynner Settles Paramount Pact, 1, 4.
The Hollywood Reporter, 13 October 1953. Mike Connolly. Rambling Reporter, 2.
The Hollywood Reporter, 4 March 1954. Rome, 4.
The Hollywood Reporter, 10 March 1954. Rome, 3.
The Hollywood Reporter, 7 April 1954. Mike Connolly. Rambling Reporter, 2.
The Hollywood Reporter, 19 May 1954. Lee Cuild. 'The King and I', 3.
The Hollywood Reporter, 24 May 1954. Mike Connolly. Rambling Reporter, 2.
The Hollywood Reporter, 10 September 1954. Mike Connolly. Rambling Reporter, 2.
The Hollywood Reporter, 2 February 1955. Leo Cuild. On the Air, 16.
The Hollywood Reporter, 19 May 1955. Mike Connolly. Rambling Reporter, 2.
The Hollywood Reporter, 27 December 1955. Mike Connolly. Rambling Reporter, 2.
The Hollywood Reporter, 5 April 1956. DeMille Musical: Wilcoxon Produces, Brynner Directs, 1, 4.
The Hollywood Reporter, 29 June 1956. 'King and I' Is Wonderful, Refreshing Entertainment, 3.
The Hollywood Reporter, 9 July 1956. London, 8.
The Hollywood Reporter, 31 July 1956. Ireland, Noonan Turning Producers, 1.
The Hollywood Reporter, 14 September 1956. Steiger Tops Exhib Poll, 8.
The Hollywood Reporter, 17 November 1956. Milton Deane. London, 3.
The Hollywood Reporter, 27 November 1956. Milton Deane. London, 3.
The Hollywood Reporter, 9 April 1957. Litvak and Brynner Set Their First Para. Indie, 2.
The Hollywood Reporter, 16 September 1957. Here and There, 6.
The Hollywood Reporter, 15 October 1957. Mike Connolly. Rambling Reporter, 2.
The Hollywood Reporter, 3 December 1957. Mike Connolly. Rambling Reporter, 2.
The Hollywood Reporter, 23 December 1957. $6,000,000 Slate Set by Romulus, 4.
The Hollywood Reporter, 27 December 1957. Here and There, 8.
The Hollywood Reporter, 19 February 1958. Jack Moffitt. 'Brothers Karamazov' Epic Picture in the Classic Mold, 3, 15
The Hollywood Reporter, 24 April 1958. Mike Connolly. Rambling Reporter, 2.
The Hollywood Reporter, 22 May 1958. 'Gladiators' Will Shoot Backgrounds in Italy, 5.
The Hollywood Reporter, 20 June 1958. Sam'l Steinman. Rome, 3.
The Hollywood Reporter, 2 July 1958. Mike Connolly. Rambling Reporter, 2.
The Hollywood Reporter, 30 July 1958. Dicker Yul Brynner to Stage B'way 'Family', 1.

The Hollywood Reporter, 25 August 1958. Bryna, U-I Appeal MPAA Award of 'Spartacus' Title to Brynner, 4.
The Hollywood Reporter, 21 August 1958. Brynner Wins Title Bout with Bryna, 1, 17.
The Hollywood Reporter, 9 October 1958. Mike Connolly. Rambling Reporter, 2.
The Hollywood Reporter, 27 October 1958. Brynner, Winner, Gives 'Spartacus' Title to Bryna, 2.
The Hollywood Reporter, 7 November 1958. Mike Connolly. Rambling Reporter, 2.
The Hollywood Reporter, 24 November 1958. $1,200,000 Para Ballyhoo Budget Given to 'Buccaneer', 3.
The Hollywood Reporter, 12 December 1958. Jack Moffitt. 'The Buccaneer' Best Film Ever Made by DeMille, 3–4.
The Hollywood Reporter, 2 February 1959. Jack Moffitt. 'Journey' Romantic Melo Tale of Hungarian Revolt, 3, 6.
The Hollywood Reporter, 10 February 1959. Mike Connolly. Rambling Reporter, 2.
The Hollywood Reporter, 3 February 1959. Sam'l Steinman. Rome, 10.
The Hollywood Reporter, 20 February 1959. Mike Connolly. Rambling Reporter, 2.
The Hollywood Reporter, 31 March 1959. Mike Connolly. Rambling Reporter, 2.
The Hollywood Reporter, 5 May 1959. Teenage Girls Prefer Their Pics in a Theatre, 3.
The Hollywood Reporter, 22 July 1959. 20th Offers Dandridge Role of 'Salammbo', 2.
The Hollywood Reporter, 2 November 1959. Brynner In Biopic of Mad Czar Paul for UA Release, 2.
The Hollywood Reporter, 16 November 1959. Sam'l Steinman. Rome, 3.
The Hollywood Reporter, 2 February 1960. Quinn Sues Brynner, UA, for $650,000, 6.
The Hollywood Reporter, 5 February 1960a. Brynner Answers Quinn Complaint, 10.
The Hollywood Reporter, 5 February 1960b. Jack Moffitt. Donen Picture Has Mass, Class Appeal, 3.
The Hollywood Reporter, 1 July 1960. Mike Connolly. Rambling Reporter, 2.
The Hollywood Reporter, 5 October 1960. James Powers. 'The Magnificent Seven' A Tough Period Western, 3.
The Hollywood Reporter, 11 October 1960. James Powers. 'Surprise Package' Based on Funny Idea but Is Miscast, 3.
The Hollywood Reporter, 9 November 1960. Mike Connolly. Rambling Reporter, 2.
The Hollywood Reporter, 19 January 1961. Brynner in State Dept. Post, 3.
The Hollywood Reporter, 2 February 1961. Italian Pix with H'wood Names Tie U.S. at Italy B.O., 1, 4.
The Hollywood Reporter, 13 February 1961. Mike Connolly. Rambling Reporter, 2.
The Hollywood Reporter, 29 March 1961. Mike Connolly. Rambling Reporter, 2.
The Hollywood Reporter, 28 April 1961. Ohio College to Honor Brynner for UN Work, 3.
The Hollywood Reporter, 10 May 1961. UA Record in Tokyo by 'Magnificent,' 3.
The Hollywood Reporter, 22 June 1961. Mike Connolly. Rambling Reporter, 2.
The Hollywood Reporter, 17 July 1961. Sordi Top Actor at Italian B.O., 3.
The Hollywood Reporter, 20 July 1961. 'Zahrain' Calls Arabs, 11.
The Hollywood Reporter, 10 October 1961. Mike Connolly. Rambling Reporter, 2.
The Hollywood Reporter, 29 May 1962. James Powers. 'Zahrain' Is Exploitable, 3.
The Hollywood Reporter, 28 June 1962. Elliot Arnold to Script Mirisch's 'Elephant Bill,' 2.
The Hollywood Reporter, 14 August 1962. Larry Lipskin. Broadway Merry-Go-Round, 4.

The Hollywood Reporter, 19 September 1962. Brynner Hosts Orphans, 6.
The Hollywood Reporter, 4 October 1962. Mike Connolly. Rambling Reporter, 2.
The Hollywood Reporter, 16 June 1978. Hank Grant. Rambling Reporter, 2.
The Hollywood Reporter, 23 August 1983. Robert Osborne. Rambling Reporter, 3.
The Hollywood Reporter, 9 January 1985. Morna Murphy-Martell. 'The King and I,' 32.
The Independent Exhibitors Film Bulletin, 29 December 1952, Studio Size-ups: Paramount, 9.
The Independent Exhibitors Film Bulletin, 9 July 1956. 'The King and I' Caresses the Eye and Ear!, 7.
The Independent Exhibitors Film Bulletin, 15 October 1956. 'The Ten Commandments' DeMille Spectacle Overwhelms the Eye, 17.
The Independent Exhibitors Film Bulletin, 17 February 1958. 'The Brothers Karamazov' One of Season's Major Offerings, 9.
The Independent Exhibitors Film Bulletin, 22 December 1958. 'The Buccaneer,' 23.
The Independent Exhibitors Film Bulletin, 16 February 1959. 'The Journey' Another Hit for M-G-M, 10.
The Independent Exhibitors Film Bulletin, 16 March 1959. 'The Sound and the Fury' Has Strong Box Office Ingredients, 11.
The Independent Exhibitors Film Bulletin, 31 August 1959. Gilt-Edge Production Supplement, 1–5.
The Independent Exhibitors Film Bulletin, 4 January 1960. 'Solomon and Sheba' Big B.O. Spectacle, 11.
The Independent Exhibitors Film Bulletin, 15 February 1960. 'Once More, With Feeling' Bright, Sophisticated Comedy, 29.
The Independent Exhibitors Film Bulletin, 10 December 1962. 'Taras Bulba,' 12.
The Independent Exhibitors Film Bulletin, 23 December 1963. 'Kings of the Sun,' 11.
The Independent Film Journal, 7 July 1956. 'The King and I,' 26.
The Independent Film Journal, 26 October 1957. Brynner Buys Novel, 49.
The Independent Film Journal, 1 March 1958. 'The Brothers Karamazov', 20.
The Independent Film Journal, 20 January 1968. Production News, 14.
The Independent Film Journal, 5 August 1971. Romance of a Horsethief, 7–8.
The Indianapolis News, 10 October 1985. Actor Yul Brynner Dies at Age 65, 56.
The Jerusalem Post, 10 January 1957. H. At the Cinema, 2.
The Jerusalem Post, 19 June 1958. Liesl Eisinger Eberhardt. Mostly for Men, viii.
The Jerusalem Post, 20 December 1960. F.D. De Mille's Last Words, 4.
The Jerusalem Post, 31 May 1965. Film Star Brynner Arrives, 6.
The Jerusalem Post, 23 December 1984. Samuel G. Freedman. When the Role Captures the Actor, 8.
The Journal News, 13 August 1972. Anna, King to Rule Sundays, 20.
The Kansas City Sun, 23 July 1961. Joseph Kaye. Bonus for Wives of Gotham's Mayors, A18.
The Korea Times, 9 March 1969. Brynner Stars as Tito In 'Battle of Neretva', 5.
The Korea Times, 16 February 1975. Aliens Win More Oscars, 5.
The Korea Times, 20 August 1978. Henry Gotlieb. Brynner Champion for 10 Mil. Gypsies, 5.
The Korea Times, 29 September 1985. Yul Brynner Hospitalized for Bacterial Meningitis, 6.

The London Standard, 10 October 1985. Emma Lee-Potter. My Sadness, by Boat Boy He Helped, 3.
The Manchester Guardian, 9 October 1953. Philip Hope-Wallace. 'The King and I,' 7.
The Manchester Guardian, 28 February 1958. The Climax of the Colossal: 'Ten Commandments,' 13.
The Manchester Guardian, 20 March 1959. If You Want to Get Ahead . . . Splitting Hairs with Mr Brynner, 22.
The Manchester Guardian, 25 June 1959. 1812 – According to Hollywood, 11.
The Montreal Gazette, 11 December 1952. Dorothy Kilgallen. The Voice of Broadway, 14.
The Montreal Gazette, January 5 1957. Phyllis Baltella. People & Things, 20.
The Montreal Gazette, 8 March 1957. Forty Years Planning for DeMille Picture, 13.
The Montreal Gazette, 24 January 1962. Dorothy Kilgallen's Voice of Broadway, 31.
The Montreal Gazette, 27 July 1962. Dorothy Kilgallen's Voice of Broadway, 11.
The Montreal Gazette, 19 January 1963. Harold Whitehead. Williams Picture First Rate, 25.
The Montreal Gazette, 1 March 1963. Records Go to Work for UN Fund, 8.
The Montreal Gazette, 9 September 1963. Bandoola to Star Brynner, 12.
The Montreal Gazette, 12 September 1966. Acting Is Not a Final Stage, 12.
The Montreal Gazette, 24 September 1968. Suzy Knickerbocker, 29.
The Montreal Gazette, 17 April 1969. Halsey Raines. Yul Brynner Is Freezing in Beautiful Yugoslavia, 49.
The Montreal Gazette, 16 October 1971. Dane Lanken. Western Blood; Eastern Horses, 42.
The Montreal Gazette, 24 October 1972. L. Ian MacDonald. Grim Reaper Poised for First Cancellations, 39.
The Montreal Gazette, 11 October 1985. Show Business Loses Two Greats, D1.
The National Tatler, 26 May 1974. Bernie Brown. How 'That Haircut' Turned Tide Of Fate Around for Yul Brynner, 7.
The New Yorker, 21 April 1951. M. Mok and Geoffrey T. Hellman. Brynner Rex, 24–5.
The New York Times, 3 February 1950. T.M.P. Narcotics and T-Men, 29.
The New York Times, 5 October 1952. Brooks Atkinson. Revisiting Siam, B1.
The New York Times, 6 February 1953. Paramount Halts 'New Kind of Love,' 16.
The New York Times, 9 February 1956. Thomas M. Pryor. Brynner Getting Chance to Direct, 38.
The New York Times, 21 June 1956. Oscar Godbout. Zanuck will Film 'Crimes of Stalin,' 35.
The New York Times, 29 June 1956. Bosley Crowther. Screen: 'The Kind and I,' 15.
The New York Times, 9 November 1956. Bosley Crowther. Screen: 'The Ten Commandments,' 35.
The New York Times, 10 November 1956. Bosley Crowther. Screen Phenomenon: DeMille's 'The Ten Commandments' Amazes the Film Industry, 1X.
The New York Times, 25 November 1956. Bosley Crowther. Eastern Western, X1.
The New York Times, 14 December 1956. Bosley Crowther. The Screen: 'Anastasia,' 35.
The New York Times, 17 October 1957. Koestler-Novel Will Be Filmed, 41.
The New York Times, 23 December 1957. Oscar Godbout. Brynner and U.A. in Multiple Pact, 18.

The New York Times, 13 May 1958. Thomas M. Pryor. Japanese Movie Will Be Adapted, 26.
The New York Times, 12 August 1958. 'The White Rajah' Planned as Film, 32.
The New York Times, 17 October 1958. Thomas M. Pryor. Brynner to Film Novel by Daudet, 34.
The New York Times, 11 November 1958. Brynner Sought for 'Billionaire,' 26.
The New York Times, 7 December 1958. A. H. Weiler. Passing Picture Scene: Drama About Czar Paul I is planned by Litvak, Brynner – Other Items, X11.
The New York Times, 20 February 1958. Bosley Crowther. Screen: A Border Incident with Hungary, 19.
The New York Times, 21 February 1959. Bosley Crowther. Screen: The Brothers Karamazov, 18.
The New York Times, 28 March 1959. Bosley Crowther. Screen: Down South, 'The Sound and the Fury' Opens at Paramount, 11.
The New York Times, 26 December 1959. Bosley Crowther. The Screen: 'Solomon and Sheba,' 7.
The New York Times, 24 November 1960. Howard Thompson. Screen: On Japanese Idea, 48.
The New York Times, 4 December 1960. John P. Shanley. Yul Brynner on a Mission for the UN, X17.
The New York Times, 24 December 1961. James Denton. Gogol Hits the Pampas, X9.
The New York Times, 12 July 1962. A.H. Weiler. 2 Paramount Releases, 19.
The New York Times, 14 October 1962. Ray Falk. On a Japanese 'Flight', X9.
The New York Times, 26 December 1962. Bosley Crowther. 'Taras Bulba' Stars Brynner and Curtis, 5.
The New York Times, 23 April 1964. Howard Thompson. Screen: A Melodrama, 34.
The New York Times, 28 October 1964. Howard Thompson. Another Western, 51.
The New York Times, 22 June 1965. Brynner Gives Up His U.S. Passport for Family's Sake, 11.
The New York Times, 20 July 1967. Alden Whitman. 'Triple Cross,' Spy Movie with All the Moves, Is Here, 30.
The New York Times, 2 November 1967. A.H. Weiler. 3 Adventure Films and a Loren Vehicle Arrive, 58.
The New York Times, 2 May 1968. Renata Adler. Screen: Spy with a Mission in the Austrian Tyrol, 57.
The New York Times, 18 July 1968. A.H. Weiler. 'Villa Rides' Arrives, 26.
The New York Times, 3 October 1969. Howard Thompson. The Screen: Spy Story, 34.
The New York Times, 17 July 1971. A.H. Weiler. 'Light at the Edge of the World', 14.
The New York Times, 19 August 1971. Roger Greenspun. Cossacks and Jews, 42.
The New York Times, 23 September 1971. A.H. Weiler. Brynner Rides Again in 'Adios, Sabata', 74.
The New York Times, 21 October 1971. Roger Greenspun. 'Catlow' Pits Cenna Against Brynner, 56.
The New York Times, 22 November 1973. Vincent Canby. The Screen: 'Westworld', 51.
The New York Times, 27 April 1977. Richard F. Shepard. The Once – and still – King Yul, C22.

The New York Times, 3 May 1977. Clive Barnes. 'King and I,' Reminder of Golden Age, 50.

The New York Times, 3 June 1978. Yul Brynner, . . . And Gypsies Now, 19.

The New York Times, 4 June 1978. Gypsies Appeal to U.N for Aid and Protection of Civil Rights, BK69.

The New York Times, 8 January 1985. Frank Rich. The Stage: Yul Brynner in 'The King and I,' C13.

The New York Times, 1 July 1985. Nan Robertson. Farewell Performance for Yul Brynner in 'The King and I,' C11.

The New York Times, 10 October 1985. Samuel G. Freedman. Yul Brynner, Theatre's 'King,' Dies, D21.

The New York Times, 31 January 1986. Nan Robertson. Brynner's Friends Reminisce at Actor's Funeral Service, B6.

The New York Times, 20 February 1986. Philip H. Dougherty. The Late Yul Brynner in Anti-Smoking Ads, D21.

The New York Times, 6 May 1988. Rita Reif. Impressionist Shows at 2 Auction Houses, C1.

The New York Times, 12 November 1989. Barbara Shulgasser. Enslaved by the King of Siam, 59.

The New York Times, 24 September 1993. Tom Hagen. Another Side of a Life's Work, Elegantly Revealed, C30.

The New York Times, 25 January 2005. Barron H. Lerner. Essay: In Unforgettable Final Act, a King Got Revenge on His Killers, F5.

The New York Times, 3 May, 2013. Kate Murphy. The Right Pose Can be Reassuring, ST10.

The Observer, 16 September 1956. C.A. Lejeune. Ruling Passion, 15.

The Observer, 24 February 1957. C.A. Lejeune. Fiction and Fact, 11.

The Observer, 29 June 1958. C.A. Lejeune. Brynner's Brothers, 15.

The Observer, 22 March 1959. C.A. Lejeune. Hungarian Goulash, 23.

The Observer, 29 March 1959. C.A. Lejeune. What's In a Name?, 13.

The Observer, 1 November 1959. C.A. Lejeune. Amour, Amour, 23.

The Observer, 3 November 1968. Yul Brynner Aids Gipsy School, 2.

The Observer, 2 November 1969. Penelope Mortimer. Fairy-Tale Plotting, 32.

The Observer, 2 February 1974. Russell Davies. That's Virna Lisi, That Was, 28.

The Observer, 4 April 1976. Russell Davies. Albee's Cadenzas, 26.

The Observer, 15 April 1979. Tom Davice. Fair Play from Rugby Envoy, 9.

The Ottawa Citizen, 6 December 1977. Noel Taylor. Brynner Upstaged by Naples in Boring Flick, 64.

The Pittsburgh Press, 24 March 1957. William Steif. The Brynner Story: Clean-Shaven Yul Creates Own Myth, 53.

The Pittsburgh Press, 2 June 1962. Thomas Blakley. Yul Brynner Rebel with Cause, 8.

The Rake, November 2015. Stuart Husband. Getting to Know Yul. https://therake.com/stories/icons/getting-to-know-yul-brynner/ (accessed 15 January 2022).

The Record, 24 January 1961. Louella O. Parsons. Jimmy Stewart and Writer Lay Sell Warner Air Force Story, 35.

The Sketch, 6 June 1951. America's Next Stage, 533.

The Sketch, 1 August 1956. Stephen Watts. Motley Notes, 108–9.
The Sketch, 26 September 1956. Reviews, 320.
The Sketch, 13 March 1957. C.A. Lejeune. Is She Or Isn't She?, 254.
The Sydney Morning Herald, 29 May 1977. Don Riseborough. Brynner Is the King of Broadway, 45, 95.
The Tatler & Bystander, 17 December 1947. Backstage, 361.
The Tatler & Bystander, 21 January 1948. The Gossip Backstage, 69.
The Tatler & Bystander, 26 September 1956. Elspeth Grant. On Gilding the Gingerbread, 618.
The Tatler & Bystander, 6 March 1957. Elspeth Grant. If only all the Films Were Like This One . . ., 438.
The Tatler & Bystander, 9 July 1958. Elspeth Grant. Brother Brynner on the Steppes, 75.
The Tatler & Bystander, 29 October 1958. Elspeth Grant. Fancied Films, 250.
The Tatler & Bystander, 1 April 1959, Elspeth Grant. They Should Have Stayed in China, 32–3.
The Tatler & Bystander, 8 April 1959. Elspeth Grant. This South Gives Birth to Such Blues, 84–5.
The Tatler & Bystander, 11 November 1959. Elspeth Grant. Two Kinds of Courage, 359.
The Tatler & Bystander, 5 October 1960. Elspeth Grant. The Picture-Stealer Supreme, 46.
The Tatler & Bystander, 24 April 1963. Elspeth Grant. Films, 226.
The Telegraph, 9 July 2020. Martin Chilton. Hollywood's King of Mean: The Bald Truth About Yul Brynner, https://www.telegraph.co.uk/films/0/hollywoods-king-mean-bald-truth-yul-brynner/ (accessed 10 March 2022).
The Times, 24 July 2004. Behind the Screen, https://www.thetimes.co.uk/article/behind-the-screen-72p8g3vzjnb (accessed 10 March 2022).
The Times, 11 January 2012. Laura Dixon. Hollywood Greats, As Seen by One of Their Own, 9.
The Times and Democrat, 11 October 1985. Michael Kuchwara. Yul Brynner Loses Battle with Cancer, 5.
The Times of India, 23 January 1958. On the English Screen: 'The Ten Commandments' Is a Magnificent Epic, 9.
The Times of India, 31 July 1958. On the English Screen: 'Karamazov' Emerges as Magnificent Picture, 7.
The Times of India, 10 January 1960. Yul Brynner's 'Weakness,' 7.
The Times of India, 9 June 1960. Superb Kendall-Brynner Musical Comedy, 5.
The Times of India, 19 December 1963. On the Foreign Screen: Mammoth Period Horse Opera, 10.
The Times of India, 24 September 1964. On the Foreign Screen: Lost and Found?, 5.
The Times of India, 8 September 1966. Jump At It, 3.
The Times of India, 7 November 1968. On the Foreign Screen: Seven Spells Adventure, 11.
The Times of India, 20 February 1969. On the Foreign Screen: Versatile Vixen, 9.
The Times of India, 19 April 1969. Santha Rungachary. Putting it Baldly, 8.
The Times of India, 11 April 1978. B.K. Joshi. Gipsies Seek UN Recognition, 14.
The Times of India, 11 October 1985. Yul Brynner Dead, 9.
The Toronto Star, 22 January 1974. Clyde Gilmour. Gadgets Steal the Show in This Espionage Drama, E6.

The Toronto Star, 22 February 1975. Frank Rasky. Yul Brynner Travels with Trappings of Stardom, F3.

The Toronto Star, 27 February 1975. Urjo Kareda. Erich Segal's Odyssey Pompous, Boring Trip, E7.

The Toronto Star, 12 December 1982. Glen Lovell. 'I'm Really a Nice Guy' Says Yul Brynner, C5.

The Vancouver Sun, 23 April 1959. Clyde Gilmour. Hungarian Revolt Forms Backdrop for 'Journey', 53.

The Vancouver Sun, 30 June 1959. Sheilah Graham. Million-Dollar Pay Cheque Means Exile for Brynner, 27.

The Vancouver Sun, 24 June 1960. Sheilah Graham. Joanne Woodward Asks Singing Role, 31.

The Vancouver Sun, 14 December 1962. Yul Versatile, 16.

The Vancouver Sun, 27 January 1972. Les Wedman. 'Catlow': Adventure 'Old As the Hills,' 35.

The Vancouver Sun, 9 September 1976. Les Wedman. A Great Movie for Robots . . . for Robots . . ., 31.

The Vancouver Sun, 9 October 1979. Rodrick Mann. Yul's Appetite Is Almost as Famous as He Is, B8.

The Wall Street Journal, 8 February 1946. Richard P. Cooke. Brocade Parade, 8.

The Wall Street Journal, 2 April 1951. Richard P. Cooke. By-Play at Bangkok, 12.

The Washington Post, 25 May 1947. 'Lute Song' Completes a Cycle, S4.

The Washington Post, 28 May 1947. Richard L. Coe. 'Lute Song' Drenches National Stage in Rare and Colorful Beauty, 13.

The Washington Post and Times Herald, 3 July 1956. Dorothy Kilgallen. Is the Great Presley Bubble Bursting?, 28.

The Washington Post and Times Herald, 2 September 1956. Ruth Waterbury. Yul: Bald, Bold and Big at Box Office, AW6.

The Washington Post and Times Herald, 22 November 1956. Richard L. Coe. Keith's Opens Here, D14.

The Washington Post and Times Herald, 15 May 1957. Dorothy Kilgallen. Polly Bergen Gets Raves in Advance, C6.

The Washington Post and Times Herald, 13 May 1958. 'Karamazov' Flops at Cannes Fete, A23.

The Washington Post and Times Herald, 25 July 1958. Louella Parsons. Yul Plans to Beat Kirk to 'Gladiators', D8.

The Washington Post and Times Herald, 18 December 1958. 'Buccaneer' at Keith's Just Right for Kids, B18.

The Washington Post and Times Herald, 20 February 1959. Richard L. Coe. The Truth Isn't in It, D8.

The Washington Post and Times Herald, 22 February 1959. Louella Parsons. Powell Wins First Permit from Castro, H4.

The Washington Post and Times Herald, 27 March 1959. Richard L. Coe. Mildew Time Down in Dixie, B13.

The Washington Post and Times Herald, 28 May 1959. Dorothy Kilgallen. Gertrude's Friends Bet on Gwen, B10.

The Washington Post and Times Herald, 30 December 1959. Richard L. Coe. One On the Aisle: Sheba Solemn, So's Solomon, B6.

The Washington Post and Times Herald, 3 February 1960. Dorothy Kilgallen. Doris-Yul Romance Keeps London Buzzing, B9.

The Washington Post and Times Herald, 7 February 1960. The Many Faces of Yul Brynner, AW10.

The Washington Post and Times Herald, 9 February 1960. Louella Parsons. Brando Sought for New 'Mutiny,' B7.

The Washington Post and Times Herald, 21 February 1960. Louella Parsons. Hollywood Is Talking About: The Galleys and the Pirates, H4.

The Washington Post and Times Herald, 14 October 1960. Richard L. Coe. 'Magnificent 7' Though, Funny, B14.

The Washington Post and Times Herald, 28 October 1960. Richard L. Coe. A Surprise, At That, C8.

The Washington Post and Times Herald, 4 December 1960. Yul Brynner's Odyssey, TV4.

The Washington Post and Times Herald, 7 May 1961. Kennedy Picks Food-for-Peace Advisory Unit, A7.

The Washington Post and Times Herald, 19 September 1961. Louella Parsons. Vale Script Continues Biblical Cycle, B10.

The Washington Post and Times Herald, 13 June 1962. Hedda Hopper's Hollywood: Grace Fetes Sinatra with Names, C7.

The Washington Post and Times Herald, 2 August 1962. Dorothy Kilgallen. Burton Pals Now See Divorce Likely, A21.

The Washington Post and Times Herald, 20 May 1963. Jack Anderson. Navy League's Backwash, B23.

The Washington Post and Times Herald, 19 December 1963. R.L.C. Mayans Now Bite the Dust, C22.

The Washington Post and Times Herald, 30 July 1964. Hebe Dorsey. Fur Shoes to Show on Winter Scene, E1.

The Washington Post and Times Herald, 8 August 1964. Philip Kopper. 'Ashiya' Airborne by Flights of Traumatic Fancy, E31.

The Washington Post and Times Herald, 11 September 1964. Louella Parsons. Bobby Darin to Be Movie, TV, and Stage Producer, B10.

The Washington Post and Times Herald, 27 October 1966. 'Return of Seven' Has Surfeit of Killing, E32.

The Washington Post and Times Herald, 13 June 1969. R.L.C. Villa Rides Again, H12.

The Washington Post and Times Herald, 13 November 1969. Dorothy McCardle. Antibeard Brynner, C2.

The Washington Post and Times Herald, 11 January 1971. Ann Hencken. Best Dressed, B1, B3.

The Washington Post and Times Herald, 21 August 1971. Kenneth Turan. Death's Sting, Etc. – All Too Evident, E1.

The Washington Post and Times Herald, 26 September 1973. Jean M. White. Run-Amok Robots in Fantasyland, D1.

The Washington Post and Times Herald, 26 November 1973. Tom Shales. Backward, Upside Down and Serpentine, B4.

The Washington Post, 14 December 1974. Sally Quinn. Brynner: Beyond the Kingly Image, F1, F3.
The Washington Post, 30 January 1975. Richard L. Coe. 'Odyssey': A Record Run, C8.
The Washington Post, 7 April 1975. Rin Schaffer. 'Save Babies' Group in High Gear, C1, 3.
The Washington Post, 10 April 1975. Hefner's 'Big Bunny' Transports 41 Orphans, A17.
The Washington Post, 7 January 1976. Tom Shales. A Final Odyssey for 'Homer,' B8.
The Washington Post, 28 July 1978. Robert Samek. Personalities, E2.
The Washington Post, 30 July 1978. Roderick Mann. Yul Brynner – The Man Who Should Be King, H3.
The Washington Post, 4 May 1979. Nina S. Hyde. Fashion notes, M3.
The Washington Post, 20 February 1981. James Lardner. Yul Brynner's Majestic 'King,' C1.
The Washington Post, 27 February 1981. Judith Martin. 'The King & I': Commanding, 11.
The Washington Post, 22 January 1985. Jeffrey Hogrefe. 'Siam,' He Said, B7.
The Washington Post, 10 October 1985. Yul Brynner, 'The King' of Classic Musical, Dies, A1, A6.
The Washington Post, 11 October 1985a. David Richards. The Once and Forever King, B1, B3.
The Washington Post, 11 October 1985b. Bart Barnes. Obituaries: Yul Brynner, 'King and I' Star, Dies, C8.
The Windsor Star, 13 May 1947. Theatre and Its People: 'The Lute Song,' 5.
Top Spot, 18 April 1959. Barbara Hutchinson. Films: The Journey, 14.
Top Spot, 25 April 1959. Journey Man – Yul Brynner and Me, 14.
Top Spot, 6 June 1959. The Eggman: Spotlight on Yul Brynner, 3.
Toronto Daily Star, 12 March 1957. By George! Baldness Not Success Key, 3.
Toronto Daily Star, 1 June 1957. Louella Parsons In Hollywood, 28.
Toronto Daily Star, 12 May 1958. Boo 'Karamazov' Film at Cannes, 21.
Toronto Daily Star, 24 May 1958. Louella Parsons In Hollywood, 26.
Toronto Daily Star, 14 March 1959. Walter Kanitz. Songs of the Gypsies, 27.
Toronto Daily Star, 4 April 1960. Bob Johnstone. Late Kay Kendall Acted Her 'Finest', 18.
Toronto Daily Star, 22 December 1962. Gerald Pratley. Outspoken Is The Word For Brynner, 22.
Toronto Daily Star, 20 December 1963. David Cobb. 'Kings of the Sun' – a Yul Epic, 12.
Toronto Daily Star, 21 December 1963. David Cobb. 'Taras Bulba': Flogging For Joy Of It, 14.
Toronto Daily Star, 1 December 1969. Dorothy Mikos. Dick Van Dyke Falls Flat Again, 25.
Toronto Daily Star, 22 February 1971. Urjo Kareda. Battle of Neretva Film Features International Cast, 20.
Toronto Daily Star, 20 October 1971. Daniel Stoffman. Fairy-Tale View of Cossacks in Romance of a Horsethief, 74.
Toronto Daily Star, 15 November 1977. Clyde Gilmour. Brynner Crime Yarn Dredged from Barrel, F1.
Toronto Star, 19 August 1984. Henry Mietkiewicz. Brynner: The Man Who Won't Be King, G1.
Town & Country, May 1951. Brailsford Felder. Siam Set to Music, 74–5, 93.

Town & Country, June 1970. A Wedding in Paris, 56–9.
Town & Country, August 1976. Deauville: An August Rite, 58–61, 95.
Town & Country, September 1976. Ave Sartoria, 136–7, 148–50.
Tribune, 5 October 1956. R.D. Smith. Long, Loud and Lovely, 8.
Tribune, 3 September 1980. Billboard, 10.
Truth, 1 July 1951. American Columnists Say . . ., 6.
Truth, 19 August 1951a. U.S. Columnists Are Saying . . ., 8.
Truth, 19 August 1951b. American Columnists Say . . ., 11.
USA Today, 24 January 1994. Donna Gable. Savalas: Tough Guy with a Soft Center, 1D.
Variety, 17 February 1943. The Moon Vine, 44.
Variety, 19 December 1945. Play Out of Town: 'Lute Song,' 44.
Variety, 31 March 1948. West End B.O. Hits Slump, 56.
Variety, 9 February 1949. WNBT's Daytime Preem Has Hausfrau Pull but Is Otherwise Below Par, 34.
Variety, 23 November 1949. 'Port of New York,' 25.
Variety, 4 April 1951. Play on Broadway: 'The King and I,' 50.
Variety, 16 July 1952. The King and I, 122.
Variety, 29 October 1952. The King and I, 66.
Variety, 10 December 1952. Advert by United Cerebral Palsy, 41.
Variety, 1 April 1953. Who Will 'Sadie' Get: Yul, Charlton or Jose?, 4.
Variety, 4 July 1956. 'The King and I,' 6.
Variety, 11 July 1956. Stalin Role Toxic, 5.
Variety, 12 September 1956. New York Sound Track, 4.
Variety, 10 October 1956. 'The Ten Commandments,' 6.
Variety, 4 December 1956. London Critics Vs. DeMille, 5.
Variety, 19 December 1956. 'Anastasia,' 6.
Variety, 10 April 1957. Brynner-Litvak Set Own 1958 Feature, 10.
Variety, 24 July 1957. Want Brynner for Sartre's 'Lucifer' Lead, 73.
Variety, 25 December 1957. Yul Brynner's Co. Sets 11 With UA, 18.
Variety, 1 January 1958. Brynner, Mirisch Pledge UA TV Tie, 23.
Variety, 5 February 1958. Japanese Plot to Be American Western, 3.
Variety, 12 February 1958. Yul Brynner Alciona $25-Mil Roll for UA, 3.
Variety, 19 February 1958. 'Brothers Karamazov,' 6.
Variety, 26 February 1958. Advert: Hail a New Hit!, 15.
Variety, 21 May 1958. Universal In on Gladiator Cycle, 13.
Variety, 4 June 1958. Acting Vs. Directing and Ne'er the Twain Shall Meet: Brynner, 2, 19.
Variety, 27 August 1958. New York Sound Track, 11.
Variety, 22 October 1958. Briefs from Lots, 25.
Variety, 26 November 1958. DeMille Even by Remote Control a Boxoffice Lure; Par Ballyhoo for 'Buccaneer' at $1,200,000, 7.
Variety, 17 December 1958. 'The Buccaneer,' 6.
Variety, 4 February 1959a. Chatter: Hollywood, 78.
Variety, 4 February 1959b. 'The Sound and the Fury,' 6
Variety, 4 March 1959. The Journey, 6.
Variety, 22 July 1959. Jean Cocteau to Make 1st Film in 5 Years, 2.
Variety, 21 October 1959. Adviser Yul Brynner, 26.

Variety, 4 November 1959a. Solomon and Sheba, 6.
Variety, 4 November 1959b, Dig Up Charlemagne and Russia's Mad Czar, 11.
Variety, 10 February 1960a. Quinn Sues Brynner on 'Magnificent 7', 15.
Variety, 10 February 1960b. 'Once More, With Feeling!' 6.
Variety, 9 March 1960. Largest Insurance Settlement, 5.
Variety, 5 October 1960. 'The Magnificent Seven,' 6.
Variety, 12 October 1960. 'Surprise Package,' 6.
Variety, 30 November 1960. Robert J. Landry. Yul Brynner's Private Roles, 7.
Variety, 8 February 1961. Marco Polo Looks to Be the Cause Of Another Involved Pic Title Hassle, 59.
Variety, 26 April 1961. New York Sound Track, 4.
Variety, 14 June 1961. Mirisch Latest: 'Idyll' in England, 17.
Variety, 5 July 1961. Clouzot Plans Three Starrers in France, 15.
Variety, 1 November 1961. International Sound Track, 12.
Variety, 16 May 1962. United Artists Product Outlook, 13.
Variety, 4 July 1962. New York Sound rack, 7.
Variety, 18 July 1962. International Soundtrack, 20.
Variety, 18 December 1963. 'Kings of the Sun,' 6.
Variety, 22 December 1963. Brynner Buys Guitry's 'Story of a Cheat,' 5.
Variety, 1 January 1964. Of 15 Films Set for UA Only Two Shooting O'Seas, 7.
Variety, 21 October 1964. 'Invitation to a Gunfighter,' 6.
Variety, 25 November 1964. Quinn's Action Vs. Yul Brynner Pic,13.
Variety, 28 July 1965. 'Morituri,' 6.
Variety, 8 December 1965. Chatter: Hollywood, 75.
Variety, 21 December 1966. 'Triple Cross,' 6.
Variety, 2 August 1967. 'The Long Duel,' 7.
Variety, 4 October 1967. International Sound Track, 26.
Variety, 8 November 1967. A Cosby Future of TV Specials, Radio Capsules, 43.
Variety, 10 January 1968. Ken Hyman Makes with Talent Pacts, 3.
Variety, 8 May 1968. Italian Film Product, 45–46, 48.
Variety, 24 July 1968. Italo Pix Biz Unites to Aid Sicily Tourism Via Taormina Film Fest, 26.
Variety, 25 July 1979. Yul Brynner Is King of Siam Backstage at Palladium, London, 99.
Variety, 5 November. Award for Yul Brynner, 106.
Variety, 3 July 1985. King Brynner Leaves Throne, Keeps Treasury, 1, 79.
Variety, 4 November 2021. Kate Aurthor. Natalie Wood Was Sexually Assaulted by Kirk Douglas, Her Sister Alleges, https://variety.com/2021/film/news/kirk-douglas-rape-natalie-wood-lana-sister-book-1235105228 (accessed 20 January 2022)
Vogue, 1 May 1964. Fashion – Vivid Beauty, 163.
Wilmington News, 27 April 1961. Yul Brynner, Ambassador Lindt, Mrs. Lord to Get Doctorates Here, 3.
Woman's Day, November 1958. Hollis Alpert. Movies, 11–12.
Woman's Day, January 1959. Hollis Alpert. Movies, 10, 12.
Yahoo Entertainment, 30 August, 2016. Gwynne Watkins. Yul Brynner's Daughter Shares Memories of Growing Up With 'The King and I', https://www.yahoo.com/entertainment/yul-brynners-daughter-shares-memories-000000740.html (accessed 11 March 2022).

Bibliography

Abramson, Leslie H. 2008. '1968: Movies and the Failure of Nostalgia.' In *American Cinema of the 1960s*, edited by Barry Keith Grant, 193–216, New Brunswick: Rutgers University Press.

Balio, Tino. 2009. *United Artists, Volume 2, 1951–1978: The Company that Changed the Film Industry*. Milwaukee: University of Wisconsin Press.

Baron, Cynthia. 2004. 'Crafting Film Performance: Acting in the Hollywood Era.' In *Movie Acting: The Film Reader*, edited by Pamela Robertson Wojcik, 83–94, London: Routledge.

Baron, Cynthia. 2008. *Reframing Screen Performance*. Ann Arbor: University of Michigan Press.

Beltrán, Mary. 2009. *Latina/o Stars in US Eyes: The Making and Meanings of Film and TV Stardom*. Chicago: University of Illinois Press.

Benshoff, Harry M. 2008. 'Movies and Camp.' In *American Cinema of the 1960s*, edited by Barry Keith Grant, 150–71, New Brunswick: Rutgers University Press.

Bergfelder, Tim. 2000. 'The Nation Vanishes: European Co-productions and Popular Genre Formulae in the 1950s and 1960s.' In *Cinema and Nation*, edited by Mette Hjorth and Scott MacKenzie, 131–42, New York: Routledge.

Berghahn, Volker R. 2001. *America and the Intellectual Cold Wars in Europe: Shepard Stone Between Philanthropy, Academy, and Diplomacy*. Princeton: Princeton University Press.

Bergman, David. 1993. 'Introduction.' In *Camp Grounds: Style and Homosexuality*, edited by David Bergman, 3–16, Amherst: University of Massachusetts Press.

Bernstein, Matthew. 1997. 'Introduction.' In *Visions of the East: Orientalism in Film*, edited by Matthew Bernstein and Gaylyn Studlar, 1–18, New Brunswick: Rutgers University Press.

Berry, Sarah. 2004. Hollywood Exoticism. In *Stars: The Film Reader*, edited by Lucy Fischer and Marcia Landy, New York: Routledge, 181–98.

Bloom, Claire. 1996. *Leaving a Doll's House*. London: Virago.

Boddy, William. 1985. 'The Studio Move into Prime Time: Hollywood and the Television Industry in the 1950s.' *Cinema Journal* 24(4): 23–37.

Braidotti, Rosi, Patrick Hanafin, and Bolette Blaagaard. 2012. 'Introduction.' In *After Cosmopolitanism*, edited by Rosi Braidotti, Patrick Hanafin, and Bolette Blaagaard, 1–7, London: Routledge.

Bret, David. 2008. *Joan Crawford: Hollywood Martyr*. Cambridge, MA: Da Capo Press.

Brown, Christopher R. 2012. 'Mad About the Boy? Hollywood Stardom and Masculinity Subverted in The Swimmer.' *Quarterly Review of Film and Video* 29(4): 356–64.

Brown, Susan, 1995. 'Alternatives to the Missionary Position: Anna Leonowens as Victorian Travel Writer.' *Feminist Studies* 21(3): 587–614.

Brynner, Rock. 1989. *Yul: The Man Who Would Be King. A Memoir of Father and Son*. New York: Simon and Schuster.

Brynner, Rock. 2006. *Empire & Odyssey: The Brynners in Far East Russia and Beyond*. Hanover, NH: Distinct Press.

Brynner, Victoria. 1996. *Yul Brynner: Photographer*. New York: Harry N. Abrams.

Brynner, Victoria. 2010. 'Introduction.' In *Yul Brynner: A Photographic Journey, Vol. 1: Life Style*, edited by Victoria Brynner and Nicolas Pages, 8–9, Göttingen: Edition 7L.

Brynner, Victoria and Nicolas Pages, eds. 2010a. *Yul Brynner: A Photographic Journey, Vol. 1: Life Style*. Göttingen: Edition 7L.

Brynner, Victoria and Nicolas Pages, eds. 2010b. *Yul Brynner: A Photographic Journey, Vol. 2: Life on Set*. Göttingen: Edition 7L.

Brynner, Victoria and Nicolas Pages, eds. 2010c. *Yul Brynner: A Photographic Journey, Vol. 3: 1956*. Göttingen: Edition 7L.

Brynner, Victoria and Nicolas Pages, eds. 2010d. *Yul Brynner: A Photographic Journey, Vol. 4: Man of Style*. Göttingen: Edition 7L.

Brynner, Yul. 1960. *Bring Forth the Children: A Journey to the Forgotten People of Europe and the Middle East*. New York: McGraw-Hill.

Brynner, Yul and Susan Reed. 1983. *The Yul Brynner Cookbook: Food Fit for the King and You*. New York: Stein and Day.

Burge, Amy. 2020. 'Introduction to the Special Issue on *The Sheik*.' *Journal of Popular Romance Studies* 9, http://www.jprstudies.org/2020/12/introduction-to-the-special-issue-on-the-sheik/ (accessed 10 March 2022).

Capua, Michelangelo. 2006. *Yul Brynner: A Biography*. Jefferson: McFarland.

Chávez, Ernesto. 2011. '"Ramon is Not One of these": Race and Sexuality in the Construction of Silent Film Actor Ramón Novarro's Star Image.' *Journal of the History of Sexuality* 20(3): 520–44.

Chekhov, Michael. (1953) 2014. *To the Actor: On the Technique of Acting*. Mansfield Centre: Martino Publishing.

Chouliaraki, Lilie. 2012. 'Cosmopolitanism as Irony: A Critique of Post-Humanitarianism.' In *After Cosmopolitanism*, edited by Rosi Braidotti, Patrick Hanafin, and Bolette Blaagaard, 77–96, London: Routledge.

Clark, Adrian and Jeremy Dronfield. 2015. *Queer Saint: The Cultured Life of Peter Watson, Who Shook Twentieth-Century Art and Shocked High Society*. London: Metro.

Clarke, Gerald. 2000. *Get Happy: The Life of Judy Garland*. New York: Delta Trade.

Cleto, Fabio. 1999. 'Introduction: Queering the Camp.' In *Camp: Queer Aesthetics and the Performing Subject – A Reader*, edited by Fabio Cleto, 1–42, Ann Arbor: The University of Michigan Press.

Cohan, Steven. 1997. *Masked Men: Masculinity and the Movies in the Fifties*. Bloomington and Indianapolis: Indiana University Press.

Cortés, Carlos E. 1991. 'Hollywood Interracial Love.' In *Beyond the Stars: Studies in American Popular Film, Volume 2: Plot Conventions in American Film*, edited by Paul Loukides and Linda K. Fuller, 21–35, Bowling Green: Bowling Green State University Popular Press.

Courtney, Susan. 2005. *Hollywood Fantasies of Miscegenation: Spectacular Narratives of Gender and Race, 1903–1967*. Princeton: Princeton University Press.

Dabell, Dawn and Jonathon Dabell. 2019. *Ultimate Warrior: The Complete Films of Yul Brynner*. Turbo Sloth.

Dayal, Samir. 2019. 'Introduction: New Cosmopolitanisms: Rethinking Race, Geography, and Belonging.' In *New Cosmopolitanism, Race, and Ethnicity: Cultural Perspective*, edited by Ewa Barbara Luczak, Anna Pochmara, and Samir Dayal, 1–24, Berlin: De Gruyter.

Derrida, Jacques. 2005. *On Cosmopolitanism and Forgiveness*. Translated by Mark Dooley and Michael Hughes. London: Routledge.
Doll, Susan M. 2005. 'Brynner, Yul.' In *International Dictionary of Films and Filmmakers 3*, 4th ed., edited by Tom Pendergast and Sara Pendergast, 167–8, Farmington Hills: St. James Press.
Donaldson, Laura. 1990. 'The King and I in Uncle Tom's Cabin, or On the Border of the Women's Room.' *Cinema Journal* 29(3): 53–68.
Drake, Philip. 2006. 'Reconceptualizing Screen Performance.' *Journal of Film and Video* 58(1–2): 84–94.
Dyer, Richard. 1979. *Stars*. London: BFI.
Dyer, Richard. 1997. *White*. London: Routledge.
Dyer, Richard. 2004. *Heavenly Bodies: Film Stars and Society*. 2nd ed. London: Routledge.
Eyman, Scott. 2020. *Cary Grant: Brilliant Disguise*. New York: Simon & Schuster.
Fenwick, James. 2020. '"Look, Ma, I'm a Corporation!": United Artists and Kirk Douglas's Bryna Productions, 1955–1959.' In *United Artists*, edited by Peter Krämer, Gary Needham, Yannis Tzioumakis, and Tino Balio, 94–111, London: Routledge.
Forster, E. M. 1927. *Aspects of the Novel*. New York: Harcourt, Brace and Company.
Fouz-Hernández, Santiago. 2011. 'Homer-otic: Male Bodies in the Epic Film Revival from *Gladiator* to *300*.' In *La piel en la palestra: Estudios corporales II*, edited by Alba Del Pozo and Alba Serrano, 27–34, Barcelona: Universitat Autònoma de Barcelona.
Frank, Marcie. 1993. 'The Critic as Performance Artist: Susan Sontag's Writing and Gay Cultures.' In *Camp Grounds: Style and Homosexuality*, edited by David Bergman, 173–84, Amherst: University of Massachusetts Press.
Gallagher, Mark. 2014. 'On Javier Bardem's Sex Appeal.' *Transnational Cinemas*, 5(2): 111–26.
Girard, Gaïd. 2018. 'Retour vers la matrice: le *Westworld* (*Mondwest*) de Michael Crichton. (1973),' TV/Series [Online] 14, https://journals.openedition.org/tvseries/2994 (accessed 10 March 2022).
Golden, Eve. 2021. *Jayne Mansfield: The Girl Couldn't Help It*. Kentucky: The University Press of Kentucky. Kindle edition.
Grant, Barry Keith. 2008. Introduction: Movies and the 1960s. In *American Cinema of the 1960s*, edited by Barry Keith Grant, 1–21, New Brunswick: Rutgers University Press.
Grewal, Inderpal. 1996. *Home and Harem: Nation, Gender, Empire, and the Cultures of Travel*. Durham: Duke University Press.
Guilbault, Jocelyne. 2017. 'The Politics of Musical Bonding: New Prospects for Cosmopolitan Music Studies.' In *Perspectives On a 21st Century Comparative Musicology: Ethnomusicology or Transcultural Musicology?*, edited by Francesco Giannattasio and Giovanni Giuriati, 100–24, Udine: Nota.
Hannan, Brian. 2015. *The Making of The Magnificent Seven: Behind the Scenes of the Pivotal Western*. Jefferson: McFarland.
Hark, Ina Rae. 1993. 'Animals or Romans: Looking at Masculinity in *Spartacus*'. In *Screening the Male: Exploring Masculinities in Hollywood Cinema*, edited by Steven Cohan and Ina Rae Hark, 151–72, London: Routledge.
Held, David. 2012. 'Cosmopolitanism in a Multipolar World.' In *After Cosmopolitanism*, edited by Rosi Braidotti, Patrick Hanafin and Bolette Blaagaard, 28–39, London: Routledge.

Hemenway, Justin. 2019. 'Audrey Hepburn's Humanitarian Legacy Continues.' UNICEF USA, April 3, https://www.unicefusa.org/stories/audrey-hepburns-humanitarian-legacy-continues/35889 (accessed 10 March 2022).

Hirsch, Foster. 2010. 'Doris Day and Rock Hudson: The Girl Next Door and the Brawny He-Man.' In *Larger Than Life: Film Stars of the 1950s*, edited by R. Barton Palmer, 147–64, New Brunswick: Rutgers University Press.

Jacobs, George and William Stadiem. 2004. *Mr. S: My Life with Frank Sinatra*. New York: HarperEntertainment.

Järvinen, Hanna. 2014. *Dancing Genius: The Stardom of Vatslav Nijinksy*. Basingstoke: Palgrave.

Järvinen, Hanna. 2020. 'Ballets Russes and Blackface.' *Dance Research Journal* 52(3): 76–96.

Jordan, Jessica Hope. 2009. *The Sex Goddess in American Film, 1930–1965: Jean Harlow, Mae West, Lana Turner, and Jayne Mansfield*. Amherst: Cambria Press.

Kaplan, Caren. 1995. '"Getting to Know You": Travel, Gender, and the Politics of Representation in *Anna and the King of Siam* and *The King and I*.' In *Late Imperial Culture*, edited by Román de la Campa, E. Ann Kaplan, and Michael Sprinker, 33–52, London: Verso.

Kelly, Gillian. 2021. *Tyrone Power: Gender, Genre and Image in Classical Hollywood Cinema*. Edinburgh: Edinburgh University Press.

Klein, Christina. 2003. *Cold War Orientalism: Asia in the Middlebrow Imagination, 1945–1961*. Berkeley: University of California Press.

Koivunen, Anu. 2003. *Performative Histories, Foundational Fictions: Gender and Sexuality in Niskavuori Films*. Helsinki: SKS.

Langella, Frank. 2012. *Dropped Names: Famous Men and Women as I Knew Them*. New York: HarperCollins.

Lant, Antonia. 1992. 'The Curse of the Pharaoh, or How Cinema Contracted Egyptomania.' *October* 59, 86–112.

Lennon, Elaine. 2012. Garbo … Auteur? *Off Screen* 16(6): https://offscreen.com/view/garbo_auteur (accessed 10 March 2022).

Leonowens, Anna Harriette. 1873. *The English Governess at the Siamese Court: Recollections of Six Years in the Royal Palace at Bangkok*. Boston: James R. Osgood & Co.

Lerman, Leo. 2007. *The Grand Surprise: The Journals of Leo Lerman*. Edited by Stephen Pascal. New York: Knopf.

Levine, Suzanne Jill. 2001. *Manuel Puig and the Spider Woman: His Life and Fictions*. Milwaukee: The University of Wisconsin Press.

Lewis, Reina. 2019. 'The Harem: Gendering Orientalism.' In *Orientalism and Literature*, edited by Geoffrey P. Nash, 166–84, Cambridge: Cambridge University Press.

Lindbergs, Kimberly. 2019. 'A Tale of Two Films: The Picasso Summer (1969).' *Cinebeats*, 8 February, https://cinebeats.wordpress.com/2019/02/08/a-tale-of-two-films-the-picasso-summer-1969/ (accessed 10 March 2022).

Lipton, Lenny. 2021. *The Cinema in Flux: The Evolution of Motion Picture Technology from the Magic Lantern to the Digital Era*. New York: Springer.

Long, Lucy M. 2018. 'Cultural Politics in Culinary Tourism with Ethnic Foods.' *Revista de Administração de Empresas* 58(39), https://doi.org/10.1590/S0034-759020180313 (accessed 10 March 2022).

Ma, Sheng-mei. 2020. *Off-White: Yellowface and Chinglish by Anglo-American Culture*. New York: Bloomsbury.

MacAdam, Henry and Duncan Cooper. 2020. *The Gladiators vs. Spartacus: Dueling Productions in Blacklist Hollywood, Volume 1: The Race to the Screen*. Cambridge: Cambridge University Press.

MacDowall, Lachlan. 2009. 'Historicising Contemporary Bisexuality.' *Journal of Bisexuality* 9(1): 3–15.

Machin, David, and Theo Van Leeuwen. 2005. 'Language Style and Lifestyle: The Case of a Global Magazine.' *Media, Culture & Society* 27(4): 577–600.

Maillard, Kevin Noble. 2018. 'Hollywood Loving.' *Fordham Law Review* 86(6): 2647–57.

Martin, Meredith. 2019. 'Staging China, Japan and Siam at the Paris Universal Exhibition of 1867.' In *Beyond Chinoiserie: Artistic Exchange between China and the West during the Late Quing Dynasty (1796–1911)*, edited by Petra ten-Doesschate Chu and Jennifer Milam, 122–48. Amsterdam: Brill.

Mathijs, Ernest and Jamie Sexton. 2011. *Cult Cinema: An Introduction*. Oxford: Blackwell.

Mayne, Judith. 1993. *Cinema and Spectatorship*. London: Routledge.

Mbembe, Achille. 2017. *Critique of Black Reason*. Translated by Laurent Dubois. Durham, NC: Duke University Press.

McDonald, Tamar Jeffers. 2013. *Doris Day Confidential: Hollywood, Sex and Stardom*. London: Bloomsbury Publishing.

McLean, Adrienne L. 1993. '"I'm a Cansino": Transformation, Ethnicity, and Authenticity in the Construction of Rita Hayworth, American Love Goddess.' *Journal of Film and Video* 44(3–4): 8–26.

Mercer, John. 2013. 'The Enigma of the Male Sex Symbol.' *Celebrity Studies* 4(1): 81–91.

Mercer, John. 2015. *Rock Hudson*. London: BFI.

Meyer, Moe. 1996. 'Introduction: Reclaiming the Discourse of Camp.' In *The Politics and Poetics of Camp*, edited by Moe Meyer, 1–22, London: Routledge.

Miltner, Kate M. and Tim Highfield. 2017. 'Never Gonna GIF You Up: Analyzing the Cultural Significance of the Animated GIF.' *Social Media + Society* 3(3): 2056305117725223.

Monro, Surya, Sally Hines, and Anthony Osborne. 2017. 'Is Bisexuality Invisible? A Review of Sexualities Scholarship 1970–2015.' *The Sociological Review* 65(4): 663–81.

Morgan, Susan, 1991. 'Introduction.' In *The Romance of the Harem* by Anna Leonowens, edited by Susan Morgan. Charlottesville: University Press of Virginia.

Morgan, Susan, 2008. *Bombay Anna: The Real Story and Remarkable Adventures of the King and I Governess*. Berkeley: University of California Press.

Myers, Robert. 2011. 'An East/West Pas De Deux: The Ballets Russes and the Orient in the Modern Western Imagination.' 미국학: *Journal of American Studies* 34: 101–21.

Naremore, James. 1990. *Acting in Cinema*. Berkeley: University of California Press.

Nava, Mica. 2007. *Visceral Cosmopolitanism: Gender, Culture and the Normalisation of Difference*. Oxford: Berg.

Neale, Steve. 1983. 'Masculinity as Spectacle: Reflections on men and mainstream cinema.' *Screen* 24(6): 2–16.

Negra, Diane. 2001. *Off-White Hollywood: American Culture and Ethnic Female Fandom*. London: Routledge.

Newton, Esther. 1972. *Mother Camp: Female Impersonators in America*. Chicago: University of Chicago Press.

Paasonen, Susanna. 2019. 'Striking Poses: The Fantastic Body of Yul Brynner.' *Screen* 60(2): 242–60.

Paasonen, Susanna. 2021. *Dependent, Frustrated, Bored: Affective Formations in Networked Media*. Cambridge, MA: MIT Press.

Paasonen, Susanna, Feona Attwood, Alan McKee, John Mercer, and Clarissa Smith. 2021. *Objectification: On the Difference Between Sex and Sexism*. London: Routledge.

Palmer, R. Barton. 2010a. 'Introduction: Stardom in the 1950s.' In *Larger Than Life: Film Stars of the 1950s*, edited by R. Barton Palmer, 1–17, New Brunswick: Rutgers University Press.

Palmer, R. Barton. 2010b. 'Charlton Heston and Gregory Peck: Organization Men.' In *Larger Than Life: Film Stars of the 1950s*, edited by R. Barton Palmer, 37–60, New Brunswick: Rutgers University Press.

Plummer, Ken. 2015. *Cosmopolitan Sexualities*. Cambridge: Polity.

Polonsky, Abraham. 2020. *The Gladiators vs. Spartacus, Volume 2: Abraham Polonsky's Screenplay*. Cambridge: Cambridge Scholars Press.

Quinn, Eithne. 2011. 'Sincere Fictions: The Production Cultures of Whiteness in Late 1960s Hollywood.' *The Velvet Light Trap* 67: 3–13.

Rantala, Varpu. 'Secular Possessions: Cinematic Iconography of Addiction.' PhD dissertation, Turku: Annales Universitatis Turkuensis, 2016. Series B 418.

Regev, Motti. 2007. 'Cultural uniqueness and aesthetic cosmopolitanism.' *European Journal of Social Theory* 10(1): 123–38.

Riva, Maria. 1993. *Marlene Dietrich*. New York: Albert A. Knopf.

Robbins, Jhan. 1987. *Yul Brynner: The Inscrutable King*. New York: Dodd, Mead & Co.

Robinson, Harlow. 2007. *Russians in Hollywood, Hollywood's Russians: Biography of an Image*. Boston: Northeastern University Press.

Rodríguez, Clara E. 2011. 'Dolores del Río and Lupe Vélez: Working in Hollywood, 1924–1944.' *Norteamérica* 6(1): 69–91.

Rövid, Márton. 'Cosmopolitanism and Exclusion: On the Limits of Transnational Democracy in the Light of the Case of Roma.' Unpublished doctoral dissertation. Budapest: Central European University, 2011.

Said, Edward W. 1994. *Culture and Imperialism*. London: Vintage.

Said, Edward W. (1978) 1995. *Orientalism: Western Conceptions of the Orient*. London: Penguin.

Sanders, George. (1960) 2015. *Memoirs of a Professional Cad*. Dean Street.

Scheibel, Will. 2013. 'Marilyn Monroe, "Sex Symbol": Film Performance, Gender Politics and 1950s Hollywood Celebrity.' *Celebrity Studies* 4(1): 4–13.

Shaw, Tony. 2007. *Hollywood's Cold War*. Edinburgh: Edinburgh University Press.

Shohat, Ella. 1995. 'The Struggle over Representation: Casting, Coalitions, and the Politics of Identification.' In *Late Imperial Culture*, edited by Román de la Campa, E. Ann Kaplan, and Michael Sprinker, 166–78, London: Verso.

Shohat, Ella. 1997. 'Gender and Culture of Empire: Toward a Feminist Ethnography of Cinema.' In *Visions of the East: Orientalism in Film*, edited by Matthew Bernstein and Gaylyn Studlar, 19–66, New Brunswick: Rutgers University Press.

Silverman, Carol. 2012. *Romani Routes: Cultural Politics and Balkan Music in Diaspora*. Oxford: Oxford University Press.
Silverman, Carol. 2015. 'DJs and the Production of "Gypsy" Music: "Balkan Beats" as Contested Commodity.' *Western Folklore* 74(1): 5–29.
Sontag, Susan. 1999. 'Notes on "Camp"(1964).' In *Camp: Queer Aesthetics and the Performing Subject – A Reader*, edited by Fabio Cleto, 53–65, Ann Arbor: The University of Michigan Press.
Straw, Will. 2011. 'Scales of Presence: Bess Flowers and the Hollywood Extra.' *Screen* 52(1): 121–7.
Studlar, Gaylyn. 1989. 'Discourses of Gender and Ethnicity: The Construction and De(con)struction of Rudolph Valentino as Other.' *Film Criticism* 13(2): 18–35.
Studlar, Gaylyn. 1997. '"Out-Salomeing Salome": Dance, the New Woman, and Fan Magazine Orientalism.' In *Visions of the East: Orientalism in Film*, edited by Matthew Bernstein and Gaylyn Studlar, 99–129, New Brunswick: Rutgers University Press.
Studlar, Gaylyn. 2011. 'Theda Bara, Orientalism, Sexual Anarchy, and the Jewish Star. Jennifer M. Bean (ed.), *Flickers of Desire: Movie Stars of the 1910s*. New Brunswick: Rutgers University Press, 113–36.
Szeman, Ioana. 2009. 'Gypsy Music' and Deejays: Orientalism, Balkanism, and Romani Musicians. *The Drama Review* 53(3): 98–116.
Talbot, Paul. 2006. *Bronson's Loose: The Making of the* Death Wish *Films*. New York: iUniverse.
Thurlow, Clifford. 2011. *Sex, Surrealism, Dalí and Me: The Memoirs of Carlos Lozano*. London: YellowBay Books.
Țion, Lucian. 2021. 'Putting it My Way, but Nicely': Neocolonialism in Feminist Clothing in Andy Tennant's *Anna and the King* (1999) and Rodgers and Hammerstein's *The King and I* (1956). In *Orientalism and Reverse Orientalism in Literature and Film: Beyond East and West*, edited by Sharmani Patricia Gabriel and Bernard Wilson, 52–66, London: Routledge.
Tlostanova, Madina. 2008. The Janus-Faced Empire Distorting Orientalist Discourses: Gender, Race and Religion in the Russian/(post)Soviet Constructions of the 'Orient.' *Worlds and Knowledges Otherwise* 2(2): 1–11.
Tonchi, Stefano. 2010. 'Man of Style.' In *Yul Brynner: A Photographic Journey, Vol. 4: Man of Style*, edited by Victoria Brynner and Nicolas Pages, 8–9, Göttingen: Edition 7L.
Van der Oye, David Schimmelpenninck. 2010. *Russian Orientalism: Asia in the Russian Mind from Peter the Great to the Emigration*. New Haven: Yale University Press.
Walkowitz, Rebecca L. 2006. *Cosmopolitan Style: Modernism Beyond the Nation*. New York: Columbia University Press.
Watts, Jill. 2003. *Mae West: An Icon in Black and White*. Oxford: Oxford University Press.
Williams, Michael. 2009. 'The Idol Body: Stars, Statuary and the Classical Epic.' *Film & History* 39(2): 39–48.
Wiseman, Thomas. 1957. *The Seven Deadly Sins of Hollywood*. London: Oldbourne Press.
Wollen, Peter. 1994. 'The Cosmopolitan Ideal in the Arts.' In *Travellers' Tales: Narratives of Home and Displacement*, edited by George Robertson, Melinda Mash, Lisa Tickner, Jon Bird, Barry Curtis, and Tim Putnam, 187–96, London: Routledge.

Index

20th Century Fox (Fox), 26, 27, 38, 46n128, 77
60 Minutes, 231

A New Kind of Love, 29
Academy Awards (Oscars), 3, 53–4, 57, 79, 108, 126, 197, 237
accents, 15–6, 19, 22, 24, 25, 28, 35, 36, 55, 69–70, 99, 118, 120, 129, 133n16, 134n51, 210
Adiarte, Parick, 57
Adíos, Sabata, 34, 116, 175–8, 183, 196, 217, 218, 219
The Advocate, 191
agents, 26, 27, 159
Ajan sävel, 83, 102n42
Alciona, 38, 39–40, 46n126, 98
Alekan, Henri, 147
Alpha Productions, 39
ambiguity, 5, 9–11, 12, 13, 76, 124, 137, 147, 156, 159, 171
Ambler, Eric, 32
American Broadcast Company (ABC), 230
American Cancer Society, 230
American civil rights movement, 37
Anastasia, 1, 9, 31, 33, 40, 64, 86, 91, 92, 93, 108–11, 148, 170, 189, 197, 203, 209, 217

animalism, 61, 76, 83, 210
animated GIFs, 237–8
Anna and the King
film, 236, 237
television series, 157, 218, 228
Anna and the King of Siam, 51
Archerd, Army, 84
Atatürk, Kemal, 31, 33
athleticism, 5, 82, 99, 112, 192
Attila, 30

baldness, 7, 12, 48, 75–81, 82, 84, 102n38, 125, 126, 155, 169, 180, 186, 201, 215, 229, 237
Ballets Russes, 60, 62
Bandoola (aka *Elephant Bill*), 40
Bara, Theda, 26, 62
Barrymore, John, 54
Battle of Neretva, 25, 34, 118, 175, 215
Beaton, Cecil, 89, 104n83
Bechdel test, 170
Belafonte, Harry, 124
Ben Hur, 97, 99
Benshoff, Harry M., 218
Bergman, Ingrid, 1, 8, 21, 42n33, 86, 92, 108–9, 170
Berry, Sarah, 36
biblical epics, 1, 30, 32, 62–4, 67–70, 99, 196, 218

Index **283**

biographies, 3, 7, 9, 11, 14n35, 15–16, 22–3, 26–8, 48, 86, 88, 145, 146, 153, 232–6
biopics, 30, 31, 32, 33, 40, 174, 232
Birkin, Jane, 116, 118, 164n115
Bloom, Claire, 8, 65, 86, 103n42, 111, 113
Bogarde, Dirk, 118
Bokiy, Alexey, 232
Bouchet, Barbara, 189, 191, 192
Bourguignon, Serge, 212
Boyer, Charles, 20–1, 35, 76, 212
Bradbury, Ray, 212
Brando, Marlon, 8, 53, 56, 129, 157, 174, 203
Bring Forth the Children, 138, 141–5
Broadway stardom, 1, 3, 16, 18, 19, 21, 29, 30, 49–50, 52–3, 57, 75, 86, 87, 223–30, 240n30
Bronson, Charles, 174, 187, 189, 191
Brooks, Richard, 33, 40, 112
The Brothers Karamazov, 8, 33, 40, 65, 86, 93, 94, 103n42, 105n96, 108, 111–3, 148, 178, 197–8
Brown, Christopher R., 215
Brown, Helen Gurley, 191
Brown, Susan, 52
brownface, 5, 9, 36, 97, 121, 124, 237
Buck, Pearl, 31, 40
Burton, Richard, 156
Bryna Productions, 46n131, 98, 194n47
Brynner, Boris, 17, 18, 41n16
Brynner, Jules, 17, 22
Brynner, Maria (Marousia), 17, 18, 41n13
Brynner, Melody, 144, 158, 159
Brynner, Mia, 144, 159
Brynner, Rock, 16, 38, 48, 138, 150, 86, 87, 144, 156, 162n47, 193n23, 234–5
Bryner, Vera, 17, 18, 24, 43n48, 148, 162n54
Brynner, Victoria, 144, 146, 164n115, 235

The Buccaneer, 12, 33, 39, 65–6, 79, 86, 93, 99, 121, 218, 220n3
Byla Productions, 33, 40, 45n104

'Cajun,' 35, 101, 107, 120, 129, 171, 237
cameos, 1, 6, 12, 30, 35, 42n33, 186, 213–15, 216, 237
camp, 12, 118, 130, 169, 175, 193, 197, 215–19, 221n62, 221n68
cancer, 24, 53, 128, 227, 230–1
Cannes Film Festival, 105n96, 113, 133n24
Capua, Michelangelo, 235
Cast a Giant Shadow, 33, 40, 78, 99, 128, 143
Catlow, 35, 116, 170, 178–9, 211
CBS, 19, 21, 29, 38, 83, 138–41, 231
celebrity, 29, 38, 90, 157, 191, 213, 216
Celebrity Parade for Cerebral Palsy, 137
Chakiris, George, 95–6, 126
charity, 102n42, 137, 143, 146, 160
Chávez, Ernesto, 58
Chekhov, Michael (Mikhail), 18, 199–201, 203
Chekhov Players, 18, 41n19, 87, 234
Chevalier, Maurice, 29
Chinese roles, 3, 19, 27, 49
Chinoiserie, 62
Chouliaraki, Lilie, 143, 144
CinemaScope, 1, 31, 54
Cirque d'Hiver, 17–18, 166
citizenship, 17, 22, 27, 42n34, 139, 146, 152
Cleopatra, 63
Clooney, Rosemary, 29
Cobb, Lee J., 111
Cocteau, Jean, 2, 18, 35, 38, 87, 89, 104n86, 141, 156, 213
Cohan, Steve, 84, 206, 217
Cold War, 3, 12, 16, 52, 107–8, 118, 131, 140–1, 152, 166, 206
Collier's, 1, 9, 24, 75, 83
colonialism, 51–2, 60, 126, 130

comedy, 12, 30, 37, 120, 196, 208–11, 216, 228
Cooper, Duncan, 98
Cortés, Carlos E., 37
Cosmopolitan magazine, 67, 75, 82, 85, 158, 191
cosmopolitanism, 5, 11, 12, 17, 28–9, 48, 60–1, 89, 119, 131–2, 148, 151, 159–60, 200, 213, 216
  as ideology, 132, 136–7, 139–40, 142–3, 145–6, 224
  as style, 137, 147, 154–8
Coward, Noël, 28, 87, 89, 210, 211, 215
The Cranes Are Flying, 113
Crawford, Joan, 86, 103n61
Crichton, Michael, 3, 35, 184, 185
Crosby, Bing, 137
cuisine, 153–4, 158, 160
cultural appropriation, 5, 58, 62, 132, 137, 148, 150–1, 160
Curtis, Tony, 8, 32, 98, 113, 115, 194n37

Daily News, 21, 76, 168
Dalí, Salvador, 87
Dan, Judy, 57
Dandridge, Dorothy, 32
Danube Films, 33
Dark Eyes, 19
Daudet, Alphonse, 31, 39
Davis, Nancy, 86
Day, Doris, 5, 137
de Laurentiis, Dino, 30, 32
Dean, James, 56, 57
Death Rage, 35, 166, 189–93
del Río, Dolores, 59
DeMille, Cecil B., 1, 2, 30, 39, 62–3, 65, 66, 73n97, 86, 100, 156
designer fashion, 155–7, 159, 160
Dickinson, Angie, 128, 147
Dietrich, Marlene, 86–7, 89, 215
Dimitrievitch, Aljosha, 147–9
Dimitrievitch, Maroussia, 148–9
Dimitrievich family, 17, 26, 86

Dominguín, Luis Miguel, 213
Donen, Stanley, 28, 35, 208
Dostoevsky, Fyodor, 111, 113
The Double Man, 35, 78, 94, 118, 161n34, 166–8, 197
Douglas, Kirk, 12, 13n17, 30, 32, 29, 44n92, 46n131, 46n136, 57, 87, 98–9, 100, 103n55, 128, 180, 187, 194n47, 221n57
drag, 12, 150, 160, 213–6, 218, 237
Drake, Albert, 58
Dumayet, Pierre, 23
Dunne, Irene, 51
Dupont, Richard, 156
Dyer, Richard, 5, 36, 60

Eastwood, Clint, 187
The Ed Sullivan Show, 148, 149
Eggar, Samantha, 181, 218
Egyptomania, 62, 73n92
Eisenstein, Sergei, 109
Ekberg, Anita, 86
Ekland, Britt, 168
Elokuva-aitta, 82–3
Empire & Odyssey: The Brynners in Far East Russia and Beyond, 235
The English Governess at the Siamese Court, 50–1
eroticism, 4, 16, 58–60, 70, 87, 91–2, 229
Escape from Zahrain, 34, 124–5, 127
European co-productions, 4–5, 119, 166, 170
exoticism, 5, 9, 27, 36, 48–9, 58, 60–2, 90, 95, 126, 137,148, 182; *see also* Orientalism

fabrication, 3, 13, 16, 24, 26–7, 51, 131, 155, 165, 235
Fairbanks, Douglas, Sr., 2, 36, 38
fan magazines, 1, 7, 8, 24, 26, 79, 81, 82, 102– 3n42, 103n43, 134n53, 165, 197
Farrow, Mia, 156, 159

Fast, Howard, 98
Faulkner, William, 120
Fellini, Federico, 33, 133n24, 222n75
femininization, 59, 80–1
Field, Shirley Ann, 96, 97, 198
The File of the Golden Goose, 35, 118, 126–7, 168–70, 175, 183, 211
film formats, 36, 62–3, 65, 67, 199, 221n57; *see also* Technicolor
fine art, 157, 227
Finney, Albert, 212
Flaubert, Gustaf, 32
Fleming, Ian, 147
Fleming, Rhonda, 138
Flight from Ashiya, 35, 93, 125–6, 157
The Flower Drum Song, 40
Fonda, Henry, 31, 118
Fonda, Peter, 186
Food Fit for the King and You, 48, 152–5
Forster, E. M., 219
Foster, Jodie, 236
France, 17, 18, 28, 23, 86, 138, 145, 146, 152, 154, 157–159
Frank, Anne, 140
French language, 15, 17, 18, 24–25, 65, 116–17, 120, 121–2, 129, 234
Futureworld, 35, 186–7
Fuzz, 35, 180, 182–3

Gabin, Jean, 31
Gallagher, Mark, 89
Gandhi, Mahatma, 30
Garland, Judy, 86
Gaslight, 21
Gautier, Benoît, 235
Gaza, 138, 142
Gaynor, Mitzi, 210
gender, 58, 80, 100, 103n55, 143, 166, 170, 182, 211; *see also* femininization; sexism
Genghis Khan, 1, 15, 32, 225, 234
 1965 film, 119
The Giant, 57

Gilmore, Virginia, 18, 19, 22, 38, 46n128, 58, 85–6, 235
Girard, Gaïd, 185
The Gladiators, 13n17, 39–40, 98–9
The Globe and Mail, 127
Goetz, William, 32
Good Morning, America, 230
gossip, 10, 12, 14n20, 29, 84–6, 88, 102n42, 193n23, 235, 241n62
 columns, 7, 8, 82, 86, 102n40
Grace, Princess of Monaco, 147, 156
Grant, Cary, 32, 42n33, 45n102, 104n77
The Greatest Story Ever Told, 32
Grewal, Inderpal, 51
The Guardian, 179, 181, 183
Guilbault, Jocelyne, 148
Guitry, Sasha, 40
The Gypsy and I, 147–8

Haber, Joyce, 86
Hammerstein, Oscar, 1, 40, 49, 51–2, 223, 227, 236
harem, 50–1, 68, 70, 210, 234
Hark, Ina Rae, 99
Harris, Ed, 237
Harrison, Rex, 51
Hastings, Phyllis, 32
Hatfield, Hurd, 87
Hayworth, Rita, 44n84, 59, 147
Hefner, Hugh, 158–9
Held, Martin, 139
Hepburn, Audrey, 29, 30, 31, 32, 146, 164n115
Hepburn, Katherine, 29, 35, 211, 212
Heston, Charlton, 8, 30, 32, 45n102, 45n103, 63, 65, 97, 99, 187, 206, 217
Hold Back the Dawn, 30
Hollywood; 3, 4, 6, 8, 10, 28, 29, 36–9, 58, 86–8, 97, 98, 100, 107, 108, 124, 131, 132, 146, 152, 156, 165, 183, 192, 196, 216, 218, 223
 clichés, 55, 61–2, 65, 67, 69, 113, 121, 153, 184, 217

Hollywood (*cont.*)
  stardom, 1, 2, 13n8, 15–16, 21, 26–7, 29, 32, 75–7, 79–80, 119–20, 151, 171, 199, 206, 236
The Hollywood Reporter, 53, 54, 86, 110, 112, 125, 226, 236
Home Box Office (HBO), 237
Hopper, Hedda, 10, 38, 49, 54, 82, 86, 89, 92, 102n40, 103n59
Howard, Trevor, 126, 147
Hudson, Rock, 5, 8, 45n102, 57, 223
human rights, 11, 136, 137, 139–40, 143, 145, 150, 152, 158, 223–4
humanitarianism, 11, 12, 131, 136–46, 159, 160
humor, 10, 100, 127, 187, 208, 215
Hungarian uprising, 108, 109, 138, 139
Hunter, Tab, 8
Hush-Hush, 2, 79
Huston, John, 30

international adoptions, 10, 144, 158–9
interracial desire, 4, 37, 50, 59, 90
intertextuality, 7, 184, 218
Interview magazine, 88
Intolerance, 62
Invitation to a Gunfighter, 4, 35, 93, 121–4, 175, 219
Ivan the Terrible, 109
Izvestia, 28

Järvinen, Hanna, 60, 194n53
The Jerusalem Post, 78
jet-set lifestyle, 9, 12, 137, 152, 156, 160, 213
Jordan, Jessica Hope, 91
journalism, 10, 22, 24, 26, 48, 49, 76, 82–4, 95, 145, 229
The Journey, 33, 40, 45n104, 80, 85, 93, 103n42, 103n60, 108–11, 123, 138, 170, 198
Judaism, 17, 26, 41n13, 117, 151

Kalazatov, Mikhail, 113
Kendall, Kay, 78, 170, 197, 208, 210
Kennedy, John, 143
Kennedy, Robert, 184
Kerr, Deborah, 9, 32, 54, 85, 109, 110, 170, 236
Khruschev, Nikita, 31
Kinematograph Weekly, 183
The King and I, 1, 4, 6, 9, 24, 29, 35, 38, 41, 48, 53–58, 62, 82, 85, 92–3, 108, 109, 111, 112, 131, 147, 189, 196, 197, 203, 209, 229, 230, 232
  stage show, 11, 3, 21, 27, 49–50, 52–3, 58, 63, 70, 77, 86, 99, 106n127, 170, 201, 204, 223–9, 231, 233, 236
King Hussein, 141
Kings of the Sun, 35, 40, 93, 95–7, 121, 123, 198, 199, 208
Kinsey, Alfred E., 88
Kismet, 30
The Kiss of the Spider Woman, 87
Klein, Christina, 52, 92, 225
Kleiner, Doris, 85–6, 146, 157, 213, 235
Koestler, Arthur, 98
Kornakova, Catharina, 17
Kramer, Stanley, 121
Kubrick, Stanley, 98
Kulik, Buzz, 33, 34, 174
Kurosawa, Akira, 39, 136, 173

La grande illusion, 120
Ladd, Alan, 39–40
Lagerfeld, Karl, 157, 159
Lancaster, Burt, 99, 187
Landon, Margaret, 51–2
Lang, Fritz, 18, 186
Lang, Walter, 1, 56–7
language skills, 22, 24–5, 50, 83, 129, 153, 158, 165, 239, 229; *see also* accents
Lavi, Daliah, 170, 179
Lawrence, Gertrude, 53, 87, 170

Lawrence of Arabia, 100, 119
Le Monde, 117, 123, 186, 229
Le Serpent / Night Flight from Moscow, 25, 33, 118
Le testament d'Orphee / The Testament of Orpheus, 35, 78, 141, 213
Leighton, Margaret, 120
Leonowens, Anna Harriette, 50–2, 57, 170
Lerman, Leo, 87, 104n73
Les mille et une vies de Yul Brynner, 43n56, 152, 235
Let's Make Love, 32
Lewis, Jerry, 79
Life magazine, 21
The Light at the Edge of the World, 35, 87, 99, 179–82, 183, 217–19
Litvak, Anatole, 1, 33, 40, 42n33, 45n104, 46n135, 108, 119, 138
location shoots, 113, 124, 127, 146, 147, 199, 217
Lollobrigida, Gina, 31, 67, 69, 86
Lom, Herbert, 30, 58
Long, Lucy M., 154
The Long Duel, 34, 126–7, 161n34, 176
Loren, Sophia, 42n33, 98
Lorre, Peter, 20–1
Los Angeles Times, 96, 98, 127, 178, 182, 183, 227
Lozano, Carlos, 87
Lucifer and the Lord, 40
Lust for Life, 30, 57
Lute Song, 3, 19, 27, 49, 62, 86, 203

MacAdam, Henry, 98
McCarthy hearings, 107
McElwaine, Guy, 159
McQueen, Steve, 171, 193–4n23
'Mad About the Boy,' 214–15
The Madwoman of Chaillot, 21, 35, 211–3
The Magic Christian, 12, 35, 213–6, 237
The Magnificent Seven, 3, 13n17, 35, 39, 40, 46n133, 98, 123, 126, 170–3, 175, 176, 184,

The Manchester Guardian, 77
Magnum Photo, 21, 138, 189, 197, 211, 217, 236–7
The Manchester Guardian, 77
Mangano, Silvia, 30
Mansfield, Jayne, 8, 31, 91, 104n95, 105n96
Marais, Jean, 18, 35
Martin, Mary, 49
Mather, Berkely, 32
Mayne, Judith, 9
Meir, Golda, 141
memes, 237
Mercer, John, 90, 100, 204
method acting, 96, 199
methodology, 6–9
Metro-Goldwyn-Mayer (MGM), 27, 33, 181, 208
Metropolis, 186
Mimieux, Yvette, 212
Mineo, Sal, 8, 14n29, 124
Miss Saigon, 58
Mission to No-Man's Land, 138
Mitchum, Robert, 32
Mr. Jones and His Neighbors, 19
Mirisch, Marvin, 95
Mirisch, Walter, 21
Mirisch Corporation, 21, 39, 40, 47n138
Modern Screen, 165
Mongolia, 22, 23–4, 28, 36, 49, 101, 153
Mongkut, Somdetch P'hra Paramendr Maha, 48, 51, 62
Monthly Film Bulletin, 123, 182
Monroe, Marilyn, 32, 86, 111
Moon Vine, 18
Morath, Inge, 21, 138, 145
Moreno, Rita, 58
Morgan, Susan, 51
Morheim, Louis, 39
Morituri, 34, 128–9, 157, 203
Moscow Art Theatre, 17, 18
Murrow, Edward R., 140

The Nabob, 39
Naumoff family, 140
Nava, Mica, 60
New Hollywood, 199
New Kind of Love, 29
New York Herald Tribune, 21, 56, 69
The New York Times, 53, 68, 108, 110, 118, 125, 129, 152, 168, 172–3, 176, 179, 183, 225, 227, 232
Newsweek, 24, 79, 84, 196, 234
Nijinsky, Vatslav, 60, 61, 73n76–7
Noiret, Philippe, 118
Norton, Elliot, 105n107, 203
Novak, Kim, 86, 138
Nureyev, Rudolf, 58, 72n61, 206

objectification, 4, 59, 61, 91, 216
The Odyssey (aka *Home, Sweet Homer*), 40, 191–2, 236
Office of War Information, 18
Olivier, Laurence, 57, 120
Onassis, Aristotle, 45n99, 156
Onassis, Christina, 156
Once More, with Feeling!, 35, 37, 78, 87, 120, 170, 197, 203, 208–10, 211
Omar Khayyam, 30
Orientalism, 4, 12, 26–7, 48–53, 57–3, 64, 68, 73n81, 84, 85, 101–1, 171, 182, 203, 225
othering, 3, 4, 26, 28, 36, 58–2, 143, 151, 206

Palestinians, 142–3
Palmer, R. Barton, 63
Paramount Pictures, 27, 29, 31, 33, 38, 82, 124, 236
Parsons, Louella, 30, 31, 82, 86, 102n40
Peil, Mary Beth, 229
Pépé le Moko, 31
peplum, 97, 101, 106n135, 218
performance style, 4, 5–6, 7, 12, 53, 107, 119, 130, 184, 191, 193, 196–9, 201–12, 215, 219
Philarmonia Hungarica, 139, 141

photography, 21–2, 42n32–3, 136, 137, 138, 141–4, 156, 235
  work as photographic model, 18, 88–9, 235
Photoplay, 80, 84, 86, 234
Picasso, Pablo, 18, 157, 213
The Picasso Summer, 212–13
Picture Show, 24
Picturegoer, 1, 2, 24, 28, 80, 82–3, 92, 98, 103n43, 111, 197
The Picture of Dorian Gray, 87
Pitöeff, Georges and Ludmilla, 18
Platt Lynes, George, 88–9
Playboy, 3, 158
Plummer, Ken, 89
Poitier, Sidney, 8, 124
Polanski, Roman, 213–4, 241n62
Polonsky, Abraham, 34, 40, 98, 105n120, 117
Ponti, Carlo, 30, 33
The Poppy is Also a Flower, 34, 128, 147
Port of New York, 4, 19–21, 35, 93, 165, 193n5
Power, Tyrone, 66–7, 94
Production Code, 12, 37, 46n117, 100, 189, 199
Pryce, Jonathan, 58
Puig, Manuel, 87, 104n76

queer, 216
  connotations, 5, 100, 169, 215, 217
  history, 88–9
Quinn, Anthony, 12, 30, 33, 39, 46n136, 47n138, 98, 99, 100, 105n120, 106n127

racism, 36–7, 44n76, 52, 58–61, 130, 132, 152, 194n53
Radin, Paul, 38
radio, 19, 21, 136, 137–8
Rain, 30
Rand, Ayn, 224
Rantala, Varpu, 6
Redbook, 24, 26, 27, 81

refugee rights, 11, 136, 138–44
Renoir, Jean, 18, 117, 129
representation (politics of), 5, 6, 10, 36, 132, 137, 206
Rescue, with Yul Brynner, 102n42, 138, 139–43, 145, 161n39
Return of the Seven, 35, 40, 173, 184, 186, 193n23
Reynolds, Burt, 182, 191
Rimski-Korsakov, Nikolai, 60
Ritt, Martin, 35, 38, 98
Riva, Maria, 87
Rivas, Carlos, 57–8
Robbins, Jhan, 232–4
Robinson, Harlow, 108
Rodgers, Richard, 1, 40, 49, 52, 227, 236
Romance of a Horsethief, 34, 116–18, 170
Romance of the Harem, 51
Romani identification and advocacy, 17, 15, 23, 26, 28, 137, 147–52, 159
 and 'gypsy' exoticism, 9, 15, 29, 49, 108, 148, 152–3, 230, 234
romantic leads, 32, 92, 94
Rossellini, Roberto, 86
Russianness, 3, 6, 16, 19, 25, 27–8, 29, 60–1, 107–11, 119, 145, 152

Said, Edward W., 26
Salmi, Albert, 111
Sanders, George, 69, 156, 198
Sartre, Jean-Paul, 40
Saturday Evening Post, 1, 23
Saunders, Terry, 57
Savalas, Terry, 80
Saxon, John, 8
Schéhérazade, 60
Schell, Maria, 8, 103n42, 111
Scheibel, Will, 90
Schneider, Romy, 130
screen violence, 100, 165–6, 172, 173, 176–8, 180–4, 186, 188, 189, 191, 217

Screenland, 83
Second World Romani Congress, 149–50, 151–2
The Secret Crimes of Josef Stalin, 31
Sellers, Peter, 216
Seven Samurai, 39, 170, 173
sex appeal, 2, 7, 12, 53, 56–7, 58, 59, 61, 66, 70, 75–6, 84–5, 88, 89–91, 94, 112, 187, 192, 206, 236
sex symbols, 3, 12, 70, 76, 80, 90–1, 100, 192, 204
sexism, 85, 103n55, 170, 211
sexuality, 37, 88–9, 90, 104n77
Sharaff, Irene, 50, 54, 57, 77
Sharif, Omar, 119–20, 147
Shatner, William, 111
The Sheik, 59, 62, 112
Shohat, Ella, 152
Sight and Sound, 123
Signoret, Simone, 31, 32
Simenon, Georges, 30
Sinatra, Frank, 128, 156
Sketch, 52
Solomon and Sheba, 12, 31, 33, 40, 67–70, 93, 94, 98, 136, 156, 198, 205
Sontag, Susan, 215
Sorbonne, 15, 21, 22, 28, 136, 234
The Sound and the Fury, 35, 79, 80, 91, 93, 120–1, 161n34, 165
South China Morning Post, 173, 230
Soviet Union, 16, 18, 28, 31, 149
Spaghetti Westerns, 175, 178
Spartacus, 13n17, 39, 98–9, 100, 221n57
Stalin, Joseph, 17, 29, 31, 33
Stanislavski, Konstantin, 17, 18
Starr, Ringo, 216
Straw, Will, 5, 204
Studio One: Flowers from a Stranger, 19
Studlar, Gaylyn, 59, 62
Sturges, John, 3, 35, 39, 173
Surprise Package, 28, 35, 91, 120, 144, 208, 210–11, 221n57
Suyin, Han, 32

Swamp Water, 18
Switzerland, 22, 40, 138
syndicated press, 8, 82, 83, 103n43, 192, 230

Taras Bulba, 4, 32, 34, 47n145, 97–8, 113–16, 130, 153, 161n34, 174, 183, 194n37, 203, 205, 208
Taylor, Elizabeth, 8, 156, 164n115
Technicolor, 4, 36, 62, 63, 65, 196, 199; *see also* film formats
television, 36, 48, 67, 80, 183, 199, 212, 227, 230
  work for, 6, 7, 19, 21, 31, 40, 42n20–1, 42n28, 50, 53, 136, 137–8, 147, 218, 228; *see also*, Rescue, with Yul Brynner
The Ten Commandments, 1, 12, 30, 33, 38, 40, 58, 62–4, 65, 66, 68, 74n116, 85, 89, 95, 99, 109, 197, 205–7, 217, 237
Thailand, 51, 57, 72n58, 154
Théâtre des Mathurins, 18
Thibault, Jean-Frédéric, 235
Thion de la Chaume, Jacqueline, 144, 157
Third Reich, 31, 128–9, 151
Thompson, J. Lee, 4, 32, 95, 208
Tilden, Lark, 86
The Times of India, 95–6, 123
Tito, Josip Broz, 118
To the Actor, 199–201
Tony Award (aka Donaldson Award), 3, 49, 53
Top Spot, 79
Toronto Daily Star, 96, 183
Towers, Constance, 76, 150
The Train, 99
Triple Cross, 34, 129–30
Truffaut, François, 212
Twitter, 236
Two Different Worlds, 33
typecasting, 10, 28, 33, 58–61, 64, 100, 107, 118, 184, 201

The Ultimate Warrior, 4, 35, 187–8, 191, 193
Ulysses, 30
Uncle Tom's Cabin, 52
United Artists (UA), 21, 38–40, 46n131–2, 47n138
United Nations (UN), 102n42, 128, 131, 136, 137–43, 146
United Nations High Commissioner for Refugees (UNHCR), 7, 9, 12, 98, 47n138, 136–8, 141, 142, 144, 145–6, 150, 156, 161n25, 224

van Cleef, Lee, 175
Valentino, Rudolph, 54, 58, 59, 60, 66, 72n63, 75–6, 81, 112
Variety, 21, 53, 98, 142
Veléz, Lupe, 59
Vidor, King, 31, 33, 67
Vietnam War, 144, 158–9
The Vikings, 89, 99
Villa Rides, 33, 34, 148, 174, 189, 213
Viva Zapata!, 174
Vladivostok, 16–17, 22, 28, 118, 232–3, 236
von Bismarck, Otto, 33
von Stroheim, Erich, 80, 129
von Sydow, Max, 32, 35, 187

Walkowitz, Rebecca L., 159
Wallace, Mike, 231
Wallach, Eli, 116, 118, 147, 171
War and Peace, 31
Warhol, Andy, 88, 156
Washington, Denzel, 236–7
The Washington Post, 22, 159, 223, 226
wax museums, 232
We're On, 19
Welch, Raquel, 182, 216
Welles, Orson, 118, 223
West, Mae, 91
Westerns, 4, 12, 39, 99, 123, 166, 170–9, 185, 188, 196, 217, 219, *see also* Spaghetti Westerns

Westworld, 3, 35, 169, 175, 179, 184–6, 187, 191, 219, 221n68, 237
What's My Line, 237
Who's Coming to Dinner, 121
Wilder, Billy, 29, 32
Wiseman, Thomas, 81
World Exhibitions, 62
World War II, 18, 62, 126, 128, 138, 151

yellowface, 5, 36, 55, 72n42
Young, Terence, 34, 119, 147
YouTube, 237, 238
Yul Brynner: A Biography, 235

Yul Brynner: A Photographic Journey, 235
Yul Brynner: Photographer, 235
Yul Brynner: The Inscrutable King, 48, 233–4
Yul Brynner: The Man Who Was King, 48, 235
Yul Brynner Head and Neck Cancer Foundation, 231
Yul: The Man Who Would Be King, 48, 234–5
Yun-fat, Chow, 236

Zorba the Greek, 100